Fallen Angels, Giants, Monsters & the World Before the Flood

How the Events of Noah's Ark and the Flood Are Relevant to the End of the Age

RICK RENNER

Fallen Angels, Giants, Monsters & the

World Before the Flood

How the Events of Noah's Ark and the Flood
Are Relevant to the End of the Age

Unless otherwise indicated, all scriptural quotations are from the *King James Version* of the Bible.

Scripture quotations marked (*AMPC*) are taken from the *Amplified® Bible, Classic Edition.* Copyright © 1954, 1958, 1962, 1964, 1965, 1987 by The Lockman Foundation. Used by permission. **www.Lockman.org**

Scripture quotations marked (*ESV*) are from *The Holy Bible, English Standard Version.* ESV® Text Edition: 2016. Copyright © 2001 by Crossway Bibles, a publishing ministry of Good News Publishers.

Scriptures marked as (*GNT*) are taken from the **Good News Translation - Second Edition** © 1992 by American Bible Society. Used by permission.

Scripture quotations marked (*NIV*) are taken from the *Holy Bible, New International Version®*, NIV®. Copyright © 1973, 1978, 1984, 2011 by Biblica, Inc.™ Used by permission of Zondervan. All rights reserved worldwide. www.zondervan.com The "NIV" and "New International Version" are trademarks registered in the United States Patent and Trademark Office by Biblica, Inc.™

All Scriptures marked (*NKJV*) are taken from the *New King James Version* of the Bible © 1979, 1980, 1982 by Thomas Nelson, Inc. All rights reserved.

Scripture quotations marked (*NLT*) are taken from the *Holy Bible, New Living Translation*, copyright © 1996, 2004, 2015 by Tyndale House Foundation. Used by permission of Tyndale House Publishers, Inc., Carol Stream, Illinois 60188. All rights reserved.

Scripture quotations marked (*RIV*) are taken from *Renner Interpretive Version*. Copyright © 2021 by Rick Renner.

Illustration and Photo Credit Acknowledgments are listed on pages 441-457.

Fallen Angels, Giants, Monsters, and the World Before the Flood —
How the Events of Noah's Ark and the Flood Are Relevant to the End of the Age

ISBN: 978-1-6675-0587-9
eBook: 978-1-6675-0588-6

Copyright © 2024 by Rick Renner
1814 W. Tacoma St.
Broken Arrow, OK 74012-1406

Published by Harrison House
Shippensburg, PA 17257-2914
www.harrisonhouse.com

3 4 5 6 7 / 28 27 26 25 24
3rd printing

Editorial Consultant: Rebecca L. Gilbert
Cover and Text Design: Lisa M. Moore

DEDICATION

This book is dedicated to Noah and his family, who lived in difficult times in the days before the Flood but who remained so faithful that they became the remnant God used to save the human population and replenish the earth. They heard the call of God and obeyed it, and today we are the fruit of their obedience. As Noah and his family built the Ark in the darkest days before the Flood — with every pound of the hammer upon the wood of that massive vessel — they also preached to the erring world around them that the judgment of a flood was about to be released and they needed to repent.

Remembering Noah's family and the price they paid also makes me think of the faithful believers in our times — times that are also quite dark. Jesus prophesied that many of the events that occurred before the Flood would be replicated at the end of the age. And just as Noah preached before the Flood, there is a replication of faithful believers and preachers who are declaring the life-saving message of salvation and deliverance — as God's plea of mercy with mankind — before a coming judgment is released upon the world of the ungodly.

Thus, I dedicate this book to Noah, to his family, and to believers and preachers everywhere today who walk holily with the Lord. They are doing their part to bring the message of repentance, deliverance, and salvation to a last-days erring generation that is teetering on the brink of a judgment that will be released in the days before us.

ENDORSEMENTS

Finally! A comprehensive look at Noah's Ark has eluded the Christian world and the archaeological world until now. The story of a Great Flood is the single most common story found in almost all religions of the world. Yet we have found no definitive proof…*until now.*

But Rick Renner's *Fallen Angels, Giants, Monsters, and the World Before the Flood* is not just another archaeological discovery detailed in a new book. Inside, you'll see mysteries unfold before you about fallen angels, giants, monsters, and UFOs. Rick does a masterful job weaving it all together without compromise. You've probably always wondered about these subjects — and now, in your hands are the answers and insights to those mysteries!

God has indeed called us to occupy until Christ comes (*see* Luke 19:13). While His return is imminent and is approaching rapidly, we must accelerate what we are called to do in these last days. Thankfully, this book will be a powerful tool in your last-days arsenal. With its foundation in Scripture, you'll find this resource invaluable in the days ahead!

Gene Bailey
Host, FlashPoint

Rick Renner is a supernatural gift to the Body of Jesus. His research is over the top and just as entertaining as it is academic. Every page of *Fallen Angels, Giants, Monsters, and the World Before the Flood* is a front-row seat and cutting-edge view of the days of Noah and the imminent return of King Jesus. Buckle your seat belt. This is one I couldn't put down and can't recommend enough in these last days.

Troy Brewer
Senior Pastor, OpenDoor Church
Author of Numbers That Preach

I cannot begin to express how much I have enjoyed reading Rick Renner's book *Fallen Angels, Giants, Monsters, and the World Before the Flood*. For years, both my dad (Charles Capps) and I studied the Scriptures regarding Genesis 6, but Rick's research, information, and revelation have filled the gaps and completed the connection between the flood of Noah and the signs of Jesus' soon return.

I believe this is a "time-released revelation" that has been waiting for this generation — for the simple reason that we are the generation seeing these very events beginning to transpire before our eyes.

Annette Capps
Bible Teacher, Author, Broadcaster

It is with great honor and profound respect that I endorse Pastor Rick Renner's *Fallen Angels, Giants, Monsters, and the World Before the Flood*. This book masterfully explores the biblical narratives of Noah's era, providing timely prophetic insights and highlighting their significance for the end times.

Rick's dedication to unveiling the complex tapestry of biblical history, paired with his solid theological understanding, gives this work remarkable depth and authenticity. It stands out as a labor of love and a significant contribution to biblical studies for those with ears to hear, offering a unique perspective on Bible stories that shape our faith and worldview.

I highly recommend this book for its deep examination of the pre-Flood world and its relevance to contemporary spiritual discourse. The parallels drawn between Noah's time and our current era are both remarkable and thought-provoking — essential for understanding the days ahead.

For both long-time followers of Rick's works and newcomers to biblical history, this book is a valuable addition to any library. Its detailed illustrations and compelling narrative are captivating, making it a must-read for anyone eager to deepen his understanding of Scripture and its implications for this critical hour.

Todd Coconato
Pastor, Teacher, Author, and Social-Media Influencer

Adding to his abundance of outstanding literary works, Rick Renner now presents a fascinating look into the distant past through *Fallen Angels, Giants, Monsters, and the World Before the Flood*. Loaded with extensive historical data and research at the very site of what is believed to be the location of Noah's Ark, Rick joins the apostle Peter in reminding us of "the world that then was." However, Rick also draws a meaningful connection to the present hour, just as Jesus did when the Savior spoke of the last days being "as the days of Noah were."

Most importantly, Rick bolsters the faith and hope of modern believers by stressing that the faithful God who delivered His people in convulsive and tumultuous times in eras past is the same God who will deliver His people still.

Tony Cooke
Bible Teacher and Author

Once again, Rick Renner has written not only a very timely book, but what I would call a "now" word for the last days that we are living in. We have all witnessed a surge in the news of late surrounding UFOs (UAPs), aliens, and other supernatural phenomena — and people are wondering what to believe. Even more importantly, people are asking what the Bible has to say about these things, and throughout this book, we are continually brought back to what the Scripture has to say.

In this book *Fallen Angels, Giants, Monsters, and the World Before the Flood*, Rick has done an incredible job studying, researching, and presenting biblical truth that will help you make sense of what otherwise can be very confusing subjects. When I think of RENNER Ministries, I think of teaching you can trust, so read this book with confidence, knowing that the Word of God is always set forth in these pages as the final authority.

Mark Cowart
Senior Pastor, Church For All Nations
Colorado Springs, Colorado

I have known and looked up to Rick Renner for over thirty-five years, and I have read virtually everything he has ever written. I can honestly say that *Fallen Angels, Giants, Monsters, and the World Before the Flood* is one of my favorite books that he has written.

No one is more eminently qualified to write a book like this. Rick is a scholar, pastor, and historian, as well as a Spirit-filled man. The combination is so rare and unique that I can't think of another individual in our generation like him. This book addresses topics that very few teachers are willing to touch in our day, but everyone wants to know more about. As you read Rick's blend of historical research, Greek exposition, and biblical theology, you will have your eyes opened to the Word of God like never before. I am so grateful for Rick Renner and this gift that he has given the Body of Christ in these days that Jesus declared would be "as in the days of Noah."

Lee Cummings
Senior Leader of Radiant Church and Radiant Network of Churches
Author, School of the Spirit, Give No Rest!, *and* Take Heed, Watch and Pray!

In a world that is becoming more confusing and chaotic, Rick Renner's *Fallen Angels, Giants, Monsters, and the World Before the Flood* serves not merely as an eyeopener, but as an end-time alarm.

Beautifully illustrated and masterfully written with Renner's signature scholarly depth, this is not just a book; it's an indispensable arsenal for anyone yearning to comprehend the signs of our times and be adequately equipped to stand firm against the rising tide of spiritual darkness enveloping our world.

As a student of Bible prophecy for more than two decades, I found that this book enriched my spirit, expanded my knowledge, and profoundly altered my perspective. I firmly believe that *Fallen Angels, Giants, Monsters, and the World Before the Flood* is an essential addition to every believer's library. The revelation contained in this book alone has the potential to stir a dormant Church and reignite a passion for the imminent return of Jesus.

Maranatha!

Alan DiDio
Host, Encounter Today

Although it grows darker in the world, it gets brighter in the Church! The best days for the Church are yet ahead of us, and we will meet them with great expectation.

In this book, Rick Renner masterfully takes you through ancient biblical history to modern and future events to echo the bright future of the Church. The extensive research, first-hand reports, and in-depth studies make this a thrilling resource that you can go to again and again to gain insight into the events that have shaped and impacted humanity of centuries past, as well as those events currently unfolding today.

Throughout the detailed study of these biblical events and their parallel to our modern times, Rick also spotlights God's longsuffering and mercy that continue to reach out to mankind, causing us to further sense the urgency with which we must labor in reaping the Father's great harvest of souls.

Rick Renner shows us that just as Noah's Ark carried Noah and his family to safety, the Ark of Christ is to be the Christian's abiding place that will safely carry us through end-time events to the epic climax of the age — the Second Coming of Jesus!

Nancy Dufresne
President, Dufresne Ministries
Murrieta, California

Rick Renner's *Fallen Angels, Giants, Monsters, and the World Before the Flood* is a breathtaking journey through the pages of Scripture and the records of history. His meticulous research and profound spiritual insights bring the ancient world to life, revealing the startling parallels between the days of Noah and our own time. This book is a wake-up call for the Church, urging us to be vigilant and prepared for the Lord's return. Rick Renner's work is a deposit of wisdom and revelation, offering hope and encouragement to believers as we navigate the challenges of the last days.

Jimmy Evans
Founder, Tipping Point
Endtimes.com

Rick Renner's *Fallen Angels, Giants, Monsters and the World Before the Flood* is an enthralling read that dives deep into the lesser-known details of Noah's Ark and the pre-Flood era. Through meticulously researched historical and biblical evidence,

Rick Renner unveils great revelation that not only impacts our understanding of the great Flood, but also gives great insights that resonate with our present and foretell our future. I was thoroughly engrossed by the revelations and could barely put the book down. *This riveting book is a must-read!*

MiChelle Ferguson
Author and Speaker
Founder, MiChelle Ferguson Ministries

We are told that we are to discern the times and seasons we live in. This is so we can be prepared, but also so we can be a part of the ultimate plan of God in the earth. Rick Renner shares insights and mysteries concerning these very times. With great depth and understanding, he unveils truths to calm us, design us, and empower us for this strategic point in history. I encourage you to glean from this significant work for the future of you and your family.

Robert Henderson
Best-selling author of The Courts of Heaven *series*

In his book *Fallen Angels, Giants, Monsters, and the World Before the Flood*, Dr. Rick Renner writes with three realms of accuracy to back up this remarkable work.

1. Theologically
2. Historically
3. Archaeologically

This topic has always been the source of many questions, especially concerning the sons of God, fallen angels, and the world before the Flood. Rick, I loved the way you looked at it from every angle. This is a great literary piece and should be in every scholar's library.

I am excited to hold this manuscript in my hands, realizing all the work and research Rick has done on this subject. This book is needed in an hour of so many lies and fables — *deception* — in relation to this topic.

Dr. Rodney Howard-Browne
President and Founder, River University, Revival Ministries International,
The River at Tampa Bay Church

Rick Renner has done it again! His latest book *Fallen Angels, Giants, Monsters, and the World Before the Flood* will open your eyes to a completely new understanding of the past. Renner's meticulous research and captivating storytelling skillfully unravel the mysteries of the pre-Flood world, shedding light on enigmatic subjects like fallen angels, giants, and the profound implications they hold for our understanding of human history.

Daniel Kolenda
President, Christ for All Nations
Pastor, Nations Church

In *Fallen Angels, Giants, Monsters, and the World Before the Flood*, my good friend Rick Renner presents a compelling and refreshing perspective on the story of Noah's Ark and the Great Flood. Through his thorough research, captivating storytelling, and biblical teaching, he brings to light evidence that supports the inerrancy and eternal truth of the Bible. This book not only sheds new light on biblical events, but also offers insightful connections to our current world and our role as Christians in it. I am grateful to Rick for sharing his unique insights and reminding us of the relevance of God's Word in our ever-changing world.

Joni Lamb
Co-Founder and President, Daystar Television Network

Rick Renner is a prolific writer and one of the great scholars of this generation. His character and integrity are of the highest standard. His books have changed countless lives, and he practices what he preaches.

From the day Rick sent me the manuscript for *Fallen Angels, Giants, Monsters, and the World Before the Flood*, I could not put it down! The research and presentation are of the highest quality, not a warmed-over rehashing of previous discoveries. It is cutting-edge, unique, and it brings greater revelation and insight concerning the world before the Flood.

I am so glad Rick chose to tackle this subject and clearly show that archaeology proves God's Word to be true and that science is not something to be feared. This book is a classic that doesn't hide the truth but exposes it. I guarantee it will open your mind to new revelations in Scripture, history, and archaeology — and it will make you think!

Dr. Larry Ollison
Pastor and Author
Larry Ollison Ministries
Osage Beach, Missouri

Fallen Angels, Giants, Monsters, and the World Before the Flood — that title should pique the interest of the most jaded among us!

Tackling a subject such as this requires someone with the investigative skills of Sherlock Holmes, the courage of Churchill, the lucidity of Shakespeare, and the patience of Job. Such a task is tailor-made for my friend Rick Renner.

Combining the writings of Church fathers, historians, and ancient manuscripts, along with the testimony of various cultural traditions, this book sheds light on what is perhaps the most intriguing of mysteries mentioned in the Bible. It brings clarity to a subject that has been shrouded in obscurity, and it provides a fascinating glimpse into antediluvian life on earth.

Most importantly, this book provides a stark warning about the current conditions and developments that we see happening in the world around us with such stunning rapidity. Events that happened before the flood of Noah have a cautionary parallel to similar events taking place right now.

In addition, they comprise an unmistakable message for us all: *Jesus is coming soon!*

Dr. Rod Parsley
Pastor and Founder, World Harvest Church
Breakthrough Media Ministries
Columbus, Ohio

In his *Fallen Angels, Giants, Monsters, and the World Before the Flood*, Rick Renner has done a phenomenal job breaking down truth concerning one of the most captivating storylines about which the world has been so ignorant.

Before reading this book, I had spent years researching this topic, but I was incredibly dissatisfied by the lack of information available. After reading it, I am thankful to finally have many of the answers I've sought after for so long. Throughout every page, Rick demonstrates a rare ability to translate a great depth of revelatory knowledge into the everyday person's language. This has been one of the most intriguing books I have ever read, and I know you will say the same after reading it.

Gabe Poirot
Gabe Poirot Ministries
Author, Speaker, and Social-Media Influencer

Rick Renner has once again masterfully written an extensive, informative, and exciting work rooted in both the Scriptures and biblical history — but this time on a subject matter many view as taboo in the Body of Christ. The subject of giants, monsters, and the mating of angels and human women may sound like something that belongs in the annals of fantasy and myth; however, in reality, it is as nonfiction as the birth of our Savior and Lord Jesus Christ. Dr. Renner not only establishes this topic's legitimacy, but intricately shows its relevancy to the Church today.

As a student of this kind of teaching myself, I highly recommend this book for all believers. The thought-provoking content found within its pages only makes one desire God that much more. If you've ever wondered about the existence of these aberrant creatures, not only will your curiosity be piqued and your questions answered, but you'll also see how it all correlates with eschatology. Don't do yourself a disservice and miss out on one of the best books written on this subject. *Get this book now!*

Dr. Frederick Price
Pastor, Author, Broadcaster

Of all the books my father has written, this one is the most unique, as he has never written a book that has even come close to this topic.

Fallen Angels, Giants, Monsters, and the World Before the Flood reads not only as prophetic insight concerning the days we're living in, but as a science book complete with archaeological facts and a treasure chest of revelation from the Word of God. I learned more in this book about mythology, history, and prophecy than I have in all his other books combined. My father has hit *a grand slam* out of the park!

It's time for us to mobilize as the Body of Christ, and this book is a wake-up call for the Church. Jesus said that in the last days, it will be as in the days of Noah. This volume will teach you how to navigate these times and will prepare you for revival!

Philip Renner
Philip Renner Ministries
Founder and President, Worship Without Limits School

You may have heard secular commentators try to explain the "unexplainable" found in the Scriptures, such as fallen angels, giants, and the Flood. Now world-class Bible teacher Rick Renner answers your questions about these and other "unexplainable" details and events from a 100-percent biblical perspective!

Sid Roth
Host, It's Supernatural! *TV program*

This is a remarkably well-researched and insightful look into the mysteries of the world before the Flood. Rick Renner dives deep into ancient texts and Scripture to unearth truths about our origins and the implications for the times we live in now. His work is both informative and deeply thought-provoking, challenging us to reexamine our place in the unseen spiritual realms surrounding us.

Mike Signorelli
Pastor, Author, Media Influencer

We have never ceased experiencing the supernatural; we simply ceased being aware of it. From medieval abuses of hyper-mysticism in the Church to the radicalized exaltation of human thought through the Enlightenment, influences in the world have relentlessly sought to blind Spirit-filled believers to the reality of the invisible realm around us.

Rick Renner's latest masterpiece *Fallen Angels, Giants, Monsters, and the World Before the Flood* proves a point I regularly share while lecturing and preaching: If we, the Church, do not appropriately educate our people (fellow Christians) on the reality and prevalence of the supernatural realm, there is a very real devil waiting outside our churches who will be more than happy to intrigue, educate, and ultimately intoxicate a generation with all manner of counterfeit spirituality.

This book is an urgent, instructional, prophetic, and aesthetically stunning wake-up call to every single believer, providing a scriptural context for the strange, weird, and bizarre events unfolding before us. Phenomena previously relegated to the stuff of science-fiction are now being heralded as fact through mainline media sources and top government officials. Prepare to be instructed, shocked, and, most importantly, prepared by what you read in this book. After all, our Lord did describe the end-times, the days we are living in, using a very specific context — that they would be "like the days of Noah."

Larry Sparks, MDiv.
Publisher, Destiny Image
Author, Pentecostal Fire *and* Ask for the Rain

Fallen Angels, Giants, Monsters, and the World Before the Flood is so much more than a book. It's a detailed account of ancient history — history that is often forgotten about, misunderstood, or shunned by some as irrelevant. However, nothing could be further from the truth, as you will discover within these pages.

What Rick Renner has accomplished with this book is an extraordinarily detailed account of the world before the Flood and quite possibly the finest writing on the subject we have to date! You are about to discover an absolute masterpiece that will move you deeply as you discover the truth about the world prior to that worldwide catastrophe.

I recommend this book to anyone who wishes to understand God to a greater degree and have a fresh hope for his or her future. In fact, this book should be compulsory reading for all high schools and colleges across the land. *We need to understand our past so we can be better prepared for our future!*

Thank you, Rick, for the incredible amount of study, research, and analyses (even on-location expeditions) that you underwent to create this phenomenally accurate book. It is my absolute honor to wholeheartedly recommend it!

Ashley Terradez
Author, Speaker, and Ministry Leader
Founder and President, Terradez Ministries International
Abundant Life TV
Global Church Family Network

It is my pleasure to endorse the newest book from my friend and ministry companion Rick Renner. *Fallen Angels, Giants, Monsters, and the World Before the Flood* compares the times we're living in *and moving into* to the days of the flood of Noah. This is different from any book Rick has written, and he has written many. The strange discoveries and events we are witnessing today are not as new as we may think. Scientists, archaeologists, and the military are discovering objects in the skies and bones of animals in the earth that we have always thought were myths or science fiction. Are they? Or are they only telling us of the world at the time of Noah and why God had to destroy it? What was seen in Noah's day are instructions for believers today as we move into the closing moments of the Church age before the unveiling of God's judgment on a Christ-rejecting world. In this book, Rick does a marvelous job of explaining a difficult subject.

Bob Yandian
Bob Yandian Ministries
Tulsa, Oklahoma

CONTENTS

CHAPTER 6

WHAT ABOUT MONSTERS?.. **131**

CHAPTER 7

WHAT TYPES OF VIOLENCE DID THE GIANTS BRING INTO THE EARTH? **151**

CONTENTS

FOREWORD

Globally noted biblical scholar and theologian Rick Renner has once again researched, documented, and published an amazing masterpiece. Taking the reader and student back to the days before and after the Flood, Rick has unearthed and revealed what has been considered by many to be one of the greatest mysteries of the Bible.

In this book, Rick will explain in detail the relationship between the sons of God and the daughters of men that procreated the ancient race of giants, which is alluded to in the Scriptures. The existence of giants in not a myth, a Jewish legend, or an embellishment written by Moses, *but it is a fact!* There is ample biblical, historical, and even secular evidence of the existence of giants. What remains a mystery is how such demi-god creatures made their appearance on Earth and why?

Get ready for a journey into ages past, which will bring to the present a mystery that Rick Renner is now making known in his book *Fallen Angels, Giants, Monsters, and the World Before the Flood.*

Perry F. Stone Jr.
Evangelist, Teacher, Author
Founder, Voice of Evangelism Ministries

FOREWORD

Imagine it! Noah's Ark has been discovered and is about to be rediscovered by you, the reader. The prophetic implications of this are monumental and astonishing, yet that is only the beginning of the journey Rick Renner takes us on in this book!

Fallen Angels, Giants, Monsters, and the World before the Flood is captivating in every way as it unveils ancient mysteries that will usher you right up to the issues of our current day. This work is both academic and convincing; not only does it offer you a master class on biblical archaeology, but it will also powerfully guide you through arenas many would consider foreign terrain or uncharted territory. Being a student of these issues myself, I was profoundly captivated by the depth, clarity, and carefully studied insights Rick communicated on every page. Refreshing is the absence of the literary clickbait and over-hyped and under-delivered style used by some when dealing with topics of this nature. Instead, this book is packed with astonishing information, page after page.

While reading it from cover to cover, I was struck by a profound thought: The Lord desires that these issues be unveiled before our generation's eyes. It is a prophetic wake-up call for our time, and no one is better equipped to deliver the message than Rick Renner! He has spent much of his life walking, filming, and researching the physical locations tied to the events contained in this book, which qualifies him as a leading voice on the matter.

As excellent as this book is, it speaks far beyond historical and geological realities. It also confronts a slumbering normalcy bias regarding where we are in the biblical timeline. The mechanisms by which God speaks to the reader are the pathbreaking clarifications about Noah's Ark, the Flood, ancient giants, monsters, Nephilim, transhumanism, and the modern resurgence of these issues. Ultimately, an underlying message within the pages ahead divulges the agenda of darkness and acts as a prophetic sign to a world attempting to go completely mad!

In contrast to simply seeing more clearly the devil's vile plans from antiquity, you will discover God's plan for man from the beginning and His strategic plan for the future. Prophetically, this book is a cry to both the Church and the world *to get ready*!

In my opinion, there is simply no other author like Rick Renner. God chose him as a once-in-a-generation voice with tenured discernment and sensitivity to the Holy Spirit, which comes across powerfully through his writings. In my estimation, Rick is a man God placed on the earth for such a time as this. I have seen what he and his wife Denise do every day for the millions of people who follow them worldwide. He is an inspiration and one of the greatest leaders and teachers of our time. His books will last for many generations to come. This one will stand out as a great masterpiece and work of revelatory excellence.

It is my great honor to endorse this book and to say I have the privilege of knowing one of God's living generals. Thank you, Rick Renner, for gifting us all with this tremendous work!

Joseph Z
Author, Broadcaster, Prophetic Voice
JosephZ.com

A SPECIAL MESSAGE

My path first crossed with Rick Renner in the shadow of the ancient kingdom of Urartu's ancient volcanic mountains within the beautiful city of Van in eastern Turkiye. Accompanied by his media team, Rick arrived — a man with a vision, intent on capturing the essence of Noah's Ark and the Flood for a television project. During those ten transformative days, I found myself amidst the rustic charm of Turkish villages and the rugged mountains of Ararat (*see* Genesis 8:4), helping with their project and sharing insights on camera alongside Dr. Renner. When he asked me to write this foreword nearly a year later, I was a bit nervous. I'm no writer, but I've spent a good chunk of my life digging into the story of Noah and the Flood.

I first heard of the claims that a boat-shaped structure was the elusive Noah's Ark from an American explorer and biblical researcher, Ron Wyatt, from Tennessee, who visited California to share his remarkable claim: *A boat-shaped formation in Turkiye was the very remains of the Ark.*

This claim sparked my curiosity as a teenager in middle school, and that has never dimmed. Years of absorbing telephone conversations with Ron Wyatt, Dave Fasold, and other Ark researchers — cumulative hours on end discussing the possibilities — led to my own journeys to the site in 1997 while in college and many more trips to the boat-shaped site after that. These experiences have deeply rooted my life in the story of Noah and his boat, so much so that I now call the town of Dogubayazit *home*, merely a half-hour's drive from where the boat-shaped object sits. The site, steeped in legend and wrapped in enigma, has become the center of my life and passion.

This passion into Noah's Ark led me to become involved in the last three geophysical surveys of the site. Using advanced technology, the scientists on these expeditions have been able to peer underground to see the possible layout with some of the walls, chambers, corridors, and hull of what I believe to be the decayed remains of the world's oldest vessel. Sharing the details of these surveys and other facts about the Ark site with tour groups and online has been something I would have never dreamed I would be doing full time. So when Dr. Renner contacted me about helping his team, I was thrilled to participate and set up their trip so that the story of Noah, the Flood, and of the Ark landing in the mountains of Ararat could be shown to a wider audience.

The story of Noah's Ark is a dual account of salvation and divine judgment upon a corrupt world, a place where the enigmatic Nephilim once tread (*see* Genesis 6:4) and men's intentions and thoughts were continually evil (v. 5). It tells of a single person who, finding favor with God (v. 8), is tasked with constructing an ark in anticipation of a global deluge. It's not an ancient myth or a made-up story from the Bronze Age, but a real event with real people and animals and a 515-foot-long wooden ship designed by God.

Even Christ, in foretelling the end times, drew a parallel to the story of Noah, asserting, "For as were the days of Noah, so will be the coming of the Son of Man" (Matthew 24:37 *ESV*). This book presents not only the stark facts and scientific investigations into the Durupinar ark site, but also delves into Rick Renner's important research on the Nephilim and their implications for our time. It is a book that enriches the discourse on Noah's Ark, enlightening and edifying the reader in an era much in need of a message of divine grace and a soon-to-come judgment.

As you read these pages, may you, too, be blessed by the enduring message of Noah and the Flood. I pray that we will all find grace in the eyes of God during these last days.

Andrew Jones
Noah's Ark Researcher
NoahsArkScans.com

ACKNOWLEDGMENTS

I have wanted to write a book on this subject for decades, and at long last, I felt it was the right time for me to dive into this amazing subject that has perplexed many who have sought solid answers from Scripture and history about this theme. To write and produce a book of this caliber has required many minds, eyes, and hands, and I want to acknowledge the roles of those who have helped me craft this book for my readers.

First, I want to acknowledge Becky Gilbert, who is the chief editor in our ministry and who carefully and diligently hovers over every word I write to make sure it correctly communicates each point I am attempting to make. Over the years, I have come to value the work of editors like Becky, and I am thankful for the way they enable a writer like me to more excellently communicate the truth of Scripture on the printed page. A big thanks to Becky for carrying out her role in this monumental task with excellence.

Second, I want to acknowledge Vincent Newfield, who was a content contributor to this book. He has done immense research of his own that verifies what I have written and has added content that was needed to more fully convey the points made in every chapter. Vincent has been an indispensable part of this project, and I am very thankful for the hours and thought he put into this book along with me.

Third, I want to acknowledge Lisa Moore, who designed every page of this book to make it sparkle more beautifully for my readers. I sat alongside Lisa as she pulled art, cropped it, enriched it, and set it in place on every page. It is a pleasure to work with a designer who is filled with the Spirit of God and who desires to produce work that gives glory to God.

Fourth, I want to acknowledge Ron Young and Danyelle Lee, who led a team, including Tori Gray, Devin Howard, Michelle Gilbert, and Krislyn Holder, as together they researched to find precisely the correct art I needed for every point that needed to be illustrated in some way. Danyelle and the team were available nonstop and promptly provided not only images and illustrations, but also solutions for points that were more difficult to illustrate, and I am so grateful.

Fifth, I want to acknowledge Pamela Page, who did the endnote research for this book. It is my practice to have a specialized researcher come behind me as I write in order to provide extra eyes that verify what I have written. To do good footnoting takes many hours, and I am thankful to Pamela for the volume of hours she spent researching vast amounts of material to correctly present the citations for this book. If you look at the endnotes in the back, you will appreciate the meticulous work Pamela did for this project.

Sixth, I want to acknowledge a team of proofreaders that includes Beth Parker, Debbie Townsley, Roni Bagby, Kalea Ellison, and also Pamela Page. Each of these individuals absorbed every word of this book to digest it and to look for anything that needed to be corrected in the text. My goal is that everything produced by my spirit, mind, and hands is done in a way that brings glory to Jesus Christ. I am thankful for these proofers who helped make sure this level of excellence was maintained.

Seventh, I want to thank Andrew Jones, the chief researcher of the Durupinar site in the mountains of Ararat, whom I appreciate and who has become a personal friend. He has also written A Special Message (*see* page xxxiii) for this book. Andrew has spent decades living in the eastern part of Turkiye as he has researched and led scientific teams to the Durupinar site to study the ruins of Noah's Ark. I am thankful for his role in helping me understand every aspect of this very important biblical site.

Eighth, I want to thank my team and film crew who regularly travel with me to the ends of the earth to document and produce resources for the Body of Christ. A big thanks to Maxim Myasnikov, Alexander Dovgan, Mark Dovgan, Nikita Lyskov, William Renner, Joel Renner, and Paul Renner (and also to Asil Tuncer), who accompanied me on my expeditions to Noah's Ark. For all their various roles as I studied the Durupinar site in the eastern mountains of Turkiye (Turkey), I am so grateful.

Ninth, I want to thank our precious family of ministry partners, whose finances, gifts, and prayers are vital to the work of the ministry we do in many parts of the world. It would be impossible for us to do anything we're doing without the support of this precious partner family. First Corinthians 3:6 says one plants, another waters, and God gives the increase. Denise and I, our family, and our ministry team do the planting; our partners faithfully water the work with their finances and prayers; and God is the One who miraculously gives the increase. All three parts are needed, and I am thankful for those who participate in every role.

Tenth, I want to thank the leadership of Harrison House Publishers — not only for being my publisher, but for genuinely caring about my family, my ministry, and me, and for allowing me to create published works in the way I dream they can be created. You are the "dream team" for me, and I am exceedingly grateful for every person we work with at Harrison House Publishers.

Last, but in a huge sense *most*, I want to thank my precious wife Denise and Paul, Philip, and Joel and their families for their support as I travel to difficult regions of the earth to document and film for others what many will never get to witness in person. My family is an amazing support, and they are *vital* to our ministry team. Thank you for your encouragement to do what is even physically challenging for me at times and for helping me and other members of the team do what is needed to produce resources for the Body of Christ.

Of course, I am most supremely thankful to the Lord Jesus Christ, who empowers me to do what He has graced me to do with my life. If it were not for His enabling touch, I would not be able to do what I do or to produce the volume of materials that flows from my heart, mind, and hands. And He has gifted me with remarkable people as a part of my team. Thank You, Lord, for all of this, and I pray that what has been produced in this book is well-pleasing to You!

INTRODUCTION

O f the many books I've written over the years, you will see that this one stands in a category that is different from the others. This is a serious work, a prophetic work, and one that I am quite excited to get into the hands of readers. Because it is different from my previous works, before you get started reading, I want to explain a few things about my *motive*, my *research*, my *arrangement of materials*, and my *desire for readers* in producing this unique book.

First, **my motive.** I have desired to write this book for many years, but — as I do generally, as a habit — I waited until the Spirit of God prompted me to do it. Finally, just in the past year, I felt Him inspiring me that the timing was correct to write and release this book.

Second, **my research.** To prepare for its writing, I carried out intense research that included studying annals of historical writings, the ancient historians who wrote them, and other scholars, statesmen, and travelers who were noteworthy in their documentations. In addition, I personally traveled multiple times with my film crew to the eastern lands of Turkiye (Turkey), to the lower mountains of the Ararat mountain range, to visit the renowned Durupinar site where the alleged ruins of Noah's Ark lay on the slope of Mount Cudi (pronounced Mount Judi). After my extensive firsthand research — and upon studying the discoveries not only of ancient voices, but of contemporary experts — I find myself convinced that the massive ship-shaped formation on the slopes of the lower mountains of Ararat is indeed the ruins of Noah's Ark.

Besides my own research and my multiple trips to the Durupinar site with my film crew, I leaned on the help of a long-term, serious Ark researcher who lives in eastern Turkiye and who has devoted decades of his life to the study of this site. But I also intensely studied the analyses of scientists, technicians, and other experts in various fields of science who have devoted many hours of study to the Durupinar site, where this massive formation lies. The combined work of all these various professionals has provided information so convincing to me that it is sufficient to substantiate what is set forth herein regarding the Durupinar site and the existence *and location* of Noah's Ark.

Also in the pages to come, you will see that I dove deep not only into the historical writings of the ancients, but also into the writings of Early Church fathers who wrote extensively about the bizarre activities in the days of Noah preceding the Flood. These Early Church fathers wrote in such a unified voice that it is impossible to ignore their unanimity about the events that led to the release of the Great Deluge that covered the earth in Noah's day. To verify the conclusions of my research, this book is supported by a substantial number of well-researched endnotes for those who wish to study the subject more deeply.

To do this research correctly, the Bible, to which I have dedicated my life, was the foundational source of my information. But in bringing to bear the surrounding details of the days of Noah before the Flood, I also considered various extrabiblical writings that were regarded as serious Bible commentary during the intertestamental years between the Old and New Testaments and during early New Testament times. These extrabiblical narratives include *The Book of Enoch*, *The Book of Jasher* (which is referred to in the Old Testament), and *The Book of Giants*.

None of these three works is considered to be a sacred, canonical book of the Bible, but it must be noted that fragments of them or, in some cases, documents in their entirety were discovered among the Dead Sea Scrolls. Scholars generally deem them to be early apocalyptical works and ancient commentary on events that occurred before the Flood.

Third, **my arrangement of materials.** To help you navigate the pages of this book, I want you to understand how I grouped the chapters. The earlier chapters begin with the Durupinar site and move to the earth's early population so you can learn why that was so important to the Flood narrative. Then I take you to the identity of the "sons of God" that are referenced in Genesis 6:2.

To further explain the intensity of man's sinful activities on the earth before the Flood, I focus next on why angels went after strange flesh, on the birth of hybrid giants (and the possibility later of hybrid *monsters*), and on the types of violence these half-human creatures brought into the earth. Finally, I bring you to the reason God chose to send the Flood and how all of this impacts the last days in which we live.

As you proceed in this book, you will see that it is loaded with art, illustrations, and various kinds of images, including specialized pieces that were created specifically for this book by noted illustrator Lev Kaplan. These images were expensive to incorporate, but my team and I felt they were necessary to assist readers in grasping the scope and the gravity of the message communicated in the pages you're about to read.

***Fourth*, my desire for readers**. It is my prayer that previously sealed mysteries will be opened to you as you read this book and that you'll understand why in our own times, it seems that darkness and delusion — very similar to the vast darkness that occurred in the days before the Flood — are being released into the earth again. Most of all, my prayer is that you will see that the Bible is completely reliable, that your prophetic role in these last days is important, and that God is calling His Church to step forward to proclaim Divine Truth to a last-days erring generation — before the age is consummated and judgment is released.

— *Rick Renner*

In 1959, an aerial photo of the Ararat mountain range passed into the hands of a cartographer named Ilhan Durupinar, a Turkish army captain, who was stunned to see a large formation in the lower mountains of Ararat that looked precisely like a massive ship. Since 1959, archaeologists, geologists, and researchers have extensively studied the site, which is now officially referred to as the Durupinar site.

CHAPTER ONE

THE DISCOVERY OF NOAH'S ARK

For thousands of years, people have read and told the story of Noah's Ark. Even major films have been produced about it by Hollywood and Christian research organizations. Some speculate that Noah's Ark was merely a legend, while others believe it to be a true account of an event that happened thousands of years ago. But the Bible makes it clear that Noah's Ark and the events preceding and following the Flood were real-life occurrences, and Scripture documents the story of it in Genesis 6-9.

Indeed, the story of the Flood and Noah's Ark is not a myth or fantasy. It was an event that really happened, and the ruins of the Ark lay visible today on the slopes of the lower mountains of Ararat. In fact, over many thousands of years, scores of people have come to this very site to see the Ark's ruins with their own eyes. There are many significant eyewitnesses from antiquity who wrote about it and documented the details of what they saw, and we will look at some of those accounts in the pages of this book. You will also see that contrary to the predominant belief that Noah's Ark landed on the *peak* of Mount Ararat, it instead landed "upon the *mountains* of Ararat," just as Genesis 8:4 tells us.

In Matthew 24:37, Jesus said, "But as the days of Noe [Noah] were, so shall also the coming of the Son of man be." According to Jesus' prophetic words in this verse, events at the end of the age will be similar to those that occurred in the days prior to the Flood. It's amazing that now we are at the end of the age, and Noah's Ark has appeared again as a glaring last-days reminder of Jesus' words in this pivotal verse.

NOAH'S ARK RE-EMERGES IN 1948 AND 1959

In earlier times, the Ark was visible, and notable people from antiquity visited it and even wrote about it.[1] But because the slope where the Ark landed was a mud-flow resulting from the abating waters of the Flood, over thousands of years, the ship became encased in hardened mud. Interestingly, an earthquake that occurred in 1948 freed the upper part of the structure from the mud, and it was at about that time that surrounding Kurdish villagers reported the ship's "sudden appearance."[2] It is fascinating that this was also the exact month and year the nation of Israel was reestablished, which was a notable sign of the end of the age.

Although local villagers noticed the emergence of the unusual formation, it was later in 1959 that it first came to the attention of authorities when it was accidentally rediscovered as a pilot was flying over the expansive Ararat mountain range in eastern Turkiye to take aerial photos for the creation of new maps for the region. When the photos passed into the hands of a cartographer named Ilhan Durupinar, a Turkish army captain, he was stunned from his study of the photos to see a

It has been noted that after an earthquake in 1948 shook the area, a local Kurdish community on the slope of Mount Cudi (pronounced Mount Judi) first noticed what appeared to be the outline of a massive ship that appeared in a mudflow.

Pictured above: Turkish army captain Ilhan Durupinar noticed the ship-shaped formation in aerial photos and passed them on to be studied by Dr. Arthur Brandenberger, a noted professor at Ohio State University.

large formation in the lower mountains of Ararat that looked precisely like a massive ship. In an interview given later by Durupinar, he stated he was absolutely convinced that the object he saw in the aerial photos was a ship. Because he believed the photos merited further research, he sent them to be studied by Dr. Arthur Brandenberger, a noted professor at Ohio State University.

Dr. Brandenberger was renowned as the expert who later studied reconnaissance photos captured in 1962 and, as a result, identified Soviet missile bases in Cuba during the Kennedy administration. After carefully studying the aerial photos of the ship-shaped formation

Pictured below: In 1960, a photo and article about the ship-shaped formation in the lower mountains of the Ararat mountain range was published in the Turkish version of *LIFE* magazine, and it was later published in the English version of *LIFE*.

Photos published in the September 1960 issue of *LIFE* magazine showed the ship-shaped formation on Mount Cudi and the rugged area around that vicinity. It is estimated that 8.5 million copies of this issue were printed and distributed.

in the lower mountains of Ararat, Dr. Brandenberger concluded: *"I have no doubt at all, that this object is a ship. In my entire career, I have never seen an object like this on an aerial photo."*[3]

Since 1959 when those early aerial photos were first taken, archaeologists, geologists, and researchers have extensively studied the site, which is now officially referred to as *the Durupinar site*. In 1960, a photo of this ship-shaped formation was published in the Turkish version of *LIFE* magazine, and it was later published in the English version of *LIFE*.[4] Soon a group of researchers arrived at the site in the lower Ararat mountains — about 18 miles south of the peak of Greater Mount Ararat — to accompany Captain Durupinar in a search for artifacts or something significant that would be related to a ship, but at that time only minor excavations occurred, which produced nothing conclusive.

THE NEXT WAVE OF INVESTIGATIONS:
RON WYATT AND HIS RESEARCH TEAM

With an estimated 8.5 million copies of *LIFE* magazine in print, a multitude of people had both seen the now-famous photo and read the article in the September 5, 1960, issue — and that multitude included an amateur archaeologist named Ron Wyatt. Moved by what he read, Wyatt began to conduct scientific tests to study various aspects of Noah's Ark. He and his two sons then took a trip to Turkiye in the fall of 1977 to do their own on-location research at the Durupinar site.[5]

After Wyatt obtained official permission to perform a study, he, with the help of others, conducted intensive research at the Durupinar site, which lasted a period of several years. His tests included metal-detection surveys, sub-surface radar scans, and chemical analyses. The results led the team to conclude that the ship-shaped formation was indeed the remains of Noah's Ark.[6]

Wyatt and his team carefully took measurements of the structure. From end to end, the formation measured 515 feet long, which is exactly 300 Egyptian cubits in length, or the same length given to Noah by God, as recorded in Genesis 6:15. They estimated that the width of this formation in the middle

Pictured above: Archaeological researcher Ron Wyatt is pictured in front of the ship-shaped formation at an early expedition at the Durupinar site.

Pictured above: A rivet found by Ron Wyatt at the Durupinar site was subjected to a chemical analysis that showed it to be made of a compound of metals.

Pictured above: After scraping one side of the ship-shaped formation, archaeologists discovered vertically positioned petrified timbers on the mud-encased object.

had originally been 50 cubits, which is also the precise measurement we see that God gave to Noah in Genesis 6:15. Due to the structure's extreme age, the sides had fallen outward, and for that reason, it is wider today. Nevertheless, when Wyatt and his team used the proper calculations, they determined that the vessel would have originally perfectly matched the dimensions provided in the Genesis 6 account.

Upon further careful examination, the team discovered vertical, mud-covered "bulges" protruding from the sides of the structure at regular intervals. They identified these to be the mud-covered ribs of the ship.[7]

Even today when one visits the site, he can see the alleged protruding ribs at regular intervals along the sides of the formation. And because of all the metal-detection surveys and subsurface radar scans performed at the site, researchers have been able to mark with precision accuracy lines on the top of the ship to show where beams still lay below the earth's surface.

At the time of this writing, the ship-shaped formation rests directly in the middle of a massive mudflow, but it is clear from studying the landscape that it has moved down the slope over time from its original location. The original landing site seems to have been about 900 feet higher in elevation than the current location. It is also important to note that the ancient name for the place where the formation was discovered was *Cudi Dagh*, and it means *the place of the landing* or *the place of descent*.[8]

Pictured above: The alleged protruding ribs of Noah's Ark can be seen at regular intervals along the sides of this ship-shaped formation. An earthquake in 1948 was responsible for unearthing the top portions of this structure.

Pictured above: Because of all the metal-detection surveys and subsurface radar scans that have been performed at the site, researchers were able to lay out lines on the top of the ship to show where beams lay below the earth's surface.

LABORATORY TESTS REVEAL PHENOMENAL FINDINGS

In the latter years of his research, Wyatt claimed that he and his team discovered a cavity on the starboard side of the ship. With permission from authorities, the team used a core drill to take samples from inside, and the excavation yielded several interesting objects, which were sent for a laboratory analysis. Some of those objects turned out to be petrified animal dung, fragments of a petrified antler, and a piece of animal hair, none of which would likely be found together, deep inside a naturally occurring geological formation.

Then there was the piece of petrified wood, which was one of the most significant discoveries of all at the formation's site. It appeared to be made of three planks that were laminated together with some kind of adhesive, similar to the technology used today to produce laminated plywood. It seems that the glue oozed from the layers, and the exterior surface of the wood was coated with bitumen (pitch), which is the tar-like material God told Noah to use to cover the exterior and interior of the Ark (*see* Genesis 6:14). All of this remarkably suggests that the builders had construction knowledge far more advanced than what was previously believed to have existed in that ancient period.[9]

A piece of petrified wood from the site appeared to be comprised of three planks "laminated" together with some kind of adhesive, similar to the technology used today to produce laminated plywood.

Wyatt also reported that the laboratory analyses revealed the petrified wood had iron nails embedded in it. Moreover, the team unearthed what seemed to be a large disk-shaped rivet. It appeared to be a rivet that had been hammered after being inserted through a hole in the ship, and laboratory analyses of the rivet showed that it was made of a combination of iron, aluminum, and titanium, which again suggests an advanced knowledge of metallurgy and engineering, far beyond anything previously believed to have existed at the time Noah's Ark was constructed.[10]

After years of working at the Durupinar site, Wyatt and his research teams concluded:

"This data does not represent natural geology. These are man-made structures. These reflections are appearing too periodic...and too periodic to be random in that type of natural pace."

The scans conducted at the site revealed the symmetry of the structure under the mud, along with a logical placement of objects. Altogether, the findings unmistakably confirmed this was a human-made structure, and most likely that it was the remains of Noah's Ark.[11]

There have been skeptics who mocked Wyatt for his research and who tried to discredit him as being nothing more than an amateur who didn't know what he was doing. But regardless of how fiercely cynics tried to discredit Wyatt, his research unleashed a flood of interest at the Durupinar site. After Wyatt's death in 1999, many others arrived to conduct their own investigations.[12]

INVESTIGATIONS OF THE DURUPINAR SITE CONTINUE — GPR AND ERT SCANS CONFIRM FINDINGS

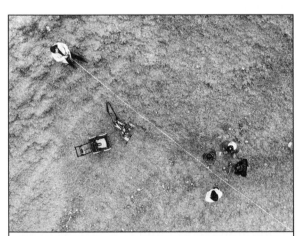

Ground-penetrating radar (GPR) and electrical-resistivity tomography (ERT) scans have been performed as a way to peer deeper into the earth to see more precisely what lies below the surface of the protruding ship-shaped formation.

Today the Durupinar site continues to be the subject of intense research and scientific investigation. Bible scholars, archaeologists, geologists, researchers, and other scientists have come from far and wide to the eastern mountains of Turkiye to study the site.

With a mountain of scientific evidence and reams of research that have been produced after Wyatt's death, it is difficult to argue with the data. Even the most severe skeptics would now find it nearly insurmountable to

Pictured above: Scans performed at the site via various scientific methods have repeatedly shown that what lies below the surface is man-made and that its measurements precisely match the biblical dimensions of the Ark as given to Noah by God in the Genesis account.

disclaim the scientific proofs that the combined research has produced over the last several decades.

The language in the following several paragraphs may seem complicated or too technical to understand from a layman's point of view — but stay with me, because the serious scientific research conducted at the Durupinar site has not been performed by mere novices or by men of means just looking to make a name for themselves or fulfill a childhood dream. From the accidental aerial photos in 1959 to the Turkish cartographer to the acclaimed professor at Ohio State, intellectual curiosity and the motivation to search out a matter with integrity have resulted in serious researchers investing their lives to build on the work and the findings of one another in a way that profoundly benefits us all, as you will see more and more clearly in the chapters of this book.

For many years, ground-penetrating radar (GPR) and electrical-resistivity tomography (ERT) scans have been carried out as a way to peer deeper into the earth to see

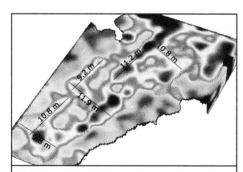

Pictured above: Scans show clear right angles that do not appear in naturally occurring geological formations, further proving that this structure is indeed a man-made object.

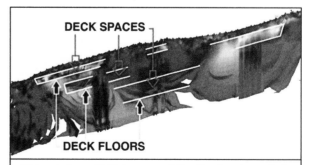

Pictured above: Multiple scans of the site also show a hull, three distinct levels, and multiple compartments or rooms. This rendering mirrors the findings and confirms that the massive object beneath the surface is not a natural formation, but man-made.

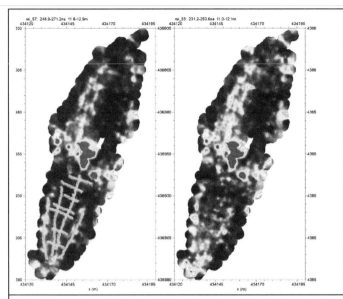

Pictured above: This recent internal analysis of the interior of the ship-shaped formation outlines distinct levels, rooms, a central corridor, and possibly even the beams for the lower structure.

more precisely what lies below the surface of the protruding ship-shaped formation.

Andrew Jones, a computer programmer and researcher, who was one of the contributors at *The Seventh International Symposium on Mount Ararat and Noah's Ark* in October 2023, as well as at the October 2021 symposium, explained some of the workings of the most recent research conducted at the Durupinar site. Jones stated in one of his writings:

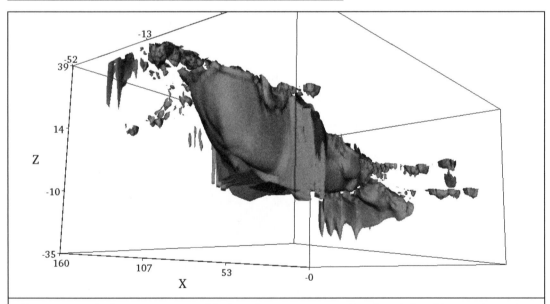

Pictured above: Viewing computer scans of the formation, even a person with no knowledge of the scanning process can easily see it is a complete ship with its underside buried deep in a mudflow. The resistivity-survey results conclusively show a buried structure, consistent in shape with the remains of a ship, including a hull, rib detail, and decks.

Ground-Penetrating Radar (GPR) has emerged as an indispensable tool in contemporary geospatial research, facilitating detailed insights into subsurface structures and potential archaeological sites . . . presenting a rigorous analysis of GPR data processed using the advanced GPR-Slice v. 7 software.

Methodological approaches encompassed noise filtration, amplitude adjustment, and enhanced signal clarity, leading to the identification of *distinct geometric patterns* [my emphasis] at a depth of 3 to 7 meters. These patterns, indicative of a unique subsurface structure, are critically examined in the context of both geological formations and potential archaeological remnants.

In addition to GPR, the expedition employed Light Detection and Ranging (LiDAR) technology, a pivotal advancement in geospatial mapping. LiDAR was instrumental in creating a detailed 3D topographical map of the Durupinar Noah's Ark site. This high-resolution map, capturing minute surface details, provided invaluable context to the GPR findings, allowing for a more comprehensive spatial understanding of the site's topography and potential structural remnants.

Lastly, the 2019 expedition results are compared with the 1987 geophysical survey. Similarities in the GPR data are shown at specific locations on the boat formation.[13]

Furthermore, remote-sensing expert, John Larsen, incorporated his ERT findings and created the formation of a three-dimensional computerized image to examine the ship-shaped formation more thoroughly. These researchers' work demonstrates that time and again, the scans and various scientific methods used have repeatedly shown that what lies below the surface is *man-made* and that its measurements *precisely fit* the biblical dimensions of the Ark as given to Noah by God in the Genesis account.[14]

The most recent analysis of the 2019 GPR scans at the Durupinar site was carried out in 2023 by a highly respected geophysicist whose renowned specialty is surveying and mapping environmental, engineering, geotechnical, infrastructural, hydrogeological, and archaeological applications and whose expert knowledge was also called upon for the development of SOPs for electromagnetic (EM), magnetic, resistivity, and other exploration methods for the Massachusetts Department of Environmental Protection (MASSDEP), formerly the Massachusetts Department of Environmental Quality Engineering (MA DEQE).

This most recent internal analysis of the interior of the ship-shaped formation clearly shows distinct levels, rooms, a central corridor, and even the possible beams and/or walls of the lower structure. None of these features would be possible in a naturally occurring geological formation, which again reveals that this is indeed a man-made object.

As a result of these multi-year investigations, there is now a growing number of archaeologists, geologists, and researchers who attest that, just as the Bible tells us in Genesis 8:4, there really is a massive ship-shaped formation lying in the lower slopes of the mountains of Ararat.

Amazingly, these multiple studies show a hull, three distinct levels, and multiple compartments or rooms. The resistivity survey results conclusively show a buried structure, consistent in shape with the remains of a ship, complete with a hull, rib detail, and decks.

Furthermore, this ship-structure looks very similar to the remains of other ships that have been discovered across the world. Viewing computer scans of the vessel, even a person with no knowledge of the scanning process can easily see it is a ship with its underside buried deep in a mudflow.[15] The location, length, and layout of the formation match the description of Noah's Ark in every detail.

With all the GPR and ERT scans that have been conducted multiple times on the mud-encased structure in the lower mountains of Ararat, growing numbers of researchers affirm that what is on the slopes is a man-made, ship-shaped object.

And these findings are so profound that TV crews have come from the Science Channel,[16] the History Channel,[17] and a growing list of other well-known media outlets to document the ship-shaped formation at the Durupinar site. Anyone who is willing to look at the site with an unbiased mind can see that the evidence is there that can confirm the ruins are indeed those of Noah's Ark.

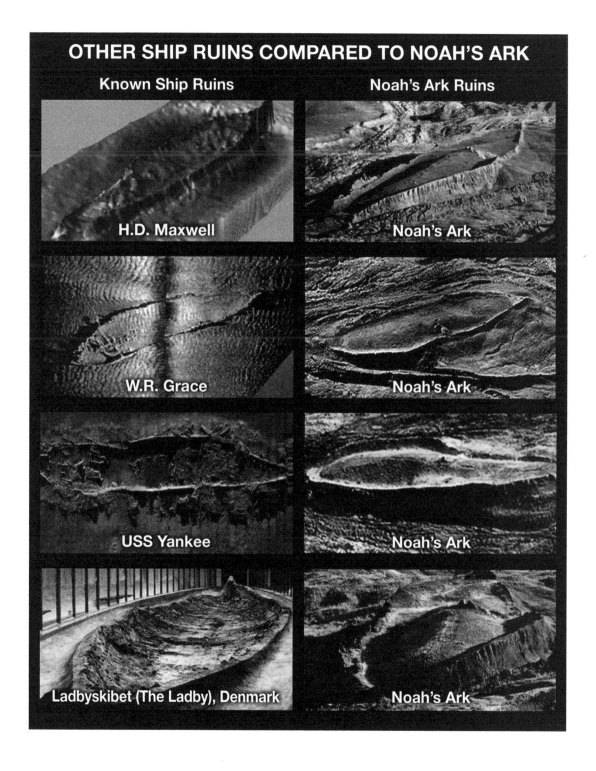

OTHER SHIP RUINS COMPARED TO NOAH'S ARK

Known Ship Ruins

Noah's Ark Ruins

H.D. Maxwell

Noah's Ark

W.R. Grace

Noah's Ark

USS Yankee

Noah's Ark

Ladbyskibet (The Ladby), Denmark

Noah's Ark

Mount Ararat consists of two peaks separated by about seven miles. The smaller peak, known as Little or Lesser Ararat, has an elevation of about 12,782 feet, and the higher peak, known as Great or Greater Ararat, has an elevation of about 16,854 feet. Historically, those who have claimed to have seen the Ark on these mountain peaks have never been able to conclusively prove their claims.

THE PEAK OF MOUNT ARARAT

There have been so-called "sightings"[18] of Noah's Ark in the past by some who claimed to have seen or visited it on the very top of Mount Ararat, which consists of two peaks separated by about seven miles. The smaller peak, known as *Little Ararat* or *Lesser Ararat*, has an elevation of about 12,782 feet, and the higher peak, known as *Great Ararat* or *Greater Ararat*, is estimated to rise to a height of 16,854 feet. Strangely, those who claimed to have seen the Ark have never been able to return to the same spot to show it to researchers, which means they have never provided verifiable proof that Noah's Ark is located on the peak of Mount Ararat.

Even movies have been produced alleging that Noah's Ark rests on the edge of a cliff or that it dangles dangerously on a crevasse on the steep slopes of Mount Ararat. Others have speculated that the Ark was split in half due to an earthquake or the impact of a glacier and that the two parts now rest on different levels on Ararat's peak. Following up on these claims, although massive sums of money have been invested by individuals who have searched for the Ark, no one has ever found it on the peak of Ararat.[19]

It should also be noted that with all the high-tech satellite technology that exists today, which is constantly capturing images of Mount Ararat and the entire surrounding region,[20] no satellite has ever produced a verifiable image of Noah's Ark on the very peak of the mountain. And if you think ice and snowpack is a problem in terms of visibility, think again. Due to climate changes over epochs of time, the ice and snow on the peak of Mount Ararat nearly melts away in the summer months, leaving only a small patch of frozen residue in the hottest months of the year.[21] This means the mountain peak is nearly completely exposed every summer. Yet even with an unobstructed view, with the absence of ice and snow, we have no known satellite image that can verify the existence of Noah's Ark on Ararat's peak.

Despite the challenges of rugged slopes and extreme altitude, reaching the peak of Mount Ararat has become popular with hordes of professional mountain climbers. Mountaineers have traveled from across the world to ascend the peak, and it has been climbed from every possible direction. Yet among the thousands of climbers, no one has come forward to claim *and verify* that he has come across the remains of Noah's Ark on the peak of Mount Ararat.

Some years ago, there was a famous video that became popular on various websites, which claimed to show the Ark on the peak of Ararat and several so-called "rooms" inside. But the individual who produced the original footage has consistently refused

Pictured above: Due to climate change, the ice and snow on the peak of Mount Ararat nearly melts away in the summer months, leaving only a small patch of frozen residue in the hottest months of the year.

Pictured above: With all the high-tech satellite technology that exists today, no satellite has ever produced a verifiable image of Noah's Ark on the very peak of Mount Ararat.

Pictured above: Professional mountain-climbers travel from across the world to ascend Mount Ararat. Yet among the thousands of climbers over the years, no one has ever come forward to verify that he has come across the ruins of Noah's Ark on its peak.

Mount Ararat is a stratovolcano that has erupted many times since the Flood. If Noah's Ark had landed on the peak of Mount Ararat, it would not have survived these multiple eruptions that have occurred since the time of the Flood. This illustration shows how the destructive blasts of a stratovolcano continually layer the sides of the slope with each eruption. A vessel landing at this location simply could not have survived these after-effects.

to identify the location where it was filmed, and he has never returned there with researchers for the sake of verification. Although the video was popular for a while, it is now generally considered to be a fraud.

In addition to all this, Mount Ararat is a stratovolcano, which has erupted many times since the Flood, making impossible the survival of a ship structure in the near vicinity. Stratovolcanoes of this type erupt with explosive force, causing magma and gases to blast out at high speed and enormous intensity. Records show that Mount Ararat had violent volcanic eruptions regularly in the period of 2,500–2,400 BC; 550 BC; 1450 AD; 1783 AD; and 1840 AD.[22] The massive eruption that occurred in 1840 was accompanied by an earthquake that killed approximately 10,000 local people and wiped out an entire village with a gigantic landslide and subsequent debris flow.[23]

In the plains below Mount Ararat are massive and deep hardened lava flows that bear witness to the devastating impact of multiple eruptions in the past. Even if Noah's Ark had landed on the peak of Mount Ararat, it would not have survived these multiple eruptions. Regardless, the Bible never said that Noah's Ark landed on the peak of Mount Ararat as many have wrongly concluded. Rather, it clearly states that the Ark came to rest "upon the mountains of Ararat" (*see* Genesis 8:4). Interestingly, on

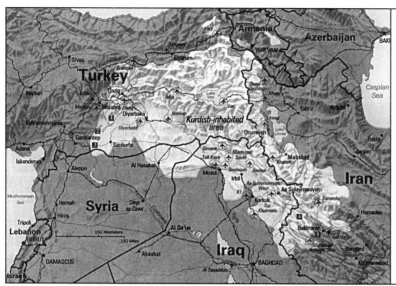

The Ararat mountain range in eastern Turkiye is geographically immense. According to the Bible, Noah's Ark came to rest somewhere in that huge range after the waters of the Flood abated. Some scholars believe the region where the Ark came to rest is also the same area where the Garden of Eden was originally located. We don't know if this is true, but it is interesting that in the same spot where God told Adam and Eve to be fruitful and multiply, He may have also told Noah and his family to replenish the earth.

the direct opposite side of the plain — about 18 miles south of Mount Ararat — is the Durupinar ship-shaped object that is nestled in the lower mountains of Ararat. Because this site is so obvious, it is perplexing that others looked for the Ark on the peak of Mount Ararat.

Again, the Ararat mountain range in eastern Turkiye is immense, extending even into Armenia and Iran. According to the Bible, Noah's Ark came to rest somewhere in that vast range after the waters of the Flood began to recede.

The remains of Noah's Ark are visible today and are located in the lower mountains of Ararat, on a slope of a mountain called *Cudi* (pronounced *Judi*). The name Cudi refers to *the place of the landing*. From the most ancient times, it has carried this name because the ancients knew it was the place where Noah's Ark had landed. After years of research, on June 20, 1987, Turkish authorities officially dedicated the slope of Mount Cudi as the site of Noah's Ark.[24]

There is one more important point about the entire region of the Ararat mountain range that must be noted. Some scholars believe the region where the Ark came to rest is also the same geographical area where the Garden of Eden was originally located. This is so important that we will come back to this possible connection as we proceed.

My team and I gathered for this photo directly on top of the ruins of Noah's Ark in the lower mountains of Ararat. The twin peaks of Mount Ararat can be seen 18 miles away in the distance beyond the flood plain that is situated below.

MY PERSONAL VISIT TO NOAH'S ARK

Having studied much of the documented material about the Durupinar site over many years, I finally decided to travel there with my media team to see and to document the site myself. From my personal experience, the following is just some of what I observed.

The terrain where the ship-shaped formation rests is extremely rugged, and the structure indeed lies in a massive hardened mudflow that has remained from the time of the Flood. As one approaches the slope and sees it from a distance, it becomes visibly clear that the formation lying on the slope of Mount Cudi is shaped like an ancient ship.

The sheer size of it — 515 feet long (or approximately 300 Egyptian cubits) — makes it difficult for a visitor to comprehend what he is seeing when he walks directly on top of it. However, with my team, a historian, and an archaeologist who has worked at the site for more than 20 years, we observed the structure from a distance and then

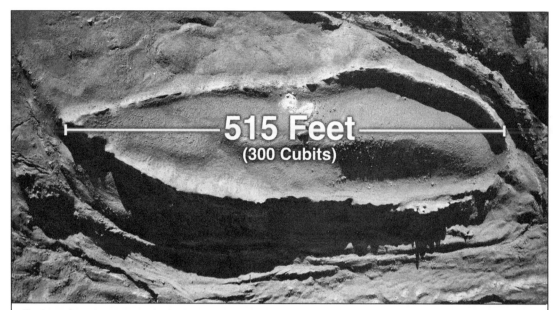

The best view of the ship-shaped formation is from overhead — that is, from the perspective of a drone — which shows the distinct image of a ship with its pointed bow at the tip and rounded stern at the bottom, exactly the shape of ships from the ancient world. This one is exactly 515 feet long (or approximately 300 Egyptian cubits).

walked the entire length and breadth of the site, even shooting drone footage as we did our own research and documentation for multiple days.

By far, the best view denoting the ship-shaped formation is from overhead — that is, from the perspective of a drone — which shows the clear image of an ancient ship with its distinctive bow at the tip and a rounded stern at the bottom, exactly like ships from the ancient world. Writers of antiquity recorded that a Kurdish village was located near the site of Noah's Ark, and today there remains a Kurdish village that has been in that area for thousands of years. In addition to our documentation of the ship, we were able to record other important aspects of the site along with archaeological evidence that I will cover in subsequent chapters.

Moving Forward

All the evidence clearly demonstrates that if one sticks with the Bible and allows it to be his guide, he will discover that what God's Word says about the Flood and the details of Noah's Ark are true and reliable. This includes what the Bible tells

God called Noah and his family to build an Ark for the saving of his family and for the preservation of the human race. No ship of this size had ever been fashioned before. The Bible tells us that the Ark was 515 feet long (300 Egyptian cubits) with multiple rooms, various compartments, and three levels. Today the ruins of this massive ship lie on the slope of Mount Cudi in the lower mountains of Ararat.

us about the bizarre activities that occurred before the Flood between the "sons of God" and the daughters of men, as is recorded in Genesis 6:2 and 4.

As we proceed, we will carefully unfold what the Bible tells us about those bizarre events that transpired in the time that preceded the Flood. I urge you to ready yourself as we take an extraordinary adventure together into the ancient past to learn about *Fallen Angels, Giants, Monsters, and the World Before the Flood.* Questions about curious, fantastic, and seemingly inexplicable happenings will be answered, while other questions will be raised to which only a speculative answer can be given. And I forewarn you that some of the content in these chapters will be hard on the emotions to read.

Indeed, Scripture tells us that due to widespread corruption and violence that abounded on earth in the time frame that preceded the Flood,[25] God brought a deluge of water on the earth to cleanse it of all the nefarious evil and rebellion that was proliferating in the world. This might cause you to ask:

- What exactly was going on during the time that preceded the Flood?
- Was it just man's sin that was so dreadfully wicked that God had to rid the earth of all but eight souls?
- Or was there something even more reprehensible taking place that brought God's judgment upon the earth at that time?

Before we delve into the subject of the Flood and the reasons God sent it, and before we discover what the Bible tells us about Noah's Ark, we must first go back in time to explore Adam's lineage and determine the approximate size of the population on the earth at the time of the Flood. The answer might surprise you!

In pages to come, you will discover that by the time the Flood came, there was already a significantly large population on the earth. The very fact that Adam and his descendants lived hundreds and hundreds of years — and that each of his descendants begat a large number of sons and daughters — makes it probable that there were already several million people living in the time before the Flood. Adam's grand lineage is what we will explore in the next chapter.

QUESTIONS TO PONDER

1. After reading about the investigations and findings of a man-made, ship-shaped structure — with internal rooms and a corridor — in the lower mountains of Ararat, what scriptures come to mind about the amazing care and plan of God for those who, like Noah, walk with Him and "find grace" in His sight (*see* Genesis 6:8)?

2. Can you speculate on why many have been diverted in their search of Noah's Ark to the *peak* of Mount Ararat instead of to the mountain *range* (the mountains of Ararat, plural) as the Scripture states (*see* Genesis 8:4)?

3. Have you ever asked the question posed in this chapter about the degree of depravity of mankind on the earth that God would visit it with such a monumental judgment from which there was no escape? In what ways is this visitation of judgment similar to what Jesus was talking about in Matthew 24:37 and Luke 17:26? Read these verses and record your thoughts so you can compare them with what you will learn along this line in the following chapters of this book.

This illustration by Gustave Doré shows the Ark in the far background as waters of the Flood begin to pour over the ancient civilization that existed at that time. When the Great Deluge was released on the earth in the days of Noah, it was so devastating that it destroyed not only all living creatures, but also nearly every hint of the civilization that existed before the Flood. The people were warned and given ample time to repent, but judgment eventually ensued according to God's own words.

CHAPTER TWO

HOW MANY PEOPLE WERE ON THE EARTH AT THE TIME OF THE FLOOD?

The lower slopes of the mountains of Ararat have been visited for thousands of years by people from all walks of life, including a long list of notable individuals who traveled there for the purpose of viewing the remains of a mammoth ship that were encased in mud but that are now protruding from the dirt.

Many early voices from history wrote that the site held the ruins of Noah's Ark. Given the number of these early witnesses, as you will see, and the fact that the structure fits the precise dimensions outlined in Genesis 6:14-16, a growing number of authoritative voices in our own time concur that the ship-shaped formation is none other than Noah's Ark.

According to Scripture, God sent a flood upon the earth to cleanse it of unthinkable evils brought on by fallen angels, horrible giants, and possibly monstrous creatures. In the pages to come in this book, we will delve into this ancient history to study the despicable and perverse deeds that gave rise to this pandemic of evil and the judgment that had to follow as a result.

Genesis 6:11 and 12 states:

The earth also was corrupt before God, and the earth was filled with violence. And God looked upon the earth, and, behold, it was corrupt; for all flesh had corrupted his way upon the earth.

Verse 12 says that "all flesh had corrupted his way." The word "corrupted" means *blemished*, and it alerts us that everyone, except for Noah and his family (*see* Genesis 6:8,9,18), had become corrupted, or blemished, by the nefarious and malevolent activities that were taking place on the earth in the days preceding the Flood.

We will look at the purity of Noah and his bloodline in later chapters, but we know that, finally, there came a time of God's judgment upon the earth and upon those "outside the Ark," and we know the Lord told Noah in advance of that monumental day:

...The end of all flesh is come before me; for the earth is filled with violence through them; and, behold, I will destroy them with the earth. Make thee an ark . . . .

— Genesis 6:13,14

Imagine God issuing this dire declaration of what was to come — what *had* to come — for those who rejected the words of His servant Noah and who refused to repent of their grave misdeeds.

We read in Genesis 6:8 that Noah had found grace in the eyes of the Lord. As a result, God made Noah a proficient shipbuilder — supplying him with blueprints, the acumen to do something that had never been done before, and *more grace*. But God also made Noah a passionate preacher of righteousness, who faithfully warned of what was to come to those around him that had not yet been contaminated with the "DNA" of the fallen angels, which we will study in more detail as we proceed. For those hearers, there was still time to repent, turn to God, and receive His provision of rescue — the Ark of safety He was preparing in advance by the hands of Noah and his family.

In the chapters ahead, we will focus on the specifics of the evil that was taking place. For now, it is important to realize that by the time God released the Great Deluge upon the planet, there was already a significantly large population on the earth. This fact becomes clear as we take a close look at some of the original text in

Genesis 5, which provides an overview of Adam and his descendants from the time of creation to the days of Noah.

ADAM AND EVE

ADAM'S FAMILY TREE:
TEN GENERATIONS FROM ADAM TO NOAH

The lineage of Adam grew rapidly during the first millennium after creation.[1] To get an understanding of the vast number of people living on the earth in the days before the Flood, we will turn to Genesis 5 to see the documented line of descendants from Adam to Noah.

> **This is the book of the generations of Adam. In the day that God created man, in the likeness of God made he him; male and female created he them; and blessed them, and called their name Adam, in the day when they were created.**
>
> **— Genesis 5:1,2**

From this point to the end of Genesis 5, Scripture documents ten generations from Adam to Noah.

> **And Adam lived an hundred and thirty years, and begat a son in his own likeness, and after his image; and called his name Seth: And the days of Adam after he had begotten Seth were eight hundred years: and he begat sons and daughters: and all the days that Adam lived were nine hundred and thirty years: and he died.**
>
> **— Genesis 5:3-5**

Notice verse 4 says that Adam "begat sons and daughters." The original text indicates he begat *many* sons and daughters. Thus, we find that after Adam and Eve begat Cain, Abel, and Seth, they also had *many* other sons and daughters whose names are not recorded in Scripture.

The Bible says that Seth was born when Adam was 130 years old, but we also know from Scripture that Adam lived 800 years after Seth's birth, and Adam and his wife produced many sons and daughters during the remainder of his life. This suggests that the potential total number of children born to Adam and Eve during his entire 930 years is nearly mind-boggling.

What is interesting is that in the 930 years Adam lived, he would have also had time to see his sons and daughters beget many of their own children. That is, he would have had time to see his grandchildren, great grandchildren, great-great-grandchildren, and even great-great-great-grandchildren and beyond. Therefore, by the time Adam finished his 930 years of life, his lineage was comprised of a colossal number of descendants.

SETH, THE SON OF ADAM

The Scripture tells us the following about Seth and his children.

And Seth lived an hundred and five years, and begat Enos: and Seth lived after he begat Enos eight hundred and seven years, and begat sons and

daughters: and all the days of Seth were nine hundred and twelve years: and he died.

— Genesis 5:6-8

According to this passage, when Seth was 105 years old, he begat a son, whom he named Enos. Scripture indicates that after the birth of Enos, Seth, like his father, also begat *many* sons and daughters. Although we don't know the exact number of sons and daughters Seth and his wife begat, the wording in the original text implies it was an enormous number.

In the 912 years that Seth lived, he, too, was old enough to see his sons and daughters produce many children. Hence, he saw his grandchildren, great-grandchildren, great-great-grandchildren, and even great-great-great-grandchildren. If we were to count only the combined descendants of Adam and Seth, whom the Bible mentions, the population of the earth at that early time would have already aggressively grown in exponential terms.

Some imagine the planet's population as ever evolving, and because of that, they subconsciously imagine the Great Flood as being catastrophic to human life on a much smaller scale than it actually occurred. Without going into detail about why a human life extended over many centuries even after the fall of Adam and Eve, if we'll just do the math, we might be astounded by the number of descendants one couple could produce over hundreds of years if they were being "fruitful and multiplying" as God instructed our progenitors in Genesis 1:28.

For example, if you and your spouse began having children at age 25 — and your firstborn followed suit, and so on — by the time you were 75 to 80 years old, you will have witnessed the birth of one or more great-grandchildren. Now multiply your 80 years of age times 10 for a total of *800 years*. If your children, their children, and *their* children, etc. had families of their own — how big would your line of descendants be at 800 years? If everyone in your bloodline had two children each, over the course of eight centuries, that number would increase to an aggregate figure totaling in the *billions*!

We know there were not likely billions of people on Earth in Noah's day, but we can conclude that it wasn't just a few thousand or even a few *hundred* thousand people who perished in the Flood. There had been a population explosion of *millions* of people — and you and I are alive today because *God saved eight*.

ENOS, THE SON OF SETH AND GRANDSON OF ADAM

The Scripture then tells us about Enos and his children.

And Enos lived ninety years, and begat Cainan: and Enos lived after he begat Cainan eight hundred and fifteen years, and begat sons and daughters: And all the days of Enos were nine hundred and five years: and he died.
— Genesis 5:9-11

Just as Adam and his son Seth begat *many* sons and daughters, Enos, who was Seth's son and Adam's grandson, additionally begat *many* sons and daughters. With each successive generation of Adam's lineage, the population of the earth abundantly multiplied exponentially as large numbers of sons and daughters were born, and generations began to *multiply*. At the age of 90, Enos fathered a son whom he named Cainan, and afterward, Cainan had many *other* sons and daughters.

Once again, no one knows exactly how many children Enos fathered, but the wording of the text indicates Enos had a large number of sons and daughters in his 905-year life.

Like Adam and Seth, Enos also lived long enough to see his sons and daughters beget a voluminous number of their own children. In fact, his 905 years of life enabled him to personally know his grandchildren, great-grandchildren, great-great-grandchildren, and even great-great-great-grandchildren. And each successive generation of those multiple children additionally begat many more sons and daughters. Thus, the burgeoning descendants of Adam, Seth, and Enos resulted in the population of the earth continuing to grow exponentially. But we're not done yet.

**CAINAN, THE SON OF ENOS, AND MAHALALEEL, THE SON OF CAINAN —
ADAM'S GREAT-GRANDSON AND GREAT-GREAT-GRANDSON**

Next, the Scriptures speak of the third and fourth generations from Adam, Cainan and Mahalaleel, along with their children.

> **And Cainan lived seventy years and begat Mahalaleel: and Cainan lived after he begat Mahalaleel eight hundred and forty years, and begat sons and daughters: and all the days of Cainan were nine hundred and ten years: and he died.**
>
> **And Mahalaleel lived sixty and five years, and begat Jared: and Mahalaleel lived after he begat Jared eight hundred and thirty years, and begat sons and daughters: and all the days of Mahalaleel were eight hundred ninety and five years: and he died.**
>
> **— Genesis 5:12-17**

These verses provide details for Adam's great-grandson Cainan and great-great-grandson Mahalaleel, which make a total of five generations, including Adam, that we've covered so far. Like their predecessors, Cainan and Mahalaleel begat *many* sons and daughters. Again, the original text signifies that they fathered a colossal number of children during the multiple centuries over which they lived.

In the 910 years that Cainan lived and in the 895 years Mahalaleel lived, they both were able to not only see their children, but also the offspring produced by their sons and daughters. Thus, they saw their grandchildren, great-grandchildren, great-great-grandchildren, and even great-great-great-grandchildren and beyond.

By the time Cainan and Mahalaleel reached the end of their lives, their lineages had grown exponentially to a number of descendants multiplied many times over. Taking into account the combined offspring of Adam, Seth, Enos, Cainan, and Mahalaleel, we see that the population of the earth was continually exploding with rapid growth.

JARED'S LIFE MARKS
AN UNPRECEDENTED ERA IN HUMAN HISTORY

From Adam to Mahalaleel, there were five generations. It is during the span of the sixth generation that it seems something unusual had begun taking place in the earth, which we will look at in this section as we continue with Adam's genealogical line, where Scripture tells us of one of Mahalaleel's sons, Jared.

And Mahalaleel lived sixty and five years, and begat Jared.
— Genesis 5:15

Jared was the son of Mahalaleel and great-great-great-grandson of Adam. The name "Jared" means *shall come down*.[2] This name was given to Jared by his father as a seemingly prophetic notation of bizarre events involving a group of fallen angels that would cause great evil on the earth.

As you will see in the pages to come, there are ancient documents that refer to this particular group of angels as *watchers*.[3] They were assigned by God to watch over and to help humans in their fallen state. But these angels became smitten by the beauty of earthly women and began lusting after them. They then abandoned their God-given posts, entered earth's atmosphere, and *came down* to cohabit and sexually mingle with mortal women.[4] The hybrid offspring produced from their union were called *Nephilim*, and these creatures were so horrific that the earth became filled with violence on account of them. Later you'll learn more about these hybrid creatures and the monstrous events that followed, which were some of the contributing factors to God's judgment of the Flood that destroyed the face of the earth.

Although this despicable activity involving the derelict angels may have already begun to take place before Jared's lifetime, it seems that his birth marked a moment when these sinister events began to become pervasive and widespread. That is why his father Mahalaleel named him "Jared," which means *shall come down*. His name served as a prophetic timestamp to signify the period when defiant, rebellious angels began to *come down* in a notable way to cohabit with women.

I am aware that this may raise some theological questions, but in the coming chapters, these questions will be answered, as you will see that the Bible, as well as noteworthy ancient sources, confirms these events. You'll also learn that both Peter and Jude wrote explicitly about this mutinous activity in their respective epistles and detailed how God Himself dealt with it.

But Jared, too, lived a very long time and begat *many* sons and daughters. Scripture tells us:

And Jared lived an hundred sixty and two years, and he begat Enoch: and Jared lived after he begat Enoch eight hundred years, and begat sons and daughters: and all the days of Jared were nine hundred sixty and two years: and he died.

— Genesis 5:18-20

Again, the specific number of Jared's offspring is not recorded, but the wording and the original text indicate large numbers. And given that Jared lived 962 years, he had ample time to father an enormous multitude. In fact, as those who lived before him, he lived long enough to see his grandchildren, great-grandchildren, great-great-grandchildren, great-great-great-grandchildren, and beyond.

Again, each successive generation from Adam begat many more sons and daughters. Thus, the combined descendants of Adam, Seth, Enos, Cainan, Mahalaleel, and Jared saw the population of the earth exponentially explode.

**ENOCH, THE SON OF JARED
AND GREAT-GREAT-GREAT-GREAT-GRANDSON OF ADAM**

Out of all of Adam's progeny, there is one who really stands out and whose life was so noteworthy, he is mentioned in the pages of the New Testament. His name is Enoch, and he was Jared's son, the seventh generation from the time of Adam. The Scripture says:

> **And Jared lived an hundred sixty and two years, and he begat Enoch: and Jared lived after he begat Enoch eight hundred years, and begat sons and daughters: and all the days of Jared were nine hundred sixty and two years: and he died.**
>
> **— Genesis 5:18-20**

These verses tell us that when Jared was 162 years old, he and his wife produced a son whom they named *Enoch*. Just as Jared's father Mahalaleel had given him his prophetic name, Jared in turn named his son Enoch, and his name bears important prophetic meaning.

The name "Enoch" means *to teach* or *to correct*.[5] This is significant because ancient sources inform us that even though the mutinous angels did not listen to him, Enoch attempted *to teach* and *to bring correction* to the angels and to those who were participating in their rebellious activities.[6]

THE LIFE OF METHUSELAH, ENOCH'S SON, WAS A DEMONSTRATION OF GOD'S LONGSUFFERING AND MERCY

We've been previewing the lineage of Adam to Noah, beginning with Adam's son Seth. *Seth* was the father of *Enos*, who was the father of *Cainan*, who begat *Mahalaleel*, who fathered *Jared*, who was the father of *Enoch* — seven generations in all so far, including Adam.

Let's continue looking at Adam's family line.

And Enoch lived sixty and five years, and begat Methuselah.
— Genesis 5:21

In addition to Methuselah, who was born when Enoch was 65 years old, Enoch begat a multitude of sons and daughters (*see* Genesis 5:22). But amazingly, Methuselah lived to the age of 969 years, securing the title of the longest life to ever be lived on the earth — with one exception, which we will see shortly.

'WHEN HE DIES, IT SHALL COME'

Like his predecessors whose names had great significance, Methuselah, too, was given a name that was packed with prophetic meaning. In the original text,

"Methuselah" means *when he is dead, it shall come* — or *his death shall bring it.*[7] Methuselah's name prophetically declared that when he died, a monumental judgment would be released into the earth, which we now know was the Flood.

God had told Enoch that when Methuselah died, his death would signal the time when judgment would come upon the earth because of the mutinous activity of the fallen angels cohabiting with mortal women, who then gave birth to a race of horrific giants that produced great violence on the earth. As long as Methuselah lived, judgment would be restrained. The fact that Methuselah lived longer than anyone else in human history was a display of God's mercy. God prolonged his life to give ample time for the humans still untainted by those rebellious activities to repent and avoid judgment.

We read in Second Peter 3:9 that it is God's *habit* to delay judgment, because He doesn't want anyone to perish. (This "habit" of God will be amply demonstrated in Chapter 8.) His delays do not guarantee people will repent, but in His mercy, God gives them ample opportunity. Again, the longevity of Methuselah demonstrates God's utter forbearance and patience.

The Bible goes on to tell us:

And Enoch walked with God after he begat Methuselah three hundred years, and begat sons and daughters: and all the days of Enoch were three hundred sixty and five years: and Enoch walked with God: and he was not; for God took him.

— Genesis 5:22-24

Like each of his forefathers, Enoch also begat *many* sons and daughters after Methuselah was born, adding even more to the burgeoning growth of the human race because he had a massive number of descendants. Remarkably, during the "short" 365 years of his life, Enoch was able to see many of his grandchildren, great-grandchildren, and likely some of his great-great-grandchildren. Thus, with the combined lineages of Adam, Seth, Enos, Cainan, Mahalaleel, Jared, and Enoch, the population of the pre-Flood world continued to extensively grow larger and larger.

But what happened to Enoch?

ENOCH'S DISAPPEARANCE IS THE FIRST OF MANY 'RAPTURES' RECORDED IN THE BIBLE

We're looking at the genealogy of Adam up to the time of Noah. The ten generations in this prophetic family line tell the fascinating story of mankind on the earth since the time of Adam and Eve and their sin that plunged all of mankind into a sinful, fallen state. But although sin had permanently entered the world and the whole human race within it, there were still marked individuals who feared God and sought diligently to walk with Him in obedient cooperation.

Let's pause for a moment to look at one such person and at an extraordinary event that took place in his life — something that had never before occurred. Genesis 5:24 tells us:

And Enoch walked with God: and he was not; for God took him.

Enoch is considered to be the first official prophet of the Old Testament. His name is said to mean *to teach* and also *dedicated*, and he was miraculously raptured into Heaven and therefore never tasted physical death.

Today there are those who scoff at the idea of a rapture — as in a rapture, or *catching away*, of the Church from Earth to Heaven. But the account of Enoch in Genesis 5:21-24 describes the first literal, physical rapture in Scripture.

What's interesting is that Enoch's experience of being supernaturally *caught away* is one of many such occurrences in the Bible. In fact, there are nine different rapture-type events recorded in Scripture — occurrences in which a person or group *experienced*, or *will experience*, a *catching away* of some type.

These recorded instances are as follows:

1. **Enoch**, who was *supernaturally, physically, caught up* into Heaven and never tasted death (*see* Genesis 5:24).

2. **Elijah**, who was *supernaturally, physically, caught up* into Heaven and never tasted death (*see* 2 Kings 2:11).

3. **Jesus**, who was *supernaturally, physically, caught up* into Heaven after His resurrection (*see* Acts 1:9-11).

4. **Philip** the evangelist, who was *supernaturally, physically, caught away* from one location to another location (*see* Acts 8:39,40).

5. **Paul**, who was *supernaturally, physically, caught up* to the third heaven and received unspeakable divine revelations (*see* 2 Corinthians 12:2-4).

6. **John**, who was *supernaturally, physically, caught up* in the spirit realm to Heaven and given the revelation of the Great Tribulation, the Millennial Reign of Christ, and the Great White Throne Judgment (*see* Revelation 4:1,2).

7. **Believers**, who, alive on Earth, will one day be *supernaturally, physically, caught away* into the presence of the Lord in the future. They will be preceded by those who have already passed away (*see* 1 Thessalonians 4:15-17).

8. The **two end-time prophetic witnesses**, who will be *supernaturally, physically, caught away* into Heaven during the time of the Great Tribulation (*see* Revelation 11:3-12).

9. The **saints**, who will be saved during the Great Tribulation and be *supernaturally, physically, caught away* into the presence of the Lord (*see* Revelation 14:14-16).

From this list, we see that six of the nine people (or groups of people) have already experienced a supernatural catching away of some kind — Enoch being the first. Exactly as Enoch was miraculously snatched into Heaven, the Bible forecasts that others in the near future will also experience a *catching away* or a *rapture*. As a matter of fact — get ready — the Church is next in line to be *supernaturally snatched* into Heaven! Indeed, a time is coming when those who live for Jesus will be *supernaturally, physically caught away*, or *snatched*, in the "twinkling of an eye" (*see* 1 Corinthians 15:51,52).

I simply do not know how anyone can argue against the rapture of the Church, for the idea of a *supernatural, physical, catching away* is clearly taught from Genesis to Revelation.

And here's something to think about concerning the rapture of Enoch. Although Enoch's son Methuselah famously lived for 969 years and is noted for being the oldest man to ever live and die on earth, Enoch is actually older. The fact that he was transported directly into God's presence without tasting death means he is still living in his physical human form in Heaven today. Hence, he holds the record for the longest life lived, which we can estimate to be at least 5,000 years![8]

Enoch Is Viewed as the First Old-Testament Prophet

Enoch's role in Scripture is so vital that Jewish sources consider him to be the first official prophet in the Old Testament. Amazingly, even though he lived during the last 300 years of the first millennia after creation, Enoch was so in sync with God's Spirit that he was able to prophetically see more than 5,000 years into the future — even beyond our present day! With supernatural accuracy, Enoch described the Lord's Second Coming when Jesus will return to the earth with His saints to pronounce judgment on the ungodly people of the world who have rejected Him and blasphemed His name.

The Bible records this prophecy in Jude 14 and 15, which is also a direct quote from *The Book of Enoch*, a book of significant importance to New Testament times that I will describe briefly in the following paragraphs and in greater detail in Chapter 3. But in these two Bible verses, Jude says:

And Enoch also, the seventh from Adam, prophesied of these, saying, Behold, the Lord cometh with ten thousands of his saints, to execute judgment upon all, and to convince all that are ungodly among them of all their ungodly deeds which they have ungodly committed, and of all their hard speeches which ungodly sinners have spoken against him.

The events Enoch experienced and the prophecies he delivered are recorded in detail in an ancient document called *The Book of Enoch*.[9] Although this book is not Scripture, it is a valuable, ancient document filled with in-depth, serious commentary about the evil events that took place on the earth in the days that preceded the Flood. These events are mentioned in Genesis 6:2 and 4.

During the intertestamental years (approximately 420 BC to 20 AD), *The Book of Enoch* was deemed to be very reliable and was widely read by Jews. In fact, during the time that Jesus lived on the earth, *The Book of Enoch* was so embraced as trustworthy that Jude, who was the younger half-brother of Jesus, quoted from it in his epistle, as we just saw.

In the coming chapters, we will peer into *The Book of Enoch* and examine some of the details it gives about the mutinous activities of the erring angels and how they made an oath to rebel against God and descend into the earth's atmosphere to sexually cohabit with women.

But now let's continue our look into the genealogy of Adam.

METHUSELAH ALSO HAD A MULTITUDE OF DESCENDANTS

So far in the ten generations that we're tracing from Adam to Noah, we've covered Adam's son *Seth*, Seth's son *Enos*, Enos' son *Cainan*, Cainan's son *Mahalaleel*, Mahalaleel's son *Jared*, Jared's son *Enoch*, and Enoch's son *Methuselah*.

After Enoch had walked in close fellowship with God and was raptured into God's presence, his son Methuselah continued to live for many years, and like his predecessors before him, Methuselah also begat *many* sons and daughters.

And Methuselah lived an hundred eighty and seven years, and begat Lamech: And Methuselah lived after he begat Lamech seven hundred eighty and two years, and begat sons and daughters: and all the days of Methuselah were nine hundred sixty and nine years: and he died.

— Genesis 5:25-27

In the 969 years Methuselah lived, he had an unparalleled amount of time to father a multitude of children. Since Adam, Seth, Enos, Cainan, Mahalaleel, Jared, and Enoch were able to see a massive number of their respective descendants, just think how many descendants Methuselah was able to see! Because he lived longer than anyone else, his lineage was potentially the largest of all.

Keep in mind, the name "Methuselah" means *when he is dead, it shall come* — or *his death shall bring it*. Thus, Methuselah's existence was a prophetic declaration that as long as he lived, judgment would be withheld. By extending the length of Methuselah's life, God gave humankind a merciful opportunity to repent and to escape the coming judgment. But when Methuselah died, his death was the announcement that God's judgment would soon be released.

**LAMECH, THE SON OF METHUSELAH
AND GREAT-GREAT-GREAT-GREAT-GREAT-GREAT-GRANDSON OF ADAM**

Among Methuselah's plethora of children, he had one son whom he named Lamech, who also begat large numbers of sons and daughters. About Lamech, Scripture tells us:

> **And Lamech lived an hundred eighty and two years, and begat a son: and he called his name Noah, saying, This same shall comfort us concerning our work and toil of our hands, because of the ground which the Lord hath cursed.**
>
> **And Lamech lived after he begat Noah five hundred ninety and five years, and begat sons and daughters: and all the days of Lamech were seven hundred seventy and seven years: and he died.**
>
> **— Genesis 5:28-31**

The ancient name "Lamech" means *one who is in despair* or *one who is despairing.*[10] It is related to the word "lament," which depicts *crying, weeping,* or *wailing.* As Jared, Enoch, and Methuselah had been given prophetic names, we find that Methuselah also gave his son Lamech a name packed with prophetic meaning.

Indeed, it was during Lamech's lifetime that there was *crying, weeping, wailing,* or *lamentation* on the earth because of the dastardly deeds of the fallen angels that were proliferating in the days before the Flood. The world in Lamech's time was in a deep state of despair and was radically devolving, growing darker and darker. As the fallen angels continued to defiantly cohabit with mortal women, who then gave birth to monstrous hybrid creatures called Nephilim, the earth became miserably dominated with bloodshed and violence. In Chapter 7, we will study ancient documents to discover more clearly what kind of bloodshed and violence the Nephilim brought into the earth.

Genesis 5:31 tells us Lamech lived 777 years, which was long enough to see his sons and daughters begat many other children. And like his forefathers, he had time to see his grandchildren, great-grandchildren, great-great-grandchildren, and great-great-great-grandchildren. Among Lamech's many offspring, he notably begat a son, whom he named *Noah.*

Of all the patriarchs mentioned thus far in this chapter — Adam, Seth, Enos, Cainan, Mahalaleel, Jared, Enoch, Methuselah, and Lamech — only Enoch and Lamech lived on the earth less than 800 years. Everyone else lived 800- to 900-plus years, and with each successive generation, the earth's population continued to rapidly increase and spiral upward in number.

Now let's look at the central character — ten generations from Adam — in the account of the Great Flood.

NOAH, THE SON OF LAMECH
AND GREAT-GREAT-GREAT-GREAT-GREAT-GREAT-GREAT-GRANDSON OF ADAM

From among Lamech's many children, he had one prominent son who would play a significant role in the plan of God and in the story of the Flood. That son's name was *Noah*, and he was among the *tenth* generation from the time of Adam.

And Lamech lived an hundred eighty and two years, and begat a son: and he called his name Noah, saying, This same shall comfort us concerning our work and toil of our hands, because of the ground which the Lord hath cursed. And Lamech lived after he begat Noah five hundred ninety and five years, and begat sons and daughters: and all the days of Lamech were seven hundred seventy and seven years: and he died.
— Genesis 5:28-31

The name "Noah" means *comfort* or *rest*.[11] Because Lamech gave Noah such a name, we understand that Lamech had received divine revelation that this was a special son whom God would use to bring *comfort* to a world of despair and lamentation due both to the nefarious activities that were occurring and to the curse of the earth that was also happening because of sin. This is made clear in Genesis 5:29, where Lamech prophetically declared of Noah, "…This same shall *comfort* us…."

There is an additional fact given to us about Noah and his own genealogy in Genesis 5, and it is found in the final verse.

And Noah was five hundred years old: and Noah begat Shem, Ham, and Japheth.

— Genesis 5:32

In Genesis chapters 6-9, we find the amazing account of Noah and the Ark he built and how he and his family — including his sons Shem, Ham, and Japheth — rode out the Flood, literally floating on a sea of destruction. In the pages ahead, we will carefully study these chapters in Genesis, but before we move on, let's review some important points about the pre-Flood patriarchs from Adam to Noah.

A Review of the Pre-Flood Patriarchs: Names, Years Lived, and Name Meanings

The following is a summary — beginning with Adam — of Adam's notable descendants, along with their respective lifespans. These individuals are paired with the original meaning of their names, and we have covered many of these names in this chapter.

NAME	YEARS LIVED	NAME MEANING
Adam	930	"man"
Seth	912	"appointed"
Enos	905	"mortal"
Cainan	910	"sorrow"
Mahalaleel	895	"the blessed God"
Jared	962	"shall come down"
Enoch	365	"to teach" or "to correct"
Methuselah	969	"when he dies, it shall come"
Lamech	777	"to despair; despairing or lamenting"
Noah	950	"comfort" or "rest"

Let's look for a moment at just five of the ten generations that preceded Noah.

Jared lived at a time when mutinous angels began to *come down* and cohabit with mortal women, who as a result gave birth to a race of monstrous giants called Nephilim. Jared was the father of Enoch and the great-great-grandfather of Noah.

Enoch was the father of Methuselah and the great-grandfather of Noah. Enoch walked with God and was the first person in history to be raptured into God's presence. He reputedly authored the earliest parts of *The Book of Enoch*, which, of course, is not Scripture but rather a document that was very respected in the intertestamental period. Among the Jews in the First Century, it was considered a reliable pre-Flood commentary.

Methuselah was the father of Lamech and Noah's grandfather. Methuselah lived longer on the earth than any other person in history. His name means *when he dies, it shall come,* and it was a prophetic declaration that when he died, a judgment would be released upon the earth. The fact that he lived such a long life demonstrates God's mercy and His deep desire that mankind repent and turn back to Him.

Lamech, Noah's father, lived during the pinnacle of despair and lamentation on the earth due to the nefarious activities of the mutinous angels and the hybrid Nephilim that were born as a result of their illicit sexual union with mortal women.

Noah, whose name means *comfort* or *rest*, was the tenth generation from Adam, and it was during Noah's lifetime that God brought an end to despair and lamentation as He released a Flood to cleanse the planet of hybrid giants and monstrous creatures who were roaming the earth and filling it with bloodshed and violence.

When we pull together the meanings of all these prophetic names, we see that God was downloading additional revelation to mankind with each subsequent generation. As each new significant player in God's plan took his place on the world scene, a new piece of the prophetic puzzle was provided. Some speculate that corporately, these ten names gave the world a message that sounded something like this:

> **Man** — because of his disobedience — **is appointed** to **mortal sorrow.** Yet our **blessed God** is good despite it all. When nefarious and mutinous angels **come down** to carry out dastardly deeds, an attempt will be made to **bring correction** to their mess. Patiently, God will restrain His retribution for a season. But eventually His forbearance will cease, signaling that His **judgment** will soon be released. Although the world grows dark and **despair** increases, **comfort and rest** will finally come.

ADAM'S SONS AND DAUGHTERS LIKELY KNEW NOAH

As a result of the extremely long lifespans of those who lived before the Flood, the lives of Adam and *generations* of his descendants overlapped one another, affording unprecedented opportunities for the generations to interact. Can you imagine the priceless, ancient wisdom that was accumulated over all those generations? With people living for several centuries, the ability to pass that wisdom on was unequaled.

The fact is, it is possible — even probable — that Adam's sons and daughters and grandchildren knew Noah. Consider the grid below and note the number in the box where each name intersects — the numbers represent the number of years these two people were alive together at the same time.

	Adam	Seth	Enos	Cainan	Mahalaleel	Jared	Enoch	Methuselah	Lamech	Noah
Adam		800	695	605	535	470	308	243	56	
Seth	800		807	717	647	582	365	355	168	
Enos	695	807		815	745	680	365	453	266	84
Cainan	605	717	815		840	775	365	548	361	179
Mahalaleel	535	647	745	840		830	300	603	416	234
Jared	470	582	680	775	830		365	735	548	366
Enoch	308	365	365	365	300	365		300	113	
Methuselah	243	355	453	548	603	735	300		777	600
Lamech	56	168	266	361	416	548	113	777		595
Noah			84	179	234	366		600	595	

By looking at this graph, you can see that Adam was still living while his great-great-great-great-grandson Enoch was alive. As a matter of fact, the godly patriarchs from Seth to Lamech were all alive simultaneously with Adam for a various number of years. If we carefully calculate Adam's lifespan side by side each of his descendants down to Lamech, we find:

• Adam was **130** when Seth was born, allowing Adam and Seth to live concurrently for **800** years.

• Adam was **235** when Enos was born, allowing Adam and Enos to live concurrently for **695** years.

- Adam was **325** when Cainan was born, allowing Adam and Cainan to live concurrently for **605** years.

- Adam was **395** when Mahalaleel was born, enabling Adam and Mahalaleel to live concurrently for **535** years.

- Adam was **460** when Jared was born, allowing Adam and Jared to live concurrently for **470** years.

- Adam was **622** when Enoch was born, allowing Adam and Enoch to live concurrently for **308** years.

- Adam was **687** when Methuselah was born, allowing Adam and Methuselah to live concurrently for **243** years.

- Adam was 874 when Lamech was born, allowing Adam and Lamech to live concurrently for **56** years.

Each of these men likely met and knew Adam. Their longevity and overlapping lifespans make it entirely possible — and even probable — that generations of Adam's grandchildren were able to personally interview him and ask about life in the Garden of Eden. They had opportunity to hear what happened in the fall of man and what it was like when Adam and Eve were evicted from the place of paradise God had created — and they could hear it from Adam himself. The many potential blessings and benefits of such longevity, overlapping lifespans, and family intersections for *generations* are mind-boggling.

WHY SUCH LONG LIFESPANS?

At this point, you may be thinking, *Why did people live such long lives before the Flood?* There are at least two possible answers for the longevity of these pre-Flood patriarchs.

The first possible answer is that after the fall of Adam and Eve when sin entered the human race, the degenerative effects of sin on the human gene pool were still minimal at that time.[12] This answer presents the idea that the effects of spiritual death upon the original God-given life that was resident even in the flesh of Adam and Eve and their lineage took time to work its "taint" and bring its decay into "the outward man" of humankind (*see* 2 Corinthians 4:16).

The second possible answer is that people lived longer because the atmospheric conditions of the pre-Flood world were very different from the conditions that existed after the Flood.[13]

In Genesis 1:6 and 7, we find that the earth was "blanketed" with a canopy of water before the Flood. This water canopy would have either absorbed or redirected a majority of cosmic and solar radiation, creating a greenhouse effect for the entire planet.

If you've ever been in a greenhouse, you know the temperature and moisture level stay the same year-round, allowing for healthy, vibrant vegetation in a warmer environment despite the colder or non-conducive weather conditions outside the "canopy." That is what the conditions were like across the earth in the pre-Flood years. Extreme high and low temperatures at the equator and in the polar regions would not have existed.

Additionally, the water canopy would have also created greater atmospheric pressure as well as an increased concentration of oxygen. These two conditions alone would have had the effects of a hyperbaric chamber that many medical professionals use today to accelerate healing and recovery. Altogether, such favorable conditions would have dramatically increased longevity in people, animals, and plants.

An example of what happens when the environment is blanketed in a canopy of water can be observed in coastal areas that have low-hanging clouds that hover along the coast. In such locations, a greenhouse-type environment is created, and that atmosphere contributes to plants and trees there living exceptionally long and often growing enormous in size.[14]

Because of the greenhouse-type environment and/or the healthier, more intact human gene pool that existed before the Flood, the world not only became populated very quickly, but people lived much longer lives. Scholars estimate that if Adam, during his 930 years of life, saw only half the children he fathered grow up — and if only half of them got married and if only half of those who got married had children — even at a conservative rate, Adam would have seen more than a million of his own descendants!

A water canopy around the earth would have created greater atmospheric pressure as well as an increased concentration of oxygen. These two conditions alone would have had the effects of a hyperbaric chamber that many medical professionals use today to accelerate healing and recovery. Altogether, such favorable conditions would have dramatically increased longevity in people, animals, and plants.

This does not include the other generations that followed from Adam. If you factor all the massive numbers of descendants born to others throughout these specified ten generations, it is very likely that there would have been millions of people living on the earth by the time of the Flood.[15] This fact shows that God's judgment of the Flood upon the earth was more devastating than most people imagine.

The purpose of this book isn't to focus on the subject of God's judgment. It is rather to guide you along the biblical narrative of a very real time when very real people were deceived *en masse* by what many believe was a demonic ploy to contaminate all human seed and to therefore abort the bringing forth of the Divine Seed. *That* Seed would be the Savior, the Son of God — the "Lamb slain from the foundation of the world" (*see* Revelation 13:8).

This holy Seed, who would come as "the seed of the woman" (*see* Genesis 3:15), would redeem mankind from the sin nature that had entered the human race because of Adam and Eve's transgression in the Garden of Eden.

And we know the Divine Seed, Jesus Christ, did come and fulfill His purpose as the Savior of the world. And it is *only by and through Him* that a person can be reconciled to God (*see* John 14:6; Acts 4:12; 2 Corinthians 5:20).

Regardless of what you believe about fallen angels, about the sexual intermingling of those angels with humans, and about a hybrid breed of giants that seems to have appeared on the scene as a result — a judgment did come upon the earth in Noah's day in the form of a great deluge of water called "the Flood," and Scripture is clear about it.

And we simply cannot deny that generations after Adam and Eve's fall and expulsion from the Garden of Eden, something else was beginning to happen on the earth so horrible that it is nearly inconceivable. It was so despicable that God took drastic measures to cleanse the earth of its horrible presence by means of a catastrophic flood.

The "sons of God" referred to in Genesis 6:2 did intentionally violate God's authority, and these sinning angels corporately and conspiratorially descended into the earth's atmosphere to commit crimes of the highest order.

But who *were* these "sons of God" in Genesis 6:2? That's what we'll discover in the next chapter!

QUESTIONS TO PONDER

1. After reading the details of Adam's descendants in Genesis 5, what are some of your takeaways? What new things have you learned that you've never heard before?

2. Before you read this chapter, what did you know about Enoch? Take a few moments to read Genesis 5:21-24; Hebrews 11:5; and Jude 14,15. How do these passages expand your understanding of this godly man and his relationship with the Lord? What is God speaking to you about his life, and what can you apply from his life to your own life?

3. The Bible reveals that the first recorded rapture was experienced by Enoch. How was his catching away similar to the soon-coming rapture of the Church? (Compare Genesis 5:22-24 and First Thessalonians 4:15-17.) Using your own words, write what the New Testament teaches about the coming rapture of the Church.

4. Have you ever thought about what the physical atmosphere and environment were like before the Flood? Based on what you gleaned from this chapter, in what specific ways do you think it was different from the atmospheric conditions in the world today? What is the significance of those differences over the course of time?

5. Had you previously contemplated the enormity of the population on the earth at the time of the Flood? Were you subconsciously under the impression that the earth was cleansed of a few thousand people when God released the deluge of water that destroyed every living thing? How has your perspective changed regarding the magnitude of this catastrophic event?

According to early rabbinical sources, when Adam and Eve were expelled from the Garden of Eden, God assigned certain angels — who were referred to as *watchers* or the "sons of God" — with the task of watching over, caring for, and helping humanity in its fallen state. There is no record of female angels in the Bible; hence, this illustration shows angels as male in gender. They were God-assigned to serve mankind, but instead, a contingency of them enticed, deceived, and abused those they were tasked with protecting.

CHAPTER THREE

WHO WERE
THE 'SONS OF GOD'
IN GENESIS 6:1–2?

In the last chapter, we learned that from the time of Adam to the days of Noah, there were ten significant individuals in ten generations through whom God was working His plan. These pre-Flood patriarchs are found in Genesis 5 in the genealogy of Adam. Here is an overview of the key people in this prophetic family line.

- **Adam** was 130 years old when he became the father of *Seth* (v. 3).

- **Seth** was 105 years old when he became the father of *Enos* (v. 6).

- **Enos** was 90 years old when he became the father of *Cainan* (v. 9).

- **Cainan** was 70 years old when he became the father of *Mahaleleel* (v. 12).

- **Mahalaleel** was 65 years old when he became the father of *Jared* (v. 15).

- **Jared** was 162 years old when he became the father of *Enoch* (v. 18).

- **Enoch** was 65 years old when he became the father of *Methuselah* (v. 21).

- **Methuselah** was 187 when he became the father of *Lamech* (v. 25).

- **Lamech** was 182 years old when he became the father of *Noah* (v. 28).

- **Noah** was 500 years old when he became the father of *Shem, Ham,* and *Japheth* (v. 32).

All the men in this list produced *many* more — *other* — sons and daughters, as we have seen. But the record only states that Noah had three sons, and there is no record of him having more sons or daughters before or after the Flood. This limitation may have been due to Noah's enormous God-given assignment and the lack of time to care for a larger family. God ultimately found only *one* family of eight (Noah and his wife, their three sons, and their sons' wives) to be free of the corruption that had affected the entire rest of the human race. But for some unknown reason, there were no more than three named children of Noah and his wife before or after the Flood.

So except for Noah, Genesis 5 says that everyone in Adam's family line had *many* sons and daughters throughout their lives. Their centuries-long lifespans provided for the exponential growth of the earth's population, and in the days just before the Flood, there was a population *explosion*. We read about this in Genesis 6:1, where it tells us "men began to multiply on the face of the earth."

I noted previously that during Adam's 930 years of life, if he saw only *half* his children grow up, and if only *half* of them got married, and if only *half* of those had children — and so on until Adam's death — even estimating conservatively, Adam would have seen tens of thousands of his own descendants! When you factor in the voluminous numbers of descendants born to everyone throughout these generations, it is likely there would have been several million people living on the earth by the time of the Flood.[1]

In Chapter 2, we also saw that during the days of Jared, dark spiritual activities were rampantly occurring between mutinous angels and the daughters of men. These angelic beings who came down to cohabit with mortal women were known by ancient rabbinical writers as *the Watchers*,[2] God-assigned watchers over mankind who became derelict in their assignment, and we will go into more detail about that in the following paragraphs.

The theological discussion of angels is very broad, and there are many different types of angelic creatures we could talk about — but that is beyond the scope of this book. For now, we are going to focus on what these beings are called in Genesis 6: the *sons of God*.

There were angelic beings that interacted with humanity, who were known as *watchers*. God authorized this category of angels to watch over, protect, and help man in his fallen state. But the books of Peter and Jude state that a group of these angels rebelled against God, abandoned their assigned posts, and descended into the earth's atmosphere to carry out sinister deeds with mortal women. The misdeeds of these rogue, rebellious angels are described by Peter and Jude, but they are also written about by ancient historical writers.

WHO WERE THE 'SONS OF GOD'?

As the population began to boom, something nefarious was also taking place. We see this revealed in the following verses.

And it came to pass, when men began to multiply on the face of the earth, and daughters were born unto them, that the sons of God saw the daughters of men that they were fair; and they took them wives of all which they chose…. There were giants in the earth in those days; and also after that, when the sons of God came in unto the daughters of men, and they bare children to them, the same became mighty men which were of old, men of renown.

— Genesis 6:1,2,4

The words "sons of God" in this passage are very important. It is interesting to note that when this phrase is used in Scripture, it denotes a direct creation of God. For instance, Adam was directly made by God, so he is referred to as a "son of God" in the genealogy of Christ (*see* Luke 3:38). Angels are also a direct creation of God.

Hence, they, too, are at times referred to as "sons of God." The words "sons of God," which appear in Genesis 6:2 and 4, were understood to be *angels* by all the Jews and rabbis from earliest times to the Third or Fourth Century. Likewise, Christians in the Early Church also held to the knowledge that these "sons of God" were angelic beings. In fact, there are no known records of any Jew or Christian believing otherwise prior to about the Third Century. It was at that time that something changed, and a new view began to take hold, and it is now called the *Sethite* view.

WERE THESE 'SONS OF GOD' THE SONS OF SETH?

The Sethite view about the phrases "sons of God" and "daughters of men" that are mentioned in Genesis 6 is that descendants of the completely "godly" sons from the line of Seth married the daughters of men, whom some allege were the completely "wicked" daughters from the lineage of Cain. There are a myriad of problems with this view that did not emerge until the time of Sextus Julius Africanus, Augustine, and others in the Second Century and in subsequent centuries. As noted previously in this book, the Genesis account states that the "sons of God" (who were celestial in origin) entered into unhallowed unions with the "daughters of men" (who were human in origin).

One writer has rightly stated, "The [theory of] 'sons of Seth' and 'daughters of Cain' fights against the intended grammatical antithesis between the *sons of God* and the *daughters of Adam.* Attempting to impute any other view to the text flies in the face of the earlier centuries of understanding of the Hebrew text among both rabbinical and Early Church scholarship. The lexicographical antithesis clearly intends to establish a contrast between the "angels" and the "women of the earth."[3] Furthermore, the words "daughters of men" in Genesis 6:2,4 does not refer only to the daughters of Cain, but to women of the entire human race, and this means all Adam's female descendants are implied in this description.

Although many argue for the Sethite view, well-known Bible scholars of recent times expressed the belief that the "angel" view is correct — including G. H. Pember, M. R. DeHaan, C. H. Mackintosh, F. Delitzsch, A. C. Gaebelein, A. W. Pink, Donald Grey Barnhouse, Henry Morris, Merrill F. Unger, and Arnold Fruchtenbaum.

THE SETHITE VIEW

However, for the sake of clarity, we will briefly look at the Sethite view to see what it is and why it is in the eyes of many so seriously flawed.

First, it must be restated that the Sethite view was a new idea that emerged in the Fourth and Fifth Centuries when Church leaders were combating Gnostic influences that caused people to become obsessed with angels. There was a need to bring correction to this obsession, but the devised correction included throwing out all long-established teachings about the "sons of God" in Genesis 6 as fallen angels who sexually mingled with mortal women. Although ancient rabbis and earlier Church fathers wrote in unison that the "sons of God" referred to fallen angels who had sexual relations with mortal women, that teaching began to be phased out or mitigated in the Fourth Century, and a new idea about this text in Genesis 6 began to be devised. In addition to trying to bring correction to the current obsession with angels, many at that time struggled, *as many do today*, with the idea that fallen angels could have physical relations with women.

The newfangled Sethite view began to assert that the "sons of God" in Genesis 6 were not fallen angels as it had been long believed — rather, they were said to be the righteous descendants of Seth who married into the wicked lineage of Cain. Proponents of this new view put forward the idea that this "merger" led to greater wickedness than the earth had seen heretofore.

In Chapter 5, you will see that many notable voices from antiquity wrote very clearly about the "sons of God" as fallen angels and about the newer Sethite view as a diversion from the established doctrine of the Church. The most ancient view of rabbis and early Church fathers was that the "sons of God" were fallen angels who sexually mingled with women. And just ahead in this chapter, you will discover that in the Old Testament, the words "sons of God" were used primarily to denote angelic hosts. When you combine this fact with what is written in Peter's and Jude's epistles, it becomes clear that the New Testament record holds to the most ancient belief as well — that the "sons of God" were rebellious angels who abandoned their posts to do the unthinkable with mortal women.

Furthermore, if the words "sons of God" and "daughters of Adam" were referring to the descendants of Seth and Cain, respectively, the question must be asked: Why did these natural unions produce monstrous giants, or Nephilim? If these were natural unions, as claimed by those who adhere to the Sethite view, the offspring of these unions should have also been normal, and they were not. These unions between human and heavenly creatures resulted in never-before-existing hybrid creatures that brought great bloodshed and violence into the earth in the days before the Flood, as we will soon see in this book.

We are told in Second Corinthians 13:1, "…In the mouth of two or three witnesses shall every word be established." In addition to the Old Testament usages and the unified writings of ancient rabbis and Early Church fathers, we have the additional inspired New Testament commentary of Peter and Jude, who each affirm that the "sons of God" in Genesis 6 were indeed fallen angels who rebelled against God, abandoned their assigned posts, and committed such atrocities that God bound them in prison for their activities. This alone is enough to obliterate the Sethite argument and to return us to the original view that the "sons of God" in Genesis 6 were fallen angels.

REASONS THE SETHITE VIEW IS UNSUPPORTED BY SCRIPTURE

- Nearly every time this term "sons of God" is used in the Old Testament, it is used to describe angelic beings or "direct creation," not humankind in general.

- The words "daughters of men" in the original language mean the *daughters of Adam*, or the *daughters of man* (or *of mankind*) and refer to ALL daughters born in Adam's line.

- Nowhere in Scripture does it say that all Seth's descendants were godly and that all Cain's descendants were ungodly. Although Cain was exiled and "cursed from the earth" (Genesis 4:11-14), God nevertheless protected him from potential deadly retribution (*see* v. 15), and in protecting him, the Lord was by default protecting his future offspring. One could equally conclude, therefore, that this idea of a perpetually cursed seed is assumed, not biblically proven.

- Adam and Eve had other sons and daughters after Seth, so to assume there were no other families on the earth besides the lineage of Cain would be an incorrect assumption.

- The ideas of the godliness of all the Sethite men, the ungodliness of all the daughters of Cain, and that the two lines were not to marry are assumed or *read into* the biblical text.

- If all the men in Seth's line were so godly, why did all of them (except Noah) die in the Flood?

Lastly, as already stated, how did the human union of Seth's sons and Cain's daughters ("godliness" and "ungodliness" in itself) produce the extreme anomaly of giants, or Nephilim?

Again, the Sethite view simply does not line up with Scripture. Nearly every use of this phrase "sons of God" in the Old Testament refers to angels, which was the long-held rabbinical understanding as well as the belief embraced by Early Church fathers, such as Clement of Rome, Justin Martyr, Irenaeus, Athenagoras of Athens, Clement of Alexandria, Tertullian, and Jerome. We will examine the writings of these and other venerated individuals in Chapter 5.

The book of Job is the oldest book in the Old Testament and contains early references to angels as the "sons of God." This illustration pictures Job as he is being confronted by God.

The Phrase 'Sons of God' Also Appears Three Times in the Book of Job

To help us understand just who the "sons of God" were in Genesis 6, let's look at two reliable sources: the Bible itself and the *Septuagint*, which is the Greek version of the Old Testament.[4] What's interesting is that in addition to Genesis 6:2 and 4, the phrase "sons of God" appears three times in the book of Job, which is understood to be the oldest book in the Bible. In each use, these words in the original language are describing *angelic beings*.

Let's look at the first two instances of this phrase in the book of Job.

Now there was a day when the *sons of God* came to present themselves before the Lord, and Satan came also among them.

— Job 1:6

Again there was a day when the *sons of God* came to present themselves before the Lord, and Satan came also among them to present himself before the Lord.

— Job 2:1

Although the topic of Job 1:6 and 2:1 is complex, note that the words "sons of God" indisputably depict *angels* who presented themselves before the Lord. In these verses, it's almost as if a spiritual curtain is being pulled back, and we are witnessing a heavenly "roll call," in which supernatural beings are checking in with God to give an account of their activities.

Later, when God answered Job out of a whirlwind, He probingly asked Job if he had been present when He laid the foundations of the earth and measured its dimensions. Of course, Job *hadn't* been there, but there was another presence there that God thought was worth our knowing about.

When the morning stars sang together, and all the *sons of God* shouted for joy.

— Job 38:7

Once again, the words "sons of God" used in this passage refers to *angels* — in this case, angels who were present and shouting for joy at the time God created the universe. Thus, we see that the words "sons of God" in both Genesis and Job are used interchangeably with *angels*.

THE *SEPTUAGINT* DEFINES THE 'SONS OF GOD' AS ANGELS

Along with Scripture interpreting Scripture, we also have the *Septuagint* to help us understand the meaning of the "sons of God." What's interesting is that in this highly respected Greek translation of the Old Testament, the words "sons of God" are translated from words that were also used to denote *angels*.[5] Therefore, in Genesis 6 in the *Septuagint*, the words "sons of God" are replaced with the word "angels." Therefore, Genesis 6:1 and 2 could be interpreted:

And it came to pass, when men began to multiply on the face of the earth, and daughters were born unto them, that the *angels* saw the daughters of men that they were fair; and they took them wives of all which they chose.

Egyptian King Ptolemy II Philadelphus of Egypt asked 70 Hebrew scholars to translate the Hebrew Scriptures into the Greek language so a Greek version of the Old Testament could be added to the Library of Alexandria.

The Library of Alexandria was one of the largest and most significant libraries of the ancient world, and it is estimated it acquired somewhere between 40,000 to 400,000 scrolls during the time of its existence.

Due to the conquests of Alexander the Great, the Greek language spread to all the lands he overcame. By the First Century, Greek became the common language of the empire, and this included the land of Israel and its people.

You may be thinking, *How reliable is the Septuagint?* The *Septuagint*, which is sometimes also referred to as *The Translation of the Seventy*, is a celebrated Greek translation of the Hebrew Scriptures developed around the Third Century BC by Jewish scholars and translators who lived in the ancient city of Alexandria in Egypt.

These distinguished Jewish intellectuals, under the orders of King Ptolemy II Philadelphus, labored to accurately translate the Hebrew Scriptures into the Greek language so that a Greek version of the Old Testament could be added to the Great Library of Alexandria. At the same time, this translation project was also a huge benefit to the Jewish population in Israel as well as to all the Jews who had been scattered throughout the world in the Diaspora.[6]

When Alexander the Great completed his conquests (circa 325 BC), the Greek language and culture had spread to all the lands he overcame. Although Hebrew was considered a sacred language, it was mostly used by Jewish intellectuals, scholars, and theologians. By the First Century, Greek became the prevalent, common language of the day that was spoken and read by the territories conquered by Alexander the

Great, and this included the land of Israel and its people.[7] The fact is, few common Jews could read or speak the Hebrew language during the Second Temple period (circa 516 BC-70 AD). This meant that the vast majority of Jews were unable to read the Hebrew Scriptures.

The creation of the *Septuagint* enabled the Jewish people throughout the world to read the Old Testament Scriptures in a language that was most common to them. Over time, the *Septuagint* became the primary version of the Old Testament used in Israel during the First Century.

Scholars concur that the *Septuagint* is the translation used by Jesus and His apostles, and when a New Testament writer quoted Old Testament Scriptures in his epistles, he nearly every time quoted from the *Septuagint* version of the Old Testament.[8]

These historical facts are vital to understand, as they demonstrate the reliability and trustworthiness of the *Septuagint*. This brings us back to the words "sons of God" in Genesis 6:2 and 4 — and in the book of Job — which were accurately translated as *angels* in the *Septuagint*.

HOW THE SONS OF GOD AND 'WATCHERS' ARE CONNECTED

As we noted at the beginning of the chapter, in addition to being called "sons of God," these angelic beings that interacted with humanity were also known as *Watchers*. It was understood by ancient Jewish scholars and writers that after Adam and Eve disobeyed God and exited the Garden of Eden, God authorized a category of angels to *watch over*, *protect*, and *help* man in his fallen state.[9] Hence, they were called the *Watchers*.

Keep in mind that from the time of Adam and Eve's fall to the time of Moses when God gave the Law, a period of about 2,500 years passed. During that era, there was no Old Testament, no New Testament, and there were also no Church leaders. According to early rabbinical sources, it was during that period that the *Watchers* — aka "sons of God" — were assigned the task of watching over and caring for humanity and assisting them in life.

Nebuchadnezzar is regarded as the greatest Babylonian king who ever ruled. He was famous for his military campaigns, and for the role he played in Jewish history. By the time of his death, he was esteemed to be one of the most powerful rulers in the world.

This idea of watchers is confirmed in the book of Daniel. When God gave king Nebuchadnezzar a dream and prophetically warned him of the consequences of continuing to walk in pride, the Scripture reveals that "watchers" were involved in carrying out God's will. You will find this term mentioned three times as that story played out in Daniel 4:13-37.

What's important to understand here is that some of these angels assigned to watch over and help mankind began to behave inordinately, lusting after earthly women, and they became so obsessed that they eventually abdicated their assignment. Early historical documents state that a group of 200 of these angels mutually swore an oath to rebel, abandon their posts, and descend into the earth's atmosphere to cohabit with mortal women. Through their unhallowed sexual unions, women with whom the fallen angels mated birthed monstrous hybrid creatures that were called Nephilim.[10] Although we do not know exactly when these vile events began, it seems these dark happenings became more prevalent during the lifetime of Jared, who was the father of Enoch.

ENOCH AND *THE BOOK OF ENOCH*

As we have seen, Adam's descendants were a prophetic family, and as each new significant player in God's plan was birthed into the world, a new piece of the prophetic picture was given. From at least the time of Jared, Noah's family was aware of the vile spiritual things that were occurring and had a keen understanding of a coming judgment. With each subsequent generation, God continued to alert them that longsuffering toward the evil interaction between fallen angels and mortal women would soon end.

Of all the pre-Flood patriarchs, Enoch held a very specific and unique role. He walked closely with God and is considered to be the first Old Testament prophet who spiritually saw the Second Coming of Christ. Although Enoch's prophetic ministry transpired more than 5,000 years ago, as a teacher of truth, his divine insights continue to instruct people today. He is believed by some to be the author of the earliest parts of *The Book of Enoch*, which is not Scripture, but it is nevertheless a document that was very respected in the intertestamental period and in the First Century.

When I first heard of *The Book of Enoch* years ago, I understood it had been written sometime between 300-200 BC and that it was a *pseudepigraphical* work, which is a literary piece attributed to an author, but which was actually composed by someone else. In biblical studies, the word *pseudepigrapha* usually refers to an assorted collection of Jewish or Christian works that are thought to be written between 300 BC to 300 AD.

In the past, *The Book of Enoch*, also known as *First Enoch* — with the first part of it often called *The Book of the Watchers*[11] — was widely considered to be a *pseudepigraphical* work dated by many to have been written between 300-200 BC. As noted, it was the opinion of historians that it was compiled by an unknown author or series of authors and not by Enoch himself.

However, more recently, some scholars have concluded that the first part of this body of work, chapters 1-36, were likely composed by Enoch himself. In this ancient text, often referred to as *The Book of the Watchers*, it is stated that Enoch entrusted these writings to his son, Methuselah, who preserved them and passed them on to subsequent generations, and eventually ended up in the hands of Noah. Although ancient sources had long referred to and quoted certain portions of Enoch's writings,[12] no copy of it was known to exist, and as time passed, scholars generally believed that it had been lost to the sands of time.

In 1773, three ancient copies of *The Book of Enoch* were found in Ethiopia and were brought back to the Western Church where it began to be passionately studied by scholars. Today it is believed by a growing number of scholars that earlier portions of it were actually written by Enoch himself. Although not canonized Scripture, it is nevertheless considered to be one of the oldest pieces of apocalyptic literature ever penned.

Then in 1773, three copies of it were found in Ethiopia[13] and brought back to the Western Church, where it began to be studied. Later, between 1946 and

This is an original photo of the Dead Sea Scrolls, also called the Qumran Caves Scrolls, which were discovered between 1946 and 1956. They are considered to be of great historical, religious, and linguistic significance because they include the oldest surviving manuscripts of entire Old Testament books, as well as the extra-biblical and deuterocanonical manuscripts.

1956, a complete copy of it was remarkably found among the Dead Sea Scrolls.[14] Interestingly, it is now believed that *The Book of Enoch* survived into Egyptian times and was even known by Moses, who carried it with him when the children of Israel exited Egypt. Although it may have been accessible for as long as a thousand years after the Exodus, no complete Hebrew copies of it survived. However, a few passages of *Enoch* from an early Hebrew text have been passed down in Aramaic fragments.

How *The Book of Enoch* came to be in Ethiopia is a story too long for this book, but in 1773 when it was discovered there and brought to Western scholars, its appearance caused a sensation in intellectual and theological circles. The conclusion of many of scholars — both then and now — is that even though the latter portions of the book may have indeed been added by outside authors, the earliest parts of the book were likely composed by Enoch himself.

Regardless of its origins, Jews and early Christians highly regarded *The Book of Enoch* and viewed it as a serious commentary on events related to activities that preceded the Flood, especially about the fallen angels and their prophesied judgment. Many concepts expressed by Jesus and Jude (Jesus' half-brother who authored the New Testament book of Jude) are directly connected to terms and ideas found in *The Book of Enoch*. Hence, it is a logical conclusion that Jesus and His natural family deemed it so serious that He and Jude (and Peter) adopted and elaborated on many important points from *The Book of Enoch*.[15]

Again, the earliest parts of *The Book of Enoch* that I'm referring to are chapters 1-36. These portions are known as the Ethiopian version as well as *First Enoch* and *The Book of the Watchers*. As already noted, it is believed by a growing number of scholars that these earlier portions were written by Enoch himself, and the manuscript, although not canonized Scripture, is nevertheless one of the oldest pieces of apocalyptic literature ever penned. Therefore, as we reference this venerated work in this chapter and in chapters to come, we will view it as a serious commentary on the events described in Genesis 6.

'IF ENOCH AUTHORED THE BOOK OF ENOCH, HOW DID IT SURVIVE THE FLOOD?'

The Book of Enoch reveals many insights into longstanding mysteries, but it also poses mysteries of its own — questions that remain difficult to answer. But the mere fact that Jude quotes directly from it and Peter refers to it speaks volumes about its need to be considered. In addition to Jude and Peter, Justin Martyr, Clement of Alexandria, Origen, Irenaeus, Tertullian, Eusebius, Jerome, Hilary, Epiphanius, and others referred to this work. And after many years of intense scrutiny, now it is generally believed that the Ethiopian version of *The Book of Enoch* is an acceptably trustworthy and valid document.[16]

Cuneiform is a writing system that was used to write several languages of the ancient Near East and vast numbers of cuneiform tablets have been preserved that contain records of ancient events. Cuneiform is the earliest known writing system, and over the course of its history, it was adapted to communicate a number of languages.

If it is true that the earliest portions of *The Book of Enoch* were written by Enoch, the great-grandfather of Noah, it would mean that these particular sections predate the Flood. If true, this raises the question: *How did this written commentary survive the Flood?*

The answer lies with Noah. When he was born, he was birthed into a prophetic family that honored and placed high value on God's divine insights and utterances. As an active member of his prophetic lineage, Noah likely received these writings as passed down from Methuselah to Lamech. Ultimately, Noah received them from Lamech his father — most likely written on cuneiform tablets — and carried them with him onto the Ark.

Think about it…

- *Noah* heard prophetic utterances from his father *Lamech*, which Lamech had received from his own father *Methuselah*.

- *Methuselah* heard prophetic insights from *his* father *Enoch* that had been passed to Enoch from his father *Jared*.

- *Jared*, whose name means *shall come down*, was alive at the time when the fallen angels began to rampantly descend from the heavens and sexually cohabit with mortal women.

Therefore, by the time Noah was born, God's prophetic words to this family had been passed down several generations, and these prophetic words included the writings of Noah's great-grandfather Enoch. Noah would have naturally revered Enoch's words and deemed them significant enough to carry them with him onto the Ark. That is how some suggest *The Book of Enoch* — that is, the earliest parts — survived the Flood.

It must be pointed out that early Babylonians and Assyrians acknowledged the pre-Flood era as a source of superior literature. In fact, one Babylonian king documented that he "loved to read the writings of the age before the Flood." Ashurbanipal, who founded the great library of Nineveh, also alluded to the great "inscriptions of the time before the Flood."

The reason I point this out is that there existed vast records written in the pre-Flood period that were buried by the waters of the Flood and that were discovered and read by ancient civilizations. Thus, it should not surprise us that it was possible for Noah to carry writings of his prophetic family with him onto the Ark to be preserved for future generations to read.

Doesn't that make you pause and ponder just how vital it is to pass important spiritual truths on to your children and grandchildren? Indeed, every one of us needs not only to pass on insights to subsequent generations, but also to treasure the precious revelations we have received from those who came before us. And in the case of Noah and his own ancestry, had he not carefully kept what had been passed on to him, much about these early events would not be known to us today.

In portions of *First Enoch*, the writer gives a riveting account of fallen angels who lusted after and cohabited with women and also describes the God-imposed incarceration on them for their deeds. Interestingly, this judgment is not only described in early parts of *The Book of Enoch*, but also in the epistles of *Peter* and *Jude*, which we will carefully examine in the pages ahead. Additionally, Enoch's writings stated that the knowledge of a coming Flood had been long-held and that the purpose of the Flood was to cleanse the earth of the evil that had infected it.

A chief seditious angel coaxed other angels in rebellion against the authority of God, and approximately 200 angels agreed to abandon their posts as watchers assigned by God. They then descended into the earth's atmosphere to cohabit with mortal women.

ENOCH DESCRIBED WHAT THE 'SONS OF GOD' HAD PLEDGED TO DO

Again, although this book of narration concerning certain world events is not a part of Scripture, *The Book of Enoch* is a seriously held commentary on the pre-Flood occurrences that was widely read and embraced by Jews in the First Century. Therefore, it is valuable in helping us understand the events of Genesis 6.

In this text, believed to predate the Flood, Enoch recorded a conversation that took place between the chief seditious angel and other angels that were led in rebellion against the authority of God. According to this ancient document, there were approximately 200 angels who agreed to abandon their posts as watchers that God had assigned to them.

We find this discourse in First Enoch 6:1-8:

First Enoch 6:1-8

And it came to pass, after the children of men had increased in those days, beautiful and comely daughters were born to them.

And the angels, the sons of the heavens, saw and lusted after them, and said one to another: "Behold, we will choose for ourselves wives from among the children of men, and will beget for ourselves children."

And Semjâzâ, who was their leader, said to them: "I fear that perhaps ye will not be willing to do this deed, and I alone shall suffer for this great sin."

Then all answered him and said: "We all will swear an oath, and bind ourselves mutually by a curse, that we will not give up this plan, but will make this plan a deed."

Then they all swore together, and bound themselves mutually by a curse; and together they were two hundred. And they descended on Ardîs, which is the summit of Mount Hermon; and they called it Mount Hermon, because they had sworn on it and bound themselves mutually by a curse.

And these are the names of their leaders: Semjâzâ, who was their leader, Urâkibarâmêêl, Akibêêl, Tâmiêl, Râmuêl, Dânêl, Ezêqêêl, Sarâqujâl, Asâêl, Armers, Batraal, Anânî, Zaqêbê, Samsâvêêl, Sartaêl, Turêl, Jomjâêl, Arâzjâl. These are the leaders of the two hundred angels, and the others all were with them.

According to this passage, a group of mutinous angels jointly swore an oath to carry out an evil deed directly opposed to the authority of God. Also notice it states that this group of wayward angels descended onto the summit of Mount Hermon.

One familiar with ancient mythology will see a striking similarity between this Enochian account and other stories from ancient legends. For example, in early mythology, celestial beings with wings are portrayed as coming down from the heavens into the earth to copulate with women who produced demigods, or hybrid creatures (giants), that were a mixture of celestial and terrestrial beings.

Indeed, early mythology and pagan religions from around the planet tell the same basic stories. Some theorists incorrectly refer to these as "ancient aliens."[17] But the story in Genesis 6:1,2, and 4 and First Enoch 6:1-8 states with clarity that this was not an event involving ancient aliens or pagan gods — rather, it was a bizarre situation that involved mutinous angels descending into the world.

The likely reason the basic elements of this story are similar to various legends around the world is, when man's languages were wildly confused by God at the Tower of Babel[18] and humans began to scatter across the face of the earth, each people group carried the tales of these events wherever they went. Over time, the original true story was adapted, changed, and twisted from its original form. Nevertheless, if you compare all the various myths from around the world, they basically tell the same story, which arguably can be traced to the real-life events that are referenced in Genesis 6:1,2, and 4.

SIMILAR STORIES, BUT THE DETAILS DIFFER SLIGHTLY

For the sake of emphasis, it must be stated again that all pagan mythology and religions have their roots in the events documented in Genesis 6:1,2, and 4 and expounded on in First Enoch 6:1-8. The Bible factually tells what took place, and other cultures and religions offer variations of what happened. The fact is that many early civilizations and cultures believed in and wrote about ancient legends that are strikingly similar to the biblical account about the "sons of God" — or fallen angels — who came down to copulate with women, who then gave birth to hybrid creatures called Nephilim.

73

The various people groups that have similar ancient stories include:

- **Sumerians,**[19] **Assyrians,**[20] **and Egyptians**[21]
- **Chaldeans**[22] **and Babylonians**[23]
- **Greeks**[24] **and Romans**[25]
- **Incas,**[26] **Mayans,**[27] **and Indians**[28]
- **Chinese,**[29] **Japanese,**[30] **and American Indians**[31]

An example of one ancient god being known by various names is Ishtar, who was also known among Akkadians, Canaanites, Egyptians, Hittites, Hurrians, Phoenicians, and Israelites by the names Athtart, Astarte, Shaushka, Ashtart, and Ashtoreth.

In nearly every culture, there are recollections and recordings of a time in civilizations past when celestial beings entered the earth's atmosphere to philander with women, who then gave birth to demigods (hybrid creatures) or giants. When the fallen angels descended with their dazzling appearance into the atmosphere of earth, they must have looked like gods to those who witnessed them. Thus, their divine appearance is the reason people at that time welcomed them and participated with them in their spiritually criminal activities.

Again, while the stories in each culture may slightly vary and use different names for those involved, the ancient account is basically the same. The following is an example of one so-called supernatural being (an unnaturally created demigod) who has been known by multiple names, in multiple regions, and was worshiped differently in various eras. Most commonly recognized this entity as "Ishtar" or "Ashtoreth."

DEITY	TIME PERIOD	CULTURE / REGION
Ishtar[32]	c. 2400 BC	Akkadian (Mesopotamia)
Athtart[33]	c. 1800 BC	Canaanite (Eastern Mediterranean)
Astarte[34]	c. 1550 BC	Egyptian (Egypt)
Shaushka[35]	c. 1500 BC	Hittite and Hurrian (Turkiye–Asia)
Ashtart[36]	c. 1200 BC	Phoenician (Eastern Mediterranean)
Ashtoreth[37]	c. 1000 BC	Israelite (Eastern Mediterranean)

Pictured above is a painting of a pantheon of the gods. Although these deities are considered mythological today, early civilizations viewed them as real and as rooted in real-life events that occurred in the past, which can be traced to the "sons of God" that are referred to in Genesis 6:2.

Greeks and Romans also shared many of the same gods, yet had different names for them. For example, in the Greek and Roman pantheon of gods, we find the following, which were the same oddly created beings with different names in Greek and Latin.

GREEK NAME	ROMAN NAME	KNOWN AS
Zeus	Jupiter	Ruler of the gods, lightening, thunder, law, and order
Hera	Juno	Queen of the gods, wife/sister of Zeus/Jupiter, marriage, childbirth, and fertility
Poseidon	Neptune	God of the seas, horses, and earthquakes
Ares	Mars	God of war
Athena	Minerva	Goddess of reason, handicrafts, war, and wisdom
Demeter	Ceres	Goddess of agriculture, crops, fertility, harvest, and the cycle of life and death
Apollo	Apollo	God of archery, arts, music, prophecy, and healing
Artemis	Diana	Goddess of childbirth, hunting, and wild animals
Aphrodite	Venus	Goddess of beauty, love, sex, and prostitutes
Hephaestus	Vulcan	God of blacksmiths, craftsmen, fire, and weapons
Hermes	Mercury	God of livestock, travelers, and speed
Dionysus	Bacchus	God of actors, drama, festivals, orgies, revelry, and wine

Although these deities are considered mythological today, to early civilizations they were viewed as real and as rooted in real-life events that occurred in the past. Such ancient events are far removed from us, but people living in antiquity were closer to the time frame in which those strange events occurred. The stories were easy for them not only to recall, but to hand down to their successive generations.

PEOPLE INVEST IN WHAT THEY BELIEVE IN

If you ponder the vast number of pagan temples erected and dedicated to various gods and goddesses over the centuries, and the enormous expense required to build and embellish them so extravagantly, you will realize the implausibility of such an unfathomable investment in something the people of that culture didn't think was real. Although they were incorrect in their conclusions to worship them, these people wouldn't have offered such lavish sacrifices and libations to these gods unless they believed these beings were real and that they were involved with controlling the universe and certain circumstances in the natural world.

Certainly, simply believing in something doesn't make it legitimate or even real. My point is, these demigod creatures were very real and were deliberately introduced to mankind through the enemy's diabolical plot to contaminate human seed.

In antiquity, cities were filled with pagan temples because the ancient world believed in them and believed that the gods needed a "house" to live in among humans. Each temple constructed and dedicated to that purpose was a consecrated place where these gods could allegedly dwell, be worshiped and experienced, and where prayers and sacrifices could be made to them. With this belief fixed in their minds, pagans enthusiastically constructed infinite numbers of temples for a pantheon of gods they worshiped in every part of the far-flung ancient world.

Some think early civilizations were simply primitive people with wild imaginations, but that was not the case in every culture. The more we study and know about these ancient cultures, the more we realize how much of life today is impacted by their innovations. For example, it was some of these same earlier civilizations that developed logic, philosophy, poetry, history, science, mathematics, geometry, literature, and various expressions of art and sophisticated architecture.[38] These were not primitive people with wild imaginations — they were individuals commemorating bizarre early events in history that led them astray.

HOW DID THESE LEGENDS SPREAD TO SO MANY CULTURES?

Of course, Noah, his wife, his sons, and his sons' wives knew very well about the despicable deeds of the disobedient angels and their offspring of Nephilim. They saw it all with their own eyes, and they prophetically understood that it was the mischief of these fallen angels and the Nephilim that caused the earth to be destroyed by the Flood.

The Tower of Babel is referred to in Genesis 11:1-9, and it was constructed at the time of Nimrod, a time when the human race spoke a single language. Although they attempted to build a city with a tower that reached into the heavens, God confounded their speech and they were scattered around the world instead.

When this noble family exited the Ark, they carried all that early history out with them into a new civilization. Again, they had personally seen and experienced much of what I have described in this book so far — so these events were very fresh in their minds.

However, later, when God confused humanity's language at the Tower of Babel and scattered the people throughout the world (*see* Genesis 11:1-9), each people group carried the same basic memories of the fallen angels and the giants with them as well. And with each passing generation, the story of what actually took place became more distorted. Some information was added, some was omitted, and the result was the creation of legends. Nevertheless, the "bare bones" of the original story can be found in each culture.

Again, the factual account of the rebellious angels and their misdeeds is found in Genesis 6:1 and 2.

And it came to pass, when men began to multiply on the face of the earth, and daughters were born unto them, that the sons of God [angels] saw the daughters of men that they were fair; and they took them wives of all which they chose.

WHY WOULD THOSE ANGELS DO IT?

At this point, you may be wondering, *Why would angels leave the perfection of their God-assigned posts to have sexual relations with earthly women?* To discover the reason, we turn to early history to see exactly what happened when sin was introduced into the world.

Just before expelling Adam and Eve from the Garden of Eden, God turned to the serpent and declared:

And I will put enmity between thee and the woman, and between thy seed and her seed; it shall bruise thy head, and thou shalt bruise his heel.
— Genesis 3:15

This is the first recorded prophecy in Scripture, and it points to Jesus as the Messiah, who would be born of a woman and whose mission would be to destroy Satan's power (*see* 1 John 3:8). This promise in Genesis 3:15 is sometimes referred to as the *protoevangelium*,[39] which literally means *the first Gospel*, as it is the first promise of redemption. This verse gloriously introduces the message of Christianity.

When God declared the promise of Genesis 3:15 and prophesied that Satan's head would be "bruised" — his authority would be broken and severed — by the Seed of the woman, Satan swung into action with a plan to corrupt the gene pool of the human race and prevent the Seed of the woman — the Messiah — from entering into the world. But the Cross and resurrection of Christ crushed Satan, nevertheless, stripped him of his authority, and forever destroyed his tyranny over humankind.

We know that the "Seed" — or offspring — of the woman prophesied here refers to Jesus Christ, who would be born of Mary. First Peter 1:23 says that He is the Incorruptible Seed of Almighty God, and it is through His death and resurrection that Satan's head was indeed "bruised" — that is, his unbridled authority over mankind through Adam's fall was eternally, irrevocably reversed. Those who repent of their sins and put their faith in Christ's finished work will be born into God's family — saved from the curse of sin and eternal death that was brought into the world, *and into all mankind*, through Adam and Eve's transgression.

When Christ crushed the head of Satan — crushed his headship and seat of power and authority over mankind — Jesus Christ the Lord would also destroy all Satan's principalities and powers, confounding all their schemes, ruining all their works, and stripping them of all their claims to rulership.

The apostle Paul wrote of this amazing victory in Colossians 2:15 (*AMPC*), where he states:

[God] disarmed the principalities and powers that were ranged against us and made a bold display and public example of them, in triumphing over them in Him and in it [the Cross].

Indeed, through the Cross and Resurrection, Christ crushed Satan's whole empire, stripped him of his authority, and forever destroyed his tyranny over humankind. Because of what Jesus did, the devil was dealt a spiritual "deathblow," and he is forever a defeated foe.

Satan heard the Lord loud and clear in the Garden of Eden when God made that prophetic declaration in Genesis 3:15. Knowing that his ultimate demise would come from the "Seed" of a woman, in Satan's mind, it meant he needed to take action to corrupt woman's seed so that such a Deliverer could never be produced through her.

At the time of man's fall, Lucifer had already lost his position in God's presence (*see* Isaiah 14:12-17; Ezekiel 28:11-19). Now operating under his new name, Satan — the master manipulator and deceiver — he seems to have seduced the sons of God (angelic beings, also known as watchers) to abandon their God-assigned posts to have sexual relations with the daughters of men. Their sexual intermingling was intended to corrupt the gene pool of the human race and prevent the Seed of the woman — the Messiah — from entering into the world.

When God declared the promise of Genesis 3:15, prophesying that Satan's head would be "bruised" — and his authority broken and severed — by the Seed of the woman, Satan swung into action and attempted to abort God's plan. Although Satan's schemes seemed somewhat successful in the beginning, they ultimately failed. God was positioned to wipe out evil and to use a small remnant of eight people who had remained pure in order to repopulate the world.

Today God is still using a remnant to wipe out evil, and if you are walking in obedience to Him, He will use you to wipe out evil in Christ's name as well. *You* can play a part in populating this world with new believers and discipling them to know their own authority in Christ to wipe out destruction by the power of His Gospel, the *Good News*.

In the next chapter, we will see what Jude and Peter graphically wrote about how the fallen angels pursued strange flesh and how God brought eternal judgment against them as a result.

QUESTIONS TO PONDER

1. Have you read Genesis 6:1 and 2 in the past and wondered who the "sons of God" were? Did you know this same phrase was also used three times in the book of Job? Who did you understand the "sons of God" to be before this chapter? Now that you know they're angels, how has your understanding of the days of Noah and the reason for the Flood changed?

2. Rabbis wrote that after man sinned in the Garden of Eden, God sent angels down to the earth to watch over, protect, and help mankind. These angels were known by the ancients as *watchers*. What does this say to you about the love and care of God for mankind — that He would send watchers to help them in their fallen state?

3. Carefully reread the passage First Enoch 6:1-8, included in this chapter, along with Genesis 6:1-4. In what ways are these passages similar? How does the excerpt from *The Book of Enoch* fill in the gaps and help you see the events of Genesis 6 differently?

4. As you read about the "watcher" angels doing the unthinkable, deceiving and exploiting those they'd been sent to protect, how has your thinking been expanded as to why God had to cleanse the earth because of the defilement that blotted it like an ink-soaked garment?

5. Why do you think humankind welcomed the descending mutinous angels into their world to begin with? There's a saying that "hindsight is 20/20." You may be surprised that humans were so readily deceived by the angels' appearances. But in what ways do we see society mesmerized and deceived today in so many ways, including by unexplainable supernatural phenomena?

By Enoch's time, angels that God had assigned to watch over and help mankind in their fallen state became enamored with the beauty of the daughters of men and willfully descended into the earth's atmosphere to take as many of them as they wanted in order to mate with them.

CHAPTER FOUR

WHEN ANGELS WENT AFTER 'STRANGE FLESH'

We have seen that the lineage of Adam grew rapidly during the first millennium, and by the time of the Flood, there were already millions of people living on the earth. As this population explosion was taking place, the *sons of God — angels* whom God had assigned to watch over and help mankind in their fallen state — became enamored with the beauty of the daughters of men, and they took as many of them as they wanted in order to mate with them.

Again, the words the "sons of God" in Genesis 6:2 and 4 is a translation of the original text that refers to *angelic beings*. This is confirmed in the highly respected Greek translation of the Old Testament called the *Septuagint*.[1] Additionally, this phrase "sons of God" also appears in Job 1:6; 2:1; and 38:7, where in each instance it describes *angelic beings*.

Along with the verification in the biblical narrative and the *Septuagint*, there is also a significant record of the fallen angels cohabiting with women found in the earliest portions of *The Book of Enoch* — those early portions are also referred to both as *First Enoch* and *The Book of the Watchers*.[2] Although that book is not a canonical

The Septuagint enabled Jewish people throughout the world to read the Old Testament Scriptures in a language that was most common to them. Scholars concur that the *Septuagint* is the translation used by Jesus and His apostles, and when a New Testament writer quoted Old Testament Scriptures in his epistles, he nearly every time quoted from the *Septuagint* version of the Old Testament.

book of the Bible, during the intertestamental period and in the time of Jesus, it was considered to be serious commentary on the events of Genesis 6. In fact, *The Book of Enoch* was viewed so seriously during the time of the New Testament that both Peter and Jude either quoted or referred to it in their respective epistles.[3]

Both Jews and Christians in the First Century were captivated with *First Enoch* because it both described past events and foretold end-times happenings. Enoch, the son of Jared, was the father of Methuselah and the great-grandfather of Noah. As previously noted, it is likely Enoch's prophetic writings survived the Flood because Noah treasured them and carried them with him onto the Ark. Thus, Noah served

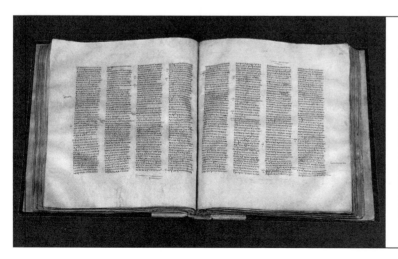

The Book of Enoch is not a canonical book of the Bible. However, during the intertestamental period and in the time of Jesus, it was considered to be serious commentary on past events, including the events of Genesis 6. *The Book of Enoch* was viewed so seriously during the time of the New Testament that both Peter and Jude either quoted or referred to it in their respective epistles.

not only as an engineer, builder, and zoologist, but also as an *archivist* who kept the cherished prophetic declarations passed on to him by his forefathers!

As we have seen, Genesis 6:1 and 2 reveals that there was a time in the earth's early history when disobedient, mutinous angels abandoned their God-assigned posts, descended into the earth's atmosphere, and began to sexually defile mortal women, who produced hybrid offspring as a result of that unholy, unauthorized union.

And it came to pass, when men began to multiply on the face of the earth, and daughters were born unto them, that the sons of God saw the daughters of men that they were fair; and they took them wives of all which they chose.

This event occurred during the pre-Flood population explosion. Although the *King James Version* says the angels took "wives" to themselves, a more accurate understanding of this wording is that these rebellious beings took women with whom *to mate*.

But it was these angels' strange obsession with human flesh that we will focus on in this chapter.

THE ANGELS' SEDITIOUS CONVERSATION WAS RECORDED BY ENOCH

By Enoch's time, this evil angelic activity was so well known that in the non-canonical book of *First Enoch*, we find recorded details of what took place. In fact, Enoch recorded a verbal exchange that occurred between Semjâzâ, who was allegedly the chief rebellious angel, and the other angels he allegedly swayed to follow him in rebellion against God.

As we saw in the last chapter, it seems that Satan enticed these angels to carry out this horrific deed so that the human gene pool would be corrupted in order to try to stop the birth of the specific "Seed" of the woman, whom God prophesied would crush Satan's head (*see* Genesis 3:15).

Here again is the seditious conversation among those sinning angels that is documented in *First Enoch* 6:1-8:

First Enoch 6:1-8

And it came to pass, after the children of men had increased in those days, beautiful and comely daughters were born to them.

And the angels, the sons of the heavens, saw and lusted after them, and said one to another: "Behold, we will choose for ourselves wives from among the children of men, and will beget for ourselves children."

And Semjâzâ, who was their leader, said to them: "I fear that perhaps ye will not be willing to do this deed, and I alone shall suffer for this great sin."

Then all answered him and said: "We all will swear an oath, and bind ourselves mutually by a curse, that we will not give up this plan, but will make this plan a deed."

Then they all swore together, and bound themselves mutually by a curse; and together they were two hundred. And they descended on Ardîs, which is the summit of Mount Hermon; and they called it Mount Hermon, because they had sworn on it and bound themselves mutually by a curse.

And these are the names of their leaders: Semjâzâ, who was their leader, Urâkibarâmêêl, Akibêêl, Tâmiêl, Râmuêl, Dânêl, Ezêqêêl, Sarâqujâl, Asâêl, Armers, Batraal, Anânî, Zaqêbê, Samsâvêêl, Sartaêl, Turêl, Jomjâêl, Arâzjâl. These are the leaders of the two hundred angels, and the others all were with them.

This ancient text further states there were 200 angels who mutually bound themselves together with an oath to abandon their God-assigned posts, descend into the earth's atmosphere, and comingle with mortal women for the angels' perverted pleasure and to produce their own offspring. This angelic brood likely understood that their violation of God's authority would invoke His judgment. Yet they allowed their lustful desire for earthly women to outweigh reason, and they chose to proceed with their evil deed.

THE BOOK OF JUDE CONFIRMS WHAT THESE ANGELS DID, AS WELL AS THEIR JUDGMENT

What is quite amazing about the bizarre activities recorded in Genesis 6 is that we are given two New Testament confirmations of what took place — by both Peter and Jude. Jude, who was the younger half-brother of Jesus,[4] provides one of those verifications, citing both the mutinous angels' actions and God's judgment against them.

And the angels which kept not their first estate, but left their own habitation, he hath reserved in everlasting chains under darkness unto the judgment of the great day. Even as Sodom and Gomorrha, and the cities about them in like manner, giving themselves over to fornication, and going after strange flesh, are set forth for an example, suffering the vengeance of eternal fire.

— Jude 6,7

Jude informs us that due to the scandalous actions of the rebellious angels, God took action and personally seized those angels and placed them in "everlasting chains under darkness" (Jude 6).

God appointed and assigned a group of angels, including these particular angels, to watch over and to help mankind in their fallen state. But a certain number deserted their divine posts in order to carry out the mischievous deeds described in Genesis 6. Jude informed us that due to their scandalous actions, God took action of His own and seized these nefarious angels, placing them in chains under eternal darkness. Furthermore, Jude stated that the appalling behavior of these mutinous angels was so bizarre and deviant that it could be likened to the depraved behavior that occurred in the cities of Sodom and Gomorrah.

Before we examine what Jude said and Peter wrote about the actions of these angels and God's response to their behavior, I must first address and clarify two important issues some people have with the idea of angels mating with women and producing unnatural offspring — i.e., the giants, or Nephilim. The first has to do with Jesus' own words concerning angels and marriage, and the second has to do with seeds producing "after their own kind" (*see* Genesis 1:11-30).

Depicted here is Jesus teaching a multitude when Sadducees posed a question to Jesus about a childless woman who had been married to seven brothers successively, one after another according to Moses' command concerning widows, until the last brother died. Jesus answered their questions, but also stated that angels do not enter into marriage in Heaven.

WHAT JESUS SAID ABOUT 'ANGELS MARRYING' IS LARGELY MISUNDERSTOOD

There are some who object to the idea that angels could sexually cohabit with women. They base their objection on what Jesus said in response to a question the Sadducees posed to Him about a childless woman who had been married to seven brothers successively, one after another, according to Moses' command concerning widows until the last brother died.

In Matthew 22:23-28, we read:

The same day came to him the Sadducees, which say that there is no resurrection, and asked him, saying, Master, Moses said, If a man die, having no children, his brother shall marry his wife, and raise up seed unto his brother. Now there were with us seven brethren: and the first, when he had married a wife, deceased, and, having no issue, left his wife unto his brother: likewise the second also, and the third, unto the seventh.

And last of all the woman died also. Therefore, in the resurrection whose wife shall she be of the seven? for they all had her.

Matthew 22:29 and 30 tells us that in response to this question, "Jesus answered and said unto them, Ye do err, not knowing the scriptures, nor the power of God. For in the resurrection they neither marry, nor are given in marriage, but are as the angels of God in heaven."

On the basis of Jesus' response in this passage, some argue that the idea of angels descending into the earth's atmosphere to mate with mortal women is impossible. But let's look at what Jesus *said* and *did not say* in these verses.

These verses exclusively address heavenly matters and what angels *don't* do, not what they *can't* do. This one passage neither pertains to, nor can it in itself refute, the angels in history who abandoned their positions and grievously sinned. Scripture and other important extra-biblical documents show that in the past, there indeed was a time when mutinous angels rebelled, descended to the earth, and sexually cohabited with mortal women. Although this activity could never take place in Heaven, Genesis 6 is not talking about angels in Heaven. It is simply retelling the sinister events that occurred in the realm of the earth just before the Flood.

It is also important to know that there is no biblical evidence for angels of a female gender, as all named angels in Scripture are male. When this group of angels mentioned in Jude were assigned to watch over humans, their watching included watching over women, and they became tempted to sexually relate to women. It seems that prior to that moment, angels had never been sexually tempted. But when they began looking at and gazing upon women, Satan seized the opportunity and caused the angels to become enamored with them. Those angels then broke rank to glut themselves sexually with women.

What I have been describing to you about these mutinous angels was the well-established opinion of many esteemed ancient voices, even from among early fathers of the Church. You will see this detailed in the next chapter.

Again, the behavior of these angelic beings was so appalling that both Jude and Peter wrote very specifically about these angels and the judgment God unleashed against them (*see* Jude 6,7 and 2 Peter 2:4). But before we resume this discourse on the angels going after "strange flesh" — and then look in Chapter 5 at what the various Church leaders said about it — there is one more important question that must be answered, and it has to do with reproduction.

God's original design was for all forms of life to reproduce "after their own kind." Later this design was violated when mutinous angels sexually engaged with mortal women, who then gave birth to unnatural, hybrid creatures.

'AFTER THEIR OWN KIND'

Some have asked the question, "How is it possible for women to give birth to hybrid giants since the Bible says everything in creation was intended and declared by God to replicate after its own kind?" Indeed, it was God's original design for all forms of life to reproduce after their own kind. Genesis states that grass, herbs, fruit trees, and everything having seed within itself was intended to replicate "after its own kind." We see this in Genesis 1:11 and 12, which says:

And God said, Let the earth bring forth grass, the herb yielding seed, and the fruit tree yielding fruit after his kind, whose seed is in itself, upon the earth: and it was so. And the earth brought forth grass, and herb yielding seed after his kind, and the tree yielding fruit, whose seed was in itself, after his kind: and God saw that it was good.

Additionally, we read that it was also God's original design for every moving creature — birds, sea creatures, and all land animals of every type — to replicate "after its own kind."

And God said, Let the waters bring forth abundantly the moving creature that hath life, and fowl that may fly above the earth in the open firmament of heaven. And God created great whales, and every living creature that moveth, which the waters brought forth abundantly, after their kind, and every winged fowl after his kind: and God saw that it was good. And God blessed them, saying, Be fruitful, and multiply, and fill the waters in the seas, and let fowl multiply in the earth. And the evening and the morning were the fifth day.

And God said, Let the earth bring forth the living creature after his kind, cattle, and creeping thing, and beast of the earth after his kind: and it was so. And God made the beast of the earth after his kind, and cattle after their kind, and every thing that creepeth upon the earth after his kind: and God saw that it was good.

— Genesis 1:20-25

The crowning achievement of creation was when God made man from the dust of the earth and breathed life into him. Just as it was with all the plants and animals He created, it was God's original design for humans to replicate "after their own kind." This is revealed in Genesis 1:26-28, which says:

And God said, Let us make man in our image, after our likeness: and let them have dominion over the fish of the sea, and over the fowl of the air, and over the cattle, and over all the earth, and over every creeping thing

that creepeth upon the earth. So God created man in his own image, in the image of God created he him; male and female created he them.

And God blessed them, and God said unto them, Be fruitful, and multiply, and replenish the earth, and subdue it: and have dominion over the fish of the sea, and over the fowl of the air, and over every living thing that moveth upon the earth.

In all these passages from Genesis, we see it was God's original design for everything to produce "after its own kind," and that is exactly what happened until fallen angels wrongly entered the picture and somehow "metamorphosed," transcending God's boundary in creation. They "mingled seed" with human beings and horribly transgressed His original design.

When those angels metamorphosed and sexually engaged with mortal women, God's original design was violated, and it resulted in women giving birth to unnatural, hybrid creatures. Equally shocking to this anomaly of creation is the fact that some believe that the giants later sexually defiled certain animals, resulting in the birth of unnatural, monstrous creatures. Although we cannot state emphatically that this actually occurred, but you will see commentary on it in Chapter 6.

Keep in mind that just because God originally wills something to be a certain way — like mankind and all creation producing after its kind — it doesn't mean it's automatically going to happen. The Bible says God "…wants all people to be saved and to come to a knowledge of the truth" (1 Timothy 2:4 *NIV*), but there have been and will be many who rebel against His will — against what He wants — and reject the truth. We see a similar principle of rebellion at work in the case of these mutinous angels who rejected God's will, abandoned their assigned places, and began to sexually cohabit with earthly women.

Again, it was — and still is — God's design for all created species to reproduce after their own kind. Specifically, His intention for human reproduction through marriage is "a godly seed" (*see* Malachi 2:15). But sexual unions between angels and human women are unnatural and were never intended by God. In Chapter 6, we will pull back the curtain even further and see what modern mankind has been working on behind the scenes and how sinister this issue of seed-tampering has become.

It is different to explain the fallen angels' ability to inseminate women to produce the Nephilim. Nevertheless, Scripture strongly suggests it, writers in antiquity have recorded it, and a large number of scholars and theologians believe it today.

Two Instances of Angels 'Transforming' Themselves in the Earthly Realm

Before we continue our discussion of the sin of the mutinous, fallen angels, whom God had originally assigned to watch over humankind in their fallen state, let's look at two instances of angels manifesting in human form at various times, as recorded in Scripture.

This painting depicts the moment when angels appeared with the Lord to Abraham as recorded in Genesis 18:1-33. The angels appeared in human form, and Abraham provided water for them to wash their feet and also provided them a meal to eat, which they ate with Abraham before journeying to the land of Sodom.

Angels as Men Before Abraham
(Genesis 18:1-33)

In this passage, three "men" visited Abraham, and one of them was the Lord Himself in human form (*see* vv. 1,10,13-33). Abraham invited them to wash their feet, rest, and eat a meal — and they did (*see* vv. 5,8).

This is the same passage in which the Lord pronounced that Sarah would bear their son Isaac. Then the other two "men" turned to make their way to Sodom and Gomorrah while the Lord remained behind with Abraham, who famously pled his case in intercession against the judgment that was about to be meted on those ungodly cities.

This illustration depicts the moment when two angels appeared to Lot at the gate of Sodom. They appeared in such a real human form that Lot washed their feet and invited them to stay all night with him at his home. Their appearance was so human-like that the men of Sodom sought to have sex with them.

ANGELS AS MEN BEFORE LOT (GENESIS 19:1-22)

In these verses, the two angels who appeared as "men" had made their way from the plains of Mamre to the gate of Sodom, where Lot sat and rose to greet them. He invited the two "men" to wash their feet and stay overnight at his house instead of in the street, where they had planned to spend the night (*see* vv. 2,3). Lot prepared a feast for the two men, "…and they did eat" (v. 3).

But the wicked men of the city — who were apparently observing Lot's greeting and invitation and noticing the two "men" — gathered around Lot's house (*see* v. 4). Known for their same-sex lust for "strange flesh," as we will see in the following section, the men demanded that Lot release the so-called "men" into the street so they could have sex with them (*see* v. 5). Lot stood outside his house to protest, and when his own well-being was threatened, the two angels who appeared as "men" forcibly opened the door, pulled Lot inside, and smote the men outside with blindness (*see* vv. 6-11).

Of course, we know that the city was soon after destroyed by these "men," who had appeared as a company of three (including the Lord) before Abraham, after which the two men — *angels transformed as men* — made their way to Lot.

In addition to these instances, there are other events recorded in both the Old and New Testaments in which angels appeared to people to encourage them, call them to action, and deliver needful information. But the particular group of angels in Genesis 6 violated their assignment and left their post to interact with women on the earth in a way that God never intended. In fact, their violation of His boundary was so horrific that those angelic transgressors are bound in chains and darkness to this very day. And, of course, we know that the entire earth had to be cleansed of the sweeping sin that blotted and contaminated nearly the entire human race.

What Is 'Strange Flesh'?

As we have already seen, the gross intermingling between the sons of God and the daughters of men was a strange and perverse deviation from God's original plan. It was so egregious and devastating in the corruption it wrought on the earth that Jude recounted parts of it in Jude 6 and 7. This profound passage states:

> **And the angels which kept not their first estate, but left their own habitation, he hath reserved in everlasting chains under darkness unto the judgment of the great day.** *Even as* **Sodom and Gomorrha** [Gomorrah], **and the cities about them in like manner, giving themselves over to fornication, and** *going after* **strange flesh, are set forth for an example, suffering the vengeance of eternal fire.**

Notice the words "even as" at the beginning of verse 7. Jude used them to link the unnatural sexual activities of angels in verse 6 with the strange activities that occurred in Sodom and Gomorrah (v. 7). These words "even as" let us know that Jude *was not* starting a different topic — rather he was drawing from the events of Sodom and Gomorrah to depict the "strangeness" of what occurred when mutinous angels copulated with women.

In fact, the words "even as" are the equivalent of saying *just as* or *in the very same way*. Thus, Jude 7 could be interpreted, "What happened with the angels was 'just as' unnatural as the deeds that took place in Sodom and Gomorrah." The words "even as" plainly mean that angels going after human flesh was "just as" unnatural and twisted as the men in Sodom and Gomorrah pursuing sexual relationships with

The men of Sodom and Gomorrah glutted themselves with illicit sexual behaviors, and Scripture calls their outrageous behaviors unnatural and strange. By giving themselves over to these actions, they moved backward into a cesspool of moral depravity.

other men. Thus, we find Jude equates the deeds of the sinning angels to the abominable, degenerate, depraved, perverted behaviors that characterized the sodomites in Sodom and Gomorrah.

Jude goes on to document that both the fallen angels and the men of Sodom and Gomorrah gave themselves to "fornication." The original meaning of the word "fornication" is so outrageous that it pictures those *who glut themselves on forbidden sexual activities and who are "a whoring" with illicit sexual behaviors*. The use of the word "fornication," along with the phrase "even as," means that *in the very same way* the men of Sodom and Gomorrah glutted themselves with illicit sexual behaviors, the sinning angels *glutted* themselves on forbidden sexual activities with earthly women. This was a sexual rampage of the angels with mortal women so vast and far-reaching in its effects that, eventually, the entire human race was blemished because of it — *with the exception of* Noah and his family.

Also notice in Jude 7 that "just as" the Sodomites were "going after" strange flesh, the fallen angels were also "going after" what was unnatural and strange. In the original language, the words "going after" actually picture *a reverting to something* or *a going backward*. This is important to note, for at that time (and in our own time), those who participated in alternative sexual lifestyles often projected their deviant behavior as more advanced and progressive. But the exact opposite was true according to Scripture: They were actually *going backward*.

The men of Sodom and Gomorrah morally *reverted* in their behavior, *going backward* into sexual encounters that were forbidden, foreign, and contrary to God's original design. Although they may have viewed themselves as progressives who were unshackled by outdated moral restraints, there was nothing progressive about it; it was a moral move backward. The Bible clearly states it was *strange* and *unnatural* for the men to burn for men rather than desire women (*see* Genesis 19).

In the same way, Jude compares the deviant behaviors of the Sodomites with the actions of the mutinous angels — indicating that the angels' seeking sexual relations with earthly women was a deviant, unnatural, and strange event that should have never occurred. Even though the angels likely thought they would gain something by engaging in their illicit behavior, they actually moved backward, producing a cesspool of moral depravity.

Although it is nearly inconceivable that angels would commit such brazen acts, Jude clearly stated that this particular group of angels did. Hence, Jude 7 uses the words "going after strange flesh" to depict both the unnatural activities of the sodomites and the unnatural activities of the mutinous angels who burned in lustful passion and left their God-given posts to sexually cohabit with human women, thus confirming the outrageous events depicted in Genesis 6:1-4.

THE BOOK OF ENOCH FURTHER DETAILS
THE DIABOLICAL DEEDS OF THE FALLEN ANGELS

Once more, let's turn our attention to *The Book of Enoch*, where we find that this early text offers a nearly parallel description of Genesis 6:1,2,4. First Enoch 6:1 and 2 says:

> **And it came to pass, after the children of men had increased in those days, beautiful and comely daughters were born to them. And the angels, the sons of the heavens, saw and lusted after them, and said one to another: "Behold, we will choose for ourselves wives [mates] from among the children of men, and will beget for ourselves children."**

Again, we find more confirmation of the angels' lustful desire for women and the fact that they went after "strange flesh" as described in Jude 7. First Enoch 7:1 and 2 adds:

> **And they took unto themselves wives [mates], and each chose for himself one, and they began to go in to them, and mixed with them…and they became pregnant and brought forth great giants….**

To demonstrate just how closely writings in *The Book of Enoch* seem to run parallel to passages in the Bible, consider once more these verses in Genesis 6:1,2, and 4:

> **And it came to pass, when men began to multiply on the face of the earth, and daughters were born unto them, that the sons of God saw the daughters of men that they were fair; and they took them wives [mates] of all which they chose…. There were giants in the earth in those days; and also after that, when the sons of God came in unto the daughters of men, and they bare children to them, the same became mighty men which were of old, men of renown.**

Interestingly, First Enoch 9:9 reiterates and adds to First Enoch 7:2:

> **And the women have brought forth giants, and thereby the whole earth has been filled with blood and wickedness.**

The Book of Enoch also informs us that in addition to defiling women, the fallen angels amplified their sinful behavior by producing offspring with the women, the Nephilim, that filled the whole earth with blood and wickedness, as we will see in the following pages, where I go into the violence and bloodshed brought about on the earth by the offspring of the angels and the women. But part of the increased bloodshed and evil possibly came as a result of the fallen angels themselves teaching humankind to make weapons of war. First Enoch 8:1-3 says:

> **And** [the sinning angels] **taught mankind to make swords and knives and shields and coats of mail, and taught them to see what was behind them, and their works of art: bracelets and ornaments, and the use of rouge, and the beautifying of the eye-brows, and the dearest and choicest stones and all coloring substances and the metals of the earth.**
>
> **And there was great wickedness and much fornication, and they sinned, and all their ways were corrupt. And** [one of them] **taught all the conjurers and root-cutters,** [one of them] **the loosening of conjurations,** [one of them] **the astrologers,** [one of them] **the signs, and** [one of them] **taught astrology, and** [one of them] **taught the course of the moon.**

If you have ever wondered where the widespread use of weapons of war came from, *The Book of Enoch* implies it was from the fallen angels. According to that book, they were the ones, at least in part, who taught humans to make swords, knives, shields, and coats of mail. Furthermore, these same mutinous angels also introduced humankind to astrology and to enchantments and the casting of spells. If that is true, it means the forbidden, occultic practices that are known and practiced today were first taught to humans by the fallen angels who were seduced by Satan to rebel against God.

In the pages to come, you will additionally discover that what the fallen angels perpetuated with humankind was not only sexually vile, but also barbarically violent. First Enoch 9:8 and 9 provides a quick summary of their mischievous activity:

> **And they** [the sinning angels] **have gone together to the daughters of men and have slept with them, with those women, and have defiled themselves, and have revealed to them these sins. And the women have brought forth giants, and thereby the whole earth has been filled with blood and wickedness.**

In addition to the abovementioned texts from *The Book of Enoch*, the notable Church father Irenaeus[5] recorded that the fallen angels also instructed humans how to participate in sexual "passions." This term is understood to mean every form of sexual behavior that was unacceptable and unnatural in the eyes of God. If what

Irenaeus wrote is true, it lets us know that the fallen angels were the source again, at least in part, from which sexually degenerate, deviant, and perverse activities were brought into the world. When these angels began to violate the authority and commandments of God, they glutted themselves on sexual activities and taught humans to do likewise.

You will see in Chapter 6 that the mutinous angels' teachings were so perverse that some believe it led to the giants' practice of bestiality. Remember from the last chapter that ancient pagan religions and cultures had their roots in their respective memories of what the fallen angels and their "demigod" offspring did and taught, as we will see more in depth as we proceed. This certainly provides an explanation for why degenerate, deviant, sexual acts were so prevalent in pagan religions in the ancient world.

THE APOSTLE PETER ALSO WROTE ABOUT GOD'S RESPONSE TO THE DEEDS OF THE FALLEN ANGELS

In addition to what Jude wrote about the treasonous angels' perverse activities, Peter also wrote about their dastardly deeds and explained how God dealt with them. It is obvious from his writings that Peter was well aware of the pre-Flood events in Genesis 6 and that he, too, had likely been impacted by the account written in *The Book of Enoch*.

It appears Peter drew on or confirmed these texts from *The Book of Enoch* as he describes these horrific happenings and how God responded. For example, consider what Peter said in these three verses.

> **For if God spared not the angels that sinned, but cast them down to hell, and delivered them into chains of darkness, to be reserved unto judgment; and spared not the old world, but saved Noah the eighth person, a preacher of righteousness, bringing in the flood upon the world of the ungodly; and turning the cities of Sodom and Gomorrha into ashes condemned them with an overthrow, making them an ensample unto those that after should live ungodly.**
>
> **— 2 Peter 2:4-6**

Notice how Peter connects "the angels that sinned" and judged by God (v. 4) with both the worldwide Flood during Noah's day (v. 5) and the judgment of the ungodly people of Sodom and Gomorrah (v. 6). There is nothing coincidental about the subject matter or placement of these three verses. The angels that sinned are the same mutinous beings described in Genesis 6 that came down from the heavens before the Flood and sexually comingled with earthly women. Those fallen angels were judged by God, who also dealt with the ungodly people of the world in Noah's day and with the sodomites of Sodom and Gomorrah who went after "strange flesh."

Without question, the sin of these angels was so detestable, Peter said that God *did not spare them* (see 2 Peter 2:4,5). The word "spare" in the original language means *to spare* or *to treat leniently*. In this case, Peter used a verb with a negative particle to state that God did not deal leniently with or spare these angels from punishment. Thus, God spared *not* — He was *not* lenient with — the mutinous angels who rebelled against His authority. Because their actions were so reprehensible, He made the irrevocable decision that these particular angels should be incarcerated until the day of the final judgment.

Peter also stated that these angels *sinned* (v. 4). The original word for "sinned" depicts *those who erred from a correct course, missed the mark of what was expected,* and are thereby *guilty*. The use of the Greek word translated "sinned" affirms that:

- These angels knew exactly what they were supposed to do.
- These angels knew that what they were doing was wrong.
- These angels willingly chose to err from a correct course; thus, they were blatantly guilty.

In fact, they were so guilty that Peter states that God "cast them down to hell" (2 Peter 2:4).

In Second Peter 2:4, the word "hell" is translated from the Greek word *tartaros*, and this is the only time it is used in the New Testament. The Greek word *tartaros* was a well-known term used in Greek and Roman mythology to depict *an underground cavern where rebellious spirits are imprisoned until the time of judgment*. This word is very familiar to anyone who knows Greek and Roman mythology, for it was

God personally seized mutinous angels and incarcerated them in an underground abyss, where they are presently and will continue to be imprisoned until the time of judgment.

used in these ancient pagan religions, preceding Peter's epistle, to describe *Tartarus*, an underground abyss where rebellious spirits were imprisoned. Again we find a connection between Genesis 6 and the stories related in pagan mythology.

These Rebellious Angels Were Placed in Chains, and God Keeps an Eye on Them to This Day

Although many allege that Tartarus is a mythological place, Peter unequivocally stated it is a real detention center where God has incarcerated the rebellious angels who sinned in Genesis 6:1,2, and 4. Peter went on to state that God "…delivered them [the fallen angels] into chains of darkness, to be reserved unto judgment" (2 Peter 2:4).

Peter further wrote that to ensure these angels never escape this place of detention, God put them in *chains*. The word "chains" here is plural and denotes *multiple chains that bind*. Thus, God did not bind them with a single chain — but to ensure they would never break free, He ordered them to be put into *multiple chains* until

Not only did God imprison rebellious angels, but He also bound them in unbreakable chains in darkness, and they are still there to this very day.

the day of eternal judgment that awaits them. God ordered these angels be locked into a subterranean abyss, and they are still chained there to this very day.

Like Jude in his epistle (Jude 1:6), Peter also stated that these angels are "reserved" in everlasting chains for judgment (*see* 2 Peter 2:4). The word "reserved" is from an original word that pictures *a watch or guard of soldiers who are positioned to protect something very important that has been entrusted to their care.*

Peter used this word very specifically to alert us that in some way, God Himself is standing attentively and perpetually on guard over this category of incarcerated, rebellious angels. Exactly how God is watching over them is not known, but Peter categorically stated that He is surveilling them to make sure they never escape this place of detention or their future judgment.

Friend, although we don't know all the details of these events written about by both Peter and Jude, we know that the Word of God is true and that rebellious angels are being determinedly detained by God unto a future day of inescapable judgment.

Taking into account the meaning in the original language, the *RIV* (*Renner Interpretive Version*) of Second Peter 2:4 says:

> **…God absolutely did not leniently go easy on or spare the angels who erred from a correct course, who failed to meet God's expectations, and who egregiously did wrong. Rather than go easy on them, on the contrary, God grabbed those rebellious angels by the scruff of their necks and handed them over in unbreakable chains into an underground dungeon — in a place void of all light and filled with a never-ending darkness — that is, to a subterranean abyss where rebellious spirits are assigned to reside until the time of judgment. And now, like a Mighty Prison Guard, God Himself perpetually and faithfully is watching over those rebellious angels to make sure they are securely kept until the judgment, which for them, will be the greatest crisis imaginable.**

I realize the material in this chapter deals with a difficult subject — both to write about and to read. The fact is, God didn't just one day decide that He was sorry and grieved that He'd created mankind (*see* Genesis 6:6). And He didn't send a catastrophic flood to destroy the face of the planet and every living thing in it just because He felt like it.

The sin taking place on the earth in Noah's day was so profoundly violent, depraved, and egregious that God swung into action to do the only thing He could do to preserve a small remnant of the human population, through which He would eventually bring forth the promised Seed — that is, Jesus the Savior of mankind and the Lamb slain from the foundation of the world.

We have covered a great deal of material in this chapter, and in the next one, you will see that the events you have just read about were well-known by and were described in the writings of reputable voices in the ancient world. In fact, some of these ancients gave insights about the fallen angels and the monstrous hybrid creatures they produced that are quite astonishing.

QUESTIONS TO PONDER

1. Carefully read Jude 6 and 7 and ask the Holy Spirit to show you the connection between the mutinous angels that abandoned their God-assigned positions and the people of Sodom and Gomorrah who went after *strange flesh*. What is He showing you?

2. Most of us know that the people of Sodom and Gomorrah were enslaved in the sin of homosexuality. But read what else the Bible specifically says about the sin of Sodom in Ezekiel 16:49 and 50 and see if you observe these things in the world today.

3. As you've been going through this chapter, have you had a difficult time accepting that angels abandoned their posts and had sexual relations with human women? Had Jesus' words in Matthew 22:30 about the angels in Heaven not marrying ever caused you confusion? How has this chapter helped you to see this subject more clearly?

4. In what way has the explanation of the mutinous angels — and how their behavior polluted the human race — helped you understand God's decision to completely rid the planet of the indescribable taint that had blanketed the earth?

5. Before reading this chapter, had you ever thought about the fact that Satan was behind the fallen angels' plot to comingle with women to create families of their own? He nearly succeeded, but God preserved a remnant who yielded to His grace and remained uncontaminated as they worked under His directives to construct a massive ark of safety that would preserve them — *and the human race* — from the catastrophe to come. Why did Satan want to irrevocably pollute the human population? How does our obedience to God today interfere with the enemy's schemes to stop the plan of God?

The above ancient engraving pictures a massive and aggressive figure from the time of Sargon I, an ancient ruler of the Akkadian Empire, whose helmet is capped with horns, a feature only attributed to god-like figures in the ancient world.

CHAPTER FIVE

WHAT ANCIENT SOURCES SAID ABOUT FALLEN ANGELS AND GIANTS

In the previous chapters, we have discovered that in the opening verses of Genesis 6, something extremely bizarre was occurring on the earth. It says that during the time preceding the Flood, the "sons of God" — which we've identified as *angels* or *watchers* — began to lust after the daughters of men. Mesmerized by the women's beauty, these angelic beings abandoned their God-assigned posts, took the women they desired, and began to cohabit with them. The result of this illicit sexual union is described in Genesis 6:4 and 5, which says:

> **There were giants in the earth in those days; and also after that, when the sons of God came in unto the daughters of men, and they bare children to them, the same became mighty men which were of old, men of renown. And God saw that the wickedness of man was great in the earth, and that every imagination of the thoughts of his heart was only evil continually.**

Although this sinister event hasn't been discussed much in modern times, details of what took place were known and documented many centuries ago by ancient scholars and Early Church fathers. Indeed, many respected Christian apologists, historians, scholars, and theologians have written about the inconceivable activities of the fallen angels and their hybrid offspring the Bible calls *giants*.

In this eye-opening chapter, you will read firsthand commentary from venerated individuals such as Clement of Rome, Josephus, Justin Martyr, Tatian, Irenaeus, Athenagoras, Clement of Alexandria, Tertullian, Commodian, Eusebius, Jerome, and Sulpicius Severus, who all believed in and confirmed the fallen-angel account of Genesis 6 to be true and wrote of the terrors brought into the world by the race of giants that was produced.[1]

GOD'S PROPHETIC WORDS WERE PASSED DOWN FROM JARED ALL THE WAY TO HIS GREAT-GREAT-GRANDSON NOAH

To briefly recap this family's prophetic influence, we know that for centuries, God had been speaking and revealing revelations to these early patriarchs about a coming judgment, and each generation successively passed these revelations on to the next.

- *Jared* shared divine insights with his son *Enoch* that the Lord had revealed to him.

- *Enoch* imparted divine insights to his son *Methuselah*, telling what the Lord had revealed to him and to his father Jared.

- *Methuselah* then shared those prophetic insights with his son *Lamech*, who in turn passed everything on to his son *Noah*.

From the time of Jared to Noah, God gave more and more revelation about how He was going to deal with the mutinous angels and the monstrous giants, who were causing barbaric violence in the earth. Because the behavior of these hybrid creatures was progressively defiling the entire human population, God prophetically declared He would send a Flood to cleanse the earth of it.

We have seen that the long, overlapping lifespans of Adam's descendants made it probable that Noah had heard with his own ears the prophetic insights from the

God told Noah that He was going to deal with the mutinous angels and giants who were causing barbaric violence in the earth. And God prophetically declared He would send a Flood to cleanse the earth of these evils. God's admonitions and warnings were never "hidden in a corner" — and neither was His plan to deal with the longstanding evil on the Earth.

mouths of his father Lamech, his grandfather Methuselah, and possibly even from his great-great-grandfather Jared — who were all living simultaneously for hundreds of years during Noah's lifetime (*see* the chart at the end of Chapter 2). Again, this should remind us of our own need to pass revelation to the next generation and to treasure the words of faithful family members who have walked with God before us.

In addition to the revelation that had been passed to Noah by his predecessors, Hebrews 11:7 informs us that Noah also heard directly from God about what was about to take place. That verse says, "By faith Noah, being warned of God of things not seen as yet, moved with fear, prepared an ark to the saving of his house…." This passage contains important insights on how Noah responded to what God revealed to him — insights we need to know and apply in our own life. Therefore, we will revisit it in the coming chapters.

WHAT SCRIPTURE DOCUMENTS ABOUT THE MUTINOUS ANGELS AND THEIR OFFSPRING THE NEPHILIM

Again, here is what the Bible tells us in Genesis 6:1,2, and 4:

And it came to pass, when men began to multiply on the face of the earth, and daughters were born unto them, that the sons of God saw the daughters of men that they were fair; and they took them wives of all which they chose…. There were giants in the earth in those days; and also after that, when the sons of God came in unto the daughters of men, and they bare children to them, the same became mighty men which were of old, men of renown.

When the rebellious angels mated with mortal women, the women birthed hybrid creatures called *giants*.

> **The word "giants" is translated from the word *nephilim*, which some suggest comes from the verb *nephal*, meaning *to fall*. This seems to imply that the Nephilim were *fallen ones*[2] — or ones who violently *fell on* people, causing them to *fall* in fear. Either way, these hybrid beings were physically enormous, possessed unnatural strength, and propagated evil and violence throughout the earth in the time before the Flood.**
>
> **When we look at Genesis 6:4 in the *Septuagint*, we find that the Greek word for Nephilim is *gigantes*.[3] This is where we derive the words "giant" and "gigantic." The use of this word in the *Septuagint* informs us that the hybrid offspring of fallen angels who mated with mortal women were *monstrous giants* that were *fallen* from God's original design. They were supersized creatures, not just in height — their arms, legs, hands, head, torso, and teeth were enormous compared to those of an average man.**

Some may argue, "That's just a myth. Giants did not really exist." But archaeological evidence says the Nephilim *did* exist, and there are reports on virtually every continent that verify gigantic hybrid creatures once roamed the earth.[4] How they appeared in each region is too broad a subject for this book, but the fact is, they really did exist.

What were the dreadful effects of these monstrous, hybrid creatures? Genesis 6:5-7 and 11 tells us.

> **And God saw that the wickedness of man was great in the earth, and that every imagination of the thoughts of his heart was only evil continually. And it repented the Lord that he had made man on the earth, and it grieved him at his heart. And the Lord said, I will destroy man whom I have created from the face of the earth; both man, and beast, and the creeping thing, and the fowls of the air; for it repenteth me that I have made them…. The earth also was corrupt before God, and the earth was filled with violence.**

Great wickedness…every imagination of the human heart was continually evil…and the earth was filled with violence. These were the characteristics of the earth and the people, giants, and fallen angels on the earth. And it all came as a result of the fallen angels who sinned with earthly women and produced monstrous hybrid creatures. We will come back to this in Chapter 14, which is entitled, "Did Jesus Prophesy It Will Happen Again?" For now, know that these ancient events are documented in Scripture, in *The Book of Enoch*, and in many other ancient historical sources.

ANCIENT SOURCES THAT VERIFY THE FALLEN ANGELS-AND-GIANTS NARRATIVE

Remarkably, there were many notable voices from early history that documented the bizarre events that occurred between fallen angels and earthly women. Ancient records from nearly the last 5,000 years show that these events were known and acknowledged to have taken place by many serious and noteworthy individuals.

In the following section, you will see an extensive and significant number of quotes from renowned apologists, historians, scholars, and theologians who each verified the account of the sinning angels who mated with mortal women, which is described in Genesis 6:1-4. To establish who each of these ancient voices are, I will first provide a brief biographical description, detailing the credibility and trustworthiness of their writings. Each brief biography will be followed by that writer's personal commentary verifying the pre-Flood events.

CLEMENT OF ROME
35 – 99 AD

Clement of Rome (also known as Pope Clement I, the fourth bishop of Rome) was a member of the church at Rome in the First Century and was said to have been ordained into the ministry by the apostle Peter.[5] He is also listed by Irenaeus and Tertullian as the bishop of Rome, who held office from 88 AD to his death in 99 AD.[6] Clement is considered to be one of three apostolic fathers of the Early Church, along with Polycarp of Smyrna and Ignatius of Antioch.

Early tradition says that Clement was imprisoned under Emperor Trajan and that during his imprisonment, he led a ministry among fellow prisoners. *The Liber Pontificalis* states that he later died during Trajan's reign,[7] being executed by having an anchor tied to him and then being thrown into the sea. In Eusebius' famous document *Ecclesiastical History*, he wrote that Clement was the third Bishop of Rome and a "co-laborer" of the apostle Paul.[8]

Clement's only credible surviving writing is called the *First Epistle of Clement*, which was an epistle that he wrote and sent to the church at Corinth. That document is one of the oldest Christian texts that exists outside of the New Testament. Later, a second epistle called the *Second Epistle of Clement* was discovered, and while it was originally attributed to Clement, it is now speculated to have been written by someone else.[9]

Clement's epistle was written in response to a dispute in the Corinthian church that involved its leaders. This letter was regarded for centuries as venerated text that exhorted the church to maintain peace as well as the traditions of the apostles.

Here Clement was emphatically one of the most formidable, legendary, and illustrious leaders of the Early Church. What he said carried great weight and his words were taken nearly as seriously as the words of the apostles with whom he personally labored.

Concerning the fallen angels and giants, Clement of Rome wrote:

> …[Angels] **metamorphosed themselves…and partook of human lust, and being brought under its subjection they fell into cohabitation with women; and being involved with them, and sunk in defilement and altogether emptied of their first power, were unable to turn back to the first purity of their nature…. But from their unhallowed intercourse spurious men sprang, much greater in stature than ordinary men, whom they afterwards called giants.**[10]

JOSEPHUS
CIRCA 37 – 100 AD

Flavius Josephus was a Jewish historian renowned for his multiple historical works, including *The Jewish War* and *The Antiquities of the Jews*.[11]

He was born in Jerusalem to a father of priestly descent and to a mother who claimed royal ancestry. He served as a general of Jewish forces during the first Jewish-Roman War until the army surrendered to the Roman leader Vespasian in 67 AD. Shortly thereafter, Vespasian became impressed by the intellectual prowess of Josephus and took him as a slave. Later, when Vespasian became the Roman Emperor in 69 AD, Josephus was granted his freedom. To show his gratitude, Josephus assumed the emperor's family's last name (Flavius), and from that point on he became known as Flavius Josephus.

Eventually Josephus became a Roman citizen and an advisor to Titus, Vespasian's son and Rome's future emperor. He even served as Titus' personal interpreter when Titus laid siege to Jerusalem in 70 AD. Jewish scholars count Josephus' works as the most important source outside of the Bible for the history of Israel.[12] To this day, his writings are considered the most accurate, trustworthy accounts — including his significant insights concerning the fallen angels who sexually comingled with earthly women. The following is what Josephus wrote concerning these mutinous beings and their offspring of giants.

> **For many angels of God accompanied with women, and begat sons that proved unjust, and despisers of all that was good, on account of the confidence they had in their own strength; for the tradition is, that these men did what resembled the acts of those whom the Grecians call giants…. [The] giants, who had bodies so large, and countenances so entirely different from other men, that they were surprising to the sight and terrible to the hearing.**[13]

JUSTIN MARTYR
CIRCA 100 – 165 AD

Justin Martyr was a philosopher who converted to Christianity and later became known as an early Christian apologist. Although the date of his birth is uncertain, it seems to fall in the first years of the Second Century. His native hometown was Flavia Neapolis, which was founded by the Emperor Vespasian in 72 AD, and its residents were mostly pagans.

Justin received a high education in philosophy, and in his written works *Apologies* and *Dialogue with Trypho*, he recorded personal details of his life that include information about his conversion and his studies in philosophy before he came to Christ. Curiously, in the first line of *Apologies*, he called himself "Justin, the son of Priscos, son of Baccheios, of Flavia Neapolis, in Palestinian Syria."[14]

Although most of his works are lost, several survived, including his *First Apology*, which was his most well-known text that passionately defended the Christian life and was used to convince the Roman Emperor Antoninus to abandon his persecution of the Church.[15]

The earliest mention of Justin is found in the *Oratio ad Graecos* by Tatian. Irenaeus quotes him twice and commented on Justin's martyrdom, confirming that Tatian was Justin's disciple. Furthermore, Tertullian, who is also included in this list of early ancient voices, referred to Justin as a philosopher and a martyr.[16]

Eusebius, who is also included later in this prestigious list, names the following significant works accredited to Justin Martyr:[17]

- The *First Apology* — an address to Emperor Antoninus, his sons, and the Roman Senate

- A *Second Apology of Justin Martyr* — an address to the Roman Senate

- The *Discourse to the Greeks* — a discussion with Greek philosophers on the character of their gods

- *On the Sovereignty of God*
- *The Psalmist*
- *On the Soul*
- The *Dialogue with Trypho*

Eusebius suggests there were other works by Justin Martyr, and from the writings of Irenaeus, we know that Justin also authored a treatise called *Against Marcion*. Justin's role in the Early Church was so significant that Epiphanius and Jerome importantly mention him in their works.

A day came in 165 AD when Justin and some of his followers were arrested for their faith. In the face of death, he was recorded to have said, "No one who is rightly minded turns from true belief to false.... If we are punished for the sake of our Lord Jesus Christ, we hope to be saved." He was later beheaded under the reign of Emperor Marcus Aurelius, the son of Antoninus Pius.[18]

Justin Martyr is revered as one of the doctors of the Early Church — an apologist and a martyr — and his name is held in high esteem to this day. He was known for his great heart and mind and is revered for his scholarly writings that are not only intellectually persuasive, but reliable and trustworthy. As many believers do today, Justin boldly contended for the faith of Jesus Christ and His Gospel in an increasingly hostile, pagan world around him.

Concerning the fallen angels, Justin Martyr wrote in his *Second Apology*:

> **...God, when He had made the whole world, and subjected things earthly to man, and arranged the heavenly elements for the increase of fruits and rotation of the seasons, and appointed this divine law — for these things also He evidently made for man — committed the care of men and of all things under heaven to angels whom He appointed over them. But the angels transgressed this appointment, and were captivated by love of women....**[19]

TATIAN
CIRCA 120 – 185 AD

Tatian — also known as Tatian of Adiabene, Tatian the Syrian, and Tatian the Assyrian — lived in the Second Century and was an Assyrian Christian. Little is known about the date and place of his birth except what he writes about himself in his treatise called *Oratio ad Graecos*. In that document, Tatian states that he was born in "the land of the Assyrians,"[20] which is the Mesopotamian area where the cities of Babylon and Nineveh are located.

His first encounter with the Christian faith took place during a lengthy visit to the city of Rome. According to his own writings, he was disgusted with pagan religions and practices, so he turned to Scripture to seek truth. As he studied the Old Testament, he came to understand the evil of paganism, and over time, he converted to Christ and became a disciple of Justin Martyr. As Justin had done earlier, Tatian eventually opened a Christian school in Rome.[21]

Eventually, he left Rome for various reasons, and it is generally believed that he resided for a time in Greece or Egypt, where he instructed Clement of Alexandria. The church leader Epiphanius reports that Tatian later established a school in Mesopotamia, and its influence reached all the way to Antioch in Assyria, to Cilicia, and to Pisidia.[22]

In Tatian's work *Oratio ad Graecos*, he vigorously argued that paganism was vile and worthless, and he praised the reasonableness and the antiquity of Christianity. As early as the time of Eusebius, Tatian was referred to honorably for his views of Moses and the Jewish law.

Among his written works was a "harmony" of the four New Testament gospels, which he called the *Diatessaron* and which became nearly the only Gospel text used in Assyria during the Third and Fourth Centuries.[23]

Tatian is believed by the Assyrian Church to have been a strong apostolic force in countries settled around the Euphrates River, and he is understood to have died in Adiabene in about 173 AD, although some project it to have been the year 180 or 185 AD.[24]

All this insight affirms that Tatian was viewed as a serious intellectual and a strong spiritual force during his time. As such, he was tremendously respected and considered to be an authority on issues related to biblical history and Scripture.

Concerning the fallen angels and giants, Tatian likely quoted Justin Martyr when he wrote:

> …[Angels] **transgressed their appointment, and were captivated by the love of women, and begat children who are those who are called demons; and besides, they afterwards subdued the human race to themselves, partly by magical writings, and partly by fears and the punishments they occasioned, and partly by teaching them to offer sacrifices, and incense, and libations, of which things they stood in need after they were enslaved by lustful passions; and among men they sowed murders, wars, adulteries, intemperate deeds, and all wickedness.**

IRENAEUS
120/140 – 200/203 AD

Irenaeus was bishop of Lyons in Gaul, a region which today is known as France. He was originally from Smyrna, which was located in the Roman province of Asia. In Irenaeus' day, Polycarp was the Bishop of Smyrna. Thus, Irenaeus knew Polycarp — the renowned disciple of the apostle John who was famously martyred for his faith in the stadium of Smyrna.

Among the works that Irenaeus authored is *Against Heresies*, which is a series of books in which he combated Gnostic errors. Another well-known book he wrote was a commentary on Paul's epistles. In addition to his monumental work *Against Heresies*, Irenaeus also wrote *The Demonstration of the Apostolic Preaching*. His influence was so great that noted scholars Hippolytus and Tertullian drew from his writings.

Additionally, he is noted for devising the three pillars of orthodoxy — *the Scriptures, tradition handed down from the apostles,* and *the teaching of the apostles' successors.* Indeed, Irenaeus' influence is still felt today, and he is counted among the Early Church fathers.[25]

Like Josephus, Irenaeus was a scholar noted for his scholarly credibility and trustworthiness. Concerning the fallen angels and giants, Irenaeus wrote in his work *Demonstration of the Apostolic Preaching*:

> **And for a very long while wickedness extended and spread, and reached and laid hold upon the whole race of mankind, until a very small seed of righteousness remained among them and illicit unions took place upon the earth, since angels were united with the daughters of the race of mankind; and they bore to them sons who for their exceeding greatness were called giants. And the angels brought as presents to their wives teachings of wickedness, in that they brought them the virtues of roots and herbs, dyeing in colors and cosmetics, the discovery of rare substances, love-potions, aversions, amours, concupiscence, constraints of love, spells of bewitchment, and all sorcery and idolatry hateful to God; by the entry of which things into the world evil extended and spread, while righteousness was diminished and enfeebled.[26]**

ATHENAGORAS OF ATHENS
133 – 190 AD

Athenagoras of Athens was converted from paganism to Christianity. This former pagan philosopher went to Alexandria, where according to Early Church historian Philip Sidetes, he eventually taught at the illustrious Catechetical School. What Athenagoras taught was central to the formulation of early Christian doctrine in the Church at that time. He, too, is considered to have been counted among the Early Church fathers and was highly respected as an early Christian apologist.

Athenagoras is referred to in several early Christian documents, and his surviving writings demonstrate his intellectual powers and competency as a philosopher and rhetorician, with a giftedness to fearlessly confront opponents. His enduring written works include the *Embassy for the Christians* (which in Latin is called *Legatio pro Christianis*) and *The Resurrection of the Dead*, which is sometimes referred to as his treatise *On the Resurrection of the Body*.[27]

Like others heretofore mentioned, Athenagoras of Athens was an intellectual giant, recognized and revered for his scholarly trustworthiness. Concerning the fallen angels and giants, Athenagoras of Athens wrote:

> …These [angels] **fell into impure love of virgins, and were subjugated by the flesh, and he became negligent and wicked in the management of the things entrusted to him. Of these lovers of virgins, therefore, were begotten those who are called giants.**[28]

CLEMENT OF ALEXANDRIA
CIRCA 150 – 215 AD

Clement of Alexandria is also considered to be one of the revered Early Church fathers. As a noted Christian theologian, he, too, taught at the Catechetical School in Alexandria, Egypt. He was also an instructor to Origen, an early Christian historian, scholar, and theologian. Clement additionally instructed Alexander of Jerusalem, an early bishop who assembled a significant Christian library in Jerusalem, which had access to many ancient records. History documents that Clement of Alexandria eventually died during the persecution of Emperor Decius.[29]

Clement rejected paganism as a young man, yet his Christian writings display an extensive knowledge of Greek and mystery religions. A noted scholar during his time, as well as a traveler and a seeker, Clement of Alexandria wrote what was well known in scholarly circles in his day about the fallen angels who mated with mortal women, who then gave birth to giants. Clement wrote in Chapters 13, 15, and 17 of his *Homily 8*:

…[Angels] **partook of human lust, and being brought under its subjection they fell into cohabitation with women…but from their unhallowed intercourse spurious men sprang, much greater in stature than ordinary men, whom they afterwards called giants…wild in manners, and greater than men in size, inasmuch as they were sprung of angels; yet less than angels, as they were born of women…not being pleased with purity of food, longed only after the taste of blood. Wherefore they first tasted flesh…all things, therefore, going from bad to worse, on account of these brutal demons, God wished to cast them away like an evil leaven, lest each generation from a wicked seed, being like to that before it, and equally impious, should empty the world to come of saved men. And for this purpose, having warned a certain righteous man, with his children, to save themselves in an ark, He sent a deluge of water, that all being destroyed, the purified world might be handed over to him who was saved in the ark, in order** [that there might be] **a second beginning of life. And thus it came to pass.**[30]

TERTULLIAN
155/160 – 220/240 AD

Tertullian was from Carthage in the Roman Province of Africa. Although it has never been proven, some suggest that, due to his expert use of legal analogies in his writings, he had been a lawyer. It appears that his conversion occurred about in 195–196 AD, and even though the details of his conversion are not known, it seems that it was sudden, decisive, and transforming. As one who had obviously experienced the power of God in his spiritual rebirth, it was with conviction that Tertullian wrote that "Christians are made, not born."

As a noted prolific writer, Tertullian became the first Christian to produce an extensive work of Christian literature in the Latin language. Moreover, he was an apologist, a scholarly historian, and a powerful theologian who used his skills to argue vehemently against heresies — particularly of a Gnostic nature. He is called the Father of Latin Christianity and the Founder of Western Theology.[31]

Amazingly, 31 of his works have survived intact,[32] along with fragments of others. His main body of written materials is comprised of the *Cluniacense, Corbeiense, Trecense, Agobardinum,* and *Ottobonianus,*[33] and his writings cover a wide theological spectrum, with a special emphasis on combating the errors of Gnostics and pagans. Tertullian is also known for his emphasis on discipline, morals, and the organization of human life on a Christian foundation. He is possibly most famous as the first writer in Latin to use the term "Trinity" to describe the Godhead.[34]

Tertullian is considered extraordinary, exceptional, and impressive in the ranks of the leaders of the Early Church. He was the predecessor of Augustine, who became the chief founder of Latin theology.[35] Jerome wrote that Tertullian lived to an old age, and his eminent writings are deemed by nearly all as being reliable and trustworthy.

Concerning the fallen angels and giants, Tertullian wrote:

> **We are instructed, moreover, by our sacred books how from certain angels, who fell of their own free-will, there sprang a more wicked demon-brood, condemned of God along with the authors of their race…there are the carcasses of the giants of old time; it will be obvious enough that they are not absolutely decayed, for their bony frames are still extant.**[36]

COMMODIAN
EXACT LIFESPAN UNKNOWN; FLOURISHED CIRCA 250 AD

Commodian was a Christian Latin poet who was supposedly originally from Roman Africa, and he flourished at about the time 250 AD. Ancient writers, such as Gennadius, who was the overseer of the Church of Massilia, referred to Commodian in his *De scriptoribus ecclesiasticis,* and Pope Gelasius mentioned him in his work *Decretum Gelasianum de libris recipiendis et non recipiendis.*[37]

Although the written works of Commodian were at some points deemed controversial, he was nevertheless noteworthy enough to be referred to by leaders of the Early Church.

Concerning the fallen angels and giants, Commodian wrote:

> **When Almighty God, to beautify the nature of the world, willed that the earth should be visited by angels, when they were sent down they despised His laws. Such was the beauty of women, that it turned them aside; so that, being contaminated, they could not return to heaven. Rebels from God, they uttered words against Him. Then the Highest uttered His judgment against them; and from their seed giants are said to have been born.**[38]

EUSEBIUS OF CAESAREA
260/265 – 339/340 AD

Eusebius of Caesarea was born either in or near Caesarea Maritima (a port in then-Roman Palestine) — the place where he was baptized and instructed in the faith and was later appointed the overseeing bishop. In addition to being considered the Father of Church History, Eusebius is regarded as one of the most learned Christians during the earliest days of Church history.

Among the many treatises he authored is *Ecclesiastical History*, which is a history of the Church from the Apostolic Age to his own time. He also wrote *The Chronicle*, *A Collection of Ancient Martyrdoms*, *Demonstrations of the Gospel*; *Preparations for the Gospel*; *On Discrepancies between the Gospels*; and a biographical work on *The Life of Constantine the Great*. Interestingly, because of special favor that Eusebius had with Constantine, he was invited to be among the delegates who attended the Council of Nicea in 325 AD, the first worldwide council of leaders of the Christian church.[39]

In addition to the abovementioned writings, Eusebius authored other documents with addresses, letters, and exegetical works that extended over the whole course of his life. These include both commentaries and an important treatise on the location and names of biblical cities and the distances between these various places. Much of what Eusebius wrote was used by church historians, such as Socrates Scholasticus,[40] Sozomen,[41] Theodoret,[42] and Jerome.[43]

Without question, Eusebius of Caesarea is among those most respected historians for accuracy, reliability, and trustworthiness. Concerning the fallen angels and giants, Eusebius wrote:

> **They** [the giants] **gave themselves wholly over to all kinds of profanity, now seducing one another, now slaying one another, now eating human flesh, and now daring to wage war with** [God] **and to undertake those battles of the giants celebrated by all; now planning to fortify earth against heaven, and in the madness of ungoverned pride to prepare an attack upon the very God of all. On account of these things, when they conducted themselves thus, the all-seeing God sent down upon them floods.**[44]

JEROME
342/347 – 420 AD

Jerome (also called Jerome of Stridon) was born at Stridon around 342-347 AD. Although the exact location of Stridon is unknown, it was likely located either in modern-day Croatia or Slovenia. He descended from Illyrian ancestry, and it seems he was converted and baptized in the city of Rome in about 360-369 AD.[45]

Jerome is celebrated as an early Christian historian, minister, scholar, and theologian, but is undoubtedly best known for his translation of the Bible into the Latin language, which is called the *Vulgate*.[46] He began in the year 390 AD, with the goal of producing an Old Testament translation based on Hebrew rather than on the Greek *Septuagint*, and he completed that work in about 405 AD.

What's interesting is that when Jerome started his Bible-translation project, he only knew some Hebrew, which is why he attempted to relocate to Jerusalem so he could strengthen his grip on the Hebrew language and enhance his knowledge of Jewish culture. Jerome fell sick on his journey and ended up in Bethlehem. He eventually learned Hebrew from a Jewish convert in the desert of Chalcis.

When a wealthy Roman learned of Jerome's endeavors, the benefactor provided the financial resources that were needed for Jerome to live in a monastery in Bethlehem.[47] There, he resided in a small compartment that was connected to the Church of the Nativity, which had been built in 326 AD at the order of Emperor Constantine.[48]

Along with his translation projects and commentaries touching on several major portions of Scripture, Jerome also wrote polemical and historical essays from a theological point of view.[49]

Jerome is the second-most voluminous writer in ancient Latin Christianity, second to Augustine of Hippo (354-430 AD) — and is renowned for his teachings on the Christian life and Christian ethics.

Indeed, his massive collection of scholarly translations and writings is what moved the Roman Catholic Church to recognize him as a Doctor of the Church, and what caused Anglicans, Lutherans, and Orthodox Christian leaders to revere him a saint.[50]

Jerome is indisputably among the greatest intellectuals in the history of the Church of all ages. His name is synonymous with knowledge, research, science, and scholarship. What he authored is still considered to be dependable, reliable, true, and trustworthy.

Concerning the fallen angels and giants, Jerome wrote in his letter to Paul of Concordia:

> **For when the first tiller of paradise had been entangled by the serpent in his snaky coils, and had been forced in consequence to migrate earthwards… afterwards sin gradually grew more and more virulent, till the ungodliness of the giants brought in its train the shipwreck of the whole world.**[51]

SULPICIUS SEVERUS
360/365 – 420/425 AD

Sulpicius Severus was born to noble parents in Aquitania, which is located in modern-day France, and he was privileged to have educational advantages that imbued him with cultural learning in Latin letters. He studied law in Burdigala (modern Bordeaux) and was known as an eloquent lawyer. In his writings, his expert knowledge of Roman law is visible.

In time, Severus became renowned as a Christian writer, and in about 403 AD, he wrote a chronicle of sacred history called *Chronica, Chronicorum Libri duo* or *Historia sacra*. He is also known for his significant historical biography of *Martin of Tours*.[52]

As one who studied law and was famous for his expert legal style in research and writing, Sulpicius Severus is considered to be a legal mind that produced histories that were well-researched, documented, and trustworthy.

Concerning the fallen angels and giants, Sulpicius Severus wrote:

> **When by this time the human race had increased to a great multitude, certain angels, whose habitation was in heaven, were captivated by the appearance of some beautiful virgins, and cherished illicit desires after them, so much so, that falling beneath their own proper nature and origin, they left the higher regions of which they were inhabitants and allied themselves in earthly marriages. These angels gradually spreading wicked habits, corrupted the human family, and from their alliance giants are said to have sprung, for the mixture with them of beings of a different nature, as a matter of course, gave birth to monsters.[53]**

In addition to all these historical and scholarly citations by revered individuals, we are also provided with two ancient documents that also speak of and verify the bizarre happenings of fallen angels and their offspring of giants. These are *The Book of Jasher* and *The Book of Jubilees*.

THE BOOK OF JASHER

The Book of Jasher is mentioned in the Old Testament, specifically in Joshua 10:13 and in Second Samuel 1:18-27. Although it is not a canonical book of Scripture,[54] it is valuable in helping us understand aspects of documented ancient history.

What's interesting is that the title *The Book of Jasher* is also known as *The Book of the Upright* (or of the *Upright One*) in the Greek *Septuagint* and *The Book of the Just Man*[55] (or of the *Just Ones*) in the Latin *Vulgate*, and many historical scholars view this book as significant.

Concerning the fallen angels and the wickedness with which they infected the world, Jasher 4:18,19 states:

> **And their judges and rulers** [referring to the fallen angels] **went to the daughters of men and took their wives by force from their husbands according to their choice, and the sons of men in those days took from the cattle of the earth, the beasts of the field and the fowls of the air, and taught the mixture of animals of one species with the other, in order therewith to provoke the Lord; and God saw the whole earth and it was corrupt, for all flesh had corrupted its ways upon earth, all men and all animals. And the Lord said, I will blot out man that I created from the face of the earth, yea from man to the birds of the air, together with cattle and beasts that are in the field....**[56]

THE BOOK OF JUBILEES

Along with *The Book of Jasher*, *The Book of Jubilees* also provides details concerning the activities of the fallen angels, or *watchers*. While its latter parts are understood to have been written in the Second Century BC, the earlier portions are believed to predate the Flood. Specifically, *The Book of Jubilees* offers details on the biblical happenings from the time of creation to Moses' day.

This ancient Jewish text is often called *Lesser Genesis*, *Little Genesis*, or *Leptogenesis,* and the Ethiopian Orthodox Church and Beta Israel view it to be a canonical book.[57]

The Book of Jubilees was well known and read by early Christians, which is evidenced in the writings by Epiphanius, Justin Martyr, Origen, Diodorus of Tarsus, Isidore of Alexandria, Isidore of Seville, Eutychius of Alexandria, and others.[58]

This ancient text was also utilized by the Essenes, who were the devoted group responsible for collecting and preserving what has become known as the *Dead Sea Scrolls.* Although no complete Greek or Latin version of *The Book of Jubilees* is known to have survived, the Ge'ez version is an accurate translation that was found among the *Dead Sea Scrolls*.[59]

Concerning the fallen angels and their brazen actions, *The Book of Jubilees* states:

> **And in the second week of the tenth jubilee Mahalalel took unto him to wife Dînâh…and she bare him a son in the third week in the sixth year, and he called his name Jared; for in his days the angels of the Lord descended on the earth, those who are named the Watchers, that they should instruct the children of men and that they should do judgment and uprightness on the earth…. [The Watchers] sinned with the daughters of men; for these had begun to unite themselves, so as to be defiled, with the daughters of men, and Enoch testified against (them) all…. But Noah found grace before the eyes of the Lord. And against the angels whom He had sent upon the earth, He was exceedingly wroth, and He gave commandment to root them out of all their dominion…. And after this [the time of the angelic disobedience] they were bound in the depths of the earth for ever, until the day of the great condemnation when judgment is executed on all those who have corrupted their ways and their works before the Lord.[60]**

What Does All This Mean?

The purpose in sharing all these historical documents written by notable ancient voices is to support that the events recorded in Genesis 6:1-4 — and corroborated in *The Book of Enoch* and other early sources — really did happen. Moreover, these happenings were nearly universally believed by both Jews and Christians of antiquity.

Make no mistake: God's Word is absolute truth, and the wickedness and violence brought into the world by fallen angels and the giants they produced through earthly women is the reason God sent the Great Flood. His intent was to cleanse and liberate the earth from all corruption and to wipe the slate clean so that humanity could have a fresh start, free of such contamination.

God commanded Noah to construct an Ark for the saving of his family and to preserve a sampling of all animal life. After the Flood, God blessed them and commissioned them to start life over again. Interestingly, He likely gave that commission in the place where life first began — in the region of the Garden of Eden, where it is believed the Ark came to rest.

With or without the corroboration of physical evidence and the supporting testimony of travelers and writers who documented their experiences, the Word of God is clear on the event of the Great Flood and the overview of events leading up to it. The fascinating detail passed on to us by these ancient writers are like colorful paint brushed on a sculpture that animates it in our imaginations, giving us a more vivid glimpse of the world as it once was.

But more than giving us a look at real-life events recorded for our benefit, the Bible provides us with an admonition from the lips of Jesus Himself, warning us that what once was will once more be (*see* Matthew 24:37). God promised never to destroy the earth by a flood again. But what about the strange events in Noah's day that led up to the Great Flood? What is God saying to us — especially to the Church — in this day?

In the next chapter, you will see that in addition to hybrid giants, monsters are also believed to have roamed the face of the earth. Amazingly, in nearly every ancient civilization, there are records on every continent of hideous beasts and monsters that instilled great fear in the hearts of men. The question is, if such creatures really did exist, how did *they* come into being?

QUESTIONS TO PONDER

1. We understand from ancient sources that the prophetic insights received by Jared and his descendants were passed down from one generation to the next. How about you and your family? What spiritual insights have your parents, grandparents, or great-grandparents passed to you? What spiritual insights has the Lord given to you that you are now passing on to your children and grandchildren?

2. Of all the quotes from the Early Church fathers and renowned leaders in this chapter, which one(s) stood out to you most? What did they say — and what details did they offer — that impacted you so greatly? Were you surprised to see so many prominent people weighing in on this topic?

3. Before reading this book, had you ever heard the term Nephilim — the Hebrew word for "giants"? Did you know it was in the Bible? What new facts did you learn about these ferocious offspring of the fallen angels and women of the earth?

4. Consider this fact: The sons of God, who lived in the perfect realm of Heaven, lusted after women who lived in the imperfect realm of earth. Clearly, they craved what they couldn't have and were discontent with what God had given them. How about you? Are you content with who and what God has placed in your life? Take time to meditate on the truths of First Timothy 6:6-11 and Hebrews 13:5. What is the Holy Spirit showing you in this sobering passage?

5. Were you surprised that so many ancient writers unanimously communicated the evil scenario of the rebellious angels and the women of the earth they comingled with? These ancients wrote independently of one another in different time periods, yet their stories are shockingly similar. How do these stories and the Genesis account affect your ideas about the plot to prevent Christ as the Divine Seed from successfully entering the earth to die for us as the spotless Lamb of God?

6. The actions of the fallen angels were diabolical, and the consequences for humankind — "save eight" — were devastating. How does this affect your view of God's determination to preserve the human race and to send to the earth a Redeemer, "born of a woman" (see Galatians 4:4 NKJV). In what ways can judgment be considered an act of mercy?

Some believe that along with the violence and bloodshed the giants brought into the earth, the giants may have also committed acts of bestiality with animals, which resulted in the birth of hybrid, monstrous creatures that never previously existed.

CHAPTER SIX

WHAT ABOUT MONSTERS?

Before we dive into this chapter, here is what we know so far. As Adam and his descendants procreated, a massive population explosion took place in the days before the Flood. And as it did, something very bizarre began to take place — something so significant that God saw fit to include it in the Bible.

> **And it came to pass, when men began to multiply on the face of the earth, and daughters were born unto them, that the sons of God saw the daughters of men that they were fair; and they took them wives of all which they chose....**
>
> **There were giants in the earth in those days; and also after that, when the sons of God came in unto the daughters of men, and they bare children to them, the same became mighty men which were of old, men of renown.**
> **— Genesis 6:1,2, and 4**

We noted in Chapter 3 that the "sons of God" were angels, some of whom left their God-assigned positions, came down into the earth, and began to cohabit with mortal women. Both Peter and Jude confirm these strange happenings in their epistles (*see* 2 Peter 2:4,5; Jude 6). From the unlawful union between these fallen angels and earthly women, giants were born, and these hybrid beings began to pollute and sully the earth in horrific ways — some of which are described in Genesis 6:5,11-13:

> **And God saw that the wickedness of man was great in the earth, and that every imagination of the thoughts of his heart was only evil continually....**
>
> **The earth also was corrupt before God, and the earth was filled with violence. And God looked upon the earth, and, behold, it was corrupt; for all flesh had corrupted his way upon the earth. And God said unto Noah, The end of all flesh is come before me; for the earth is filled with violence through them; and, behold, I will destroy them with the earth.**

Make no mistake: The "great wickedness," "violence," and "corruption" that filled the whole earth was a direct result of the nefarious activities of the fallen angels and the giants they produced through their illicit sexual unions with earthly women. That is why God saw fit to place all these verses together in the same context with Noah and the Flood.

These strange goings-on between the sons of God — *fallen angels* — and the women of earth was clearly understood and documented by Jewish rabbis and scribes, ancient historians, and Early Church fathers all the way up to the Fourth Century AD, and we saw many of those accounts in Chapter 5 of this book. God's reason for bringing the Flood was to totally cleanse the earth of all the violence and corruption that abounded because of the dreadful deeds of the fallen angels and the giants.

THE BOOK OF ENOCH SUPPORTS AND EXPOUNDS ON THE GENESIS 6 NARRATIVE

In addition to the biblical narrative, we have seen that portions of *The Book of Enoch* also describe these same heinous activities. Again, while *The Book of Enoch* is not Scripture, the earliest portions — which includes the first 36 chapters — was probably written by Enoch, the great-grandfather of Noah. It is also referred to as *First Enoch* and *The Book of the Watchers*, offering historical value and insights that are believed by many to predate the Flood. This early text helps us understand what the ancients believed regarding the events of this early history, and it was widely read by those living in the intertestamental period (circa 420 BC to 20 AD), as well as by people in the First Century AD. In fact, those living in Jesus' day were so familiar with *First Enoch* and considered it such a serious commentary on the events recorded in Genesis 6 that Peter and Jude quoted it or referred to it in their New Testament writings.

The Book of Enoch provides insightful commentary on what took place in the days just prior to the Flood. Here again in First Enoch 6:1-8 is a review of the conversation recorded between the leading rebellious angel and the other angels he coaxed into rebellion against God.

First Enoch 6:1-8

And it came to pass, after the children of men had increased in those days, beautiful and comely daughters were born to them.

And the angels, the sons of the heavens, saw and lusted after them, and said one to another: "Behold, we will choose for ourselves wives from among the children of men, and will beget for ourselves children."

And Semjâzâ, who was their leader, said to them: "I fear that perhaps ye will not be willing to do this deed, and I alone shall suffer for this great sin."

Then all answered him and said: "We all will swear an oath, and bind ourselves mutually by a curse, that we will not give up this plan, but will make this plan a deed." Then they all swore together, and bound themselves mutually by a curse; and together they were two hundred.

And they descended on Ardîs, which is the summit of Mount Hermon; and they called it Mount Hermon, because they had sworn on it and bound themselves mutually by a curse.

And these are the names of their leaders: Semjâzâ, who was their leader, Urâkibarâmêêl, Akibêêl, Tâmiêl, Râmuêl, Dânêl, Ezêqêêl, Sarâqujâl, Asâêl, Armers, Batraal, Anânî, Zaqêbê, Samsâvêêl, Sartaêl, Turêl, Jomjâêl, Arâzjâl. These are the leaders of the two hundred angels, and the others all were with them.

Today many theorize that "ancient aliens" came to the earth at some point in early history, but these proposed theories do not match the biblical account. It is the Bible that provides the facts of what really took place — all other versions contained in all ancient mythology and pagan religions are a fragmented retelling of the true events recorded in Genesis 6:1-4 and corroborated in *The Book of Enoch*.

As we've noted in previous chapters, nearly every ancient civilization and people group have oral and/or written legends describing how celestial beings descended to earth and slept with mortal women, who then gave birth to giants or demigods. Although the details of the stories differed slightly as they were retold from culture to culture, they contained the same basic account everywhere, and the reason for these multicultural retellings was that they were based on real events that occurred in history.

SOME BELIEVE THERE WERE ALSO 'MONSTERS' BEFORE THE FLOOD

I'm not stating this as fact, but in addition to the fallen angels sexually comingling with women to produce a race of giants, some believe the criminal activities of those giant offspring eventually gave rise to an untold number of *monsters.*

They claim that along with the violence and bloodshed the giants brought into the earth, the giants, like their fallen-angel predecessors, may have *also* transgressed God's boundaries, committing acts of *bestiality* with animals and impregnating them, which resulted in the birth of hybrid, monstrous creatures that, like the giants born of women, had never previously existed. Although I do not categorically state this to be the case, because it is believed by some, I am including it in this chapter.

Ancient documents, such as the earliest portions of *The Book of Enoch*, not only show the origin of the giants — also known as the Nephilim — but also detail the giants' activities as they grew in numbers on the earth. Immediately after revealing the angels' plot and oath to unite with mortal women and create their own children, First Enoch 7:1-5 also tells us:

> **And all the others together with them took unto themselves wives, and each chose for himself one, and they began to go in unto them and to defile themselves with them, and they taught them charms and enchantments, and the cutting of roots, and made them acquainted with plants.**
>
> **And they became pregnant, and they bare great giants....** [The giants] **consumed all the acquisitions of men. And when men could no longer sustain them, the giants turned against them and devoured mankind.**
>
> **And they** [the giants] **began to sin against birds, and beasts, and reptiles, and fish, and to devour one another's flesh, and drink the blood.**

According to this ancient text, the giants devoured everything man produced, which included all the crops and animals mankind raised. When these harvests of men's labors no longer satisfied them, the giants began to turn against other giants and humans and began to eat their flesh and drink their blood. Their evil escalated even further, as the text suggests here, as the giants began to "sin against" — which some interpret to mean *sexually defile* — the animals.

This same view seems to be reiterated in the earliest parts of *The Book of Jubilees* and *The Book of Jasher*, which as we noted in Chapter 5 are both believed to predate the Flood and thusly focus on the details of the pre-Flood world.

Jasher 4:18 and 19 from *The Book of Jasher* states:

> **And their judges and rulers** [referring to the fallen angels] **went to the daughters of men and took their wives by force from their husbands according to their choice, and the sons of men in those days took from the cattle of the earth, the beasts of the field and the fowls of the air, and taught the mixture of animals of one species with the other, in order therewith to provoke the Lord; and God saw the whole earth and it was corrupt, for all flesh had corrupted its ways upon earth, all men and all animals. And the Lord said, I will blot out man that I created from the face of the earth, yea from man to the birds of the air, together with cattle and beasts that are in the field....**

And the following passage, Jubilees 5:2, from *The Book of Jubilees* states:

> **And lawlessness increased on the earth and all flesh corrupted its ways, alike man and cattle and beasts and birds and everything that walks on the earth — all of them corrupted their ways and their orders, and they began to devour each other.**

If the giants (Nephilim) did sexually defile the animals, then what took place in those pre-Flood days was *bestiality*. For the record, God repeatedly forbade this detestable behavior, as recorded in Exodus, Leviticus, and Deuteronomy, as it is forbidden today. Take, for example, this passage from Leviticus 18 — a passage that warns against all types of sexual perversion. Here, God Himself said:

> **A man must not defile himself by having sex with an animal. And a woman must not offer herself to a male animal to have intercourse with it. This is a perverse act. Do not defile yourselves in any of these ways, for the people I am driving out before you have defiled themselves in all these ways. Because the entire land has become defiled, I am punishing the people who live there. I will cause the land to vomit them out.**
>
> **You must obey all my decrees and regulations. You must not commit any of these detestable sins. This applies both to native-born Israelites and to the foreigners living among you. All these detestable activities are practiced by the people of the land where I am taking you, and this is how the land has become defiled. So do not defile the land and give it a reason to vomit you out, as it will vomit out the people who live there now.**
> — **Leviticus 18:23-28** *NLT*

Twice in these six verses, God said that the people living in the land of Canaan *were* indeed committing bestiality. This behavior was definitely happening on the earth at the time Israel was taking possession of the Promised Land, and this vulgar defilement is one among many reasons that God drove the people of Canaan out of the land. Furthermore, God said any man or woman who sexually mated with an animal was to be put to death, and the animal was to be killed too (*see* Exodus 22:19; Leviticus 20:16).

Again, some believe that along with the violence and bloodshed the giants brought into the earth, they also committed acts of *bestiality*, and from this abhorrent and forbidden act, monstrous hybrid creatures were created. As outlandish as it sounds, accounts of this horrific activity are nearly universally described by ancient civilizations in the pagan world.

DID ANCIENT HYBRID CREATURES LIKE THESE REALLY EXIST?

Just as nearly all ancient mythologies and pagan religions tell the same basic story of winged, celestial beings who descended to Earth and philandered with women, who then birthed giants, or demigods, a study of early civilizations around the world shows that nearly every ancient people group also recorded similar stories of strange beasts and monsters coexisting with the giants and humans. Although these creatures appear with different names in various cultures, they are essentially the same beasts.

For example, the ancient civilizations of the Akkadians, Assyrians, Babylonians,[1] Canaanites, Chaldeans,[2] Cimmerians, Egyptians,[3] Elamites,[4] Greeks,[5] Hittites,[6] Medes,[7] Mitannians,[8] Palmyrenes, Parthians,[9] Persians,[10] Phoenicians, Romans,[11] Sasanians,[12] Summerians,[13] Uraratians,[14] and all civilizations all the way to India[15] and as far north as the Vikings[16] all possess ancient records that depict similar monstrous beasts, and their writings spoke of these creatures as being real.

Representations of all these monstrous creatures — and numerous others — can be found in cave drawings, primeval structures and formations, stone tablets, and in a sundry of ancient artifacts. Again, although they have different names in the records of various ancient cultures and religions, they are essentially the same creatures.

But the big question is this: *Did hybrid beasts (monsters) like these really exist in the ancient world?* Did the giants — who were birthed through the illicit sexual union of fallen angels and mortal women — really defile the animals and beget hideous creatures? No one knows the answer with any degree of certainty.

It should be noted, however, that the odds of these same hybrid beasts appearing regularly in nearly all ancient civilizations that had little contact with each other are statistically unlikely. Furthermore, the chances of these stories being told so consistently without a thread of truth behind them is nearly zero.

As I previously noted, some have wrongly concluded that these ancient civilizations were simply primitive people with wild, over-active imaginations. However, many of these early cultures are still impacting our lives today by their innovations. These are the same people who developed logic, philosophy, poetry, history, science, mathematics, literature, art, and architecture.

So rather than write these earlier civilizations off as merely having hallucinatory revelations, remember that many were intelligent cultures who documented all kinds of history that is considered reliable by archaeologists and historians today. Why would they be considered reliable in many of their historical records, but discounted in what they wrote about *monsters* that they said once roamed the earth in the days before the Flood? It's certainly something to think about.

The 'Mixing of Seed' Today Has Been Engaged

The "mixing of seed" — or the cross-breeding of species on the earth before the Flood — seems far-fetched and illogical in today's world, but it's not entirely implausible. What I'm about to write concerning the modifying or "re-engineering" of much of our food supply, for example, is not an exact analogy of the mixing of human seed with the seed of angels — or of giants' seed with the seed of animals. But I want you to understand that similar interference with and modification of the creation of God is not a completely foreign concept on the earth today.

The mixing of seed is simply not something new. It was going on in the days of Noah, and it is happening again right now across the globe, albeit not in the exact same way, by the same mechanism. For example, on a smaller scale, perhaps you've seen the letters "GMO" on food packaging, which stands for Genetically Modified Organism. Or maybe you've read label notifications to consumers indicating the product contains bioengineered ingredients.

Genetically modifying our food supply is a practice that started in the 1980s, but entered overdrive in the late '90s. It seems that just about every food known to man has been — or is in the process of being — genetically modified. From soybeans, corn, and cotton to rice, tomatoes, and potatoes, plant seeds of all kinds are being genetically altered to be more disease resistant, have a longer shelf life, and produce higher yields. The problem is that the jury is still out on the long-term effects of all these bioengineered foods we're consuming.

Also, as strange as it sounds, researchers and scientists are additionally pursuing the modifying of animals. And at the time of this writing, they are even performing hybrid experimentation with animals *and* human beings, and some of the results are alarming. Take, for example, the mixing of human DNA with that of pigs to create the first human-pig hybrid embryos. By isolating certain human chromosomes and fusing them with the genetic material of swine, researchers are "growing" things like hybrid human hearts, livers, kidneys, and pancreases for organ-transplant patients. While many such hybrid experiments are done with the sincere hopes of helping those in desperate need of a transplant, the potential dangers and ethical violations of such endeavors, unchecked, are troubling to contemplate.

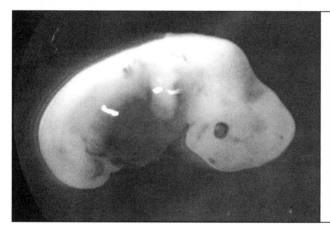

The mixing of human DNA with pigs is occurring to create the first human-pig hybrid embryos. By isolating certain human chromosomes and fusing them with the genetic material of swine, researchers are "growing" things like hybrid human hearts, livers, kidneys, and pancreases for transplant patients. While many such hybrid experiments are done with the sincere hopes of helping those in desperate need of a transplant, the potential dangers and ethical violations of such endeavors, unchecked, are troubling to contemplate.

Although this experimentation with hybridization is certainly not a new phenomenon, its recent levels of strangeness have raised many ethical and moral concerns. Bioengineers have moved beyond the creation of a mule, for example, which is the breeding of a male donkey and female horse, and have begun to fabricate numerous radical combinations, such as:

- The Liger: Male lion crossbred with a female tiger
- The Zonkey: Zebra crossbred with a donkey
- The Zebroid: Zebra combined with a horse (Zorse) or other animal
- The Jaglion: Male jaguar crossbred with a female lion
- The Leopon: Lioness combined with a male leopard
- The Wholphin: Male false-killer whale crossbred with a female bottlenose dolphin

These are just a few of the mixed breeds — albeit not the mixing of species — *that we know about* that have been created. What is being attempted in laboratories across the world — and some in secret, remote locations — violates natural laws and takes us into the realm of what was once thought to be the stuff of science fiction. And where does all this stop? At what point have we crossed a line and gone too far? Only God knows the far-reaching consequences of such tampering. And although our "seed-mingling" mechanism today is scientific and not "celestial," these practices seem oddly similar to what was taking place in the time frame before the Flood.

OTHER GENETIC EXPERIMENTATION TODAY

We're looking at the hybridization of plants and animals in a society that has already succeeded in creating both genetically modified plants and crops, as well as "bioengineered" animals of several kinds. The truth is, some of the ancient accounts of human-animal hybridization are moving from the realm of what many call mythology to becoming a tangible reality today. For instance, one leading genetic researcher has stated, "In ancient civilizations, chimeras were associated with God." He went on to say that our ancestors thought the chimeric form could "guard humans."

Although outlandish, this kind of dialogue is actually occurring as idealistic messages are being sold by certain bioengineers in hopes of having their genetic experimentations funded by private investors.

EXAMPLES OF NEWLY CREATED HYBRID ANIMALS

Liger

Leopon

Zebroid

Zonkey

Jaglion

Wholphin

> **To a great degree, these scientists who are manipulating genetic material are "playing God," and the use of a gene-editing tool known as CRISPR is a perfect example. Essentially CRISPR, which is short for "clustered regularly interspaced short palindromic repeats," is a technology that research scientists use to selectively modify the DNA of living organisms. It enables technicians to "edit out" certain genetic characteristics in organisms and then reconnect the DNA chain.**
>
> **In other words, just as a film editor slices a scene out of a movie and splices the remaining scenes together, bioengineers are slicing and splicing chromosome coding from the DNA of organisms to custom-create new, specialized organisms. But are those involved in these newer genetic-modification techniques ignoring the possibilities of creating *new* diseases, inserting errors into the human gene pool, and causing permanent, negative changes that could be passed down for generations?**

Scientists in the field of genetic engineering are largely allowed to *self-regulate* their research and experiments. In other words, "every man does what seems right in his own eyes" (*see* Judges 21:25), which is a scary thought.

> **Steven Walker, the Director of U.S. Defense Advanced Research Projects Agency (DARPA) said, *"All these technologies, they are dual use. You can use them for good, and you can use them for evil...."* [17]**

Of course, this is true of *any* advance in medicine or technology, but given the deceitfulness of the human heart and the moral depravity of man without God, the consequences of people operating in this realm of science *as a law unto themselves* could be devastating beyond comprehension.

Let me be clear in saying that these events are not coming down the road — *they are happening right now*, which in itself is a sign that we are living in the days just before the coming of Christ. Remember, Jesus said, "As it was in the days of Noah, so it will be at the coming of the Son of Man" (Matthew 24:37 *NIV*). The "mixing of seed" and the ongoing manipulation of the genetic coding of plants, animals,

Science, including certain branches of psychiatry, is familiar with what some call demonic activity and others simply call a sleep phenomenon — an experience with an *"incubus"* — that is, a phenomenon in which a "male" demon is believed to have sexual intercourse with sleeping women. We know demon spirits roam the earth today, but those who are living *in Christ* have absolute authority and dominion over all these powers.

and humans is eerily reminiscent of the defiling of humans on the earth in the days before the Flood.

SCIENTIFIC *AND* CELESTIAL?

We have no evidence of celestial-human comingling that has resulted in weird pregnancies, but since Jesus said what occurred before the Flood would be replicated in the last days, some wonder about the scope of pre-Flood occurrences that will occur again in history as we near the end of the age. Is it possible that celestial-human interactions could occur again before this age is culminated? Some ministries who take calls from the public are testifying that women are calling in increasing numbers for prayerful help because they claim to have been sexually defiled by demon spirits, especially during the night. This trend with incoming calls from women who have been reputably stable and commonsensical people is notable, and it's alarming — it certainly makes one wonder what is happening and why it's happening with greater intensity.

Even science, including certain branches of psychiatry, are familiar with what some call demonic activity and others simply a sleep phenomenon — and that is, an experience with *"incubus."* I'll not go into detail here, but make no mistake: This "phenomenon" is a demonic attack that believers in Jesus Christ who know who they are in Him should not fear, but should instead exercise God-given authority over.

But has the current rise in wickedness in the earth opened a "portal," as some are claiming, that is allowing this kind of sinister demonic activity to have greater influence in our sphere? The current number of claims of assault by so many women adds strength to the argument of a few that some of the supernatural mutinous events that occurred before the Flood could eventually be replicated in our time.

GOD ADDRESSED THE MINGLING OF SEED

Again, we turn to *The Book of Enoch* and *The Book of Jasher* for possible additional insight. Again, while these works are not a part of Scripture, the earliest portions of both texts were considered reliable commentary on pre-Flood happenings. First Enoch 7:5 states that the giants began to sin against (or possibly sexually defile) the animals, and Jasher 4:18 notes that the fallen angels "…taught the mixture of animals of one species with the other, in order therewith to provoke the Lord."

God is against and forbids the mixing of seed. In Leviticus 19:19 (*NKJV*), He declared:

You shall keep My statutes. You shall not let your livestock breed with another kind. You shall not sow your field with mixed seed….

The term "Pandora's box" is a metaphor for something that, once opened, releases evil into the world. Much of the bioengineering currently taking place could prove to be a similar "opening" that will release great evils.

Clearly, this was one of the primary reasons why the earth became exponentially corrupt, and all flesh corrupted itself. It was this widespread corruption of "all flesh" that moved God to bring the Flood to cleanse the earth (*see* Genesis 6:12,13).

Unnatural conditions like these and violations of God-given commands gave rise to giants — *and perhaps monsters* — that were *not* born "after their own kind" according to the Lord's plan. And the mixing of human and animal DNA today is unnatural according to divine design — it is a "mixture" similar to that which provoked the Lord to anger in the days before the Flood. It provoked Him for different reasons than just mere hybridism. That one act of rebellion by the fallen angels not only violated God's boundaries in creation, it unleashed a "Pandora's box" of violence, bloodshed, perversion, and sorceries on a level the world had not theretofore known.

Again, the "mixture" that is taking place in research today is scientific, not celestial, yet it appears to be on a fast track to increasing levels of strangeness. And as I submitted to you previously, it is at least *possible* that as wickedness increases, a "portal" to the spirit realm will be opened wider than ever before that could thusly allow a similar *celestial* mixing of seed after the manner of the days of Noah before the Flood.

145

Because the pre-Flood world was teeming with outlandish perversities, violence, and corruption, God chose to send a flood to destroy all of it, with the exception of Noah and his family of eight that had remained pure. It's easy to see that Satan himself lured the mutinous angels into rebellion against God. And he did it to destroy mankind that was created in God's image and crowned with His glory. But the enemy's chiefest aim was to prevent the birth of the Divine Seed, who would bruise his head, remove his authority, and deal him a crushing defeat.

'ALL FLESH HAD BECOME CORRUPTED'

The pre-Flood world was teeming with outlandish perversities, violence, and corruption. It's no wonder the Bible says, "...God looked upon the earth, and, behold, it was corrupt; *for all flesh had corrupted his way upon the earth*" (Genesis 6:12). All flesh — human beings, animals, and, literally, *all flesh* — had become corrupted by the rampant perversion initiated by the fallen angels and then propagated by the giants. Only Noah and his family of eight had remained pure from the defilement that was occurring on the earth at that time.

Some ask, "If all of this is true, where are skeletal remains of these giants and beasts?" The fact is, many unexplainable skeletal remains *have* been discovered, but the Bible tells us in Second Peter 2:4 that the destruction of the Flood was so vast that hardly a remnant of what existed before the Flood remained afterward. Indeed, the Flood was devastating beyond our ability to imagine. When God opened the windows of Heaven and all the fountains of the great deep were broken up (*see* Genesis 7:11), He wiped the slate clean of these nefarious pre-Flood beings.

Consider what the Bible says in Genesis 7:19-23 (*NLT*):

...The water covered even the highest mountains on the earth, rising more than twenty-two feet above the highest peaks. All the living things on earth died — birds, domestic animals, wild animals, small animals that scurry along the ground, and all the people. Everything that breathed and lived on dry land died. God wiped out every living thing on the earth — people, livestock, small animals that scurry along the ground, and the birds of the sky. All were destroyed. The only people who survived were Noah and those with him in the boat.

The fact that all flesh had corrupted itself — including the animals — makes it clearer why God supernaturally brought the animals to Noah that were to be placed on the Ark. Is it possible that so many animals had been sexually defiled that only God knew which ones had DNA that was free of this wicked mingling of the seed? If there was sexual defilement occurring between the giants and animals who then birthed monstrous beasts as a result, it would certainly stand to reason that God had to handpick the animals and bring them to Noah for preservation (*see* Genesis 7:15).

Jesus Declared That Pre-Flood History Would Repeat Itself

As we continue this study, bear in mind the sobering words Jesus spoke when He was asked about the conditions of the world just before His coming. He said:

But as the days of Noah were, so also will the coming of the Son of Man be.

— Matthew 24:37 *NKJV*

According to Jesus, many of the same events that were taking place in Noah's day just prior to the Flood will resurface at the end of the age before the Lord returns. The scientific mixing of seed today is not celestial in nature. However, some wonder in light of Jesus' words if the former might occur again as we near the end of the age.

But think about it. In what ways are those sinister events of old *already* being replicated in our own day?

- Do you see human beings becoming more monster-like in their behavior and physical appearance as they modify themselves, even surgically (and in many cases, beyond recognition)? *Have you ever seen a person so modified that you were genuinely startled by his or her "monstrous" appearance?*
- Do you see a continual rise of sexual defilement on many levels in society? *Would you have ever imagined that people would become so defiled by seducing spirits that they would question their gender and try to alter their physical makeup to match a mental delusion?*
- Do you see the very things that were once taboo now being embraced and celebrated? Do you see this to the degree you can also fathom the possibility that bestiality could become normalized in last-day's society that has gone off track? *Who would have ever thought decades ago that it would become legal to butcher physical bodies — even those of children — in an attempt to change one's gender? If the lid of reason has been lifted in that sphere, what would stop the legalization of bestiality or legal marriage to animals in the future?*
- Do you see transhumanism on the rise that is attempting to produce new variations of human beings? *Years ago, the idea of transhumanism — which is human integration with machinery and computers — was the stuff of science fiction, but now it is really happening. You can search for yourself and see that there is a growing movement of elitists from across the globe working to create a supposedly "advanced," post-human society in which mankind, "with machines," will live forever.*

Indeed, Jesus said that what was occurring in the world in the days before the Flood would be replicated in some way before His coming. Although the exact way these things occurred in the time frame before the Flood may not be precisely replicated — in essence, Jesus stated many of these abnormalities will be repeated in various ways as we speed toward the end of the age.

In the next chapter, we will delve into the annals of history to see what was written in ancient documents about the types of violence and bloodshed that were released in the world because of the giants (and perhaps other monstrous creatures) that roamed the earth in the days before the Flood. Some of it may be emotionally hard to read, but the information is critical in understanding the dire condition of all humankind in Satan's attempt to prevent the Seed — Jesus Christ and Satan's ultimate nemesis — from entering the human race.

QUESTIONS TO PONDER

1. As you come to the close of this chapter, what is your greatest takeaway from all that you read?

2. Have you ever taken a mythology class, watched a movie where mythology was a main theme, or maybe read up on it out of curiosity? What monsters do you remember seeing or hearing about? How does this chapter change your thought process to know that the creatures presented in mythology may have an actual, biblical basis in reality?

3. Take a few moments to reread the section "Some Believe 'Monsters' Also Existed Before the Flood." What is your takeaway from the passages in *The Book of Enoch*, *The Book of Jasher*, and *The Book of Jubilees*? How do the verses in Leviticus 18:23-28 make what the passages stated in these three extra-biblical books seem more likely to have happened?

4. The idea of the days of Noah being replicated at the end of the age (*see* Matthew 24:37) is a sobering thought that provokes many questions about the "monsters" that many in ancient civilizations wrote about concerning pre-Flood history. What do you think that ancient scenario might look like in a depraved end-time society?

5. The enemy seeks to debase God's creation, mankind, and rob us of the glory God crowned us with — glory he forsook as Lucifer, one of God's chief angels in Heaven. Everything the devil touches becomes twisted and perverted from God's original design. In what ways might God's enemy, and ours, "touch" a last-days culture to debase it and make it "monstrous"?

Due to a brood of angels who rebelled against God, abandoned their posts, and comingled with mortal women, Genesis 6:4 says hybrid giants were born that brought widespread bloodshed and violence into the period before the Flood.

CHAPTER SEVEN

WHAT TYPES OF VIOLENCE DID THE GIANTS BRING INTO THE EARTH?

Today if you were to visit the lower slopes of the Ararat mountains near the border of Iran and eastern Turkiye, you could visibly see what many believe are the ruins of Noah's Ark protruding from the ground. I have spent many days on location researching this site for myself, and along with others who have investigated it, I am personally convinced the ship-shaped object is indeed the remains of Noah's Ark.

When we consider all the cumulative scientific research conducted since 1959 at the Durupinar[1] site in the lower mountains of Ararat, there are growing reasons to believe this mud-encased formation on the slope of Mount Cudi[2] really is Noah's Ark. Although the massive object has been deteriorating for more than 5,000 years, the remains serve as natural evidence that the Flood of Noah really did take place.

In previous chapters, we have noted that in almost every ancient civilization, there are legends regarding the days preceding this momentous event — retellings of celestial beings that came down to earth and sexually comingled with earthly women, who then gave birth to demigods or giants. Likewise, these same ancient civilizations have stories of *monsters*, besides the giants, that also roamed the earth in the pre-Flood world. Some allege these creatures were produced when the giants — otherwise known as the Nephilim — began to sexually defile the animals, who then birthed hideous, hybrid creatures referred to, in general, as monsters. Although they had different names in various parts of the world, these creatures were basically the same *in their descriptions* from culture to culture.

Some try to dismiss these stories of celestial beings, giants, and strange, monstrous creatures as merely mythological nonsense. However, many of the ancient peoples who wrote about these creatures and events were extremely brilliant. They are the authors and originators of mathematics, logic, various sciences, the arts, and architecture. Again, they were not given to wild imaginations, but they wrote about what they really believed existed at some point, either in their current societies or as handed down to them from those in their ancestry.

The Source of the Problem and the Purpose for the Flood

Again, nearly all pagan mythology and pagan religions can be traced to Genesis 6.

And it came to pass, when men began to multiply on the face of the earth, and daughters were born unto them, that the sons of God saw the daughters of men that they were fair; and they took them wives of all which they chose…. There were giants in the earth in those days; and also after that, when the sons of God came in unto the daughters of men, and they bare children to them, the same became mighty men which were of old, men of renown.

— Genesis 6:1,2,4

We've seen that the words "sons of God" actually refer to mutinous *angels* who abandoned their God-assigned posts in order to engage in illicit sexual relations with mortal women. And from those women, giants were born — fierce, mighty men of renown, as we have also seen. Both Peter and Jude wrote convincingly, by the Spirit, about these events, expounding on how God dealt with those rebellious angels.

Thus, the *source* of the problems in Noah's day was the mutinous actions of the fallen angels and the actions of the giants they produced through forbidden unions with mortal women. The Bible is clear about what was going on and how God felt about it. Scripture says:

And God saw that the wickedness of man was great in the earth, and that every imagination of the thoughts of his heart was only evil continually.

And it repented the Lord that he had made man on the earth, and it grieved him at his heart.

And the Lord said, I will destroy man whom I have created from the face of the earth; both man, and beast, and the creeping thing, and the fowls of the air; for it repenteth me that I have made them.

— Genesis 6:5-7

This illustration depicts the Ark in the background, floating on waters of destruction after the Great Deluge flooded the entire world in the days of Noah.

Great wickedness filled the earth, and every thought of people's hearts was evil continually. This "grieved" God's heart, which in the original language means God *was deeply hurt and vexed inside.* It was out of this intense distress of soul that God chose to bring the Flood to cleanse the earth of the infestation of giants, monstrous creatures, and all the wickedness that was rampant at that time among man *and* beast (*see* Genesis 6:12).

Through Noah and his family, God enacted a plan to save a sampling both of humanity and of the animals that were genetically pure. Through the Ark, which Noah obediently built with God-instructed precision, God preserved him and his family and the animals on board, and He gave them the grace to start life over again free of these evil contaminants.

Violence and Corruption Plagued the Pre-Flood Population

Genesis 6:11-13 elaborates further, in addition to every thought and imagination of man being evil continually, the all-encompassing problems that plagued humanity.

The earth also was *corrupt* before God, and the earth was filled with *violence*. And God looked upon the earth, and behold, it was *corrupt*; for all flesh had *corrupted* his way upon the earth. And God said unto Noah, The end of all flesh is come before me; for the earth is filled with *violence* through them; and, behold, I will destroy them with the earth.

The word "corrupt" appears in this passage three times, and in each case, it is translated from an original word that depicts something that has been *blemished*, *marred*, or *ruined*. It not only refers to the spiritual rot that was in the world at that time, but also to the blemishing and marring of the human gene pool that was occurring because of fallen angels engaging in sexual relations with earthly women. Through this angelic-human mixture, a pollution of human DNA was taking place, resulting in the birth of a contaminated, twisted race of hybrid giants. Again, some allege a similar kind of genetic contamination was taking place in the animal kingdom as this new race of giants began to violate and defile the animals.

This planet-wide defilement had become so pandemic in the days preceding the Flood that "all flesh had corrupted his way" (*see* Genesis 6:12). The words "all flesh" show that the inclination of all humanity at that time was to participate in the evil that was taking place. But, importantly, the words "all flesh" can also encompass the animal kingdom (*see* Genesis 7:15,16; 8:17).

As previously noted, the likely reason people willingly engaged in wickedness was, when the celestial beings descended from the heavens, it looked as if "gods" had come down from another dimension. Consequently, people were mesmerized and enamored by their presence.

Remember, Second Corinthians 11:14 states that Satan has the ability to transform himself into an "angel of light." What was happening at that early moment

As rebellious angels entered the physical realm of earth, they outwardly appeared as glorious, celestial beings — angels of light — and were wrongly, idolatrously perceived by humans to be celestial gods who had entered their atmosphere to bless them. However, Satan's intention was their destruction — but first he would attempt to pollute the seed of humankind.

in Earth's history was dark, devious, deceptive, and almost completely successful. As those rebellious angels were entering the physical realm of earth, they outwardly appeared as glorious, celestial beings — *angels of light*. It seems the people were so dumbfounded by the angels' godlike presence that they opened their arms to welcome them and even began to worship them. This also seems to be the time when pagan religions of idolatry were birthed.

In addition to corruption, Genesis 6:11 and 13 says that the earth was "filled with *violence*." The words "filled with violence" show that the byproduct of the fallen angels intermingling with mortal women and animals was widespread violence. In response to the indescribable wickedness in the earth, God said:

And, behold, I, even I, do bring a flood of waters upon the earth, to destroy all flesh, wherein is the breath of life, from under heaven; and every thing that is in the earth shall die.

— Genesis 6:17

If worldwide corruption, violence, and unprecedented perversities really did occur as stated in Scripture and in the authoritative writings I have recounted, are there any other authoritative sources that describe the *kind* of violence the giants brought to the earth?

Here's What We Can Ascertain From Early Sources About the Giants' Potential Role in the Pre-Flood Violence in the Earth

In addition to what the Bible reveals in Genesis 6 and what we can ascertain from other ancient documents that have been previously mentioned, there were also highly respected Church fathers who spoke of the giants and described the types of violence they brought into the earth.

Consider the quote below by Eusebius, who is considered the Father of Church History.

EUSEBIUS OF CAESAREA
260/265 – 339/340 AD

We saw in Chapter 5 that Eusebius was regarded as one of the most reliable, trustworthy Church fathers, who authored many extraordinary commentaries on the Scriptures. His influence served to strengthen the Church and advance the Gospel to such an extent that he was referred to as the "Father of Church History."

Addressing the topic of the giants, Eusebius wrote the following:

> They [the giants] **gave themselves wholly over to all kinds of profanity, now seducing one another, now slaying one another, now eating human flesh, and now daring to wage war with** [God] **and to undertake those battles of the giants celebrated by all; now planning to fortify earth against heaven, and in the madness of ungoverned pride to prepare an attack upon the very God of all. On account of these things, when they conducted themselves thus, the all-seeing God sent down upon them floods.**

According to Eusebius, the giants brought great violence into the earth, which included them spewing all kinds of profanity, as well as seducing and slaying each other, eating human flesh, and even planning to wage war against God Himself. These facts are reiterated by another venerated leader, Clement of Alexandria.

CLEMENT OF ALEXANDRIA
CIRCA 150 – 215 AD

We saw in Chapter 5 that Clement was a revered scholar, theologian, and Christian historian who served as a teacher of teachers — the famed Origen being one of his pupils.

Clement was an intellectual who possessed a broad range of knowledge, including classical Greek history and literature. But he was more widely reputed in his time as a great Christian thinker.

Like Eusebius, Clement of Alexandria also weighed in on the issue of the giants, stating:

> **...When irrational animals fell short, these** [evil] **men** [giants] **tasted also human flesh. For it was not a long step to the consumption of flesh like their own, having first tasted it in other forms.**[3]

When Clement wrote that "irrational animals fell short," he was stating that when the giants had eaten of all the various animals and were no longer satisfied, they began to eat human flesh. Thus, not only were the giants *murderers*, but they were also *cannibals*.

These details are confirmed in *The Book of Enoch*.[4] Again, even though it is not a canonized part of Scripture, *The Book of Enoch* was a highly respected and widely read commentary for hundreds of years — including during the First Century — on the activities of the pre-Flood world.

The fact that some of the apostles were very familiar with and even quoted from the early portions of this document (*First Enoch*) speaks volumes of its commentarial value. With so many early commentators weighing in with reports of the atrocious pre-flood activities occurring on the earth, it is worth considering that these retellings are accurate and true.

THE BOOK OF ENOCH

The respected *Book of Enoch*, as I've stated, is a historical commentary that some believe was written, at least in part, by a man who walked with God and whom God "took" so that he didn't taste natural death (*see* Genesis 5:24). The *Book of Enoch* is in no way canonical; nevertheless, its testimony of ancient events has retained a level of respect over epochs of time that makes it worthy of our consideration.

Regarding the violence of the giants, *The Book of Enoch* states in First Enoch 7:2-5:

> **And they** [the women] **became pregnant, and they bare** [gave birth to] **great giants...who consumed all the acquisitions** [work, possessions] **of men. And when men could no longer sustain them, the giants turned against them and devoured mankind. And they began to sin against birds, and beasts, and reptiles, and fish, and to devour one another's flesh, and drink the blood....**

When the text states the giants "consumed the acquisitions of men," it means that they consumed all the accessible food that mankind had harvested through farming, as well as the meats they produced through raising animals.

The words "when men could no longer sustain them" mean the people were no longer able to appease the appetites of the giants with natural foods. It was at that point the giants turned on and began to kill and eat other giants, and they eventually began to eat human beings. The text also states the giants drank blood, which is an important point we will return to in the following paragraphs.

Considering such claims, could one ascertain that the celebrated ancient author Homer, who gave us both the *Iliad* and the *Odyssey*, actually penned his stories based on early, real-life events? For example, is it possible that the cyclops from the island of Sicily and the clan of cannibalistic giants known as the Laestrygones, who attacked and began eating Odysseus' men, were modeled after incidents that really took place?

It is certainly something to think about. Although I cannot state this with certainty, it is undeniable that stories like these mirror the recorded deeds of ancient giants and could somehow be connected.

In any case, the combined testimonies of Eusebius, Clement of Alexandria, and *The Book of Enoch*, uniformly state that the violence of the giants was linked to their *appetites*. When the plant and animal life around them no longer satisfied their hunger, the giants turned on each other and began slaying and eating one another — and eventually murdered humans, eating their flesh and drinking their blood. This is the earliest known act of cannibalism in history.

There is another valuable quote I want to include, and it is from the distinguished Jewish historian Josephus, whose works are so accurate and reliable they are categorized as the most important source on Israel's history outside of the Old Testament.

JOSEPHUS
CIRCA 37 – 100 AD

As a traveler, historian, and scholar, Josephus is among the most noteworthy of ancient writers. His works are still widely read and studied today both by Christian and Jewish students of history, who consider the works of Josephus to be accurate and therefore trusted.

In addition to his insights on fallen angels, Josephus wrote about the giants, and he tells us something very interesting about what Noah did when the violence and bloodshed of the giants were proliferating in the world.

> **But Noah was very uneasy at what they** [the giants] **did; and, being displeased at their conduct, persuaded them to change their dispositions and their acts for the better; but, seeing they did not yield to him, but were slaves to their wicked pleasures, he was afraid they would kill him, together with his wife and children, and those they had married; so he departed out of that land.**[5]

THREE ANCIENT BOOKS WITH INFORMATION ON THE GIANTS

For additional insights on the violence brought on by the giants, we can turn to three early documents that are believed to be *antediluvian*, which means they are texts that predate the Flood. These include *The Book of the Watchers*; *The Book of Jubilees*; and *The Book of Giants*. We've looked briefly at passages from these three works, but the following paragraphs provide a brief background on each of these ancient texts and are accompanied by corresponding excerpts detailing the giants' acts of violence.

 *The Book of the Watchers*, as we have already seen, is a compilation of the earliest portions of *The Book of Enoch,* which encompasses chapters 1-36. It is believed to be a pre-Flood work that was reputedly composed by Enoch, the great-grandfather of Noah. It describes how 200 angels agreed to rebel against God and mutually swore an oath to descend into the earth's atmosphere to sexually intermingle with the daughters of men, which produced offspring that the Bible calls giants.

Again, regarding the violence of these hybrid beings, *The Book of the Watchers*, in First Enoch 7:2-5, says:

> **And they** [the women] **became pregnant, and they bare** [gave birth to] **great giants...who consumed all the acquisitions** [work, possessions] **of men. And when men could no longer sustain them, the giants turned against them and devoured mankind. And they began to sin against birds, and beasts, and reptiles, and fish, and to devour one another's flesh, and drink the blood....**

According to this ancient account, the giants introduced bloodshed and violence into the earth due primarily to their unceasing appetite for blood. First Enoch 8 states that these fallen angels also taught humanity secret knowledge for which they were not prepared to know or deal with, including how to make weapons of war, as well as engaging in sexual fornication, seduction, and all manner of immorality, sorcery, and divination, as well as a perversion of various sciences, which we saw in the writings of

Irenaeus in Chapter 5 — "…roots and herbs, dyeing in colours and cosmetics, the discovery of rare substances, love-potions…."

The Book of Jubilees is also believed to be an *antediluvian* document that seems to have been best preserved in Ethiopia. An incomplete Latin version was discovered in 1861,[6] and fragments of it written in Greek are scattered among the writings of various Byzantine chroniclers such as Syncellus, Cedrenus, Zonoras, and Glycas. *Jubilees* focuses on and gives similar details of the pre-Flood events found in the book of Genesis, and for this reason it is also known as *Lesser Genesis* or *Little Genesis*.[7]

Jubilees 5:2 in *The Book of Jubilees* also provides information on the widespread corruption and violence taking place on the earth just before the Flood.

> **And lawlessness increased on the earth and all flesh corrupted its way alike — men and cattle and beasts and birds and everything that walks on the earth — all of them corrupted their ways and their orders, and they began to devour each other.**

Early Christian leaders such as Epiphanius, Justin Martyr, Origen, Diodorus of Tarsus, Isidore of Alexandria, Isidore of Seville, and Eutychius of Alexandria were all very familiar with *The Book of Jubilees*. Although no complete Greek or Latin version of it is known to have survived, what's considered to be an accurate translation was found among the *Dead Sea Scrolls*.[8]

The Book of Giants is a third ancient text believed to date back to the pre-Flood days. Fragments of it were also found among the *Dead Sea Scrolls* in 1947,[9] and it is said to contain an expanded rendition of *The Book of the Watchers*. In this narrative, God sends watchers to help fallen man, but the divinely commissioned angels stray from their God-assigned posts in order to sexually mate with mortal women. As a result of their unsanctioned union, the women give birth to giants, who bring great misery upon the earth. Although Enoch is said to have tried to teach and persuade these fallen angels to do right (as Noah is purported to have done later with the unruly giants), they refused to listen, so God eventually sent the Flood upon the earth to cleanse it of this spiritual infection.

A passage from Chapter 15 of *The Book of Giants* offers additional insights concerning the giants.

> **Therefore God, knowing that they were barbarized to brutality, and that the world was not sufficient to satisfy them, for it was created according to the proportion of men and human use…but they, on account of their [evil] nature, not being pleased with purity of food, longed only after the taste of blood. Wherefore they first tasted flesh….**

If what the ancients wrote about the barbarous giants is true, the world was not fashioned for the appetites of giants, which is why their hunger would never have been satisfied. While *The Book of Giants* is not a canonical part of Scripture, it is an authentic piece of ancient literature, which shares events that occurred before God sent the Flood, including stories of the fallen angels and their incarceration by God — and of the giants and their own judgment along with the people of the earth who allowed themselves to be deceived and defiled by Satan's ploy to use the angels who were willing to rebel. Thus, it can be viewed as an ancient commentary to show what life was like during antediluvian times.

MOST ANCIENT TEXTS WERE RECORDED ON CLAY TABLETS

Many scholars believe the early portions of these three ancient texts were written by Noah's relatives. Of course, Noah didn't have paper or parchment volumes of these books in his possession, for at that time, most writing was done on clay cuneiform tablets. Such tablets with ancient, engraved writings are some of the most abundant types of early artifacts in the world. In fact, there are hundreds of thousands of such tablets.

Take, for example, the Bisitun inscription found in the Zagros Mountains in Iran, which features a trilingual inscription written in Persian, Akkadian, and an Iranian language known as Elamite. It records the deeds of the Achaemenid king Cyrus the Great (reign 521–486 BC), which is the same king in Scripture about

Pictured here is a stone found at the site of Bisitun Pass in Iran, which features a trilingual cuneiform inscription that records the deeds of the Achaemenid king Cyrus the Great (r. 521–486 BC), which is the same king in Scripture Isaiah prophesied (*see* Isaiah 44:28) would be used by God to allow His people to return to the land of Israel after their Babylonian captivity (*see* the book of Ezra).

whom Isaiah prophesied (*see* Isaiah 44:28) God would use to allow His people to return to the land of Israel after their Babylonian captivity (*see* the book of Ezra).[10]

Information on cuneiform tablets was engraved on a slightly soft piece of clay with a pointed tool and then allowed to dry.[11] This is likely the type of documentation Noah carried with him onto the Ark, and that's how these tablets survived the Flood.

Giants committed violent crimes, which included murder, cannibalism, and the consumption of blood. While the fallen angels couldn't restrain their sexual desire for women, the Nephilim (or giants) couldn't restrain their physical appetite for blood. Such was the extent of their lust and lack of self-control that God sent a great Flood to rid the land of these wanton creatures and those who had been defiled by them.

Although *The Book of the Watchers, The Book of Jubilees,* and *The Book of Giants* are not canonized books of the Bible, they offer valuable commentary regarding things related to Scripture. Regarding the giants, these three books contain a unified record of their violent crimes, which included murder, cannibalism, and the consumption of blood. It seems that while the fallen angels couldn't restrain their *sexual desire for women*, their offspring, the Nephilim or giants, couldn't restrain their *physical appetite for blood.*

The Ban on Blood Consumption Was the First Post-Flood Law Established by God

You will notice a common thread running through all three of these ancient sources, and that is that giants were murderous cannibals that not only ate other giants, but also ate human beings and drank human blood. With this in mind, consider the first law God issued after the Flood, which is found in Genesis 9:3 and 4. The following is what God told Noah, his family, and all who would be born after them.

> **Every moving thing that liveth shall be meat for you; even as the green herb have I given you all things. But flesh with the life thereof, which is the blood thereof, shall ye not eat.**

Of all the laws God could have issued just after Noah and his family exited the Ark, it is no coincidence God's first law was a ban on the consumption of blood. Later, this same prohibition was repeated in the Law of Moses, where it is written:

> **And whatsoever man there be of the house of Israel, or of the strangers that sojourn among you, that eateth any manner of blood; I will even set my face against that soul that eateth blood, and will cut him off from among his people. For the life of the flesh is in the blood....**
> **— Leviticus 17:10,11**

Without question, the "eating of blood" was one of the atrocities committed by the giants before the Flood — and a contributing factor as to why God brought the Flood upon the earth. God's command not to eat flesh with blood in it was the equivalent of Him saying, "Rule number one is that you're not to drink blood. We will not return to the carnage and chaos that has just been destroyed. Now and forever more, leave behind the drinking of blood!"

This chapter gives a small glimpse into the various types of violence giants brought into the earth. When God saw that the earth was filled with violence through the activities of fallen angels and giants, He decided to cleanse the earth through a flood.

In the next chapter, we will look closely at a very important declaration God made in the midst of all the mayhem produced by the mutinous angels and the giants. It is found in Genesis 6:3, which says, "And the Lord said, My spirit shall not always strive with man, for that he also is flesh: yet his days shall be an hundred and twenty years."

Over the years, there has been much debate and speculation about the meaning of this mysterious verse, but in the pages to come, we will remove the mystery and decipher specifically what the Lord was saying to mankind on the earth in the days of Noah.

QUESTIONS TO PONDER

1. In Genesis 6:17 and Genesis 7:4,21-23, what is God repeatedly saying about those living on the earth at that time — both people and creatures? What does this tell you about the scope of the Flood, and how does it shape your understanding of this catastrophic event?

2. According to the historian Eusebius, not only did the giants bring great violence into the earth, but they also sought to wage war against God Himself! What does God prophesy will happen in Revelation 19:19-21 at the very end of the age?

3. Now that you've read seven chapters of this book, how is your understanding of the fallen-angel activity before the Flood different than when you first started? Is there something in the Bible that makes more sense to you now that you can factor in the actions of the mutinous angels and the giants they produced? If so, what is it?

Pictured here are the ruins of Noah's Ark at the Durupinar site in the lower mountains of Ararat. Even after more than 4,000 years of earthquakes, mudslides, and weathering, the ruins of the Ark can still be observed encased in the mud, but through multiple ground-penetrating radar scans and numerous ERT scans conducted by archaeologists, geologists, researchers, and scientists, the interior of the site has been studied extensively.

CHAPTER EIGHT

WHAT DOES THE PROMISE
OF 120 YEARS MEAN?

After years of studying about the Durupinar site on the lower slope of Mount Cudi, where Noah's Ark is believed to reside, my team and I were finally able to travel to eastern Turkiye to personally visit the ship-shaped formation and conduct some firsthand investigations of our own.

Although I had studied everything I could find about the site for many years before traveling there, I was finally able to see the so-called ruins of Noah's Ark for myself. What's more, a researcher who has devoted 20 years of his life to studying the site was able to set aside time in his schedule and help my team and me make the most of our visit.

As one meticulously examines the site, he can see what appears to be the mud-encased ribs of the ship protruding from the top of the structure, which is now exposed due to multiple earthquakes over the years that have unsettled millennia of dried mud that encased the mammoth vessel. Likewise, the erosion of the soil around the sides reveals regularly spaced vertical anomalies, which appear to mark the ribs of the structure as well as the very distinct bow and stern of the ship. Artistic renderings have been created to illustrate how the ship's ribs are connected to parallel beams, and those renderings help us understand the ruins that are visible today. Although the ribs are no longer clearly visible due to deterioration, earlier excavations on one side of the ship actually revealed what appeared to be the ribs of the ship.

Amazingly, even after exposure to thousands of years of earthquakes, mudslides, and weathering, the exterior ruins of the Ark can still be observed encased in the mud in the lower mountains of Ararat. And through multiple GPR and ERT scans conducted by archaeologists, geologists, researchers, and other scientists, the *interior* of the site has also been studied extensively. The results reveal unequivocally that the enormous structure within the earth is man-made and in no way a natural, geological formation. Indeed, as we've seen, the dimensions of the structure precisely fit those of Noah's Ark as described in Genesis 6!

The account of Noah's Ark could be no account at all without an account of the Flood, the judgment of which precipitated the building of the Ark for the preservation of the "eight," along with every species of animal that had not been contaminated by the wickedness God's creation had endured for hundreds of years.

As we saw in Chapter 2 in the prophetic genealogy of Adam's lineage, God foretold the judgment of the Flood for many years before this catastrophic event occurred. Referring to the meaning of the name "Methuselah" — who was recorded as the oldest human being on earth — God said, in effect, *"When he dies, it will come."*

We'll investigate the ultimate manifestation of this prophetic word and God's longsuffering toward sinful man in the pages of this chapter.

God Drew a 'Timeline in the Sand' Before Sending Judgment

Immediately after we are told about the "sons of God" (also known as fallen angels), who saw the daughters of men and began to come down from the heavens to have sexual relationships with them, the Bible tells us in Genesis 6:3 that God's toleration of the situation would eventually come to an end.

And the Lord said, My spirit shall not always strive with man, for that he also is flesh: yet his days shall be an hundred and twenty years.

As seen in this illustration, God gave Noah a plan to build the Ark when Noah was 500 years old, which gave him a time span of 100 years to build it. In that span of 100 years, faithful Noah also became a passionate preacher of righteousness. Every swing of his hammer was a prophetic proclamation of a timeline that would eventually reach an end.

In this verse, the word "man" is translated from a word that refers to *all of mankind*, which alerts us to the widespread number of the earth's inhabitants that had gone astray because of the angelic interference. In fact, the activity of these mutinous angels and the giants they fathered through mortal women had so corrupted mankind that God said He would not always "strive" with man. This was God's way of prophetically declaring that a time was soon coming when He would no longer endure the wickedness on the earth. Thus, He set an expiration date for His patience regarding the evil that was taking place.

God went on to say that man's days "…shall be an hundred and twenty years" (Genesis 6:3). This was the equivalent of Him saying, "I'm giving those of you who are untainted 120 years to turn to Me and repent." If the population not yet affected by the hybridism of "angels with humans" did not turn back to God by that point, His patience with the situation would end and they would be consumed by the judgment to come. Thus, God gave humanity 120 years from that point forward to turn back to Him.

Noah was known in his time as "a preacher of righteousness" and he pleaded with those around him to repent. With every pound of the hammer to put a board into place, Noah warned all those around him of their need to return to God to avoid the coming judgment. But, unfortunately, rather than heed his message, the people mocked him and nonchalantly continued their lives oblivious to the fact that they were living in the shadow of an approaching judgment.

In rabbinic literature, it is written that God gave this specific amount of time because He wanted people to know exactly how long they had to repent.[1] The space of 120 years was ample time for the remnant to turn from wickedness, live reverently before the Lord, and forego judgment.

NOAH BUILT THE ARK AND PREACHED REPENTANCE FOR 100 YEARS

The Bible tells us that when Noah was about 500 years old, he and his wife became the parents of Shem, Ham, and Japheth (*see* Genesis 5:32). It seems that about that same time, God also famously instructed Noah to begin building the Ark (*see* Genesis 6:13,14). In Genesis 7, we read more about the time frame of the events surrounding the Great Flood.

And Noah was six hundred years old when the flood of waters was upon the earth.

— Genesis 7:6

Since the Flood was unleashed when Noah was 600, and he began building the Ark when he was 500, he had a span of 100 years to construct this enormous vessel. Nevertheless, God's warning clock had already been ticking. According to Genesis 6:3, He pressed the start button 120 years before the Flood. A careful calculation of these years shows us that God's initial warning was given about 20 years *before* He instructed Noah to start building the Ark.

It seems that during those 20 years, God was watching to see if anyone was seriously responding to His warning. It may be that when He saw no movement toward repentance, He spoke to Noah and instructed him to begin building the ark of safety from the judgment to come. Because Noah was from a prophetic lineage and had received the prophetic writings of his forefathers, he knew God's words were sure and that, just as He had spoken, He would eventually deal with the fallen-angel situation that defiled humankind with sin and rebellion against God and produced a race of giants on the earth that wreaked havoc with all of creation. However, at the age of 500, Noah was hearing from God about what to do about the Flood that was approaching.

According to Second Peter 2:5, Noah was known in his time as "a preacher of righteousness." Therefore, as he and his sons built the Ark, he pleaded with those around him to repent. With every pound of the hammer to put another board into place, Noah warned his erring audience of their need to return to God and avoid the coming judgment. A hundred years of steadfast building means there were also 100 years of steadfast preaching. Unfortunately, rather than heed his message, the people nonchalantly continued their lives, oblivious to the fact that they were living in the shadow of an approaching judgment.

Those 120 years were intended to be a last-chance window of opportunity for people to repent before the gavel of God's justice came slamming down. Such a long period clearly displays God's forbearance, but eventually God's patience abruptly came to an end. Scripture tells us that *only* Noah's family of eight remained untainted by the sinister events that were occurring in the world around them. By the time the

120 years ended, he and his family were surrounded by a sea of humanity that had been directly or indirectly sexually defiled by the fallen angels. Hence, their DNA was tainted, and the world in which they lived was miserably filled with bloodshed and violence brought about by the giants.

THE RECORD SHOWS GOD IS NOT IN A RUSH TO JUDGE

What's interesting about the story of Noah is that it is the first display of a distinct pattern of God's remarkable patience toward mankind. Here, He gave humanity a space of 120 years to repent before taking severe action, which demonstrates that He is rarely in a rush to judge. In fact, the Scripture record shows that in most cases, God moves slowly, giving each person — or group of people — ample opportunity to repent and avoid judgment. He has never been desirous of seeing people perish. Indeed, judgment is always God's last resort or course of action.

Second Peter 3:9 is a vivid picture of God's heart of mercy.

The Lord is not slack concerning his promise, as some men count slackness; but is longsuffering to us-ward, not willing that any should perish, but that all should come to repentance.

This verse says God is never tardy or delayed in fulfilling what He has said is coming. It is because of His patience that He often delays bringing judgment because it is never His wish that anyone perish and be eternally separated from Him (*see* Ezekiel 33:11; 2 Peter 3:9). Of course, that does not mean everyone will be spared from judgment. The only way a sinning person or group of people can circumvent His judgment and receive His mercy is to positively respond to His kindness (*see* Ephesians 2:4-7).

GOD HAS ALWAYS GIVEN AMPLE TIME
FOR PEOPLE TO REPENT

From Genesis to Revelation, the record is clear that God is never in a rush to bring judgment, but always gives a person (or people) "space" to repent before He takes alternative action. Lamentations 3:22 aptly says, "It is of the Lord's mercies that we are not consumed, because his compassions fail not." Out of His compassion, He waits and waits and waits — regularly providing a space of time for repentance to occur because He never desires to bring judgment.

172

There are some who claim God's judgment falls quickly, and they mistakenly use one or more of the following examples to prove it. However, if you ponder these cases closely, it becomes clear that God's kindness provided each of these people sufficient *time* to repent before alternative action was taken against his or her sin.

God mercifully expelled Adam and Eve from the Garden of Eden lest they eat of the tree of life and be forced to live forever in a fallen human state (*see* Genesis 3:22-24). Although Scripture does not state what happened to them spiritually afterward, their long lives provided time for them to repent.

Adam and Eve were the original human case of rebellion and sin. Yet in their situation, they were immediately confronted with God's kindness and patience. After they sinned and were no longer clothed with God's glory, rather than damn them with no hope of recovery, God covered their nakedness with the skins of animals (*see* Genesis 3:21).

Then the Lord mercifully expelled them from the Garden of Eden lest they would eat of the tree of life and be forced to live forever in a fallen human state (*see* Genesis 3:22-24). Although Scripture does not state what happened to them spiritually afterward, the remaining years of their long lives provided *time* for them to repent.

God allowed Cain to move to the land of Nod where he continued his life (*see* Genesis 4:16). Although the Bible does not state Cain repented, God's kindness and patience provided time for him to do so.

Cain committed the first murder in human history against his own brother, Abel (*see* Genesis 4:8). But God's kindness marked him so that no one would kill him in retaliation (*see* Genesis 4:15). Not only did God protect him, but He also allowed Cain to move to the land of Nod, where Cain continued his life (*see* Genesis 4:16). Although the Bible does not state whether Cain repented, God's kindness and patience nevertheless provided *time* for him to do so.

God demonstrated His great patience by providing substantial time for Eli and his sons to repent before judgment would have to come. Although they did not repent, God gave them ample time to do so.

Eli's sons sinned egregiously against God and His people, and Eli sinned by not restraining his sons, who for a very long time had been stealing from the offerings and fornicating with women who served at the tabernacle.

In a few paragraphs, you will see how God demonstrated His patience toward the family of Eli, providing substantial *time* for them to repent before judgment fell.

Although they ultimately did not turn to God in repentance and change their behavior, God did not rush to bring about judgment.

David committed adultery with Bathsheba, and God waited a year before dispatching the prophet Nathan to confront David about his sin, thereby giving him and Bathsheba nearly a year of time to repent before a time of judgment.

David and Bathsheba were guilty of adultery and the murder of Uriah (*see* 2 Samuel 11:1-27). Yet even though their actions were abominable, God provided *time* for them to repent before alternative action was taken.

In fact, God waited about a year before dispatching the prophet Nathan to confront David with his sin (*see* 2 Samuel 12:1-15), thus giving them nearly a year of *time* to repent.

As we have seen in all the examples so far, God is slow to bring judgment, and is instead patient, giving those who have sinned time to turn to Him in repentance and to receive His mercy.

God's judgment on Ahab and Jezebel did not come quickly. Because they were regularly confronted and warned about their wickedness by the prophet Elijah, God mercifully provided time for each of them to repent before taking alternative action.

Ahab and Jezebel are noted as two of the most wicked people in the Old Testament. In fact, the Bible states there was never a more wicked king in the history of Israel than Ahab (*see* 1 Kings 21:25), and Jezebel killed many prophets of God (*see* 1 Kings 18:13).

Yet God's judgment on this wicked couple did not come quickly. Instead, they were both regularly confronted and warned by the prophet Elijah concerning their wickedness. Before judgment fell on Ahab (*see* 1 Kings 22:29-39) and afterward on Jezebel (*see* 2 Kings 9:30-37), God had mercifully provided *time* for each of them to repent before taking alternative action.

Judas Iscariot is well known as the notorious betrayer of Jesus. Judas' betrayal of the Lord was infamously fulfilled in the Garden of Gethsemane. Although it seems Judas' end came abruptly, it did not.

In God's great kindness, He brought Judas into Jesus' inner circle and provided three years of time for him to be loved unconditionally, face himself, deal with his character flaws, and be changed. But regrettably, Judas did not repent.

A study of Judas' life shows that his character was fatally flawed from the beginning, but in God's great kindness, He brought Judas into Jesus' inner circle and thusly provided three years of *time* for him to be loved unconditionally, to face himself, and to deal with his character flaws and be changed. Regrettably, although he was filled with remorse for his predicament, he did not repent, but ended his own life as "the son of perdition" (*see* Matthew 27:3-5).

Ananias and Sapphira had significant time to think about what they were doing and to make a course correction, which means God provided them ample time to repent before judgment dramatically fell on them.

Ananias and Sapphira are often used as examples of God's judgment falling quickly on those who sin, but a deeper look at their story shows that God's kindness provided significant *time* for them to repent before judgment came. The Bible says they agreed together to sell a piece of land for a certain price and then to lie to the apostles, saying they were giving the whole amount to the ministry when the truth was, they kept part of the money for themselves (*see* Acts 5:1-11).

Ananias and Sapphira had significant *time* to think about what they were doing and to make a course correction. It took time for them to agree to sell the land, and it took time for them to come to an agreement that they would lie about what they were doing. It also took time to prepare documentation for a legal sale of property, and it took time for them to collect the funds from the sale. During the entire process, which may have been lengthy, they deliberately proceeded with a plan to deceive. This means they had *time* to rethink what they were doing. God provided them ample *time* to repent before judgment dramatically fell on them.

A woman Jesus identified by the name Jezebel in Thyatira was seducing the congregation into compromise and error, but Christ provided her substantial time to make things right before He took alternative action to bring correction to the situation.

In the **Church at Thyatira**, there was a woman named Jezebel who was unthinkably seducing the congregation into compromise and error. A superficial reading of the text in Revelation 2:18-28 may cause one to think God's judgment quickly fell on this woman and her co-conspirators. However, a deeper study reveals that Christ gave her at least three opportunities to repent, providing her substantial *time* to make things right before He took alternative action to bring correction to the situation.

WHAT DOES IT MEAN THAT JESUS' FEET WERE COMING IN JUDGMENT LIKE *BURNING BRASS*?

Christ's feet of brass demonstrate that He doesn't rush to judgment. Rather, He moves slowly enough to give each church or person an opportunity to avoid judgment by repenting before suffering the consequences of continued error or sin.

In this last description of God's kindness and longsuffering toward those who are in violation of His moral absolutes, we have a very vivid, graphic illustration of God's desire to be "slow to judge" as He waits patiently for an erring one to turn and change his or her behavior.

The messages of Jesus to the seven churches in the book of Revelation are preceded by a picture of Christ having "feet like unto fine brass, as if they burned in a furnace" (Revelation 1:15). The word for "brass" here is from an unusual Greek word that is a compound of two Greek words. The first word describes *an alloy of copper, mixed with either tin (bronze) or zinc (brass)* and is used frequently in ancient writings. The second word is the Greek word for *frankincense*, which was the chief fragrance used by priests in temple worship in Jerusalem. But since frankincense isn't an alloy that can mix with metal, the words "like unto fine brass" provide an allegorical message about Christ.

Brass is a symbol of judgment, which tells us that Christ is prepared to bring judgment when it is necessary. But brass is very heavy, and it is difficult to quickly move an object made of this metal. The fact that Jesus' feet were like brass sends the message that when Christ moves to bring judgment, He does so slowly in order to provide "space to repent" before releasing judgment.

In Scripture, brass is a symbol of *judgment*, and here Jesus' feet are "like unto brass." This tells us that Christ is prepared to bring judgment when it is necessary. Those who resist Jesus' commands will discover that He will ultimately trample every plan and purpose of man that stands against the character of God. But brass is very heavy, and it is difficult to quickly move an object made of this type of metal. The fact that

Frankincense was used in connection with intercession and prayer, and it implies Jesus' feet were drenched in the incense of prayer. Although He was poised to bring judgment if necessary, Jesus is, has been, and always will be interceding in prayer and pleading for His people to hear Him and repent before He arrives with judgment.

Jesus' feet were like brass sends the message that when Christ moves to bring judgment, He does so *slowly* in order to provide "space to repent" before judgment must be released (*see* Revelation 2:21).

Additionally, notice Revelation 1:15 says Jesus' feet looked "as if they burned in a furnace." This wording tells us the bronze had not yet been set. In other words, the decision-making process was still being "forged in the crucible." The metal had been heated and poured forth, but because it still glowed brightly, we know that the hardening process was not yet complete.

Although Christ is pictured as moving forward to bring rebuke, correction, or even judgment, the decision to judge the situation with finality had not yet been reached. It was still in the crucible. Slowly lifting one foot at a time, Jesus wasn't rushing to judgment. Instead, He was moving slowly enough to give each church (or person) an opportunity to avoid judgment by repenting before suffering the consequences of continued error or sin.

Because the Greek word for *frankincense* is so often used in connection with intercession and prayer, it implies Jesus' feet were drenched in the incense of prayer. Although He was poised to bring potential judgment if necessary, Jesus *is, has been,* and *always will be* interceding in prayer and pleading for His people to hear Him and repent before He must arrive with judgment.

Again, the biblical record clearly shows that God is not willing that any perish (*see* 2 Peter 3:9), but that everyone is always given time to repent before more severe action is taken. Because this principle is so important, let's take some time to look more closely at the patience and longsuffering God showed to Eli and his sons Hophni and Phinehas, as well as the forbearance He extended to Jezebel, before judgment fell on each one of them for their refusal to repent.

God gave Eli and his sons a specific duration of time in which to repent and to make things right. It was only *after* they would not repent that judgment was released. Depicted here is Eli falling to his death when judgment finally came.

ELI AND HIS SONS: AN OLD TESTAMENT EXAMPLE OF GOD GIVING TIME TO REPENT

As I already briefly mentioned, in First Samuel, we find that Eli was serving as the judge and priest in Israel — and his sons, Hophni and Phinehas, were serving under him. Hophni and Phinehas were vile and did not have a relationship with the Lord. They were unthinkably stealing from the offerings and committing fornication with the women who served in the tabernacle.

The Scripture says:

Wherefore the sin of the young men was very great before the Lord: for men abhorred the offering of the Lord.

— 1 Samuel 2:17

This verse states that the atrocious behavior of Eli's sons caused worshipers to "abhor the offering of the Lord." In other words, Hophni and Phinehas' conduct was so well-known and hurtful that people stopped coming to the tabernacle because they could no longer tolerate the injurious behavior of Eli's sons. Consequently, God was deeply exasperated with them and with Eli their father, who was well-aware of what they were doing, but wouldn't correct or remove them from their positions of authority.

Exactly how long God tolerated the actions of Eli, Hophni, and Phinehas before judgment was released is not known. But a careful reading of Scripture — especially where it reveals that Eli was 98 years old and blind when God brought judgment (*see* 1 Samuel 4:15) — indicates God was patient and gave them a lengthy period of time to repent before judgment was finally unleashed.

Again, judgment is never God's first choice. In the case of Eli and his sons, God did not rush to judgment, but gave them a specified duration of time in which to repent and make things right. If a person (or group of people) spurns God's lovingkindness and patience and is unwilling to cooperate, eventually the mercy clock stops ticking, and God brings correction to the situation. That is precisely what happened to Eli, Hophni, and Phinehas.

Once God saw that Eli was not going to exercise authority to stop his sons from doing what they were doing — and that the two younger men would not repent — time ran out and the clock of God's forbearance stopped ticking. It was only after they were given space to repent, and it was clear that they would not change, that a time came for judgment to be released. According to Scripture, their judgment came all at once when all three men died in a single day (*see* 1 Samuel 4:11-18).

Again, God is never in a rush to dole out punishment, but when behavior becomes so foul that it detrimentally affects the outcome of God's people and God's plan, eventually a time will come when He will deal with such a situation in a more severe way.

Just like Jezebel in the Old Testament who fell from her window and died in judgment, Christ gave time for a woman identified by the name Jezebel in Thyatira to repent before judgment fell. But after the Lord gave her and her accomplices ample "space" to repent, they chose not to comply, and the clock of God's patience stopped ticking and they were judged.

JEZEBEL: A NEW TESTAMENT EXAMPLE OF GOD GIVING TIME TO REPENT

Turning to the book of Revelation, we see that God's patience was extended to a woman named Jezebel along with a group of her accomplices who were a part of the church of Thyatira. After praising this congregation of believers for their charitable works, their faith, and their patience, Jesus proceeded to tell them:

Notwithstanding I have a few things against thee, because thou sufferest that woman Jezebel, which calleth herself a prophetess, to teach and to seduce my servants to commit fornication, and to eat things sacrificed unto idols. And I gave her space to repent of her fornication; and she repented not.

— Revelation 2:20,21

This Jezebel was a woman of prominence in the church of Thyatira. She claimed to be a prophetess and used her position to wrongly influence and seduce God's people into a doctrine of compromise.

The word "seduce" in verse 20 is translated from a Greek word that describes *moral wandering*. It pictures *a person or group of people that have veered from a solid path*, and as a result of veering morally, they have lost their moral anchor and are now *adrift*. Apparently, what Jezebel was endorsing was causing the believers in Thyatira to veer from a righteous path to commit fornication and "to eat things sacrificed unto idols" (v. 20).

The word "fornication" and the phrase "to eat things sacrificed to idols" categorically mean this Jezebel was advocating that the church quit living so separately from the world and begin to re-enter pagan temples to sacrifice to idols, which was the very environment where fornication took place. She allegedly claimed that by doing so, it would give the believers a better standing with their pagan neighbors. But this doctrine of compromise was bringing a deadly spiritual disease right into the heart of the church in Thyatira.

Essentially, Jezebel's doctrine of compromise declared, "It's okay to lower your standards. You don't have to live such a restrictive, separate lifestyle. Learn to blend in with the world and become more inclusive and accommodating of other people's practices. If you learn to blend in instead of living so separately, you will gain more acceptance by pagans."

While compromising God's standards may have bought a temporary reprieve from persecution, it removed God's power and holiness from that church. The fact that Jezebel was wrongly influencing believers to blend in and re-engage with the world deeply grieved Christ's heart. Yet He did not rush to judge her. Instead, Christ stated, "I gave her space to repent" (Revelation 2:21).

WHAT DOES IT MEAN TO BE GIVEN 'SPACE TO REPENT'?

The Greek tense of Jesus' words denotes, "*I have given* her space to repent." This informs us that Jesus *had already* spoken to Jezebel in the past and *had already given* her an opportunity to repent. He had even warned her that she had a limited amount of time left to make things right before judgment would be released. In His great mercy, Christ said He gave her "space" to repent.

> **In the original text, the word "space" describes *a time, a season,* or *a specified duration of time*. The use of this word was the equivalent of Jesus saying, "I've spoken to her in the past, and I've already given her a warning. I've made it clear to her that she has been given a limited amount of time to repent."**
>
> **Also notice this word "repent." It is from an original Greek word that describes *a change of mind that results in a complete, radical, total change of behavior. It also means to completely change or to turn around in the way one is thinking, believing, or living*. It is *a total transformation affecting every part of a person's life, both inside and outside, resulting in a behavioral change*.**

When God calls on a person or people to *repent*, He is asking for more than an emotional response. He is calling for an inward change of thinking that results in an outward change in conduct. Sadly, although Jesus had already given Jezebel a specified amount of time to repent, she ignored Christ's warnings and continued down a path that ultimately led to judgment. In fact, Revelation 2:21 specifically says "she repented not."

In the three oldest known manuscripts of the New Testament, the phrase "she repented not" in the original Greek text says, "She *willed* not to repent." Even though Jezebel had heard the Holy Spirit tell her to repent, and she knew that time was running out on Christ's patience, she willfully chose *not* to cooperate and knowingly kept doing the very things He instructed her to stop doing.

Jezebel Was Given a *Third* Chance

In His great mercy and His hesitancy to rush to judge, Jesus offered her what appears to be a third chance to repent and to avoid judgment. This additional opportunity is found in verse 22, where Jesus warned, "Behold, I will cast her into a bed, and them that commit adultery with her into great tribulation, *except* they repent of their deeds" (Revelation 2:22).

Scripture makes it clear that God is not willing for anyone to perish, but eventually the "mercy clock" stops ticking and time runs out. This is the scenario that played out in the days of Noah before the Flood. God, in His mercy, extended mankind 120 years to turn from their wayward activities and to return to Him. But although God gave them "space" to repent before the consequences of judgment came, nearly all of humankind corrupted its way, refused to listen, and experienced judgment as a result.

Notice the word "except" in this verse. This word signifies *one more chance*. Even with all the evil that Jezebel and her followers had done and the trouble they'd caused in the church, Jesus patiently let her know that she still had one more opportunity to repent before the clock of His forbearance stopped ticking. This word "except" also shows that Jesus' warning was *conditional*. In other words, *a judgment may or may not happen, depending on how she and her followers responded*. If the conditions of Christ's demand were met and the parties involved changed, the pending judgment would be prevented.

Furthermore, this word "except" indicates that Jezebel and those who were engaged in sin with her would be judged *except* or *unless* they repented. Once again, this shows Christ is not in the habit of rushing to judgment, and judgment is never God's first choice where mankind is concerned. In His kindness, He extends for each of us a season or a specified duration of time in which to self-correct before judgment ensues.

What happened with Jezebel and her followers would depend entirely on how they responded. But after the Lord's pleading and giving her and her accomplices ample "space" to repent, they would not comply. Therefore, the clock of His long-suffering stopped ticking, and they were judged.

These examples illustrate the scenario that played out in the days of Noah before the Flood. In His mercy, God gave mankind 120 years to turn from their wayward activities and to return to Him. In typical fashion, God gave them "space" to repent before consequences of judgment would be forthcoming.

As God gave humanity 120 years to repent, Noah pleaded and preached to anyone who had ears to hear in that dark generation. Preachers carry out the task of preaching from a pulpit, but Noah's pulpit was the Ark itself. The sounds of its construction reverberating in the ears of sinners among the pre-Flood population were a constant reminder that God's Spirit would not always strive with the violence and corruption that was in the world.

GOD GAVE THE PEOPLE OF THE PRE-FLOOD WORLD A PERIOD OF 120 YEARS TO REPENT

Returning to the Genesis 6 narrative, we see that when humanity had erred far from God's plan, He gave them the space of 120 years to repent. He declared:

...My spirit shall not always strive with man, for that he also is flesh: yet his days shall be an hundred and twenty years.

— Genesis 6:3

Just as God gave space to repent to Jezebel, Eli's sons, and everyone else in creation, He gave the people of the pre-Flood world space to repent as well. Again, it was as if God had said, "I'm setting a timer for 120 years, and when the clock stops ticking, if the people have not repented and returned to Me, I'll have to deal with this messy situation in a different way."

Meanwhile, as God gave humanity 120 years of "space" to repent, Noah pleaded and preached to anyone who had ears to hear in that dark generation (*see* 2 Peter 2:5). Again and again, he urged people to repent and to return to God and, thus, avoid divine judgment.

Today, preachers carry out the task of preaching from a pulpit, but for Noah, his pulpit was the Ark itself. The sounds of its construction reverberating in the ears of sinners among the pre-Flood population was a constant reminder that God's Spirit would not always strive with the violence and corruption in the world.

In Matthew 24:38 and 39, Jesus said:

For as in the days that were before the flood they were eating and drinking, marrying and giving in marriage, until the day that Noe [Noah] entered into the ark, and knew not until the flood came, and took them all away; so shall also the coming of the Son of man be.

For 100 years, Noah preached and warned that judgment was coming. The building of the Ark was a visible reminder to the watching world that God's clock of patience would soon run out of time, and the Flood would come. Sadly, people shrugged it off and went about their daily routines nonchalantly, as if nothing was going to happen. It is likely they regarded Noah as someone who was mentally ill. Or maybe they had heard so much about a "so-called" coming Flood, but never saw any evidence of it, that they became numb to Noah's preaching.

Think of all the lost people today who have heard the message that Jesus is coming and the end of the age is here. They have heard this kind of warning from friends, churches, and media, and yet they shrug it off, going about their lives nonchalantly, as if they have heard no such warnings. Jesus said the people in Noah's day ignored the warnings, going about "eating and drinking, marrying and giving in marriage" (Matthew 24:38). He then prophesied, "That's the same exact way it's going to be before the coming of the Son of man."

Do you know people who have been forewarned that Christ is coming and time is running out — yet they continue to live their lives as if they've heard nothing? Everything is "business as usual" — eating and drinking, marrying, and being given in marriage — while friends, pastors, and preachers plead with them to take their warnings seriously. We are indeed witnessing a duplicate moment in time of what occurred in the days of Noah.

God requires us to warn every person of what is coming — just as Noah warned the people of his day. If we do our best to warn people of what is coming, as Noah did in his generation, and they do not heed our warnings, our pleading with them frees us from being accountable for their eternal destiny. Their choice to ignore God's warnings and reject His merciful gift of salvation will be their own burden to bear.

Because the people spurned God's warnings and His patience, the clock eventually stopped ticking, and the Flood came just as they had been warned. Everyone was lost except Noah's family of eight who had hearkened to the voice of the Lord. Regardless of the people's failure to heed the warnings, Noah believed God and faithfully carried out His divine mission.

Do you see the parallel of Noah's day with today — a time when those who preach Christ and His coming are deemed as fanatical, overreactive, and even mentally ill? Regardless of how the world perceives the believer in Christ, we must faithfully carry out our own assignment "...warning every man and teaching every man in all wisdom that we may present every man perfect in Christ Jesus (Colossians 1:28).

LIKE NOAH, WE ARE CALLED TO WARN OTHERS OF THE COMING JUDGMENT

Peter tells us something very important that connects the Flood to the end of times. In Second Peter 3:6 and 7 (*NLT*), he says, "...[God] used the water to destroy the ancient world with a mighty flood. And by the same word, the present heavens and earth have been stored up for fire. They are being kept for the day of judgment, when ungodly people will be destroyed."

Like Noah, our job is to warn others of this coming judgment. We do it with the words of our mouth and the way we live our life. Ezekiel 3:18 and 19 alerts us of our responsibility to warn people of God's coming judgment. Here, God says:

When I say unto the wicked, Thou shalt surely die; and thou givest him not warning, nor speakest to warn the wicked from his wicked way, to save his life; the same wicked *man* shall die in his iniquity; but his blood

will I require at thine hand. Yet if thou warn the wicked, and he turn not from his wickedness, nor from his wicked way, he shall die in his iniquity; but thou hast delivered thy soul.

There is a day of judgment coming — a moment in time when every person who has ever lived will stand before God and give an account for his life (*see* Romans 14:12; Revelation 20:11-15). Since we have the knowledge that the wicked are going to perish without Christ, God requires us to warn them of what is coming — just as Noah warned the people of his day. If we do not love them enough to tell them of the coming judgment, God will hold us accountable, and their life's blood will be on our hands.

On the other hand, if we do our best to warn people of what is coming, as Noah did in his generation, and they do not heed our warnings, our pleading with them frees us from being accountable for their eternal destiny. In that case, the consequences of their choice to ignore God's warnings and reject His merciful gift of salvation will be on them, not us.

BE READY TO GIVE AN ANSWER FOR THE HOPE THAT'S IN YOU

Without question, we are living in the last of the last days. The infrastructure of the coming Antichrist kingdom seems to be falling into place rapidly before our eyes, and it is as if the Holy Spirit is telling God's people, "Places! Places, everyone! Sound the alarm that Jesus is coming, and share the Good News of salvation that comes only through Christ."

Just as He called Noah, God has called you and me to be "preachers of righteousness" in this hour. Through the apostle Peter, He instructs us:

…Be ready always to give an answer to every man that asketh you a reason of the hope that is in you with meekness and fear.
— 1 Peter 3:15

The words "be ready always" are translated from Greek words that mean *to be ready* or *to be prepared*. It pictures an attitude of one who is *set to go, eager, prompt,* and *raring to get started*. It describes the perpetual mindset of *being ready* — and having such a *readiness* also implies *preparation*. Inherent in this command to *be ready* is that one must do everything in his ability to be equipped for the moment when he is called to action. This means to the best of our ability, we must:

> • *Know what we believe.*
>
> • *Know why we believe it.*
>
> • *Know what the Bible teaches* when we try to reach people with the Gospel.

Furthermore, First Peter 3:15 states we must be ready "to give an answer" to those who inquire more deeply about the message of hope we share with them. The word "answer" here is translated from the Greek word that means *to answer back, to reply, to respond, to explain,* or *to defend.* It is the same word the apostle Paul used in Philippians 1:16 and 17 when he wrote that he had been "...set for the *defense* of the gospel." By using this word, Paul acknowledged that part of his God-given responsibility was to *answer* questions put to him about the Gospel. Peter used this same word to unmistakably let us know that we must be ready to give an *answer, explanation,* or even a *defense* about what we believe to every person who asks about the hope we are sharing.

Peter went on to say that those we are trying to reach may "ask" for clarification about the message. The word "ask" here is translated from a word that pictures a *demand* for an answer to satisfy an insatiable longing to know something. Peter thus alerted us that when non-Christians finally work up the nerve to inquire more deeply about the message we're sharing, we must be ready to give them faith-filled, intelligent answers.

Even if they do not take the message seriously or they shrug it off as though nothing has been said, God nevertheless expects us to warn others of the truth. By doing so, we will have fulfilled our God-given responsibility.

The need for repentance — a 180-degree turning to Christ and a change in one's previous manner of life or behavior — is as critical today as it was in the days of Noah. God asks for this *turning to Christ* from a wicked generation in order to save them from eternal damnation in hell. Contrary to the thinking of many today, repentance is a *gift* that brings rewards in this life and in the life to come. God patiently waits for the unsaved, as well as the erring believers, to turn to Him because He loves mankind and because His love is longsuffering, patient, and kind (*see* 1 Corinthians 13:4; James 5:7).

120 YEARS: DOES GENESIS 6:3 ESTABLISH
A NEW LIFESPAN FOR MAN?

Let's look again at Genesis 6:3.

And the Lord said, My spirit shall not always strive with man, for that he also is flesh: yet his days shall be an hundred and twenty years.

Some interpret this as a promise that we can live up to 120 years. Although this is certainly a possibility, in the context here, that is not what God is stating. Rather than reduce man's lifespan from 900-plus years to 120 years as some have believed, God was actually giving a "space" of 120 years for the people of earth to repent.

> **But that space of 120 years to repent doesn't mean we can't live a long, healthy, happy, productive life here on Earth! In fact, there is no reason someone can't live 120 years or even longer if he does what is necessary to take care of his body — *and his soul* (*see* 3 John 2) — to achieve a longer life. The fact is, there are *many* scriptures that promise exceptionally long physical life *if* the right conditions are met, and we will look at that shortly.**

Unfortunately, many raised in traditional churches grew up hearing that God only promised us 70 or 80 years of life. They were incorrectly told, based on Psalm 90:10, that this is the limitation of life.

The days of our years are threescore years and ten; and if by reason of strength they be fourscore years, yet is their strength labour and sorrow; for it is soon cut off, and we fly away.

Because of incorrect teaching, there are generations who have lived and died believing that 70 — or possibly even 80 — years of age is the scope of what God has promised. But the truth is that Psalm 90:10 was written to the children of Israel who rebelled against God in the wilderness and forfeited their privilege to enter into the Promised Land.

Rather than let this disgruntled generation wander in misery for decades on end, God limited their misery and essentially said, "This particular (rebellious) generation will live no more than 70 to 80 years because I do not want them to wander in misery

189

Rather than let a disgruntled generation wander in misery for hundreds of years, God limited their misery and essentially said, "This particular (rebellious) generation will live no more than 70 to 80 years because I do not want them to wander in misery for years on end." This limitation had to do with God's mercy, and it was not a longevity limitation that applies to all God's people for all time.

for years on end." Thus, this limitation of life had to do with God's mercy — it was not a promise to be claimed by all God's people.

When the next generation of Israelites who cooperated with God entered the Promised Land, *many* of them lived much longer than the 70- to 80-year lifespan referred to in Psalm 90:10. This shows how vital it is to understand *who* God is speaking to and *why* He is saying what He is saying.

THE BIBLE REPEATEDLY PROMISES LONG LIFE
TO THOSE WHO LOVE AND OBEY THE LORD

Let me be clear: The Word of God is filled with promises of a long, vibrant life for those who walk with and honor the Lord. Longevity is His blessing to the faithful. Consider this promise in Psalm 91:16.

With long life will I satisfy him, and shew him my salvation.

> The word "long" here is from a word that *speaks of length*, and it implies *longevity*. The word "life" denotes *days*. As a phrase, the word "long life" depicts *long days* or *a very long life*. Also notice the word "satisfy," which means *to have enough, to have plenty of*, or *to be fully satisfied*. If you want a verse to claim longevity, this one clearly guarantees it, and it is founded on the condition of *abiding in the shadow of the Almighty (see* Psalm 91:1). Those who do so can live until they reach the point of *satisfaction*.

The blessing of long life is assured throughout the Scriptures, and it is offered to anyone who chooses to walk with God and obey His commandments. I encourage you to spend time meditating on these extraordinary promises.

> Thou shalt keep therefore his statutes, and his commandments, which I command thee this day, that it may go well with thee, and with thy children after thee, and that *thou mayest prolong thy days upon the earth,* which the Lord thy God giveth thee, for ever.
>
> — Deuteronomy 4:40
>
> Ye shall walk in all the ways which the Lord your God hath commanded you, that ye may live, and that it may be well with you, and that *ye may prolong your days* in the land which ye shall possess.
>
> — Deuteronomy 5:33
>
> Now these are the commandments, the statutes, and the judgments, which the Lord your God commanded to teach you, that ye might do them in the land whither ye go to possess it: that thou mightest fear the Lord thy God, to keep all his statutes and his commandments, which I command thee, thou, and thy son, and thy son's son, all the days of thy life; and that *thy days may be prolonged.*
>
> — Deuteronomy 6:1,2
>
> I call heaven and earth to record this day against you, that I have set before you life and death, blessing and cursing: therefore choose life, that both thou and thy seed may live: That thou mayest love the Lord thy

> God, and that thou mayest obey his voice, and that thou mayest cleave unto him: for he is thy life, and *the length of thy days....*
>
> — Deuteronomy 30:19,20
>
> Honour thy father and thy mother: that *thy days may be long upon the land* which the Lord thy God giveth thee.
>
> — Exodus 20:12
>
> And if thou wilt walk in my ways, to keep my statutes and my commandments, as thy father David did walk, then *I will lengthen thy days.*
>
> — 1 Kings 3:14
>
> My son, forget not my law; but let thine heart keep my commandments: for *length of days, and long life, and peace,* shall they add to thee.
>
> — Proverbs 3:1,2
>
> Hear, O my son, and receive my sayings; and *the years of thy life shall be many.*
>
> — Proverbs 4:10
>
> For by me [wisdom] *thy days shall be multiplied,* and *the years of thy life shall be increased.*
>
> — Proverbs 9:11
>
> The fear of the Lord *prolongeth days....*
>
> — Proverbs 10:27
>
> Thou shalt come to thy grave in *a full age,* like as a shock of corn cometh in his season.
>
> — Job 5:26

In addition to having these marvelous promises to claim as a believer, it must be noted that now even medical science declares that if certain conditions could be met to drastically slow down the aging of cells, it could be possible for the human body to live up to 1,000 years.[2] As astounding as that sounds, if these purported studies have any merit, it tells me that the stewardship of our health and well-being (spiritually and naturally) is more important than many have realized. It also tells me that the way most people have been thinking about aging and "old age" probably needs to change. The Bible indicates in many places the tremendous power our thought-life has on our overall well-being. And Proverbs 23:7 says that as a person thinks in his heart, "so *is* he."

But these medical studies, if reliable, could remarkably place life expectancy closer to the number of days people were living in the time before the Flood. And, of course, God's Word is life itself — it is teeming and overflowing with the life and nature of God Himself — and it is God's power *unto* our healing, deliverance, wholeness, soundness, preservation, safety, and welfare in every area of our lives if we'll believe and embrace it (*see* Romans 1:16).

Indeed, God promises a long, satisfying life to the faithful, and He does not ever limit His blessings of long life to 70 or 80 years — or even to 120 years, as some claim. According to Psalm 91:16, God will give you as many years as you want, or until you are *satisfied*.

SEVERAL POST-FLOOD PATRIARCHS LIVED WELL OVER 100 YEARS

Abraham lived to be 175 years old, and he did not end his life as an old, weak man, but instead, he was physically strong to his very last breath.

But what about Bible patriarchs and matriarchs *after* the Flood — after the days of Noah in which people's lifetimes transcended *centuries*? This truth of physical longevity is evident in the lives of several post-Flood patriarchs, including Abraham, Moses, and Job.

Concerning Abraham, Genesis 25:7 and 8 says:

And these are the days of the years of Abraham's life which he lived, an hundred threescore and fifteen years. Then Abraham gave up the ghost, and died in a good old age, an old man, and full of years; and was gathered to his people.

Moses lived 120 years. His eyesight was clear, his mental acuity was sharp, and his physical body was still strong all the way to the end of his earthly life.

One "score" is 20 years, so if Abraham's life was 100 plus 3 score and 15 years, he lived to be 175 years old. He did not end his life as an old, weak man, but instead, he was physically strong to his very last breath.

What about Moses? Deuteronomy 34:7 says:

And Moses was an hundred and twenty years old when he died: his eye was not dim, nor his natural force abated.

Here again, we see Moses lived well beyond the 70- to 80-year limitation of Psalm 90:10. This verse states Moses lived 120 years, and his eyesight was clear, he possessed mental acuity, and all his mental and physical faculties were sharp and strong — just like Abraham — all the way to the end of his earthly life.

Then there is the man called Job, who lived at about the same time as Abraham, which would place his lifetime at about 350 years after the Flood. Regarding Job, the Bible says that after he was tested and tried by the enemy during a difficult season of his life, he received double of everything he had lost.

Job lived a long life, and he did not die a sick, weak man. Instead he was completely — doubly — restored by God and when he finally died, he was satisfied and full of days.

After this lived Job an hundred and forty years, and saw his sons, and his sons' sons, even four generations. So Job died, being old and full of days.
— Job 42:16,17

"...they that wait upon the Lord shall renew their strength; they shall mount up with wings as eagles; they shall run, and not be weary; and they shall walk, and not faint."

— Isaiah 40:31

In addition to all the years Job lived leading up to all the difficulties he faced, he went on to live another 140 years. His life was not cut short, and he did not die a sick, weak man. He was satisfied and "*full* of days."

Abraham, Moses, and Job were not the only people to live long lives after the Flood. The Bible says Terah, Abraham's father, lived 205 years (*see* Genesis 11:32); Isaac lived to be 180 (*see* Genesis 35:28); and Jacob, who was the father of the 12 tribes of Israel, lived to be 147 (*see* Genesis 47:28). And just in case you're wondering about a modern-day, contemporary story of extreme longevity, at the time of this writing, Jeanne Louise Calment is said to hold the world's record for the "longest person in modernity," living to the age of 122 years and 164 days.[3]

Psalm 103:5 says, in effect, that God will "renew your youth like the eagle's," which pictures supernatural age renewal for those who walk with God. And Isaiah 40:29-31 promises that those who wait on the Lord will experience a supernatural strengthening on many levels, including living long and strong!

These verses say:

He giveth power to the faint; and to them that have no might he increaseth strength. Even the youths shall faint and be weary, and the young men shall utterly fall: but they that wait upon the Lord shall renew their strength; they shall mount up with wings as eagles; they shall run, and not be weary; and they shall walk, and not faint.

These verses promise that those who "wait upon the Lord" will have *power* instead of faintness, *strength* instead of weakness, and *renewed strength* instead of frailty. Moreover, they will soar like an eagle, they will run and not be weary, and they will walk and not faint. Hence, this is God's guarantee that whoever "waits upon the Lord" can live long and live strong all the way to the conclusion of his or her life!

AGE DOES NOT LIMIT ONE'S USEFULNESS TO GOD

It is a grave mistake for older, more mature people to believe they are irrelevant due to their age. How tragic to move off the playing field and sit on the sidelines before one reaches an age that holds greater anointing and revelation than he or she has ever known in the past.

The apostle John was one such example of someone who lived to receive commissions, insights, and knowledge from the Lord for his *decades*. In other words, rather than leave the earth before his time, John remained, and his seasons of usefulness continued *and flourished* until he died at an old age and was finally present with the Lord (*see* 2 Corinthians 5:8).

At the age of 92, John was sent to the island of Patmos as a prisoner of the emperor Domitian. In a cave on that hostile island, the elderly apostle found himself isolated from mainstream society. But his isolation was suddenly invaded when he was caught up into the realm of the spirit and beheld Christ in all His splendor. On that day, Jesus — the One who correctly calls Himself the "KING OF KINGS, AND LORD OF LORDS" (Revelation 19:16) — stepped into that lonely hole in the earth and revealed Himself to John as John had never seen Him before. (*See* Revelation 19:1-16.)

The apostle John received the book of Revelation in his 90s on the island of Patmos. When he was finally released, he returned to Ephesus to continue providing guidance and oversight to the churches in Asia Minor.

Remember, John was known as "the disciple whom Jesus loved" (*see* John 13:23; 19:26; 20:2; 21:7,20), and he had no doubt carried precious memories of Christ in his heart from those early days of walking with Him as one of the first disciples. But a moment came at the age of 92 when John had an encounter with Christ far beyond anything he ever previously knew — a revelation that superseded all his previous experience and knowledge.

So rather than becoming irrelevant and moving off the playing field, John stayed in the game, took a pen in his hand, and recorded the book of Revelation. Then when Emperor Domitian died and John was released from Patmos when he was in his mid-90s, he returned to the city of Ephesus to continue his leadership over the churches. Remarkably, it was after his release from Patmos in the later years of his life that he penned the gospel of John, First John, Second John, and Third John.

Oh, how we need to understand there are anointings, insights, and revelations that we are only capable of receiving at a more mature age. Sadly, most do not reach the age at which they can enter and experience the greatest anointings and revelations that God has reserved for them. God's plan is for us to go from strength to strength (*see* Psalm 84:7) and for each of us to run a long race of many years. Even though much of what takes place in the early part of our life is *weighty* in eternal value and significance, it is merely preparation for greater things God has planned for us in our latter years.

In our time, people's perspective on age is changing, and as a result, many are living longer. All around us is a cloud of contemporary witnesses who have run long races and who are still running strong and serving *robustly* into years way beyond what others may consider to be "the norm." And because of their remarkable examples, it is quite evident that running a long and strong race and becoming more valuable and usable is possible as we age with God's grace.

So don't buy into the lie that God only promised 70 or 80 years of life. If you aim only for 70 or 80 years, that is probably what you'll get. But if you aim for a longer life — even 120 years or more — you will come much closer to it. I encourage you to determine to run a long race! Aim to stay spiritually vibrant, physically fit, engaged in God-given relationships, and on track with God's Word and His Spirit. All of these are vital for longevity. Choose to keep edging forward with the various assignments God has given you and determine not to veer from the race until you can confidently say, "I have finished my race!" (*See* 2 Timothy 4:7.)

But while we rejoice at God's promises of longevity and see that there are many Bible verses that guarantee it if we'll embrace them as our own, Genesis 6:3 is not a verse about longevity. Again, it is the declaration that God gave humanity, granting them a "space" of 120 years to repent before the judgment of the Flood would be released.

But, again, the fact that the "promise" of 120 years in Genesis 6:3 pertains to a space of time in Noah's day to repent — and not to the longevity of man — doesn't mean we can't claim the many other Bible promises of long life! I listed previously in this chapter many such promises, and not only did God make absolute declarations in His Word pertaining to longevity, we also see many Old Testament patriarchs who lived very long lives *after* the Flood.

I say this to encourage you — not to take the wind from your sails! God didn't say "120 years" in Genesis 6:3 specifically concerning the lifespan of man, but all things are possible to those who believe (*see* Mark 9:23). So why not embrace the verses we read on long life, take them into your spirit, and foster them by meditating on them continually and speaking them from your lips?

And then exercise stewardship where the care of your physical body is concerned. Show the Lord "your faith by your works" (*see* James 2:18) by eating right, exercising, getting adequate sleep, and having medical checkups from time to time.

Just as you feed on God's Word and maintain an active prayer life to stay spiritually and emotionally strong — you have to take care of your body to stay physically strong. Some hear a few Bible messages on faith and healing, and they begin to presume they can eat whatever they feel like eating and continually drive themselves with very little downtime to provide the selfcare they need for their physical well-being.

But never forget that *you* are the steward of your own life — the steward of the resources of your time, money, efforts, and energy. And that includes the resource of your physical health. Mark 12:30 says, "…Thou shalt love the Lord thy God with all thy heart, and with all thy soul, and with all thy mind, and with all thy strength…." No one else can take this responsibility for you — it is something only you can do.

In the next chapter, we will see that the Flood was intended to cleanse and purify the earth of the wickedness that was abounding everywhere in the antediluvian age.

QUESTIONS TO PONDER

1. When we receive God's mercy, it means we don't get what we deserve. What else does the Bible say about the mercy of God? Take a look at what the insights these passages offer and record a specific instance of God's mercy in your own life.

   - Psalm 86:15; 103:8; 145:8
   - Ephesians 2:4,5
   - Titus 3:4-7
   - Micah 7:18
   - Luke 1:50
   - Lamentations 3:22,23
   - James 2:13
   - Joel 2:12-14

2. If Jesus were to speak to you right now about things you're doing *right,* what do you think He would celebrate with you about?

3. If Jesus were to speak to you right now about activities you need to repent of and change, what would they be? If God has given you a space to repent of sin, don't wait any longer. Humble yourself before the Lord and ask Him to give you His grace to do the right thing. Cooperate with the promptings of His Holy Spirit and allow Him to transform your soul.

4. The Bible says Noah preached about the coming Flood and called on hearers to repent while there was still an opportunity to do so. As you work and go about your daily routine, what are you doing to tell people about the fact that we are rapidly approaching the end of the age? Are you warning them to escape the coming wrath by repenting and accepting Jesus as their Savior and Lord?

5. First Peter 3:15 says you should always be ready to give a reason for the eternal hope you have in Jesus. To help you prepare for the people God is going to bring across your path, take time now to jot down some of the amazing ways Jesus has transformed your life. What opportunities are you taking to help others who are in need of God's love and delivering power?

This photo shows my team and me pictured at the steeply turned upward bow of the ancient ship-shaped formation in the lower mountains of Ararat. On multiple trips, my team and I worked with the chief researcher of the Durupinar site to document the Ark and areas surrounding it that are related to the story of Noah and the Flood.

CHAPTER NINE

A FLOOD TO CLEANSE THE EARTH

The lower slopes of the mountains of Ararat have been visited for thousands of years by people of all walks of life, including many notable individuals, who documented seeing the remains of a mammoth ship, which is now encased in mud, mostly still beneath the earth. Given its biblical location (*see* Genesis 8:4) and the fact that its dimensions precisely match those outlined in Genesis 6, there are many who now conclude this ship-shaped structure is none other than Noah's Ark.

God's Word is holy, infallible, and needs no real defense. But evidence of the Ark is evidence of the Flood. According to Scripture, God decided to flood the entire earth to cleanse it of the unthinkable evils brought about by the fallen angels, giants, and, some say, monstrous creatures. By the time of the Flood, the world had become filled with violence and corruption because of the activity of these mutinous angelic beings and their hybrid offspring — giants — which were created through the angels' illicit unions with mortal women. Genesis 6:5,11,12 paints a vivid picture of what was happening in the pre-Flood world.

> **And God saw that the wickedness of man was great in the earth, and that every imagination of the thoughts of his heart was only evil continually....**

The earth also was corrupt before God, and the earth was filled with violence. And God looked upon the earth, and, behold, it was corrupt; for all flesh had corrupted his way upon the earth.

We've seen that the words "all flesh had corrupted his way" tell us that everyone, except the remnant of Noah and his family, seems to have willfully participated in the perversion that was taking place on earth and had thereby become defiled.

THE BOOK OF ENOCH CORROBORATES THE GENESIS 6 ACCOUNT

As noted in a previous chapter, the earliest parts of *The Book of Enoch* — which is also referred to as *First Enoch* or *The Book of the Watchers* — support the Genesis 6 account, which says that the sons of God (angels) abandoned their God-assigned positions and began to sexually comingle with earthly women. Again, even though *The Book of Enoch* is not a canonical book of the Bible, it was considered a very serious pre-Flood commentary to people living during the intertestamental period between the Old Testament and the time of those living during the time of Jesus.

Consider once again the following excerpts from First Enoch 6:1,2 and First Enoch 7:1,2 in *The Book of Enoch* that mention the mutinous angels' plan and the outcome of it.

> **And it came to pass, after the children of men had increased in those days, beautiful and comely daughters were born to them. And the angels, the sons of the heavens, saw and lusted after them, and said one to another: "Behold, we will choose for ourselves wives from among the children of men, and will beget for ourselves children...."**
>
> **And they took unto themselves wives, and each chose for himself one, and they began to go in to them, and mixed with them...and they became pregnant and brought forth great giants....**

In addition to these insights, First Enoch 8:1-3 also reveals that those nefarious angels began to teach humanity things like the art of warfare and how to operate in occult practices.

> **And [they] taught mankind to make swords and knives and shields and coats of mail, and taught them to see what was behind them, and their works of art: bracelets and ornaments, and the use of rouge, and the beautifying of the eyebrows, and the dearest and choicest stones and all coloring substances and the metals of the earth. And there was great wickedness and much fornication, and they sinned, and all their ways were corrupt. And** [one of them] **taught all the conjurers and root-cutters,** [one of them] **the loosening of conjurations,** [one of them] **the astrologers,** [one of them] **the signs, and** [one of them] **taught astrology, and** [one of them] **taught the course of the moon.**

Then in First Enoch 9:8 and 9, we find another brief summary of what the fallen angels did.

> **And they have gone together to the daughters of men and have slept with them, with those women, and have defiled themselves, and have revealed to them these sins. And the women have brought forth giants, and thereby the whole earth has been filled with blood and wickedness.**

When you understand just how much these mutinous beings poisoned mankind and polluted the earth through the violence of the giants they fathered, it is no wonder that God sent the Flood to cleanse the world of all its wickedness.

GOD WAS DEEPLY GRIEVED BY ALL HE SAW

God saw how widespread the wickedness was on the earth and that every imagination and thought in people's hearts was constantly evil (*see* Genesis 6:5). Verses 6 and 7 tell us:

> **And it repented the Lord that he had made man on the earth, and it grieved him at his heart. And the Lord said, I will destroy man whom I have created from the face of the earth; both man, and beast, and the creeping thing, and the fowls of the air; for it repenteth me that I have made them.**

God warned that He would destroy the world with the Flood because of the intermingling of the fallen angels and earthly women — and possibly the defilement of the animals — that was producing giants (and allegedly monstrous hybrid beasts) on the earth.

In the last chapter, we learned that God graciously provided mankind 120 years to repent (*see* Genesis 6:3). It was as if He set a timer on His patience and mercy, and once that timer ran out, if people hadn't turned back to Him, they would face judgment.

During that period, Noah called for people to repent and turn back to God (*see* 2 Peter 2:5). But the entire time Noah was preaching his message of repentance, the intermingling of the fallen angels and earthly women — and possibly the alleged defilement of the animals — continued, producing more giants and monstrous hybrid beasts on the earth.

God was grieved by what He saw, as recorded in Genesis 6:13.

…God said unto Noah, The end of all flesh is come before me; for the earth is filled with violence through them; and, behold, I will destroy them with the earth.

Noah Found Favor in God's Eyes Because He Walked With God and Remained Pure

Remarkably, amid all the mess taking place on Earth, one man stood out among the millions, and his name was Noah. The Bible tells us in Genesis 6:8-10:

But Noah found grace in the eyes of the Lord. These are the generations of Noah: Noah was a just man and perfect in his generations, and Noah walked with God. And Noah begat three sons, Shem, Ham, and Japheth.

Notice verse 9 states that Noah was "perfect in his generations." Most people read this to mean Noah was morally and spiritually pure, which is true — but the word "perfect" in this verse is translated from an original word that means *complete, whole, undefiled,* or *without blemish.* It is this very word that is often used in Scripture to describe the *unblemished* sacrifices being offered in the Temple. So when the Bible says that Noah was "perfect" in his generations, it most likely refers to the fact that Noah's *genes* were *unblemished* because he and his family had walked with God and refrained from intermingling with the fallen angels.

Noah and his family demonstrate how God has *always* and *will always* have a remnant set apart for Himself. Even in the midst of extremely corrupt generations in Noah's day, there was still a remnant of people who had kept themselves pure and continued to walk with God.

God Told Noah About the Coming Judgment and Showed Him How To Be *Saved* Through It

Because Noah walked in close relationship with the Lord and kept himself pure from the criminal spiritual activities that were taking place, God personally alerted him concerning the coming Flood and gave him a precise plan of action to build an ark for the saving of his family — and for the preservation of the animals that God would bring to him.

God downloaded to Noah the blueprints for building the Ark, instructing him in Genesis 6:14-16:

Make thee an ark of gopher wood; rooms shalt thou make in the ark, and shalt pitch it within and without with pitch. And this is the fashion which thou shalt make it of: The length of the ark shall be three hundred cubits, the breadth of it fifty cubits, and the height of it thirty cubits. A window shalt thou make to the ark, and in a cubit shalt thou finish it above; and the door of the ark shalt thou set in the side thereof; with lower, second, and third stories shalt thou make it.

The story of Noah and his family demonstrate that God *has* always and *will* always have a remnant. God alerted Noah of the coming Flood and gave him a precise plan of action to build an ark for the saving of his family — and for the preservation of the animals that God would bring to him.

Along with these specifications given to Noah for the saving of his family and the preservation of humankind, there are two more important facts that can't be missed in the narrative of Noah, and they are that: 1) God is the One who brought the Flood; and 2) the Flood destroyed absolutely every living creature on the earth — except for Noah and his family and the animals that were preserved with them on the Ark. In Genesis 6:17 and 18, God said:

And, behold, I, even I, do bring a flood of waters upon the earth, to destroy all flesh, wherein is the breath of life, from under heaven; and every thing that is in the earth shall die. But with thee will I establish my covenant; and thou shalt come into the ark, thou, and thy sons, and thy wife, and thy sons' wives with thee.

Next, God revealed to Noah His divine plan for saving the animals.

And of every living thing of all flesh, two of every sort shalt thou bring into the ark, to keep them alive with thee; they shall be male and female. Of fowls after their kind, and of cattle after their kind, of every creeping thing of the earth after his kind, two of every sort shall come unto thee, to keep them alive. And take thou unto thee of all food that is eaten, and thou shalt gather it to thee; and it shall be for food for thee, and for them.

— Genesis 6:19-21

Finally, after God gave Noah all these words of instruction and explanation, we find that Noah received God's warning very soberly and began to obey everything God had commanded him to do.

Thus did Noah; according to all that God commanded him, so did he.
— Genesis 6:22

As we have seen in this chapter, from Genesis 6 and from *The Book of Enoch*, we have a biblical and an extra-biblical account of what was occurring in the days of Noah just before the Flood.

Now let's look at further respectable ancient documentation of the existence of the Ark and the events that took place before the Flood.

ANCIENT VOICES WHO CONFIRMED
THE EXISTENCE OF NOAH'S ARK

Since the account of Noah's Ark and the Flood is real, it would stand to reason that there would be reliable, ancient voices in history who wrote about it. Indeed, there *are* many reputable ancient voices who documented their personal visits to the ruins of the Ark or the experiences of others they knew who had visited the site.

In the following pages, you will see what early writers of antiquity as well as venerated individuals up to the Twentieth Century wrote about the actual physical remains of the Ark. These people were ambassadors, antiquarians, archaeologists, archbishops, bishops, Church fathers, geographers, historians, librarians, mathematicians, philosophers, teachers, theologians, travelers, tutors, and scholars.

In these entries, you will read quotes about the Ark, along with a few entries that, although they are not direct quotes, they are from notable individuals who referred to others who viewed the physical remains of the Ark in the mountains of Ararat.

To help you better understand the significance of each person and the weight of his testimony, I've provided a brief biography of each one, and following these descriptions, I've supplied you with the particular reference they have given concerning Noah's Ark. This will serve to verify the trustworthiness of the voices who testified of what they saw — or who had a solid reference of someone who saw the Ark clearly visible in the lower mountains of Ararat.

BEROSSUS
330/323 – 281/275 BC

Berossus was born before or during the time Alexander the Great reigned over Babylon (330-323 BC). He was a Babylonian historian and priest of the Babylonian god Marduk. His priesthood position is important to note because, by his ability to employ the use of ancient Babylonian records and texts that are now lost, he published a famous work called the *History of Babylonia* in about 290-278 BC. Fragments of this work were either quoted or referred to by Pliny the Elder, Censorinus, Flavius Josephus, and Marcus Vitruvius Pollio.[1] In *History of Babylonia*, Berossus recorded that *pilgrims were going to a mountain to carve amulets from the petrified pitch that covered the Ark.*

Concerning the Ark, Berossus wrote:

> **The vessel being thus stranded in Armenia, some part of it yet remains in the Corcyræan mountains of Armenia; and the people scrape off the bitumen, with which it had been outwardly coated, and use it to make amulets to guard against poison.[2]**

ABYDENUS
(DATES UNCERTAIN)

Abydenus was a Greek historian who wrote, probably between the years 80-40 BC, a history of Assyria and Babylonia that was entitled, *On the Assyrians*. The first writer to quote him was Eusebius, who cited Abydenus in his *Praeparatio Evangelica*, and he is also quoted in fragments that Cyril of Alexandria wrote in a treatise against the apostate Emperor Julian. Moreover, fragments from Abydenus' work can also be found in the writings of Syncellus. Indeed, Abydenus was a scholar with a distinguished and renowned status.[3] He spoke with knowledge about the Ark landing in the country of Armenia (geographically, modern-day eastern Turkiye) and noted, as did Berossus, that *people regularly visited it to take bitumen from it that they would use to make wooden amulets.*

Concerning the Ark, Abydenus wrote:

...In Armenia the ship supplied the people of the country with wooden amulets as antidotes to poison.[4]

NICOLAUS OF DAMASCUS
CIRCA 64 BC – 1 AD

Nicolaus of Damascus was a widely respected Greek historian and philosopher who lived during the Augustan age of the Roman Empire. He was born about 64 BC in Damascus, and in life, he became a close friend of Herod the Great. Sophronius wrote that Nicolaus served as tutor for the children of Mark Antony and Cleopatra.[5] His influence was so great that he accompanied Herod Archelaus to Rome to argue for the younger Herod's claim to the throne after the death of his father, Herod the Great. Nicolaus' brother served as a steward in the court of Herod. Although most of Nicolaus' literary works are lost, we know that his most important work was 144 books that covered universal history.[6] His writings are significant, for in them, *he referred to the remains of Noah's Ark as still existing in his time.*[7]

JOSEPHUS
CIRCA 37 – 100 AD

As noted in Chapter 5, Flavius Josephus was a Jewish historian renowned for his multiple historical works, including *The Jewish War* and *The Antiquities of the Jews.* To this day, his writings are considered in Israel to be the most accurate histories of the Jewish people outside the Old Testament.[8]

Josephus was born in Jerusalem to a father of priestly descent and to a mother who claimed royal ancestry. He served as a general of Jewish forces during the first Jewish-Roman War until the army surrendered to Vespasian in 67 AD. Shortly thereafter, Vespasian became impressed by the intellectual prowess of Josephus and took him as a slave. Later, when Vespasian became the Roman Emperor in 69 AD, Josephus was granted his freedom. To show his gratitude, Josephus assumed the emperor's family's last name (Flavius), and from that point on, he became known as Flavius Josephus.

Eventually Josephus became a Roman citizen and an advisor to Titus, Vespasian's son and future emperor. He even served as Titus' personal interpreter when he laid siege to Jerusalem in 70 AD. Jewish scholars count Josephus' works as the most important source for the history of Israel.[9] His writings are considered the most accurate, trustworthy accounts — including his significant insights concerning the fallen angels who sexually comingled with earthly women, who then gave birth to hybrid giants that roamed the earth before the Flood. He also referred to the writings of other ancient historians that he respected, who categorically stated that *the remains of Noah's Ark could still be seen in the mountains of Ararat.*

Concerning the Ark, Josephus wrote:

Now all the writers of barbarian histories make mention of this flood, and of this ark; among whom is Berosus [Berossus] the Chaldean. For when he is describing the circumstances of the flood, he goes on thus: "It is said there is still some part of this ship in Armenia, at the mountain of the Cordyaeans; and that some people carry off pieces of the bitumen, which they take away, and use chiefly as amulets for the averting of mischiefs."[10]

SEXTUS JULIUS AFRICANUS
CIRCA 160 – 240 AD

Sextus Julius Africanus was a historian of the late Second and early Third Centuries, who was also an extensive traveler in a period of time when traveling was uncommon for most. He is important because of his profound influence on fellow historian Eusebius, as well as his continued influence on later writers of Church history and on the whole Greek school of chroniclers. Although Africanus referred to himself as a native of Jerusalem, the *Suda*[11] — a large, Tenth Century Byzantine encyclopedia of the ancient Mediterranean world — states that he was a Libyan philosopher.

Although little of his personal life is known, scholars consider Jerusalem as his *birthplace* and say that he later lived in and helped restore the nearby village of Emmaus, which explains his knowledge of historic Judea. One early tradition placed his life during the reign of Gordian III (238-244 AD), while another places him earlier, in the reign of Severus Alexander (222-235 AD).[12]

In any case, in about the year 215 AD, Africanus traveled to parts of Greece and to Rome and also studied in Alexandria at the famous Catechetical School of Alexandria. He knew Greek and even wrote in that language, but he also understood Latin and Hebrew. Although earlier in his life, he had been a soldier and a pagan, he wrote all his works as a Christian, and they include a five-volume work called *Chronographiai*, a composition that deals with the time frame from the Creation to the year 221 AD.

Although that work is no longer in existence, extracts are found in Eusebius' work called *Chronicon*, and Eusebius deemed it so reliable that he also used it when he compiled early lists of bishops. Fragments of Africanus' *Chronographiai* can also be observed in the writings of Syncellus and Cedrenus and in *Chronicon Paschale*, along with Eusebius' use of additional extracts in his works in other documents and letters.[13]

Many other works are also ascribed to Julius Africanus, some of them dealing with agriculture, liturgiology, medicine, military science, natural history, tactics, veterinary science, and even spiritual matters of a miraculous nature. But very importantly, this revered scholar wrote that *the Ark was still visible in his lifetime on the lower mountains of Ararat.*

Concerning the Ark, Africanus categorically wrote:

When the water abated, the ark settled on the mountains of Ararat.[14]

HIPPOLYTUS OF ROME
CIRCA 170 – 235 AD

Hippolytus of Rome was one of the most important Second- to Third-Century Christian theologians. Some suggest he came from Rome, while others speculate that his origins may have been Palestine, Egypt, Anatolia, or another region of the Middle East. Both Eusebius of Caesarea and Jerome said Hippolytus' place of service could not be specifically identified. In his work *Bibliotheca*, Photios I of Constantinople describes him as being a disciple of Irenaeus.

Indeed, Hippolytus was distinguished for his learning and eloquence, and when Origen, who was a young man at the time, heard him preach, he was greatly impacted by his messages. Regardless of his mysterious origins, Hippolytus' voice became nearly synonymous with authority in the Early Church.[15]

Although there are various tales of his death, it is most likely that during the persecutions of Emperor Maximum Thrax, Hippolytus was exiled to Sardinia and then died there as a martyr in the mines.[16] During the time of Pope Fabian (236-250 AD), his body was sent to Rome. *The Chronology of 354* states that he was interred in Rome in 236 AD and that his funeral was conducted by Justin the Confessor.

Scholars assert Hippolytus' principal work was the ten-volume piece called the *Refutation of All Heresies,* which was printed with the title *Philosophumena* among the works of Origen. Hippolytus' voluminous writings, which can be compared with those of Origen, embrace the biblical spheres of *exegesis, homiletics, apologetics, polemics, chronography,* and *ecclesiastical law.*

But of the best-preserved works of Hippolytus are the *Commentary on the Prophet Daniel* and the *Commentary on the Song of Songs.* Many of his compositions are listed by Eusebius of Caesarea and Jerome.[17]

Scholars generally credit Hippolytus with an important work called the *Apostolic Tradition,* which contains the earliest known ritual of ordination. His chronicle of the world is a chronology starting from Creation and going to the year 234 AD, and this work was later used as a foundation for other chronographical works in the East and West.[18]

Many other documents, including *The Blessing of Jacob, The Blessing of Moses,* and *The Narrative of David and Goliath,* were also attributed to Hippolytus.

This brilliant, scholarly man in the Early Church also wrote emphatically that *the Ark, along with its full dimensions, was still visible to be seen in his day in the mountains of Ararat.*

Concerning the Ark, Hippolytus wrote:

> **This Noah, inasmuch as he was a most religious and God-loving man, alone, with wife and children, and the three wives of these, escaped the flood that ensued. And he owed his preservation to an ark; and both the dimensions and relics of this ark are, as we have explained, shown to this day in the mountains called Ararat.[19]**

EPIPHANIUS
CIRCA 310 – 403 AD

Epiphanius was either born into a Romaniote Christian family or seems to have become a Christian in his youth. He was a Romaniote Jew[20] who was born in a small settlement near Eleutheropolis (modern-day Beit Guvrin in Israel) and later lived as a monk in Egypt, where he came into contact with and was educated by Valentinian groups. Afterward, he returned to Roman Palestine, where he founded and oversaw a monastery.[21]

He was known to communicate in Hebrew, Syriac, Egyptian, Greek, and Latin and was also recognized as a strong defender of orthodoxy. Epiphanius' best-known work is called the *Panarion*, which was a compendium of 80 heresies that included pagan religions and philosophical systems. His work entitled, *Ancoratus* conversely was a compilation of the teachings of the church, which contradicted heretical teachings nevertheless. Epiphanius traveled widely to combat various heresies and was present at the synod in Antioch in 376 AD and at the Council of Rome in 382 AD.

In reputation, Epiphanius was a zealous minister and a respected ascetic whose works are considered an invaluable resource for the history of theological ideas. His orthodox views conflicted with those of the Roman emperor Valens, who was reported to have embraced Arianism, which purports that Jesus was created by God and is therefore not purely divine. The Arian sect was therefore deemed as heretical by mainstream denominations of Christianity and most certainly by Epiphanius and his followers.

He is either quoted or referred to by Jerome. Beginning in either 365 or 367 AD, Epiphanius became bishop of Salamis in Cyprus and served there for 40 years until his death.[22] It is significant that this knowledgeable and reputable man noted that *the remains of Noah's Ark still existed and could be seen in the mountains of Ararat.*

Concerning the Ark, Epiphanius wrote:

> **...Even to this day the remnants of the Ark are still shown in the region.**[23]

214

JOHN CHRYSOSTOM
CIRCA 347 – 407 AD

John Chrysostom was born in Antioch in Roman Syria and is acknowledged as an important Early Church father, who eventually became the archbishop of Constantinople. Although there are disputes about the faith of his mother, his father was a high-ranking military officer who died soon after his birth, which left him to be raised by his mother.

In the year 368 or 373 AD, he was water-baptized, and because of his mother's influential connections in the city, he was educated under the notable pagan Libanius, from whom he acquired skills for a career as a rhetorician. Over time, he developed a love for the Greek language and literature and eventually became a lawyer. As he grew older, he became deeply committed to his Christian faith and studied theology under Diodore of Tarsus, who founded the re-constituted School of Antioch.

In Antioch, Zeno of Verona appointed John to be a reader in the church, and in 381 AD, John was ordained by Meletius of Antioch to be a deacon. Later, he was ordained by Evagrius of Antioch as a presbyter and became instrumental in bringing reconciliation to the spiritual leaders in Antioch, Alexandria, and Rome for the first time in 70 years.[24]

While in Antioch, Chrysostom grew in popularity because of his eloquence in preaching and was given the title "golden-mouthed," which is also what the name "Chrysostom" means. He was especially loved for his insightful expositions of Bible passages, and among his most valuable works are his homilies on various books of the Bible. Additionally, John was one of the most prolific authors in the Early Christian Church, and in the fall of 397 AD, Eutropius nominated him to be appointed archbishop of Constantinople.

For various reasons, he was eventually exiled to several remote locations and ended up dying at Comana Pontica in September 407 AD.[25] Generally, John Chrysostom was and is still considered to be one of the most important and respected Early

Church fathers, renowned for his brilliant mind and intellectual trustworthiness. Indeed, *this scholar of the Early Church also referred to the surviving remains of Noah's Ark in the mountains of Ararat.*[26]

FAUSTUS OF BYZANTIUM
CIRCA 390 – 500 AD

Faustus of Byzantium was an Armenian historian of the Fifth Century who wrote the *History of the Armenians* — a series of volumes that described the military, socio-cultural, and political life of Armenia in the Fourth Century.[27] Faustus' historical writings were substantial and deemed to be important and serious. Knowing that he was a serious scholar and venerated historian, whose work focused on the early Armenian regions of the Ararat Mountain range, makes it even more significant that he reported *the true experiences of a bishop who traveled to the lower mountains of Ararat and saw firsthand the remains of Noah's Ark.*[28]

ISIDORE OF SEVILLE
CIRCA 560 – 636 AD

Isidore of Seville was a Hispano-Roman scholar, theologian, and the archbishop of Seville in Spain. He was born to parents who both belonged to families of high social rank and who were instrumental in the conversion of the Visigothic kings from Arianism to Chalcedonian Christianity. Isidore's older brother, Leander, preceded him as archbishop of Seville; his younger brother served as the bishop of Astigi; and his sister provided administration to more than 40 convents.[29]

Isidore was educated in a school in Seville that was composed of teachers who taught the trivium, quadrivium, and classical liberal arts. He mastered Latin and became familiar with Greek and Hebrew. It was after the death of his elder brother that Isidore was appointed bishop of Seville. He used the resources of education to counteract Gothic barbarism throughout his service as bishop. He also presided over the Second Council of Seville in 619 AD, a provincial council that was attended by eight other bishops from southern Spain, and in 624 AD, he presided over an additional important council.

His fame is due to his work entitled *Etymologiae*, which is an encyclopedia that assembles extracts of many books from classical antiquity that would have otherwise been lost. Remarkably, Isidore is regarded as "the last scholar of the ancient world"[30] who dedicated his life to extracting significant historical information from ancient classical works. *He emphatically stated that the remains of Noah's Ark existed in the mountains of Ararat.*

THEOPHILUS OF EDESSA
695 – 785 AD

Theophilus of Edessa was an astrologer and scholar who lived in Mesopotamia. Later in life, he served as court astrologer to Abbasid Caliph al-Mahdi — then he also later became a *Maronite Christian* who became known for translating numerous books from Greek to Syriac, including the *Iliad*,[31] as well as works by Aristotle and possibly Galen.

Theophilus' life is described in the Syriac *Chronicle of Bar Hebraeus* (1226-1286 AD), where it states that he served the Caliph al-Mahdî, who esteemed him because of his superiority in the art of astrology. It also chronicles a story that spoke of Theophilus as having prophetic abilities.

This noteworthy scholar wrote that *he knew that the Emperor Heraclius camped at a village on the slope of the Ararat mountain range, who then climbed it to see the still visible ruins of Noah's Ark.*

Concerning the Ark, Theophilus wrote:

> Then (Byzantine Emperor) Heraclius turned back and encamped at a village…where the ark stopped during the flood, in the time of Noah. He climbed the mountain…and examined the location of the ark.[32]

HAYTON
(Also Known as HETHUM or HAITHON)
1213/1224 – 1271 AD

Hayton was a king of Little Armenia, and throughout his reign, he followed a policy of friendship and alliance with the Mongols. Known for his widespread travels in western and central Asia, Hayton often went on long, adventurous journeys that took him through dangerous lands and put his life at risk.[33] During his widespread travels, he personally witnessed many sites from the ancient world. Pertinent to our study, it is believed that *Hayton referred to the resting place of Noah's Ark as being in the mountains of Ararat.*

SIR JEAN CHARDIN
1643 – 1713 AD

Jean Chardin was born in Paris as the son of a wealthy merchant and jeweler. For a profession, Jean was himself a jeweler, but eventually he became a traveler and penned a ten-volume work called *The Travels of Sir John Chardin*, which is still considered to be one of the finest works of early western scholarship on Safavid Iran and the Near East.

In 1664, Chardin began working for the East Indies and began journeying through Constantinople along the Black Sea, finally arriving in Persia. Being impressed with him, the Shah appointed Chardin to be his official agent for the purchase of jewels. In mid-1667, Chardin visited India and stayed until 1669 when he returned to Persia. In the next year, while in Paris, he wrote a book of the events he witnessed in Persia and entitled the book, *Le Couronnement de Soleiman Troisième*.[34]

In 1671, Chardin journeyed again to the east to Constantinople, but because of a power struggle in the city, Chardin escaped across the Black Sea, and began an adventurous journey through Caffa, Georgia, Armenia, and on to Isfahan, where he stayed four years. His journeys took him from the Caspian Sea to the Persian Gulf and down the Indus River, where he visited multiple Indian cities. He finally returned to Europe in 1677.

Chardin wrote four volumes covering his travels, but it was his first volume — *Journal du Voyage...de Chardin Isfahan en Perse et aux Indes Orientales* — that contained stories of his journeys from Paris to Isfahan. Both simple and graphic, Chardin's writings were a faithful account of what he saw and heard, which many scholars have acknowledged as quite valuable. In fact, Sir William Jones stated that Chardin wrote the best account of the Muslim nations that was ever published to that time.[35]

Because of the persecution of Protestants in France, Jean Chardin moved to England where he was appointed court jeweler and knighted by Charles II. He carried on a considerable trade in jewels and was called "the flower of merchants." Shortly thereafter, he was elected to be a fellow of the Royal Society, and eventually the king sent him as envoy to Holland, where he stayed several years. On his return to London, he devoted his time to Oriental studies and wrote his observation of Holy Scriptures. Chardin died in London in 1713, and a funeral monument to him now exists in Westminster Abbey that bears the inscription *Sir John Chardin – nomen sibi fecit eundo*, which means, "He made a name for himself by travelling."[36]

Chardin's literary work was praised by Montesquieu, Rousseau, Voltaire, and Gibbon. Scholars in Persia affirmed the importance of his writings, and John Emerson wrote that Chardin's "information on Safavid Persia outranks that of all other Western writers in range, depth, accuracy, and judiciousness."

In life, Jean Chardin journeyed far and wide and wrote detailed reports of the places and people he encountered along the way. He was and is a trusted, reliable witness, and his works have been used as a source for diverse studies on Near Eastern history, government, economics, anthropology, religion, art, and culture. And this factual, faithful, respectable writer affirmed the testimony of Josephus, Berossus, and Nicolaus of Damascus in their descriptions of the Ark. Equally important, *he noted that people were still coming to see it and to take tokens from where it rested in the mountains of Ararat.*

Concerning the Ark, Sir Jean Chardin wrote:

> **Authors, as Josephus, Berosus, or Nicholas of Damascus, who assure us that the Remainders of the Ark were to be seen, and that the People took the Pitch with which it was besmear'd.**[37]

ADAM OLEARIUS
CIRCA 1599 – 1671 AD

Adam Olearius was a German scholar, mathematician, geographer, and librarian. He was born at Aschersleban, later studied at Leipzig, and afterward became the librarian and court mathematician to Frederick III. In 1633, he was appointed secretary to ambassadors Philipp Crusius and Otto Bruggenmann, who was dispatched to Muscovy and Persia for business developments related to the silk trade. Adam's travels took him to Hamburg, Lubeck, Riga, Dorpat, Reval, Narva, Ladoga, Novgorod, and Moscow, where a treaty was signed with Tsar Michael Romanov of Russia.[38]

Olearius and his team started afresh from Hamburg on October 22, 1635, and arrived in Moscow on March 29, 1636. He left Moscow on June 30 for Balakhna near Nizhniy Novgorod, to where they had already sent agents (in 1634/1635 AD) to prepare a vessel for their descent of the Volga. Their voyage down the great river and over the Caspian Sea was slow and hindered by accidents, especially when the ship was grounded near Darband in November. After a three-month delay, they finally reached the Persian court at Isfahan in August 1637 AD and were received by the Safavid king, Shah Safi.

While traveling homeward, Olearius used the opportunity to make a geographical chart of the Volga River, which was so impressive that Tsar Michael Romanov tried to persuade him to enter his service. But Olearius chose to return to Gottorp to become a librarian to the duke. While under the duke's supervision, Olearius was enriched with important manuscripts, rare books, and valuable works of art.[39]

Olearius went on to author many books on a wide array of subjects, deemed as reliable and trustworthy, which included extensive observations he made during his many travels, along with his meetings and connections with powerful people in the course of his life. In his writings, *Olearius factually reported Armenian and Persian stories that testified of those who had seen the physical ruins of Noah's Ark.*

CLAUDIUS JAMES RICH
1787 – 1821 AD

Claudius James Rich was a British Assyriologist,[40] businessman, traveler, and an antiquarian scholar. He knew Greek, Latin, Hebrew, Persian, Syriac, and several modern European languages, and was also fluent in Turkish and Arabic. The research he conducted was considered a key to understanding Mesopotamian archaeology.

In 1811, Rich was dispatched to Baghdad to examine the ruins of Babylon. While there, he sketched the site and made a survey of the area. He excavated inscribed bricks and had underground cavities explored. His findings were later published in *Memoir on the Ruins of Babylon* and then expanded and republished as *Second Memoir on Babylon.*

In addition to his momentous work in ancient Babylon, Rich visited multiple sites of ancient Mesopotamia, collected antiquities that were purchased by the British Museum, and eventually became the founder of Mesopotamian antiquarian studies in England.[41] As a renowned scholar of scholars, Claudius James Rich gave his life searching for factual insights to antiquity, and *he wrote convincingly about those who had seen the remains of Noah's Ark.*

TSAR NICHOLAS ROMANOV II
1868 – 1918 AD

Tsar Nicholas II and his family's dynasty, the House of Romanov, began their 300-year rule when Michael Romanov became the first Romanov Tsar in 1613. Throughout its lengthy reign, the House of Romanov had many famous rulers, including Peter the Great, Catherine the Great, and Alexander I, among others.

As a young man, Nicholas married Alexandra, the granddaughter of England's Queen Victoria, and within weeks, his father, Alexander III died. Nicholas II was then coronated as the new Tsar of Russia, and he and his wife produced four daughters — Olga, Tatiana, Maria, and Anastasia — and one son, Alexei, who was next in line to the imperial throne after him. However, Nicholas II would be the last Tsar to rule Russia.[42]

History shows that his period of rulership was plagued by political and social unrest. Indeed, after his unsuccessful handling of the Russo-Japanese War of 1904-05 and the uprisings of Russian workers in 1905 that were filled with widespread accusations of police brutality, many came to view Nicholas II as a weak and indecisive leader. Because of these and many other factors, discontentment began to grow even more among the working classes of Russia.

When a document of abdication was placed before him on March 2, 1917, Nicholas placed his signature upon it.[43] In that surreal moment, 300 years of the Romanov dynasty abruptly came to an end. This act was strangely in sync with the overthrow of monarchies that was occurring all over Europe at that same time. But the overthrow that occurred in Russia would turn out to be the bloodiest of them all. Sixteen months later, on the nights of July 16 and 17 in 1918, the upper royal family and their attending doctor and servants were executed by a firing squad in the basement of a large home in Ekaterinburg (Yekaterinburg), Russia.

During the days preceding those revolutionary times, *Tsar Nicolas II heard reports of the ruins of Noah's Ark in the mountains of Ararat and sent an expedition of 150 men to an area near the Iranian border in the Ararat mountain range to document Noah's Ark on his behalf.*

THE SILK ROAD
CIRCA 130 BC – 1450 AD

The Silk Road seems to have officially opened during the Chinese Han dynasty, and it remained operational until the Ottoman dynasty cut off trade with the West. This ancient trade-route system played a leading role in linking the Middle East and Asia with the Western world, serving as a major conduit for Chinese merchants to export silk and other precious goods to Western buyers in the Roman Empire and afterward in the kingdoms of Europe.

Historians tell us the Silk Road began in northcentral China near Xi'an (modern Shaanxi province) and ran along the renowned Great Wall of China, across the Pamirs, through Afghanistan, and into the Levant (Syria, Jordan, Israel, Sinai Peninsula, and northeast Africa) and Anatolia, which includes Asia Minor and the Turkish/Armenian regions. Altogether, the length of the Silk Road was about 4,000 miles.

What's interesting is that as the Silk Road made its way east, it ran right along the top ridge of what today is the border of Iran. This same mountain ridge road is located only a few thousand feet above the Durupinar site where Noah's Ark is located on the slope of Mount Cudi in eastern Turkiye.[44] For centuries, as travelers journeyed on this ancient road in the lower mountains of Ararat, they would frequently detour from the road to go down the mountain to see the Ark because it was so accessible. To remember their visit, they would chip off small wooden pieces from the vessel as a souvenir. This practice is widely noted by the trustworthy, ancient voices previously mentioned.

The Ark came to rest on Mount Cudi, which is in the lower mountains of Ararat. The ship-shaped formation encased in the earth has been studied extensively for years, leading many to conclude that it is indeed the remains of Noah's Ark.

HISTORY AND ARCHAEOLOGY CORROBORATE SCRIPTURE

Isn't it remarkable that there are so many records of trustworthy voices from over 2,000 years of history that declare the existence of Noah's Ark on the lower mountains of Ararat? Amazingly, all these historical testimonies agree that "…the ark rested…upon the mountains of Ararat," just as it says in Genesis 8:4.

In the coming chapters, we will examine present-day Mount Ararat, and see numerous reasons the Ark could never have landed there. Clearly, it came to rest — and appears to still be resting — on Mount Cudi, which is in the *lower* mountains of Ararat. The ship-shaped formation encased in the earth has been studied extensively for years, leading many to conclude that it is indeed the remains of Noah's Ark. As we have seen, GPR and ERT scans verify its length of approximately 515 feet and that the interior of the structure has multiple rooms and three distinct levels — all which exactly fit the description we read in Scripture.

The remains of the Ark testify that the Bible is true and that it can be trusted. They also support that the events of Genesis 6 really did occur — including the intermingling of fallen angels and earthly women who produced giants.

The biblical account is real — not a fantasy or a myth. The pre-Flood world was filled with violence and corruption. God sent the Flood to cleanse the earth and give Noah and his family the assignment to start life all over again.

In the next chapter, we will see what the Bible specifically says about the construction of Noah's Ark.

QUESTIONS TO PONDER

1. In Genesis 6:13-18, God outlined a "plan of salvation" for Noah and his family. Noah accepted, trusted in, and obeyed God's word, and Noah and his family were saved. According to Romans 10:9 and 10, what is God's plan of salvation for you, your family, and all of mankind? (*Also consider* John 3:16-18.) Have you accepted and are you trusting in God's only way of salvation (*see* John 14:6)? Are you sharing this plan with others?

2. How important and valuable is it to keep yourself pure and uncontaminated from the things of this world? Look at how God specifically answers this question in James 1:27; Second Timothy 2:20-22; First John 5:21; Matthew 5:8; Psalm 15:1-5 and 24:3,4. What is the Holy Spirit revealing to you in these passages?

3. Because Noah walked with God and kept himself from all the perversion taking place, God alerted him of the coming destruction. What does God promise again and again in the following passages that He will do for you if you walk closely with Him and reverently seek His presence? Read Amos 3:7; Psalm 25:14; First Corinthians 2:9,10; and John 16:13-15.

4. Noah was different from other people on the earth. In fact, the Bible says he was "perfect in his generations" (*see* Genesis 6:9). What did you understand this statement to mean prior to this lesson? How has its actual meaning changed your perspective of Noah and of God's purpose in bringing the Flood?

5. Did you know that in addition to Scripture, there are many trusted historical sources that verify the story of Noah, the Ark, and the worldwide Flood? How is your faith impacted after seeing so many people document the existence of the Ark over the course of millennia?

This artistic rendering is designed to illustrate the enormous dimensions of the Ark. If the Ark described in the Bible were proven to have been found, it would need to meet these exact specifications: 300 cubits long, 50 cubits wide, and 30 cubits high. Some argue the idea of a worldwide flood is a fabricated story, but in virtually every culture and civilization around the world, there are accounts of a global, cataclysmic flood and a ship that saved a chosen family from that flood, which devastatingly covered the face of the earth.

CHAPTER TEN

WHAT DOES THE BIBLE TELL US ABOUT NOAH'S ARK?

In virtually every civilization of the world, there are documented stories of a global flood. Of all the Flood accounts, the best source is the Bible, which tells us how God gave Noah very precise dimensions for the Ark and told him to construct it to have three stories and multiple rooms. Additionally, Noah and his family were to gather food for themselves and for the selection of animals that God Himself would bring to them.

Regarding the specifications of the Ark, God told Noah in Genesis 6:14-16:

Make thee an ark of gopher wood; rooms shalt thou make in the ark, and shalt pitch it within and without with pitch. And this is the fashion which thou shalt make it of: The length of the ark shall be three hundred cubits, the breadth of it fifty cubits, and the height of it thirty cubits. A window shalt thou make to the ark, and in a cubit shalt thou finish it above; and the door of the ark shalt thou set in the side thereof; with lower, second, and third stories shalt thou make it.

These dimensions are so specific that if the Ark described in the Bible were proven to have been found, it would need to meet these exact specifications. That is, it would have to be 300 cubits long, 50 cubits wide, and 30 cubits high.

In the last chapter, we discovered the writings of many notable ancients who either wrote about their personal visits to the site of Noah's Ark or about the experiences of others they knew who had visited the Ark. These written testimonies are significant, as they verify that the ruins found in the lower mountains of Ararat match the biblical dimensions. Equally important, the remains of the Ark testify that the Bible is true and that it can be trusted. They also confirm that the events of Genesis 6 really did happen.

Indeed, the world before the Flood was different from the world we're living in today — yet our current society is becoming oddly similar to that pre-Flood period. In the days of Noah, fallen angels, giants, and *perhaps* monsters roamed the earth, causing great bloodshed and violence on a scale the world hadn't previously known. This violence included giants killing other giants and murdering human beings — and, even worse, the giants resorted to cannibalism and were eating each other as well as eating human flesh and drinking blood.

It was because of such violence and corruption that God sent the Flood to cleanse the earth and give Noah and his family the assignment to start life all over again.

Again, this biblical account is *real* — it is not a fantasy or a myth.

Flood Legends Abound Around the World

Some argue that the idea of a worldwide flood is a fabricated story. But the fact is, in virtually every culture and civilization of the world, there are accounts of a global flood that brought cataclysmic destruction to the earth. One scholar has estimated that there are nearly 270 stories of the Flood from around the world,[1] and all of them share a varying degree of common elements with the biblical account.

The following is an alphabetized listing of just a few places in the world where a combined nearly 270 variants of the story of Noah's Ark have been found:[2]

- *Africa*
- *Ancient Greece*
- *Australia*
- *Baltic nations of Estonia, Latvia, Lithuania*
- *The lands of the Bakshir people*
- *China*
- *Egypt*
- *Hawaii*
- *India*
- *Indonesia*
- *Iran*
- *Ireland*
- *Japan*
- *Korea*
- *Malaysia*
- *Mesoamerica, including the lands of the Aztecs and Incas*
- *Mesopotamia, including Iraq and Syria*
- *Nordic countries of Norway, Sweden, Finland, and Iceland*
- *North America*
- *Philippines*
- *Polynesia*
- *Siberia*
- *South America*
- *Taiwan*
- *Thailand*
- *Areas of the United Kingdom*
- *Vietnam*
- *The lands of Welsh-speaking people*

It is important to note that even though there is resistance to the idea of a worldwide flood, there are many modern-day, secular scientists and historians who state unabashedly that the majority of ancient cultures have stories of a global flood. Consider, for example, these quotes from prominent contributors who spoke at *The Seventh International Mount Ararat and Noah's Ark Symposium* in October 2023:

Dr. Faruk Kaya, Vice Rector Professor of Agri Ibrahim Cecen University, has recently said:

Legends, myths, and narratives about the Flood event, which holds a place in the common memory of humanity, can be found even in the most isolated societies worldwide. The Flood event, although with differences in content, has been ingrained in many cultures, except for certain regions in Africa and Asia, alongside the three major Abrahamic religions: Judaism, Christianity, and Islam.[3]

Dr. Randall W. Younker, Professor of Archaeology and History of Antiquity at Andrews University, recently noted:

Whatever one's personal beliefs, the fact remains that many peoples throughout the centuries — even the millennia — have believed in such a story. They believe there was some sort of Great Flood and that humans — and animals — were saved by a boat, an ark. It is a story of judgment, a story of mercy and salvation, a story of new beginnings, a story of hope for the future.[4]

Dr. Mehmet Teyfur, Professor of Agri Ibrahim Cecen University, also stated:

One of the strongest proofs of the global flood that wiped out all people on earth except Noah and his family is the ubiquity of flood legends in the folklore of human groups from around the world. All the stories told are very similar to each other. Local geography and cultural elements may be present, but they all seem to tell the same story. The strongest evidence for these common messages is religious sources. The only reliable way to understand common, similar flood legends is to recognize that all people alive today, even if they are geographically, linguistically, and culturally separated, are descendants of a few real people who survived a real global flood in a real boat.[5]

Findings like these from *The Seventh International Mount Ararat and Noah's Ark Symposium* are so important and relevant that we will refer to this and similar gatherings of intellectuals throughout the coming chapters. For now, realize that the Great Deluge was a real event, which is why similar stories exist in cultures around the world. Those who deny that it occurred are actually fulfilling Bible prophecy. As Peter said, "They *deliberately* forget that God…used the water to destroy the ancient world with a mighty flood" (2 Peter 3:5,6 *NLT*). With all the mounting evidence available to confirm its existence, it must be assumed that those who don't believe in the reality of the Flood and the Ark Noah built simply don't *want* to believe.

This illustration depicts the story of a king that is taken from *The Epic of Gilgamesh*. This body of work is preserved in an ancient text that is older than the Bible and tells of a storm with torrential rains that produced a flood so immense that it flattened the lands. It further reports that when the waters eventually receded, the survivors on a ship exited, made a sacrificial offering, and began to repopulate the world.

THE EPIC OF GILGAMESH

Of all the well-known, extrabiblical accounts of Noah's Ark and the Flood, there is one that is very important, and it is known as *The Epic of Gilgamesh*.[6] This early Babylonian version of the Flood story was originally found on cuneiform tablets in the ancient ruins of Nineveh, which was at one time the capital of the Assyrian empire. The cuneiform tablets that make up the *Epic of Gilgamesh* were discovered in the excavated ancient library of King Ashurbanipal in Nineveh (668-627 BC), and the tablets date to approximately 750 BC.[7]

The fact that there is a list of other kings that was found in the fragments of other tablets in the same excavations confirms that there really was a King of Uruk named Gilgamesh who lived in approximately 2600 BC.[8] Equally important to note is that in recent times when the waters of the Euphrates River became significantly diminished, the tomb of Gilgamesh appeared from where it laid below the Euphrates, again verifying that Gilgamesh was a real figure in ancient history.[9]

The Epic of Gilgamesh is said to have been written about 2,500 years before Christ and is referred to in numerous works of antiquity, which confirms that the tale is *very* ancient. Although no perfectly intact set of cuneiform tablets of *The Epic of Gilgamesh* has been found, modern-day scholars have enough pieces of it to compile a narrative. Here's how the writer of *The Epic of Gilgamesh* began:

> **I will proclaim to the world the deeds of Gilgamesh. This was the man to whom all things were known; this was the king who knew the countries of the world. He was wise, he saw mysteries and knew secret things, he brought us a tale of the days before the flood. He went on a long journey, was weary, worn-out with labour, returning he rested, he engraved on a stone the whole story.**[10]

This particular tablet that contains the story of the Flood tells of a man who built an ark for the saving of his family and animals.[11] It relates the story of a great deluge that covered the earth and of a huge ship with multiple decks that was constructed to keep a sampling of human and animal species alive.

Remember, this was written by someone with likely *no* knowledge of the Genesis narrative penned in about 1500 BC, which many believe occurred nearly 1,000 years after the writing of *The Epic of Gilgamesh*. Although there are some differences in the presentation of the Gilgamesh story that do not concur with the biblical event, there are also striking similarities.

According to the ancient Gilgamesh text, a god (or gods) spoke to the builder of the ark and said:

Into the midst of it thy grain, thy furniture, and thy goods, thy wealth, thy woman servants, thy female slaves...the animals of the field all, I will gather and I will send to thee, and they shall be enclosed in thy door.[12]

Pictured here is a fragment of *The Epic of Gilgamesh*, which is believed to have been written about 2,500 years before Christ and is referred to in numerous works of antiquity. Although no perfectly intact set of cuneiform tablets of *The Epic of Gilgamesh* has been found, modern-day scholars have enough pieces of it to compile a narrative that matches the biblical account on an impressive number of points. (*See* page 234 for a list of those common details.)

FLOOD STORY SIMILARITIES BETWEEN THE BIBLE AND *THE EPIC OF GILGAMESH*

This ancient narrative written by Gilgamesh reports that a storm with torrential rains arrived and produced a flood so immense that it "flattened the lands." *The Epic of Gilgamesh* also describes in some detail how the waters eventually receded, and all the survivors on the great ship exited and made a sacrificial offering.

Although Gilgamesh's retelling of events contains some variances compared to the biblical narrative, it is interesting to see how this vivid account of the Flood from *outside* of Scripture has so many similarities to the biblical account.

The following is a compilation of 19 items that show the parallels between the Genesis account and the account contained in *The Epic of Gilgamesh*.[13] Are these 19 items and events mere coincidences, or are they a corroboration of the Genesis account?

- Because of mankind's great wickedness, God (or "the gods" in the Gilgamesh story) decided to annihilate humanity.

- A good man was directed by God (or "the gods") to build a seafaring vessel to save himself, a small group of others, and a sampling of animals.

- Carpenters and certain others worked on the project.

- The ship had several decks that were segregated into various compartments. It also had one door and at least one window.

- Very large quantities of bitumen (pitch) were used in building the ship.

- The builder brought his relatives and "all the beasts and animals of the field" on board.

- The builder's God (or "the gods" according to Gilgamesh) determined when the Flood was to begin, and He (or "the gods") sealed the door of the boat once everyone was inside.

- The increasing waters overwhelmed the people outside the ship.

- The waters and winds were so fierce that they flattened the face of the land.

- The flood lasted a number of days.

- Eventually, the storm ceased, the waters calmed, and the flood stopped.

- The builder opened a window of the vessel.

- The ship ultimately lodged on top of a mountain.

- The builder sent out a dove and later a swallow that both flew away but came back to him.

- He also sent out a raven that did not return.

- Once the waters began to abate, the builder began releasing animals in various directions.

- After leaving the ship, he sacrificed sheep and offered incense to his God (or "the gods" according to Gilgamesh) at a mountain altar.

- God (or "the gods") smelled the sweet odor of the sacrificial animals and was pleased.

- The ship's builder received a blessing from God (or "the gods" according to Gilgamesh).

This is only one of approximately 270 various flood stories from around the world. What would be the odds of varying cultures around the world, with virtually no contact with each other, all relating at least the same basic components of a common story if it did not have some basis in a real-life event?

SIMILARITIES AMONG ALL THE FLOOD STORIES

Let's take a few moments to look at the various accounts of the Flood from around the world and see how similar they are to the biblical narrative. By identifying 12 major elements from the Genesis account and measuring it with the other versions from around the world, we can determine how similar other flood stories are to what the Bible tells us about Noah's Ark and the Flood.

The following graph depicts the 12 major biblical elements of the Genesis account of the Flood and Noah's Ark compared to the percentages of similarities with other stories from around the world of a great flood.[14]

	10%	20%	30%	40%	50%	60%	70%	80%	90%	100%
There was a catastrophic flood									95% of the stories	
The flood was global									95% of the stories	
There was a favored family								88% of the stories		
Survival was due to a ship							70% of the stories			
Animals were also saved						67% of the stories				
The family was forewarned						66% of the stories				
The flood was due to wickedness					60% of the stories					
Survivors landed in a mountainous region					57% of the stories					
Birds were sent out			35% of the stories							
Survivors offered a sacrifice	13% of the stories									
Eight people were saved	9% of the stories									
A rainbow was mentioned	7% of the stories									

This illustration shows Noah's family loading the Ark with the animals. We have seen that Noah was from a prophetic family who walked with God and was informed about a coming judgment. Noah was "perfect in his generations," which means his genes were uncontaminated — a sharp contrast to the rest of society, which had become completely decadent and defiled.

Here we see that from the hundreds of flood legends from around the world, nearly *90 percent* of them agree that there was a flood, that the flood was global, and that there was a favored family saved from the worldwide devastation. Of all the versions of the Flood, nearly *70 percent* of them agree that a favored family was forewarned of the coming disaster, their survival was due to a ship, and the ship also contained animals.

There could not be such a voluminous number of flood stories from nearly every nook and cranny of the world if there had never been an actual flood. But how did the account of the Flood make its way to the nations of the world? The answer leads us to the Tower of Babel.

We know that after Noah, his wife, and his sons and their wives exited the Ark, they began to scatter and repopulate the earth. Noah had three sons: Shem, Ham, and Japheth, who all boarded the ship with their wives, along with Noah and his wife. The Bible documents that Ham had Cush, Mizraim (Egypt), Phut, and Canaan — and Cush was the father of a man named Nimrod. That makes Nimrod, whose name means *rebellion*, Noah's great-grandson. It is Nimrod who began to build the Tower of Babel (*see* Genesis 10:1-10; 11:1-4). His defiance and deeds were so nefarious that to put an end to his scheme, God confused everyone's language and scattered the people further across the earth.

Keep in mind that these same people who were scattered were very familiar with the bare bones of the story of the Flood as well as Noah and the Ark. As they traveled across the earth, they carried this knowledge with them everywhere they went.

Over time, some elements were added, and some were taken away — but the basic components of the story remained the same. Nevertheless, of all the accounts of the Flood and Noah's Ark, the most accurate account is the narrative found in the Bible.

OF ALL THE PEOPLE OF THE EARTH, ONLY NOAH AND HIS FAMILY WERE GENETICALLY PURE

So far, we have seen that the reason God sent the Flood was rampant evil brought into the earth by the activity of mutinous angels who abandoned their God-assigned posts and began to sexually comingle with the daughters of men. The outcome of their illicit union was the Nephilim — a hybrid race of giants that brought great violence and corruption into the world.

How did God react when He saw the wickedness of man growing increasingly worse? Genesis 6:5-9 tells us:

And God saw that the wickedness of man was great in the earth, and that every imagination of the thoughts of his heart was only evil continually. And it repented the Lord that he had made man on the earth, and it grieved him at his heart.

And the Lord said, I will destroy man whom I have created from the face of the earth; both man, and beast, and the creeping thing, and the fowls of the air; for it repenteth me that I have made them.

But Noah found grace in the eyes of the Lord. These are the generations of Noah: Noah was a just man and perfect in his generations, and Noah walked with God.

Remember, Noah was from a prophetic family that walked with God and had been informed about a coming judgment. We saw that the word "perfect" is from a word that carries the idea of something that is *whole, undefiled,* and *without blemish.* It is the same word used throughout the Old Testament to describe the condition of the sacrifices that were offered in the Tabernacle and Temple of God. The fact that Noah was "perfect in his generations" means his genes were uncontaminated.

His life was in sharp contrast to the rest of society, which had become completely depraved and defiled. Genesis 6:11 and 12 tells us:

The earth also was corrupt before God, and the earth was filled with violence. And God looked upon the earth, and, behold, it was corrupt; for all flesh had corrupted his way upon the earth.

Seeing that the condition of the world was getting worse and no one was turning back to God with a heart of repentance, God said to Noah:

...The end of all flesh is come before me; for the earth is filled with violence through them; and, behold, I will destroy them with the earth.
— Genesis 6:13

Although God had patiently given ample time for the humans on the earth to repent and return to Him, only Noah and his family ultimately remained pure and unblemished in their generation. The time clock counting down the 120 years of God's patience was coming to an end. Very soon He would set in motion His plan to cleanse the earth of all pervasive evil and launch His rescue mission to save Noah, his family, and a sampling of the animals.

God Revealed the Ark's 'Blueprint' to Noah and Told Him What To Take on Board

At this point, God revealed His divine plan to Noah regarding the construction of the Ark.

Make thee an ark of gopher wood; rooms shalt thou make in the ark, and shalt pitch it within and without with pitch.
— Genesis 6:14

What was so special about "gopher wood"? Certain facets of the Ark's construction — the exact materials used and specific details concerning the workmanship — are unknown even today. But the following might help you better comprehend the magnitude of detail God communicated to Noah to ensure that His Ark of Safety would be built precisely, to specification, and would effectively preserve the last remaining eight humans on Earth so that His purposes could be fulfilled.

> The term "gopher wood" has been a mystery for some time. In the Hebrew language, the letters equivalent to G and K are so similar that inexperienced Hebrew "scholars," such as those translating the *King James Version* of the Bible, were likely prone to erroneously insert a G instead of a K in some places. Such an error would have resulted in the words in Genesis 6:14 being transcribed as GOPHER wood instead of KOPHER wood. If that is the case, "gopher wood" is a misreading and scribal error.
>
> The term "kopher" is the Hebrew word for *pitch* or *bitumen*. Hence, "kopher wood" describes any wood that is covered with pitch or bitumen. Based on Scripture, as well as on the samples found at the Durupinar site in 1987, it seems likely that Noah used an advanced process to fabricate laminated wood and then covered that wood with kopher (pitch or bitumen), just as God instructed. This made the wood especially water repellant and watertight and served to preserve the vessel for many centuries.[15]

Once God specified the building material, Genesis 6:15-20 tells us He continued His instructions to Noah, saying:

> And this is the fashion which thou shalt make it of: The length of the ark shall be three hundred cubits, the breadth of it fifty cubits, and the height of it thirty cubits. A window shalt thou make to the ark, and in a cubit shalt thou finish it above; and the door of the ark shalt thou set in the side thereof; with lower, second, and third stories shalt thou make it.
>
> And, behold, I, even I, do bring a flood of waters upon the earth, to destroy all flesh, wherein is the breath of life, from under heaven; and every thing that is in the earth shall die. But with thee will I establish my covenant; and thou shalt come into the ark, thou, and thy sons, and thy wife, and thy sons' wives with thee.
>
> And of every living thing of all flesh, two of every sort shalt thou bring into the ark, to keep them alive with thee; they shall be male and female. Of fowls after their kind, and of cattle after their kind, of every creeping thing of the earth after his kind, two of every sort shall come unto thee, to keep them alive.

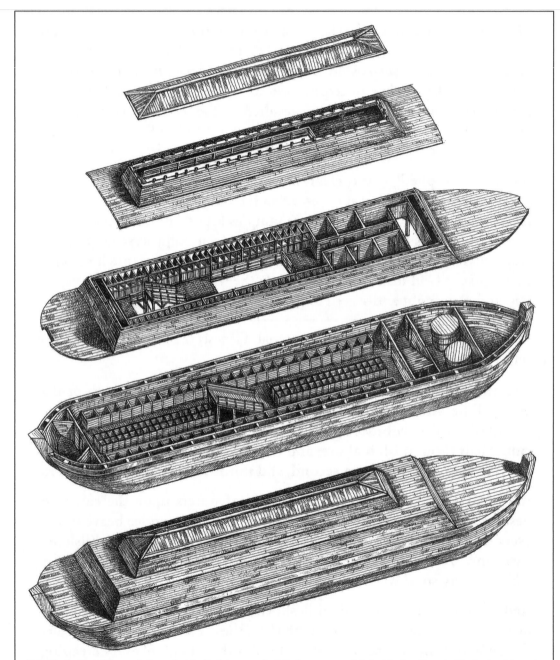

This illustration shows what we find in Scripture — that God gave very detailed instructions to Noah about how to build the Ark, which was 300 cubits long by 50 cubits wide by 30 cubits high with three levels and a single door and a single window.

Notice God told Noah that animals of every kind "shall come unto thee" (v. 20). This strongly indicates that Noah and his family did not have to go on an expedition to find the animals they were to bring onboard the ship. Instead, it appears God Himself selected the animals to be brought onto the Ark by placing an instinctual "tug" in each of them to come to Noah from across the earth. Only God knew which animals had not been contaminated at that time, so He Himself brought the pure animals to Noah. Noah's assignment was to preserve them on the Ark so that after the Flood, they could reproduce in the new world and replenish it.

Of course, Noah, his family, and the animals would need to eat, so in Genesis 6:21, God said:

And take thou unto thee of all food that is eaten, and thou shalt gather it to thee; and it shall be for food for thee, and for them.

Just as wise people prepare for an approaching hurricane or a severe winter storm, Noah and his family stockpiled the necessary rations of food for themselves and the animals, and they gathered enough to sustain themselves for what would be just over a year of confinement on the Ark. Imagine the effort and the faith that was needed to carry out such a task. However, just as he'd done concerning everything else God had instructed him to do, Noah obeyed God completely.

Thus did Noah; according to all that God commanded him, so did he.
— Genesis 6:22

CALCULATING THE ARK'S SIZE AND CONSTRUCTION

Looking once more at Genesis 6:15, we see that God told Noah to make the Ark 300 cubits long by 50 cubits wide by 30 cubits high. This raises the question: *What was the length of a cubit?* Did Noah use the Egyptian cubit, Hebrew cubit, or another cubit measurement from the Mesopotamian world?

Remember, it was likely Moses who penned the narrative of the Ark's construction, and Moses had been reared by his adoptive mother in the Egyptian Pharoah's household, which meant he had been schooled in Egypt's finest institutions.[16] Thus, being familiar with the Egyptian cubit,[17] Moses likely used the Egyptian cubit in Genesis 6:15, which was approximately 20.6 inches by modern-day measurements.

If we use this measurement equivalent to calculate the God-given dimensions for the Ark, we can estimate the measurements for the Ark to be as follows:

THE LENGTH OF THE ARK
The length of the Ark was to be 300 cubits.
Multiply 300 by 20.6 inches, and it comes to 6,180 inches
or approximately 515 feet long.

THE WIDTH OF THE ARK
The width of the Ark was to be 50 cubits.
Multiply 50 by 20.6 inches, and it comes to 1,030 inches
or approximately 85 feet wide.

THE HEIGHT OF THE ARK
The height of the Ark was to be 30 cubits.
Multiply 30 by 20.6 inches, and it comes to 618 inches
or approximately 50 feet high.

THE TOTAL SIZE OF THE ARK
This means the Ark was to be approximately 515 feet long
by 85 feet wide by 50 feet high.

THE INTERIOR OF THE ARK
Genesis 6:14 and 16 says God instructed Noah to make "rooms" inside
the Ark and that the structure was to consist of "lower, second,
and third stories."

The rooms in the Ark served as compartments for the animals as well as living quarters for Noah and his family. They were also used to store all the food provisions for everyone on board. The purpose in talking about these specifications and calculating the Ark's dimensions is because if the ruins of Noah's Ark were to be found in our time, they would need to meet these biblical stipulations. Any structure found that doesn't match these dimensions simply could not be the genuine Ark.

This photo shows the ship-shaped formation of the Ark as it rests on the lower slopes of Mount Cudi in the Ararat mountain range today. ERT and GPR scans show the levels and compartments of the formation's interior, which as yet lies beneath the earth's surface.

EVIDENCE CONFIRMS MOUNT CUDI IS THE LANDING PLACE OF THE ARK

In the lower mountains of Ararat on the slope of a mountain called Cudi, there really is a massive, ship-shaped formation embedded in the earth that exactly matches the biblical dimensions God provided to Noah in the Genesis account.

As we have noted in previous chapters, ground-penetrating radar (GPR) and multiple electrical-resistivity tomography (ERT) scans conducted over the past few decades have convinced several geologists to conclude that this object is *not* a natural geologic formation, but a manmade object encased in a mudflow.[18]

At *The Seventh International Symposium on Mount Ararat and Noah's Ark*[19] conducted in Agri, Turkiye, in October 2023, many notable archaeologists, geologists, researchers, and other scientists attended and were invited to give insights on the region as well as share views of the ship-shaped formation on Mount Cudi. A short time after the symposium, articles released in newspapers around the world stated that

The Seventh International Symposium on Mount Ararat and Noah's Ark was conducted in Agri, Turkiye, in October 2023.

the boat-like structure and other artifacts from this location on the slope of Mount Cudi date to the time of Noah's Ark (well over 4,000 years ago).[20]

Interestingly, just as the blueprint God gave to Noah was 515 feet long and had multiple rooms and three stories, the compiled research shows that the massive ship-shaped object on Mount Cudi is precisely 515 feet long, contains multiple rooms or compartments, and has three distinct stories.

Although many have suggested that the Ark's shape was something like a large rectangular box, that is likely an inaccurate assumption. The ship-shaped formation on the slopes of Mount Cudi precisely fits the specifications of ancient ships built in antiquity, having a very sharp bow on the front and a rounded stern in back. In fact, everything about this massive, manmade object matches what would be true of any ship from the ancient past.

THE PRESENCE OF DROGUE STONES POINTS TO EVEN MORE PROOF OF THE ARK'S EXISTENCE

In addition to the ruins of the ship resting on the slopes of Mount Cudi, researchers have found approximately 26 massive drogue stones[21] scattered across the valley situated just beneath where the Ark landed.

A drogue stone is a huge rock with a round hole carved through the top part so that a rope could be placed through the opening, and it could then be suspended from the side of a ship. Drogue stones were similar to ancient anchors, and such stones were hung from the sides of a ship to balance it in bad weather. These stones trailed behind seafaring vessels on a long line and served to slow a ship down in a storm, keeping it from propelling down the slope of a wave and crashing into the next one. Thus, they prevented the ship from capsizing.[22]

Researchers have found 26 massive drogue stones scattered across the valley that is situated just beneath where the Ark landed. A drogue stone is a huge rock with a round hole carved out of its top so that a rope could be placed through the opening, and it could then be suspended from the side of a ship to balance it in bad weather.

History reveals that drogue stones were a feature of nearly all ancient ships and were so prevalently used in the ancient maritime world that they have been found at various locations along the Nile River and in the Mediterranean Sea.[23]

Interestingly, all surviving ancient examples of drogue stones are identical to the ones located in the plain below the Ark location in the Ararat mountain range. The only exception is that the drogue stones from Noah's Ark are gargantuan, and the reason they are so enormous is, those giant stones needed to be proportionate to the giant size of the Ark.

Logically speaking, there is no reason for 26 massive drogue stones to be anywhere near eastern Turkiye in the Ararat mountain range — that is, *unless* a massive ship at some point sailed through that area. Bear in mind that there are no bodies of water anywhere nearby.

The Mediterranean Sea is approximately 1,300 miles away.

The Black Sea is approximately 600 miles away.

The Caspian Sea is approximately 500 miles away.

Despite the fact that there are no nearby bodies of water, and it seems impossible that a ship has ever sailed through the region, the fact remains that there are at least 26 massive drogue stones present on the plain. Clearly, Noah's Ark experienced the fiercest kinds of weather conditions. Therefore, this enormous vessel required a great number

A drogue stone is a huge rock with a round hole carved out of its top so that a rope could be placed through the opening, and it could then be suspended from the side of a ship to balance it in bad weather.

Imagine the support that would be necessary to brace a massive vessel like the Ark amidst the catastrophic destruction God brought upon the earth. It is evident that no detail was omitted in God's plan of escape for Noah and his family.

of drogue stones that were abnormally large in order to stabilize it through months of stormy weather "at sea."

Toward the end of its voyage as the waters grew calmer and began to recede, the Ark no longer needed the extra weight of the drogue stones that hung from the sides of the ship. At that point, it is likely Noah and his sons began to cut the ropes on which the stones

This illustration depicts a compilation of several of the massive drogue stones in the valley below the resting place of the Ark. Since early Christian times, crosses have been carved into these massive stones — some bearing eight crosses in memory of Noah and his family of eight people who survived the Flood.

had been strung, leaving a trail of stones in the present-day valley below the Ark's ruins. Today if you were to follow this trail of stones, you could fairly well determine the path of the Ark as it sailed up into the lower mountains of Ararat and finally landed on the top of what is called Mount Cudi.

The reason drogue stones exist in this region is because there really was a Great Flood and an Ark, and God caused the floodwaters to carry the Ark into this area. Those stones were once attached to the sides of the Ark to keep it stable in the roughest waters in the history of the world at the time. Noah obeyed everything God told him to do, and as a result, he and his family were not destroyed by the Flood. They literally floated on the waters of destruction until the Ark came to rest in the lower mountains of Ararat.

After thousands of years and many earthquakes and mudslides, the location of the Ark has changed. Having been carried by and subsequently encased in a mudflow, the Ark presently rests about 900 feet lower in elevation than its original landing place, which is a few thousand feet below the ancient Silk Road.

As we noted in the last chapter, the renowned Silk Road[24] ran along the top of the ridge that borders present-day Turkiye and Iran. This road was so heavily traveled that the ruins of the Ark became common knowledge, causing many travelers to detour from the path to get a personal view of the Ark's remains. Ancient writers confirmed this fact and further stated that it was customary for people to chip off small pieces of bitumen (or the hardened exterior tar) from the ship to make amulets as souvenirs.

One of the routes in the Silk Road network of roads ran along a ridge at the top of Mount Cudi, which is now the location of the border that separates Turkiye and Iran. In ancient times, this road was so heavily traveled that the ruins of the Ark became common knowledge, causing many travelers to detour from the path to get a personal view.

Today the Ark's ruins can be found at the Durupinar site, which

Near the Durupinar site, where the ship-shaped formation rests, is a massive marine fossil field that is covered with seashells, sand dollars, and fossilized starfish — all evidence that a "sea" once covered the area.

by the way is also a massive, marine fossil field[25] that is covered with fossilized seashells, sand dollars, and fossilized star fish — all evidence that a "sea" once covered the area. Altogether, the ruins of the Ark itself, the presence of massive drogue stones, and the millions of marine fossils are all evidence of a global flood.

Scripture reveals so much about Noah's Ark — its exact dimensions, much of the materials used in construction, the ship's content as it began its critical voyage, and even its *purpose*. But nearly equally telling concerning the reality of this massive ship are the archaeological remains left beneath the earth's surface in the mountains of Ararat, where God explicitly stated the Ark landed (*see* Genesis 8:4).

The core philosophy of archaeology is the quest to understand human past by what workers in this field discover in our present. But the quest is not without price, as what can be found of "human past" is not usually lying in plain eyesight or arm's reach. When I read of the modern discoveries surrounding the Ark in the Ararat mountain range — *and I have seen most of these items of discovery, including the marine fossils, myself!* — I am reminded of another Old Testament verse of Scripture: "It is God's privilege to conceal things and the king's privilege to discover them" (Proverbs 25:2 *NLT*).

On the other end of our searching out a matter, what a thrill it is to discover some magnificent witness of the hand of God on the affairs of man and of His great love toward His human creation. Concerning the very apparent remains of a massive ship at the Durupinar site, I acknowledge this privilege of discovery with the profoundest gratitude. In the next chapter, we will dive deeper into what both the Bible and history tell us about the Ark's landing place.

QUESTIONS TO PONDER

1. Were you aware God told Noah that the animals would come to him (*see* Genesis 6:20)? What does this say to you about the animals and God's connection with them? How do you imagine the animals interacted with Noah and his family on the Ark?

2. Had you ever thought about Noah needing to take food onto the Ark for him, his family, and the animals (*see* Genesis 6:21)? How does this fact — and the fact that there were multiple rooms and three stories in the Ark — reshape the way you envision the time spent on the Ark by Noah and his family?

3. Did you know that there are stories of the Flood in virtually every civilization and culture around the world? What does the fact that all these stories exist say to you about the Flood? What does it say about the Bible? Why do you think people in the secular world — which includes our public schools and universities — rarely talk about the existence of these Flood stories?

4. In the pre-Flood world, there were many unthinkable activities taking place. For example, angelic beings from other dimensions were coming to earth and sexually comingling with women, who were then giving birth to a hybrid offspring of giants — who allegedly sexually violated the animals, thereby producing a myriad of monstrous hybrid creatures. Can you see any similarities between these pre-Flood activities and things taking place in the world today? If so, what are they?

5. Of all the information you learned in this chapter, what is most interesting or astonishing to you? Was it the use of the Egyptian cubit, the size of the Ark, the presence of drogue stones near the ruins, or something else?

6. What are you seeking God about that has been "concealed" where you're concerned, but you believe God wants you to discover it? Look up Jeremiah 33:3 and write out what you're imagining God to show you that has been hidden from your understanding but that you believe will soon come to light.

Pictured here (left to right) are William, Paul, Rick, and Joel Renner standing on top of the ruins of Noah's Ark with Greater Ararat behind in the distance. Many expeditions have been carried out in search of Noah's Ark — and one hypothesis after another has been purported about where the Ark actually landed. Although some believe it lies on the upper slopes of Mount Ararat, it is now known that it lies 18 miles south on the slopes of Mount Cudi in the lower part of the Ararat mountain range.

CHAPTER ELEVEN

WHERE IS THE LOCATION OF NOAH'S ARK?

O ver the years, many expeditions have been carried out by individuals in search of Noah's Ark. There have even been movies filmed and documentaries made with people purporting one hypothesis after another about where the Ark actually landed. Although their claims have never been proven, some have testified that they have personally seen the Ark on Mount Ararat. Others have speculated that the Ark was broken into two parts, perhaps due to an earthquake or the movement of a glacier, and that now these massive fragments lie high up on the slopes of Mount Ararat trapped beneath the ice.[1]

The truth is, those who claim to have seen the Ark on the peak of Ararat have never been able to identify its location or to take others to see it. Although some of these so-called sightings featured in various media have generated a lot of interest, they have been proven to be fraudulent.[2]

As we noted in Chapter 1, due to contemporary climate change, the ice and snow on the peak of Mount Ararat is virtually gone in the summer months — yet even with the absence of snow and ice, no satellite imagery has produced a single solid bit of evidence of Noah's Ark. Even with the surge of mountain climbers in recent years who have journeyed to Mount Ararat to ascend its peaks from every imaginable angle during the summer, no one has come forward to claim and verify that they have encountered the remains of Noah's Ark.

Does the Bible specifically say what happened to the Ark and *where* it landed? Is there tangible evidence today showing where Noah and his family disembarked and settled in the new world? Just how devastating was the Flood?

This illustration depicts Noah and his sons constructing the Ark. According to the Bible, Noah was about 500 years old when he began to build the Ark, and he and his family worked continually on this massive construction project for 100 years.

NOAH WAS AN ARK-BUILDER AND PREACHER OF RIGHTEOUSNESS FOR 100 YEARS BEFORE THE FLOOD

To retrace the biblical facts of Noah's story, we begin in Genesis 5:32, which informs us that Noah was 500 years old when he began having children, and he became the father of Shem, Ham, and Japheth. It is believed that at this same age of 500, Noah began to build the Ark (*see* Genesis 6:10-14). For about 100 years, he worked on this massive construction project, and according to Second Peter 2:5, it was during this time that Noah became an active "preacher of righteousness." This means for 100 years, he preached to all who would listen, pleading with them to repent and escape the coming judgment.

Remarkably, even with the unprecedented level of evil operating in the world, God gave humanity 120 years to repent and turn back to Him (*see* Genesis 6:3). Nevertheless, even though God is never in a rush to judge, nor is He willing that any perish, eventually His longsuffering has a stopping point. According to His own words of warning, this is what happened concerning the people of the pre-Flood world. When the clock counting down God's patience ran out of time and the Ark was completed, "…The Lord said unto Noah, Come thou and all thy house into the ark; for thee have I seen righteous before me in this generation" (Genesis 7:1).

It is interesting to note that God spoke to Noah and prompted him and his family to get on board the Ark *seven days* before the Flood event actually began. God said, "For yet seven days, and I will cause it to rain upon the earth forty days and forty nights; and every living substance that I have made will I destroy from off the face of the earth" (Genesis 7:4). Again, just as Noah obeyed God's instructions to build the Ark, "…Noah did according unto all that the Lord commanded him" (Genesis 7:5).

THERE WAS ONLY ONE WAY INTO THE ARK

When God instructed Noah to build the Ark, He said, "…The door of the ark shalt thou set in the side thereof…" (Genesis 6:16). Notice it was not door*s*, plural. It was "the door," singular. Thus, there was only *one way* into the Ark, and it was through the single door God designed as the entrance. The Bible states that once Noah, his family, and all the animals were inside, God Himself supernaturally shut the door (*see* Genesis 7:16), sealing Noah and his family and the animals safely inside.

This is a powerful picture of what happens to us when we repent of our sin and confess that Jesus is our Lord and Savior (*see* Romans 10:9,10). In that instant, we are placed in Christ, and "…if any man be in Christ, he is a new creature: old things are passed away; behold, all things are become new" (2 Corinthians 5:17). There is no safer place than being in Christ! He is our Ark of Refuge where we are protected and carried through the storms of life.

There was only one door into the Ark, and the Bible states that once Noah, his family, and the animals were inside, God Himself supernaturally shut the door, sealing Noah and his family and the animals safely inside. Just as Noah's Ark had only one door to enter, Jesus is the only Door to enter into salvation — and anyone sealed inside Christ is provided protection from the destruction that swirls all around us in the world.

And just as Noah's Ark had only one door to enter, Jesus is the only Door to enter and be made right with God. In John 14:6, He declared, "...I am *the* way, *the* truth, and *the* life: no man cometh unto the Father, but by me." As hard as this statement may seem to some, Jesus is not *a* way — He is *the only way* to be saved and made right with the Father.

Noah's Ark brought salvation to all who entered it, exemplifying the saving work Christ accomplished through His death, burial, and resurrection (*see* 1 Peter 3:18-22). Just as God used a wooden boat to rescue all who entered it in the ancient world, He is using a wooden cross to save all who put their faith in Christ today. In Noah's day, only those who entered the Ark were saved. Today, only those who enter into Christ through faith are saved.

Likewise, in the same way God shut the door and sealed Noah and his family safely inside the Ark once they passed through the door, when a person enters into Christ, the Spirit of God seals him safely inside the Person of Jesus. Anyone sealed inside Christ is provided protection from the destruction in the world that swirls all around us, just like the Ark of old did for Noah and his family.

Thus, when a person is in Christ, even if a flood of trouble seems to rise around him, he can be kept safe and sound. That believer has the supernatural ability to float even on waters of destruction! Amazingly, the same waters that destroyed the rest of the earth caused Noah and his family to rise higher and higher and sail above it all.

THE DAY NOAH ENTERED THE ARK

The Bible reveals several specific details regarding the day Noah and his family entered the Ark. First, it makes a general statement, saying:

And Noah was six hundred years old when the flood of waters was upon the earth.

— Genesis 7:6

Then it gives us some particulars regarding what took place the day Noah boarded the ship.

And Noah went in, and his sons, and his wife, and his sons' wives with him, into the ark, because of the waters of the flood.

Of clean beasts, and of beasts that are not clean, and of fowls, and of every thing that creepeth upon the earth, there went in two and two unto Noah into the ark, the male and the female, as God had commanded Noah.

And it came to pass after seven days, that the waters of the flood were upon the earth.

— Genesis 7:7-10

Here we see that Noah was 600 years old when he entered the Ark, which means his three sons that boarded the Ark were at least 100 years old. Along with these four men, their four wives also entered. We're also told that the animals boarded the Ark on the same day as Noah, coming in two by two — the male animals and their female counterparts. And Genesis 7:10 confirms the words God spoke in Genesis 6:7. Seven days after everyone was on board, God brought the Flood. And verse 11 says there was a great breaking up of the deep and an opening of the heavens.

In the six hundredth year of Noah's life, in the second month, the seventeenth day of the month, the same day were all the fountains of the great deep broken up, and the windows of heaven were opened.

— Genesis 7:11

FALLEN ANGELS, GIANTS, MONSTERS, AND THE WORLD BEFORE THE FLOOD

Dr. Henry Morris, respected lecturer and author of scientific and biblical textbooks, noted the following concerning this very different weather pattern on the earth and its long-term effects.

The Noahic flood marked a great discontinuity, both in the course of human history and in the normal operation of natural processes that God had established supernaturally in the beginning. The rates of most geological processes (such as erosion, sedimentation, tectonism, and volcanism) were vastly accelerated during the year of the flood. God finally allowed the flood to run its course, after which all these rates gradually slowed, though much 'residual catastrophism' persists even to the present day.[3]

THE 'FOUNTAINS OF THE GREAT DEEP' WERE BROKEN UP

While many talk about the rain that poured through the "windows of Heaven" — which we will examine in a few moments — we must understand that the floodwaters also came from below. Indeed, there have been many serious discussions about what the Bible means when it states that "the fountains of the deep were broken up." One source has noted:

> On the day the flood began, there was a "breaking up" of the fountains, which implies a release of the water, possibly through large fissures in the ground or in the sea floor. The waters that had been held back burst forth with catastrophic consequences.
>
> There are many volcanic rocks interspersed between the fossil layers in the rock record — layers that were obviously deposited during Noah's flood. So it is quite plausible that these fountains of the great deep involved a series of volcanic eruptions with prodigious amounts of water bursting up through the ground. It is interesting that up to 70 percent or more of what comes out of volcanoes today is water, often in the form of steam.[4]

256

This same source further states that there is a catastrophic plate-tectonics model for the Flood, which suggests that when the Flood began, the ocean floor rapidly rose up to 6,500 feet as a result of a sudden increase in temperature as horizontal movement of the tectonic plates accelerated. This abrupt change would have spilled the seawater onto the land and caused massive flooding. This, very possibly, is what is meant by the "fountains of the great deep" being "broken up."[5]

Just imagine what occurred when vast reservoirs of water stored beneath the earth's crust suddenly began breaking through the surface at random places everywhere. To help us grasp what is meant by the "the fountains of the great deep" being broken up, another researcher commented:

> It is sometimes assumed that these fountains, or springs, were hydrothermal vents, similar to those which occur in the middle of modern oceans where crustal plates are moving apart and a new sea-floor is being generated. Such vents are known from quite early in the geological record....
>
> It seems best to conclude that the earth was flooded through the outbreak of subterranean waters.... The Flood did not come upon the land progressively, moving inwards from the coasts and upwards from the valleys, but everywhere at the same time. Nor did it merely cover the land; it burst through it. There was no possibility of men and animals at higher elevations escaping to the mountains. The land was broken up, almost instantaneously submerged, and as the initial violence subsided, replaced by new land.[6]

Regarding the earth's crust and the totality of the Flood's destruction, this same source states:

> So far as the land was concerned, the Flood was not only universal in its extent but total in its destructiveness. The high mountains of the pre-Flood land were broken down, not merely covered. If this exegesis is correct, we shall find no buried, undestroyed remains of the previous earth, such as coastlines, valley and mountain topography, roads and buildings, no geological boundary representing the surface of the old, covered by sediments of the new. The earth which then existed exists no longer (*see* 2 Peter 2:6)....

[And] **if the entire crust of the pre-Flood earth was destroyed, so, inevitably, was everything that lived on it. The destruction was so violent that even insects and birds could not escape. Whatever visited the earth's crust when the fountains of the deep broke open made survival just as impossible for creatures that flew in the face of the firmament as it did for creatures that crept on the ground. The earth was destroyed and every animal moving on the face of the ground totally obliterated.[7]**

In one moment, it appears that as the Flood commenced, hydro-geysers began bursting through the ground everywhere, and the force of these random, all-encompassing explosions of water meant there was no escaping the Great Deluge. That is what the Bible documents in Genesis 7:21-23 and Second Peter 2:5.

This Gustave Doré illustration depicts the Ark floating in the background as the Flood destroys the entire civilization. The depths of the deep were broken up and giant hydro-geysers violently erupted upward to thrust volumes of water all at once into every part of the earth.

THE FLOOD WAS A GLOBAL, CATACLYSMIC EVENT

Second Peter 2:5 says, "And [God] spared not the old world, but saved Noah the eighth person, a preacher of righteousness, bringing in the flood upon the world of the ungodly."

The word "old" in "old world" is translated from the term from which we get the word "archaic." It denotes what is *original, ancient,* or *old in terms of time and age.* The word "world" is translated from a word that describes *the ordered world, a civilization, culture,* or *society.* When these words are combined to form the phrase "old world," it is a depiction of *an entire ancient civilization that is no longer existent,* and we know, in this case of the days of

258

Peter wrote that the entire civilization that previously existed was entirely wiped out by the Flood, which was a terrific deluge of water coming down and over the face of the entire earth. It was not a regional flood, as some argue, but a worldwide flood with waves so mighty that they covered the entire face of the earth until it was completely washed over. The depths of the deep were broken up, and giant hydro-geysers violently erupted to thrust volumes of water all at once into every part of the earth. There would be no escaping this violent overthrow of the sin that degraded the earth.

Noah, its extermination was due to the Great Flood at the time of Noah, a flood that engulfed the entire ancient world and completely destroyed it.

Thus, Peter informs us that the entire civilization that previously existed was entirely wiped out by a cataclysmic flood. God's justice is so steadfast that when the world of Noah's day persisted in their egregious, sinful behavior and refused to repent, God judged that entire ancient civilization. In fact, He judged it so entirely that He wiped it out — leaving only a handful of Noah's family surviving.

In Second Peter 2:5, Peter went on to write about God "bringing in" the flood upon the world of the ungodly. These words "bringing in" are interpreted from a Greek word that denotes *the letting loose of wild and vicious dogs to literally rip a victim to pieces, limb from limb.* By using this word, Peter illustrates what the Flood did to the ancient civilization that existed in the antediluvian days. Namely, the Flood was like ferociously wild dogs that literally tore the old world to pieces until nothing remained of it. This explains why so few skeletal remains, if any, have been found intact from that earlier age.

This brings us to the word "flood" in Second Peter 2:5, which is translated from the Greek word *kataklusmos*, a compound of the preposition *kata* and the word *kludon*. The preposition *kata* means *down,* and the word *kludon* means *to wash,* as *a wave washes over land.* As Peter used it in this verse, the word *kataklusmos* depicts *a complete deluge of water coming down and over the face of the entire earth.* Hence, this was not a regional flood, as some argue, but a worldwide flood. The word *kataklusmos* emphatically pictures *waves so mighty that they covered the entire face of the earth* until it was *completely washed over.* God's judgment of that earlier civilization meant not a single remnant of it would survive or remain in place.

The Greek word *kataklusmos* is where we derive the English word "cataclysmic," and certainly the word "cataclysmic" is fitting to describe what happened when the depths of the deep were broken up and giant hydro-geysers violently erupted to thrust volumes of water all at once into every part of the earth.

'THE WINDOWS OF HEAVEN WERE OPENED'

In addition to the foundations of the deep being broken up and releasing unimaginable, explosive destruction, the Bible also states that "...the windows of heaven were opened" (Genesis 7:11), and they also contributed to the floodwaters that came upon the earth.

I want to note that Genesis 7:11 is the very first mention of the "windows of Heaven" in Scripture. This is very important because, in interpreting Scripture, there is a principle called *the law of first mention.* The first time a particular word, phrase, or concept is mentioned in the Bible, it sets a precedence for its meaning.

In this case, we see that when the "windows of Heaven" were opened in the days of the Flood, the result was a superabundance of rain that began pouring and pouring through. In fact, so much rain fell through these windows over the course of 40 days and nights that "...the waters prevailed exceedingly upon the earth; and all the high hills, that were under the whole heaven, were covered" (Genesis 7:19).

Thus, the "windows of Heaven" are like a spiritual portal, and every time they are opened, something comes pouring through in superabundance. Again, this is the precedent that is set in Genesis 7:11: The windows of Heaven opened, and a superabundance of rain poured through them, covering the earth completely with water.

Illustrated here is the supernatural appearance of manna. Rabbinical sources assert that manna fell in such abundance from the "windows of Heaven" each day that it spread over more than 2,000 square cubits, with a depth of 50 to 60 cubits. If this was the case, one day's supply of manna was so abundant, it would have been enough to feed the children of Israel for 2,000 years.

By studying biblical references to the "windows of Heaven," we can find out what always happens when they are opened. The windows — or "doors" — of Heaven appears in Genesis 7:11, Psalm 78:23, and Malachi 3:10. Every time these windows (or doors) of Heaven open, miraculous things happen, and some type of superabundance comes pouring through.

MANNA POURED THROUGH THE WINDOWS OF HEAVEN
FOR THE CHILDREN OF ISRAEL

The significance of the windows of Heaven becomes even clearer when we recall how manna poured through them for the children of Israel. Approximately two months after the Israelites left Egypt, their food provisions began to run low, and supplies were rationed. As their stomachs ached for food, they dreamed of the meals they had left behind in Egypt and began to complain and murmur amongst themselves. In their dissatisfaction, they even accused Moses of leading them into the wilderness to kill the entire assembly with hunger (*see* Exodus 16:3).

Although God had delivered the children of Israel from Egyptian bondage, they demonstrated ingratitude and a lack of faith. Yet despite their thankless attitude, God came through for them once again and told Moses, "...Behold, I will rain bread from heaven for you..." (Exodus 16:4).

Theologian John Gill wrote that the manna that rained down was so plentiful that it came as thick as a shower of rain.[8] Thus, God not only provided manna through the windows of Heaven — He *amply* provided it. Psalm 78:23-25 records that God "...opened the doors of heaven, and had rained down manna upon them to eat..." (vv. 23,24). The rest of that passage says, "....Man did eat angels' food..." (v. 25).

The psalmist tells us two important truths about this supernatural provision:

> • The doors (windows) of Heaven were opened (v. 23).
>
> • When the doors (windows) were opened, manna *rained down* upon them (v. 24).

First, the psalmist informs us that when the manna fell, the "doors of Heaven" were opened. This phrase "doors of Heaven" refers to the "windows of Heaven" — a heavenly portal that opens at God's command. *Second*, the psalmist records that when this manna began falling, it "rained down." This shows that when Heaven's portal opens, whatever comes through it does so *in superabundant measures*.

Rabbinical literature asserts that manna fell in such abundance each day that it spread over more than 2,000 square cubits (one cubit being approximately 18 to 20 inches), with a depth of 50 to 60 cubits. If this was the case, then one day's supply of manna would have been enough to feed the children of Israel for 2,000 years!

Although it is impossible to know exactly how much manna came pouring through that heavenly portal during those 40 years, we can make a rough estimate. If the Israelites numbered approximately 3,000,000 people at the time of the Exodus, as many Bible scholars believe, it is estimated that they would have needed *4,500 tons* of manna every day. If they gathered 4,500 tons a day every day for 40 years, that means an estimated *65,700,000 tons* of manna supernaturally appeared on the ground over that period of time.

If your city woke up tomorrow to find 4,500 tons of beautiful, freshly-baked, nourishing manna lying on the ground all over the city — free to anyone who wanted to go out, pick it up, and take it home — it would be a worldwide sensation. Scientists would fly in from around the world to study it; journalists would write about it; and every major news program would cover the story. However, for the children of Israel, the miracle of the manna was an everyday event that occurred for 40 years — that's how long the windows of Heaven remained open over them! An entire generation of young children was born during that time period, and they grew up thinking it was *normal* for 4,500 tons of manna to appear each morning out of thin air (*see* Exodus 16:35)!

BLESSINGS WILL POUR THROUGH THE WINDOWS OF HEAVEN FOR THOSE WHO OBEY GOD IN GIVING

A third example of the windows of Heaven is found in Malachi 3:10. Here, God promises to those who bring "all the tithes into His house" that He will "...open you the windows of heaven, and pour you out a blessing, that there shall not be room enough to receive it."

So just as the windows of Heaven were opened and rain kept pouring and pouring in Noah's day — and just as the windows of Heaven were opened in the wilderness and manna kept pouring and pouring to feed God's people — when you obey God by sowing your finances, your financial giving becomes a key that opens the windows of Heaven, and blessings will keep pouring and pouring into your life through that heavenly portal until you will not have room enough to receive them!

In summary, we have three biblical accounts for the windows of Heaven being opened.

1. *First*, the windows of Heaven opened and poured out superabundant rain that covered the earth during the time of the Flood.

2. *Second*, that heavenly portal opened for a span of 40 years, and tons of manna poured through in superabundance, providing nourishment for God's people.

3. *Third*, God promises to open the windows of Heaven to pour out immeasurable blessings on all those who willingly give Him their tithe.

Again, the precedent-setting example of the windows of Heaven is first found in Genesis 7:11. When these windows are opened, superabundance is going to pour out, as it did in the days of Noah.

For 150 days — or approximately 5 months — the floodwaters continued to be great, mighty, powerful, and strong all over the face of the earth, dominating and destroying everything in their path.

THE FLOODWATERS DOMINATED AND DEVOURED EVERYTHING ON EARTH

The combined effects of the "fountains of the deep" breaking up and the torrential rain pouring down nonstop through the windows of Heaven resulted in cataclysmic destruction that filled the entire earth.

Regarding the rain, the Bible says, "And the rain was upon the earth forty days and forty nights" (Genesis 7:12). To give a bit of perspective, according to the World Meteorological Organization, the French island territory of Réunion in the Indian Ocean holds the record for the greatest amount of rainfall in a 24-hour period. The town of Foc-Foc received 71.8 inches of rain (1,825 millimeters or nearly 6 feet) on January 7-8, 1966, during the passage of tropical cyclone Denise.[9] Imagine that amount of rain many times over falling *everywhere on the earth* for 40 days nonstop. Add to that the explosive eruption of water geysers ripping through the earth's crust — and you have a global Flood with indescribable ramifications.

THE FLOODWATERS PREVAILED OVER THE EARTH, BUT NOT OVER THE ARK

In Genesis 7:17-20, God gives us these additional details concerning the Flood.

And the flood was forty days upon the earth; and THE WATERS INCREASED, and bare up the ark, and it was lift up above the earth. And THE WATERS PREVAILED AND WERE INCREASED GREATLY upon the earth; and the ark went upon the face of the waters. And THE WATERS PREVAILED EXCEEDINGLY upon the earth; and all the high hills, that were under the whole heaven, were covered.

Fifteen cubits upward DID THE WATERS PREVAIL; and the mountains were covered.

There are several key facts in these verses. First, we see that the waters of the Flood continued to *increase* more and more. With each passing day, the waters rose higher and higher, devouring and dominating everything in their path. Verse 17 could even indicate that after the first 40 days of the Flood, the water on the earth had reached the level needed to finally float the massive Ark.

Also notice the word "prevailed" (or "prevail"), which appears three times in three verses. Over and over, the Scripture says the waters *prevailed*, and the word "prevailed" in the original text carries the idea of being *great, mighty, powerful*, or *strong*. It is a picture of the floodwaters forcefully dominating the earth and subjugating everything therein *except* the Ark containing Noah, his family, and selected animals. In other words, *not one living creature outside the Ark* was able to resist or withstand the indomitable force of the Great Deluge that God sent as His judgment upon the earth.

Genesis 7:19 informs us that the waters were so strong, they rose until "...all the high hills under the whole heaven were covered." The fact that the Bible says *all* the high hills were covered with water clearly indicates that the Flood was *global*, and not local or regional, as some people allege. Indeed, Scripture states that the mountains were covered with 15 cubits of water. If we use the Egyptian cubit (approximately 20.6 inches), we calculate that the highest mountains were covered with more than 25 feet of water.

How much damage can water do? To give some perspective, let's look to a few of the many documented events of catastrophic rapid erosion, which are simply mindboggling. For example, the "Little Grand Canyon" of the Toutle River in Washington State

This is a photo of the "Little Grand Canyon" in Washington State that was cut by a mudflow originating in a single day from the crater of Mount St. Helens. The catastrophic and abrasive action of the water formed a new canyon system several miles long and about 140 feet deep. Imagine the effect of water gushing and coursing nonstop for the duration of the Flood and how it catastrophically reshaped the earth.

was cut by a mudflow that originated from the crater of Mount St. Helens. In one single day — March 19, 1982 — the catastrophic and abrasive action of water cut through pumice and rockslide deposits, forming a new canyon system several miles long and about 140 feet deep.[10] "Little Grand Canyon" is estimated to be about *one-fortieth* the size of the renowned Grand Canyon in Arizona.

Other examples of catastrophic flooding include the formation of Engineer's Canyon near Mount St. Helens, Washington, and the creation of the Channeled Scablands in the eastern half of Washington State. While a single-day mudflow cut a 100-foot-deep gorge to create Engineer's Canyon, the Scablands were formed by a glacial ice dam that burst, releasing a volume of water equal to Lakes Eerie and Ontario combined. In a matter of weeks, water rapidly cut through hard, basaltic bedrock, cavitating the terrain and creating a new delta more than 200 square miles in size.[11]

These are real, observable events that took place, not just textbook theories. And where Noah's Flood is concerned, rather than choosing the Bible *or* science, we have the Bible *and* science working together to confirm the intensity and far-reaching effects of that worldwide flood.

Just imagine what resulted from the explosive power of water bursting through the crust of the earth and pouring from the skies across the entire planet. This immeasurable amount of water gushing and coursing nonstop throughout the duration of the Flood catastrophically reshaped the earth, much as we see it today.

WHAT EXACTLY DID THE FLOOD DESTROY?

If anyone has ever had a doubt about whether anything or anyone survived the Flood, the following verses quickly put that question to rest. Take a moment and count how many times the words "all" and "every" appear in this passage. These words appear six times collectively, and this emphatically means that absolutely every organism and every entity with breath in its lungs was destroyed by the Flood.

And ALL flesh died that moved upon the earth, both of fowl, and of cattle, and of beast, and of EVERY creeping thing that creepeth upon the earth, and EVERY man: ALL in whose nostrils was the breath of life, of ALL that was in the dry land, died.

This illustration shows the Flood covering the face of the earth. For 150 days the floodwaters continued to be great, mighty, and overpowering over all the face of the earth, dominating and destroying everything in its path.

And EVERY living substance was destroyed which was upon the face of the ground, both man, and cattle, and the creeping things, and the fowl of the heaven; and they were destroyed from the earth: and Noah only remained alive, and they that were with him in the ark.

And the waters prevailed upon the earth an hundred and fifty days.
— Genesis 7:21-24

In verse 24, we are informed that the waters *prevailed* on the earth for 150 days. For a fourth time the word "prevailed" is included in Genesis 7. In the original text this word means *great, mighty, powerful*, or *strong*. This means that for 150 days — or approximately 5 months — the floodwaters continued to be great, mighty, powerful, and strong all over the face of the earth, dominating and destroying everything beneath it.

Realize that this was not just an ordinary rainstorm that lasted 40 days and nights. This was a catastrophic event in which "all the fountains of the great deep were broken up" in addition to the torrential rain that poured from the heavens (*see* Genesis 7:11). According to Genesis 7:24 and 8:3, the explosive action of all the "fountains" continued and did not stop for 150 days, which means the earth was boiling beneath the floodwaters for about 5 months. This makes it clear why Peter wrote, "…The world that then was, being overflowed with water, perished" (2 Peter 3:6).

God Remembered Noah and Everyone With Him

After the account of the horrific deluge that destroyed all life left on the earth, the story takes a different turn as it focuses on Noah and all who were safely with him inside the Ark.

And God remembered Noah, and every living thing, and all the cattle that was with him in the ark: and God made a wind to pass over the earth, and the waters asswaged;

The fountains also of the deep and the windows of heaven were stopped, and the rain from heaven was restrained; and the waters returned from off the earth continually: and after the end of the hundred and fifty days the waters were abated.

— Genesis 8:1-3

In these three verses, we find that God began the process of reversing the Flood after His judgment had been meted upon the earth. He caused wind to pass over the entire planet, and the blowing wind seems to have set certain weather conditions into motion, initiating the evaporation phase of the water cycle and pushing the water in specific directions as God set in motion restoring the earth and "starting over" with a mere eight undefiled souls.

Genesis 8:1 says the waters "asswaged" (assuaged), which in the original text means they began *to subside, to abate,* or *to decrease.* For Noah and his family, it became a waiting game as the water began to abate. Although they could do absolutely nothing to change their situation, they trusted in God's ability to bring the Great Deluge to an end.

The fact that the waters were going down was a direct result of God turning off the water flow from below the earth and from the heavens above. The Bible says that after 150 days the waters were abated. We are not sure how much time it took for the waters to rise 25 feet above the highest mountains, nor how long it took for the water to be completely turned off and to return to its place from off the earth. The word "asswaged" in Genesis 8:1 simply describes the process of the waters slowly beginning to wane and decrease from the face of the earth.

Where Did Noah's Ark Land?

Where Noah's Ark landed is answered in Genesis 8:4.

...After the end of the hundred and fifty days the waters were abated. And the ark rested in the seventh month, on the seventeenth day of the month, *upon the mountains of Ararat.*

— Genesis 8:3,4

Mount Ararat is a double-peaked mountain consisting of two stratovolcano cones, with the larger peak known as Greater Ararat and the smaller one referred to as Little Ararat. There have been many violent and massive eruptions since the time of the Flood, and if the Ark had landed on the peak of Mount Ararat, it would have either been blown to bits by eruptions or completely covered with lava.

As we have already established, the Bible never says the Ark landed on the peak of Mount Ararat, but that it came to rest in *the mountains* of Ararat.

As I noted in Chapter 1, it is impossible that Noah's Ark would have landed on the peak of modern-day Mount Ararat. In its present form, Mount Ararat is a double-peaked mountain consisting of two stratovolcano cones. The larger peak is known as *Greater Ararat*, and the smaller one is referred to as *Little Ararat*.

As previously stated, there are some who argue that the Ark landed on the peak of Mount Ararat as it exists today. But if that were the case, the Ark would have been destroyed due to numerous massive, violent eruptions since the time of the Flood.[12] In fact, if the Ark had landed on the peak of Mount Ararat, it would have either been blown to bits by eruptions or completely covered with lava. Therefore, the possibility of legitimate Ark sightings would have been nil. Besides the fact that the Ark remains lie on Mount Cudi, this stratovolcano issue is another reason it is futile to look for the Ark — even remnants of the Ark — on Ararat's peak.

Another reason Noah's Ark couldn't have landed on Mount Ararat as we know it today has to do with its *altitude*. Although the peak's height at the time of the Flood would not have been the same height as it is today, it still would have been nearly impossible to safely descend or to scale without special equipment due to the steep terrain. Yet as we learned in Chapter 9, many ancient people wrote of visiting the

The mountains of Ararat encompass a region that in early times was known as the Urartu Kingdom, which has been identified by many as the general vicinity of the Garden of Eden.

ruins of the Ark (in the lower Ararat mountain range). If the Ark had been on the top of modern-day Mount Ararat, as some argue, the ancients would have still needed special equipment to get there — equipment that did not exist during their lifetimes.

The fact that Noah's Ark is not on top of Mount Ararat explains why so many who have searched there have been unsuccessful. *They've been climbing the wrong mountain and looking in the wrong place!*

To be clear, the mountains of Ararat were, and still are, a large *range* of mountains. And in early times, the entire region was known as the *Urartu Kingdom*. Interestingly, the word "Ararat" in the Assyrian language is translated *Urartu*. It was in about 1105 AD that the word "Urartu" evolved into the word Ararat. Equally important, the region of Urartu has been identified by many as the general location of the Garden of Eden.[13]

Wouldn't it be just like God to bring Noah and his family all the way back to Eden, the starting place of humanity? Just as God spoke to Adam and Eve and said, "…Be fruitful, and multiply, and replenish the earth…" (Genesis 1:28), it seems that God brought Noah and his family back to the same place and spoke to them, once again saying, "…Be fruitful, and multiply, and replenish the earth" (Genesis 9:1).

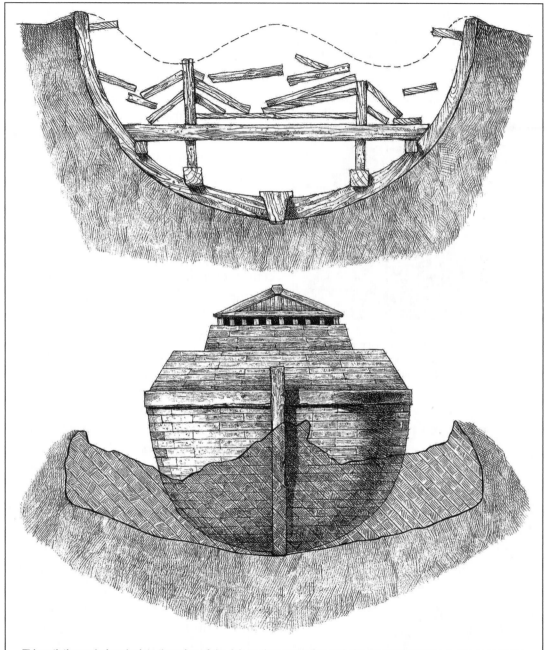

This artistic rendering depicts the ruins of the Ark as they are today and also how the vessel would appear if the sides of the ship were re-placed into their original positions. Scientific studies show that if this could be done, the width would again perfectly match the dimensions provided in the biblical narrative for Noah's Ark.

Above: This photo shows the protruding ribs of the ship-shaped formation at the Durupinar site. Below: This illustration shows what scans have revealed about the structure of Noah's Ark at the Durupinar site.

MOUNT CUDI AND THE CITY OF MESHA

As has been established in previous chapters, on the slope of Mount Cudi lie the mud-encased ruins of Noah's Ark. Over thousands of years, the sides of the ship have fallen outward, but scientific scans and illustrations demonstrate that if these fallen sides were put back into their original positions, even the width of the ship would perfectly match the biblical dimensions of the Ark. Artistic renderings based on ground-penetrating radar and ERT scans show the interior of the ship that includes a central corridor, multiple rooms and compartments, and three distinct levels. And the protruding ridges that appear vertically at regular intervals on the sides of the ship allow one to see the solid ribs of the Ark that have survived to this present time.

As previously noted, there is a lower mountain in the Ararat mountain range known as Mount *Cudi*, which, as I've said, is pronounced *Judi* in Turkish and Arabic and, interestingly, means *the place of the landing*. It is also referred to as Mount Mashu and *Cudi Dagi*, which means *mountain of the Kurds*. Ancient writings identify the upper slope of Cudi as the original resting place of Noah's Ark. This mountain reaches an elevation of approximately 7,000 feet,[14] and in ancient times, a Silk Road route once tracked along the top of the ridge. Today that landmark shares a border with Turkiye and Iran.

This lower mountain in the Ararat mountain range was where Noah's Ark landed, a fact confirmed by the writings of Berossus, a Chaldean priest from the Third Century, who stated that when the Flood ended, the Ark rested there in a place that later came to be called *the place of the landing*. (For a review of what Berossus wrote, please refer to Chapter 9.)

But there's even more to this story.

In Genesis 10, we read the genealogy of Noah's sons *Shem, Ham,* and *Japheth.* Scripture informs us about the first settlement built after the Flood, which was called *Mesha.* Genesis 10:21 indicates Shem was the forefather of all the sons of Eber, and verse 30 suggests they dwelled toward Sephar, a mountain of the East, having come "from Mesha."

> One meaning of the name "Mesha" is *to be drawn from water*, which would be a fitting name for people who had been taken from the raging waters of the Great Deluge. What is interesting is that traditional Kurdish names for the mountain are *Masher Dag* and *Mashur Dag*, which, respectively, mean *Doomsday Mountain* and *Resurrection Mountain*. Other documents state that Shem lived in a place called *Dilmun*, which means *the abode of the dangling (dried up)*.[15] Again, this is also a fitting description for those left high, dry, and safe — *rescued* — on the mountain after the Flood.

The Epic of Gilgamesh states that the Ark came to the "Mountains of Mashu," where the builder of the Ark lived — and that one could see "twin peaks as high as the wall of heaven that guard the rising of the sun." Precisely as described in this writing, there are rocky twin peaks that can be seen from atop the slope of Mount Cudi. Directly below these distinct peaks are ancient ruins that some scholars believe are the ruins of Mesha-Naxuan — the first post-Flood city built by Noah and his family.

Illustrated here is the Ark resting on Mount Cudi with the twin peaks rising above it in the background, just as described in ancient history. A growing number of scholars believe that after the Flood, Noah and his family built a settlement below the twin peaks that are depicted in this illustration. They believe that Noah's family took materials from the Ark to construct certain parts of the settlement. They allegedly used parts of the ship's hull, planks, and beams, which they stripped from the Ark to build roofs, and they melted down bitumen to seal the roofs from rain.

The Epic of Gilgamesh states that Gilgamesh came to the "Mountains of Mashu" where the builder of the Ark had lived. As we have already learned, a part of the slope at the Durupinar site is called Mashur even to this day. Gilgamesh also stated that in Mashur, one could see "twin peaks as high as the wall of heaven that guard the rising of the sun." Today rocky twin peaks can be seen from atop the slope of Mount Cudi, and some allege that the ruins of *Mesha-Naxuan* — purported to be the first post-Flood city built by Noah and his family — lie below the mountain and were said to, in their day, "guard the rising of the sun," exactly as Gilgamesh claimed.

In his *Antiquities of the Jews*, Josephus quotes Moses of Chronensis, an Armenian historian, as saying the city of Mesha-Naxuan was built at "the place of the first descent." This fits well with the archaeological evidence that has been found, and now there is a growing number of scholars who believe Noah and those who survived the Flood descended from the upper slope of Cudi and built a settlement after the Flood. Some also speculate that they used materials from the Ark to construct various aspects of the structures there. This is believed to include parts of the ship's hull as well as planks and beams that were said to be stripped from the Ark to build roofs. Still others claim Noah and the Flood survivors used the melted down bitumen to seal the roofs from rain.[16]

This area today is called *Meshur*, which is a modern derivative of the biblical name *Mesha*. The ancient ruins believed to be Mesha-Naxuan, the first post-Flood city, are found there, and although no one is currently permitted to go there because it's so close to the border of Iran, if one *were* able to climb to the base of those cliffs, he would indeed see the ruins of ancient dwellings.[17] Equally astounding is the presence of ancient gravesites scattered throughout the area.

It is remarkable that there really are twin mountain peaks just as Gilgamesh wrote, and below them the possible location where survivors of the Flood allegedly built the first post-Flood settlement. Most who have direct knowledge of this information don't think it's mere coincidence that the rocky, double-peaked mountain above the ruins of the ship-shaped formation exactly fits the description in the Gilgamesh narrative.

THE MEASUREMENTS OF THE RUINS REVEAL THAT THE ARK WAS LIKE A CLASSIC, ANCIENT SHIP

It should be noted that in the 4,000-plus years since the Flood, the Ark — which came to rest in a mudflow — has slidden approximately 1,200 feet down the side of the mountain from its original resting place. Every spring when rain comes and mud begins to move, the whole mountainside shifts. Scans of this formation show a huge boulder situated inside the ancient remains — perhaps as a result of an earthquake, causing the rock to roll into the ship.

Consequently, because this boulder seems to have permanently secured this ship-shaped formation, the only thing that *doesn't* change on this ever-changing slope is the strange formation positioned firmly in the middle of the mudflow.

Something that is very interesting about these ship-shaped ruins is that they fit the description of a classical ancient ship. Ships in antiquity were referred to in three measurements:

- First, was the *length*, which is a hard number, or an actual measurement, in length.
- *Second*, was the *width*, which always referred to the average width of the ship at its mid-point.
- *Third*, was the *height*, which included the hull and the superstructure.

Remarkably, the dimensions of the ship-shaped formation on Mount Cudi, near what is believed to be the ruins of the ancient city of Mesha, are precisely the measurements of Noah's Ark provided in the Bible. Although greatly deteriorated, the ship formation is still very visible, and the 26 massive drogue stones that have been discovered in the valley below are additional authenticating evidence that this ancient ship formation is the actual ruins of the Ark.

THESE RUINS ARE THE *REAL DEAL*

Today if you were to travel to the lower mountains of Ararat — to the smaller mountain called Cudi — you would discover a boat-shaped object embedded in the earth with dimensions that exactly fit those given to Noah by God in Genesis 6:14-16. As we conclude this chapter, let's quickly review (on page 278) these measurements and specifications God gave to Noah:

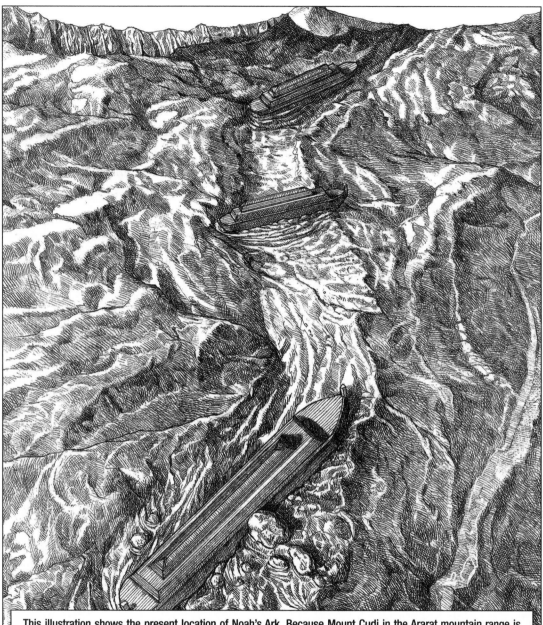

This illustration shows the present location of Noah's Ark. Because Mount Cudi in the Ararat mountain range is prone to heavy rains that produce mudslides, it is estimated that the Ark has slidden a distance of about 1.9 miles over the past 4,000-plus years and currently rests at 6,500 feet above sea level, which is approximately 900 feet lower in elevation than its original location. While the slope's features are constantly changing each spring due to fresh mudflows, the ship-shaped formation buried in the earth remains consistently positioned year after year.

- In Genesis 6:15, we read that God instructed Noah to build the Ark 300 cubits in length. Using the Egyptian cubit (20.6 inches) and multiplying it by 300 would make the Ark approximately **515 feet long**. *The ship-shaped formation in the lower mountains of Ararat is approximately 515 feet in length.*

- In Genesis 6:15, God instructed Noah to build the Ark 50 cubits in width. Using the Egyptian cubit (20.6 inches) and multiplying it by 50 would make the Ark approximately **85 feet wide**. *Although the sides of the ship-shaped formation in the lower mountains of Ararat are now fallen out due to deterioration, the original size has been determined to be approximately 85 feet in width.*

- In Genesis 6:15, God instructed Noah to build the Ark 30 cubits in height. Using the Egyptian cubit (20.6 inches) and multiplying it by 30 would make the Ark approximately **50 feet high**. *The ship-shaped formation in the lower mountains of Ararat is approximately 50 feet in height.*

- In Genesis 6:14, God instructed Noah to make **many rooms** inside the Ark. *GPR and ERT scans show that the ship-shaped formation in the lower mountains of Ararat has multiple rooms.*

- In Genesis 6:16, God instructed Noah to make the Ark with **three stories** inside. *GPR and ERT scans show the ship-shaped formation in the lower mountains of Ararat is comprised of three levels.*

Thus, this nautical-design formation in the lower Ararat mountains of eastern Turkiye has the length of the Ark, the width of the Ark, the height of the Ark, and the rooms and levels of the Ark, *because it is Noah's Ark!*

We touched briefly on the settlement Noah and his family allegedly built in what became known as *Meshur* (Mesha in the Bible) in eastern Turkiye. In the next chapter, we will examine more closely what took place when Noah and his family exited the Ark after the Flood.

QUESTIONS TO PONDER

1. What new fascinating facts did you learn in this lesson about Mount Ararat, the Ararat mountain range, Mount Cudi, and the city of Meshur/Mesha? What aspects thrilled you the most? And what do you think about the possible connection between lower Urartu (the Ark's resting place) and the Garden of Eden?

2. Have you ever heard someone say that the Flood was *local*, not global, and that it only destroyed the region of Mesopotamia? How does Genesis 7:19-24 completely refute this notion, and why did the Flood have to be worldwide to accomplish God's purpose?

3. Did you ever stop to think about the water that burst upward from the ground? When you hear the Bible say, "…All the fountains of the great deep were broken up…" (Genesis 7:11), what kind of scientific phenomenon or event does this seem to indicate? And what type of chain reaction of destruction do you think was likely unleashed?

4. Describe the parallels you can see between Noah's Ark and Jesus as the Savior of every believer in Christ (include any scriptures that come to mind). With Christ Himself represented by the Ark symbolically, what would you say about the fact that entering through one solitary door of the Ark was the only way Noah and his family could be saved?

5. Are you certain that you are safe in the "Ark" of Jesus Christ? Have you accepted His gift of salvation? If not, today is a great day to make things right with God! Just take a moment right now and say, *Father, I ask You to forgive me of all my sins. I believe that Jesus Christ is Lord and that He took the penalty for all the wrong I've done or ever will do. Jesus, come into my life. Wash me clean with Your precious blood. I want to live safely in You. Thank You, Father, for hearing and answering my prayer. In Jesus' name I pray, amen.*

Noah, his family, and a sampling of animals endured the roughest sea weather in the history of the planet as the Ark sailed on the rising and turbulent waters of the Great Flood. Finally, the waters began to abate, Noah and his sons began to cut the ropes that held the drogue stones, and the Ark slowed for landing on what is now known as Mount Cudi in the Ararat mountain range.

CHAPTER TWELVE

THE EXIT FROM NOAH'S ARK

As we have seen again and again throughout these chapters, the record of a worldwide flood — and in many cultures, the existence of an ark — is enshrined in virtually every civilization around the world. In *The Antiquities of the Jews*, noted and highly revered First Century historian Flavius Josephus stated:

Now all the writers of barbarian histories make mention of this flood and of this ark; among whom is Berosus the Chaldean. For when he is describing the circumstances of the flood, he goes on thus: "It is said there is still some part of this ship in Armenia, at the mountain of the Cordyaeans [referring to the Kurds]; and that some people carry off pieces of the bitumen, which they take away, and use chiefly as amulets for the averting of mischiefs."

Josephus went on to add:

> Hieronymus the Egyptian also, who wrote the Phoenician Antiquities, and Mnaseas, and a great many more, make mention of the same. Nay, Nicolaus of Damascus, in his ninety-sixth book, hath a particular relation about them; where he speaks thus: "There is a great mountain in Armenia, over Minyas, called Baris, upon which it is reported that many who fled at the time of the Deluge were saved; and that one who was carried in an ark came on shore upon the top of it; and that the remains of the timber were a great while preserved."[1]

Indeed, Noah's Ark came to rest in the lower mountains of Ararat on a smaller mountain called Mount Cudi, which, as we've seen, is pronounced *Judi* in Turkish and Arabic. Despite the fact that the closest body of water — the Black Sea — is hundreds of miles away, the lower slope of Mount Cudi contains the ruins of an ancient, massive, classical ship that once sailed through the region. The proof of this event

Pictured here is a massive drogue stone — one of at least 26 of them that have been found in the valley below the ruins of Noah's Ark. These anchor-like stones once hung from the sides of that large ship to balance it and keep it from capsizing during the Flood. It seems that as Noah and his sons realized the Ark was coming to a place of landing, they slowly began cutting the ropes of these stones, thus leaving a trail of them in the valley below. If one follows the trail of these drogue stones, he or she can determine the path of the Ark as it sailed into the region and came to rest atop Mount Cudi in the Ararat mountain range.

and the Ark's location is further substantiated by the presence of 26 massive drogue stones in the valley below the ruins.

These anchor-like stones once hung from the sides of that large ship to balance it and keep it from capsizing during the Flood. It seems that as Noah and his sons realized the Ark was coming to a place of landing, they slowly began cutting the ropes that secured these stones, thus leaving a trail of them in the valley below. If one follows the trail of these drogue stones, he or she can determine the path of the Ark as it sailed into the region and came to rest atop Mount Cudi in the Ararat mountain range.

The Bible says that when the Flood was over, and the ground was dry:

...God spake unto Noah, saying, Go forth of the ark, thou, and thy wife, and thy sons, and thy sons' wives with thee.... And Noah went forth, and his sons, and his wife, and his sons' wives with him.
— Genesis 8:15,16,18

Remarkably, after being on the Ark for a little more than a year, Noah and his family and all the animals exited into what would be a new world. The post-Flood planet was a very different place than the pre-Flood version. The power of water and the synergistic effects of volcanism, earthquakes, and other geophysical effects had reshaped the earth in indescribable ways. Yet through it all, Noah responded with a heart of worship to God, and God blessed him and all the surviving creation with supernatural ability to replenish the earth. We will explore all this and more in the pages of this chapter.

It Took a Great Deal of Time for the Floodwaters To Dry Up

As we saw previously, Noah was 600 years old when the floodwaters came on the earth (*see* Genesis 7:6). In fact, Genesis 7:11 tells us precisely, "In the six hundredth year of Noah's life, in the second month, the seventeenth day of the month, the same day were all the fountains of the great deep broken up, and the windows of heaven were opened." Higher and higher the floodwaters rose, increasing upon and dominating the planet for 150 days (*see* Genesis 7:24).

What's interesting is that it took the same amount of time for the floodwaters to decrease as it did for them to increase. The Bible tells us in Genesis 8:2 and 3:

This illustration shows a dove with an olive branch in its mouth. The Bible tells us that Noah opened a window of the Ark to release a raven and then a dove. The raven never came back, the dove flew out and returned twice, the second time with an olive branch in its beak, which alerted Noah that the floodwaters were abating and there was vegetation that was beginning to bloom with new life. Seven days later, Noah sent the dove out a third time, and it never returned.

The fountains also of the deep and the windows of heaven were stopped, and the rain from heaven was restrained;

And the waters returned from off the earth continually: and after the end of the hundred and fifty days the waters were abated.

In the book of Job, which is understood to be the oldest book of the Bible, God identifies Himself as the One "… who shut in the sea with doors, when it burst forth and issued from the womb" and who fixed its limit saying, "…This far you may come, but no farther, and here your proud waves must stop!" (Job 38:8,11 *NKJV*).

What happened after God turned off the waters from above and below? The floodwaters continued to decrease, and in the tenth month, the tops of the mountains could be seen (*see* Genesis 8:5). Noah waited 40 more days and then opened the window of the Ark and released a raven and then a dove. Although the raven never came back, the dove flew out and returned twice, the second time with an olive branch in its beak (*see* Genesis 8:6-11). This alerted Noah that the floodwaters had abated and there was vegetation that was beginning to bloom with new life. Seven days later, Noah sent the dove out a third time, and it never returned.

For the first time in many months, Noah and his family saw a glimpse of the world after the Flood. The ground was finally visible, but it still needed more time to be completely dried. Therefore, Noah and his family remained inside the Ark for another period of time before it was finally time for them to disembark from the ship.

And it came to pass in the six hundredth and first year, in the first month, the first day of the month, the waters were dried up from off the earth: and Noah removed the covering of the ark, and looked, and, behold, the face of the ground was dry. And in the second month, on the seven and twentieth day of the month, was the earth dried.

— Genesis 8:13,14

It is not known if the entire earth was completely dried at that point or if the land was only navigable on foot where the favored family landed. Whatever the case, the water-soaked land took quite a bit of time to dry. In the meantime, Noah and his wife and his sons and their wives were all schooled in patience by the Lord Himself.

This illustration shows Noah and the animals as they entered the Ark at God's command. Noah and his family didn't go into or exit the Ark one day earlier or one day later than God had instructed, demonstrating their strict obedience to every one of God's commands.

GOD TOLD NOAH EXACTLY WHEN TO ENTER AND EXIT THE ARK

In Genesis 7:1, we find the *beginning* of the Flood and the point at which Noah and his family were instructed by God to enter the Ark.

And the Lord said unto Noah, Come thou and all thy house into the ark; for thee have I seen righteous before me in this generation.

Seven days later, the windows of Heaven were opened, pouring forth torrential rains, and the fountains of the deep were broken up, activating explosive hydro-geysers across the earth. The combined effects of these two reservoirs releasing massive quantities of water ultimately destroyed every living creature on the face of the earth, including those that flew in the skies above.

Remarkably, just as God had informed Noah and his family precisely when to *enter* the Ark, He also told them when to make their *exit*. This is recorded in Genesis 8:15-17:

And God spake unto Noah, saying, Go forth of the ark, thou, and thy wife, and thy sons, and thy sons' wives with thee. Bring forth with thee every living thing that is with thee, of all flesh, both of fowl, and of cattle, and of every creeping thing that creepeth upon the earth; that they may breed abundantly in the earth, and be fruitful, and multiply upon the earth.

Note that Noah and his family didn't go into or exit the Ark one day earlier or one day later than God had instructed. This tells us that Noah was careful to move only with divine direction. Likewise, it's imperative that we learn to stay put until we receive a prompting from the Lord to make a move. Many times, people get into trouble because they move prematurely and get ahead of God, or they wait and move too late and miss His divine opportunity. That is why we need to learn to be still and listen for the voice of the Holy Spirit — going when He says to go and staying when He says to stay.

The Post-Flood World Was Nothing Like the Pre-Flood World

Notice the words "bring forth" in God's command to Noah as they exited the Ark: "Bring forth with thee every living thing that is with thee…" (Genesis 8:17). In the original Hebrew text, these words carry the idea of *ordering the animals out, by force if necessary*. This implies that a number of the animals may have been wary of leaving the Ark. The fact is, they had been cooped up on that ship for a year and may have been quite shaken by the experience.

Even if God did put many of the animals into a state of hibernation during their time on the Ark, as some suggest, those animals had been through quite an ordeal. Imagine trying to sail through the biggest waves, heaviest rains, and loudest thunder in human history. More than likely, the animals could sense they were entering a different world than they had known before. It was for that reason that Noah had to forcibly "bring forth" at least some of them from the Ark.

And Noah went forth, and his sons, and his wife, and his sons' wives with him: Every beast, every creeping thing, and every fowl, and whatsoever creepeth upon the earth, after their kinds, went forth out of the ark.
— Genesis 8:18,19

When the door of the Ark opened and everyone walked out for the first time, the new world they saw before them was very different from the one they previously knew. Again, the earth's surface had been reshaped by the combined catastrophic effects of the windows of Heaven pouring forth torrential, nonstop rain and the explosive release of water from within the earth.

The world that Noah, his family, and all the animals had known had been ripped apart and put back together by the plan and the command of the Lord. According to Peter's words in Second Peter 3:6 (*NKJV*), "…The world that then existed perished, being flooded with water."

 Creationist, apologist, and engineer Henry M. Morris stated that the process of such a cataclysmic event simply cannot be explained by theories of uniformitarianism — although many have tried to consign the worldwide Deluge as a "happenstance of nature."

"The 'present processes' of uniformitarian scientists could never create anything, neither could they ever produce the cataclysmic changes of the flood."
— Dr. Henry Morris[2]
Founder of the Institute for Creation Research

If you examine the scientific evidence at our disposal, you will no doubt conclude that our present world was not shaped just by the gradual, slower-paced rates of erosion, sedimentation, volcanism, and tectonism that we see. It was shaped by super-accelerated catastrophism on a scale no one has ever seen. For example, present-day Mount Everest, which is estimated to be 29,035 feet above sea level, was formed toward the end of, or after, the Flood by the collision of tectonic plates and the related thrusting upward of the land — the same way most mountains were formed. We know this is true concerning Mount Everest because the uppermost sections of

The rock that comprises the uppermost part of the mighty Himalayas is well-bedded with fragments of common marine invertebrate shells, such as trilobites, brachiopods, ostracods, and crinoids.

the mountain are composed of water-deposited layers teeming with countless marine fossils.

Marine fossils — which make up about 95 percent of all fossils[3] — can be found throughout the mighty Himalayas, as well as in the Rocky Mountains and the strata of the Grand Canyon. Sedimentary rocks throughout the canyon are abounding with oceanic fossils such as crinoids, brachiopods, and sponges.[4] In the Santa Cruz Mountains near California, the fossilized remains of a 25-foot whale were unearthed.[5]

The fact that marine fossils are found in the upper layers of mountains around the world is evidence that the rock sediment was once covered with ocean water. These well-preserved fossils could have only been formed by rapid, catastrophic events that

The tsunami event that rocked the world on December 26, 2004, not only caused the death of an estimated quarter of a million people, but there were also thousands of individuals who were never found. The tsunami was generated by an earthquake off the coast of Indonesia that generated massive waves — ranging from 30 to 100 feet in height — which traveled at an upward speed of nearly 500 miles per hour.

destroyed ocean organisms and then quickly buried them. The fossil-laden material would have then been transported and/or uplifted through tectonism and seismic activity.

If you've ever seen the effects of a local flood, you know that inordinate amounts of water are quite devastating to the landscape affected. That water moves houses, vehicles, buildings, and bridges — it uproots trees and alters landscapes. The tsunami event that rocked the world on December 26, 2004, is a powerful demonstration of the force and swiftness with which water and other geophysical forces can eradicate entire communities and every trace of human life. Not only did it cause the death of an estimated quarter of a million people, but there were also tens of thousands of people who were never found. The tsunami was generated by an undersea earthquake that struck off the coast of the Indonesian island of Sumatra. That quake, with a magnitude of 9.1, generated massive waves — ranging from 30

Depicted here are the fountains of the deep that were broken up, activating explosive hydro-geysers across the earth. The combined catastrophic effects of the windows of Heaven thrusting torrential, nonstop rain and the explosive release of water from within the earth totally reshaped the earth's surface. These water-releasing reservoirs ultimately destroyed every living creature on the face of the earth and that flew in the skies above.

to 100 feet in height — which traveled at an upward speed of nearly 500 miles per hour, devastating coastal communities of nearly a dozen countries including India, Sri Lanka, Thailand, Indonesia, and areas of northern Africa and the Maldives.[6]

Since that is true of one tsunami event, try to imagine the devastation that occurred when fountains deep within the earth opened and huge hydro-geysers began to violently blast water upward through the earth's crust and into the atmosphere simultaneously all over the world. Add to that the nonstop torrential rain that fell for 40 days and nights, which the Bible says made the water rise 15 cubits (about 25 feet) above the highest mountains (*see* Genesis 7:20).

Then when the hydro-geysers stopped blasting water into the air and the rain stopped falling from the heavens, strong currents and waves continued to reshape the face of the earth. Finally, when the waters began to subside, as is always the case in a large flood, the receding waters were also devastating as they carried soil, rock, trees, debris, and pre-Flood structures away into the recesses of history, never to be remembered again. It is impossible to overstate the consequences of such a worldwide cataclysmic event.

Second Peter 2:5 says that God "…spared not the old world, but saved Noah the eighth person, a preacher of righteousness, bringing in the flood upon the world of the ungodly." We have seen that the Greek word for "flood" here depicts *a complete deluge of water coming down and over the face of the entire earth*. This Greek word pictures *waves so mighty that they covered the entire face of the earth* until it was *completely washed over*. Thus, we are informed by Scripture that the Flood literally tore the old world to pieces until nothing remained of that ancient civilization.

REGARDLESS OF THE MESS, NOAH CHOSE TO WORSHIP AND GIVE GOD HIS BEST

As the hull of the Ark scraped against the earth and came to land on the peak of the lower mountains of Ararat, there was probably shouting, rejoicing, and weeping among Noah's household because their long journey was finally coming to an end. Think of how grateful Noah and his family must have been toward God. In His mercy, God…

- Warned them of the coming Flood.
- Gave them instructions about how to build the Ark to survive.
- Caused the animals to come to them.
- Kept the Ark from capsizing in the midst of the world's largest waves.
- Stopped the rain and sealed up the fountains of the deep, enabling the ground to dry out.

Still, when Noah and his family disembarked from the Ark, they were confronted with a devastated world. Not only was it strangely different, but there was also no one else on the planet available to help them start over again. As they pondered it all, surely it must have been overwhelming for them to realize the task that was before them. In one moment, they were thankful to have survived the catastrophic event, but in the next, they were jarred to the reality of the challenges of starting life over in a world so completely different than what they'd ever known.

By God's grace, Noah and his family pushed past their myriad of emotions and chose to worship God. They expressed their gratefulness by offering sacrifices, and at the same time, they sought God's help to begin again in their challenging post-Flood environment. The Bible says:

And Noah builded an altar unto the Lord; and took of every clean beast, and of every clean fowl, and offered burnt offerings on the altar.

— Genesis 8:20

Although Noah could have done many other things upon exiting the Ark, this passage states the first thing he did was to offer sacrifices to the Lord. As the leader of his family and head patriarch of the post-Flood world, he, along with his wife and his sons and their wives, worshiped and expressed their heartfelt thanks to God for carrying them through the Flood.

The evidence for Noah's acts of sacrifice is found near the Ark's original landing site on the top of Mount Cudi. There a massive stone still lies, which served as an ancient altar once used by Noah and his family for the sacrifice of animals. The local Kurdish people who live there and who have traced their roots to that area for thousands of years say that from ancient times, that stone has been identified as the place where Noah offered those first sacrifices after the Flood.[7]

A closer look at this massive stone reveals a human-made channel cut

Noah built an altar to the Lord when he, his family, and the animals exited the Ark. In this photograph taken by one of my team, I am sitting atop an ancient stone altar near the landing site of the Ark. The local Kurdish people who have lived on this mountain for thousands of years state that it is the very altar upon which Noah offered his sacrifice to God.

Close examination of this massive sacrificial stone reveals a human-made channel cut right across the top and center of it, which allowed blood from animal sacrifices to flow off its sides. It is entirely possible that this massive stone is the very altar Noah used to offer the first sacrifices after he and his family exited the Ark.

right across the top and center of it, which allowed blood from animal sacrifices to flow off its sides. This stone altar, which is just a few hundred feet from the Ark's original landing place, has been in this same location for thousands of years. It is entirely possible — in fact, it is probable — that this massive stone is the very altar Noah used to offer those first sacrifices after he and his family exited the Ark.

God had been extremely merciful to Noah and his family, and Noah was vitally aware that he and his family were on the receiving end of a great manifestation of the mercy of God. The sacrifices on that altar were Noah's way of thanking God for mercifully saving him and his family from the cataclysmic deluge that destroyed everything living on the earth.

God Was Deeply Touched by Noah's Worship and Made a Covenant With All of Creation

When Noah and his family offered their sacrifices in worship to God, and the smoke of their offering billowed into the air and ascended into His nostrils, God was moved to respond. Genesis 8:21 and 22 records His response:

And the Lord smelled a sweet savour; and the Lord said in his heart, I will not again curse the ground any more for man's sake; for the imagination of man's heart is evil from his youth; neither will I again smite any more every thing living, as I have done.

Noah offered a sacrificial offering to God — perhaps at the massive, sacrificial stone altar that remains to this day near the original site of the landing of the Ark — and Noah and his family looked up into the sky and saw the first rainbow, which was the physical sign in the sky of God's covenant promise that the earth will never again be destroyed by a worldwide flood. This promissory sign can, of course, still be seen in the sky today.

While the earth remaineth, seedtime and harvest, and cold and heat, and summer and winter, and day and night shall not cease.

The Lord added further clarification of His pledge to humanity and creation in Genesis 9:8-11.

And God spake unto Noah, and to his sons with him, saying, And I, behold, I establish my covenant with you, and with your seed after you; And with every living creature that is with you, of the fowl, of the cattle,

and of every beast of the earth with you; from all that go out of the ark, to every beast of the earth.

And I will establish my covenant with you, neither shall all flesh be cut off any more by the waters of a flood; neither shall there any more be a flood to destroy the earth.

So in Genesis 8:21 and Genesis 9:11, God made a promise that He would never again destroy the earth with a worldwide flood. Some misconstrue this to mean God promised He would never destroy the earth again, but that is not what He said. Clearly, God stated that He would not destroy the earth again with a *flood*. The Bible unmistakably teaches that at some point in the future, the world will be refined by fire. In fact, Second Peter 3:7 says this present world is "…kept in store, reserved unto fire against the day of judgment and perdition of ungodly men."

Nevertheless, God will not allow a global flood to annihilate the earth again, and He sealed this promise to mankind and creation by giving us a tangible token of His covenant: the rainbow. Scripture tells us in Genesis 9:12-17:

And God said, This is the token of the covenant which I make between me and you and every living creature that is with you, for perpetual generations: I do set my bow in the cloud, and it shall be for a token of a covenant between me and the earth.

And it shall come to pass, when I bring a cloud over the earth, that the bow shall be seen in the cloud: And I will remember my covenant, which is between me and you and every living creature of all flesh; and the waters shall no more become a flood to destroy all flesh.

And the bow shall be in the cloud; and I will look upon it, that I may remember the everlasting covenant between God and every living creature of all flesh that is upon the earth.

And God said unto Noah, This is the token of the covenant, which I have established between me and all flesh that is upon the earth.

As Noah was making his sacrificial offering to God — perhaps at the massive, sacrificial stone altar that remains to this day near the original site of the landing of the Ark — Noah and his family looked up into the sky and saw the first rainbow. This

God gave the rainbow as a perpetual reminder of His covenant that He would never again destroy the earth with a Flood. Not only did God promise never to destroy the world again by water, but He also declared a blessing over Noah and his family and all the animals that had escaped the Great Deluge.

physical sign in the firmament of God's covenant promise that the earth will never again be destroyed by a worldwide flood can, of course, still be seen today.

When I personally stood on that massive sacrificial stone and looked up into Heaven, I was moved by the reality that I may have been standing in the very spot where Noah and his family offered their sacrifices and where the rainbow appeared for the first time. Just think about it; God gave the rainbow as a perpetual reminder of His covenant that He would never again destroy the earth with a flood.

To say that the Lord is faithful is nearly an understatement. In Revelation 19:11, He is called *Faithful and True*, and Proverbs 30:5 says, "Every word of God is pure: He is a shield unto them that put their trust in him." Every word from God can be depended on and will prove true, and when God made a covenant with Noah with the sign of the rainbow as a seal, Noah knew he could count on the Faithful and True to keep His word that He would never destroy the earth again with a flood.

To be clear, if the Great Flood of Noah's day was local or regional as some have alleged, it would have implications that God has repeatedly broken His covenant since then because of the countless local and regional floods that have resulted in the loss of life. Likewise, if the Flood had been local or regional, people could have simply moved to higher ground in another area and escaped it — including Noah and his family — making the building of the Ark unreasonable and unnecessary. But the fact is, the Flood was global, covering the highest known mountains with nearly 25 feet of water and exterminating all forms of life on earth and in the sky (*see* Genesis 7:20-23).

Many scholars believe the Ark came to rest in the area that was originally the vicinity of the Garden of Eden. When people hear and see the word "garden," they tend to imagine that Eden was just a small plot of land featuring an assortment of flowers, plants, and trees. But due to the geographical markers provided in Genesis 2, it is likely that the Garden of Eden was significantly larger than imagined and was spread out over as many as 1,500 square miles. That's about 960,000 acres and approximately the median size of Rhode Island and Delaware.

GOD SPOKE THE SAME BLESSING OVER NOAH AND HIS FAMILY THAT HE SPOKE OVER ADAM AND EVE

Noah's sacrificial offering so pleased God that not only did God promise never to destroy the world again by water, but He also declared a blessing over Noah and his family and all the animals that had escaped the Great Deluge. The Bible says that God smelled the sweet savor of Noah's sacrifice:

...God blessed Noah and his sons, and said unto them, Be fruitful, and multiply, and replenish the earth.

— Genesis 9:1

As I have noted, the Bible states that Noah's Ark came to rest on the *mountains* of Ararat (*see* Genesis 8:4). And as we saw in Chapter 11, the mountains of Ararat were, and still are, a large *range* of mountains that in early times were a significant part of the *Urartu Kingdom*. The word "Urartu" evolved into the word *Ararat* in about 1105 AD, and the region of *Urartu* (or Ararat) has been identified by many scholars as the supposed original location of the Garden of Eden.

When people hear and see the word "garden," they tend to imagine that Eden was just a small plot of land featuring an assortment of flowers, plants, and trees. But because of the geographical markers given to us in Genesis 2, it is much more likely that the Garden of Eden was large, and a part of it was in the same vicinity in which the Ark came to rest.[8]

The following is how the Bible describes Eden.

And a river went out of Eden to water the garden; and from thence it was parted, and became into four heads.

The name of the first is Pison: that is it which compasseth the whole land of Havilah, where there is gold; and the gold of that land is good: there is bdellium and the onyx stone. And the name of the second river is Gihon: the same is it that compasseth the whole land of Ethiopia.

And the name of the third river is Hiddekel: that is it which goeth toward the east of Assyria. And the fourth river is Euphrates.

— Genesis 2:10-14

With the exception of the Euphrates River, the names of the four rivers in this passage — Pison, Gihon, Hiddekel, and Euphrates — have changed over time. For instance, Josephus cites that the Pishon (Pison) and Gihon Rivers were called the *Ganges* and *Nile Rivers*, respectively, by the Greeks.[9] And the Hiddekel River is another name for the *Tigris River*, which is confirmed in Daniel 10:4. If you were to draw a square, using the four rivers as boundary lines, the area of Eden may have been as large as 1,500 square miles!

Researchers generally believe the headwaters of all four of these rivers were located in what is today eastern Turkiye, in the very area where the Ark landed when the waters of the Flood began to recede. Most scholars estimate that the Garden of Eden began in the highlands of Armenia and went southward to where a number of these rivers emptied into the Persian Gulf.[10]

If the Garden of Eden was indeed located in this region — which would include the area where the Ark came to land in the mountains of Ararat — it means God, the Great Master Planner, who is given to dates, times, and places, caused the currents of the Flood to carry the Ark, with Noah and his family, to the same general area where He had first placed Adam and Eve at the time of creation. If that is true, it means that when Noah and his family exited the Ark in the mountains of Ararat, God amazingly spoke the same exact words to them that He had spoken more than 1,600 years earlier to Adam and Eve in the Garden of Eden.

The Bible states that after God created mankind in His image and placed them in Eden:

…God blessed them, and God said unto them, Be fruitful, and multiply, and replenish the earth, and subdue it: and have dominion over the fish of the sea, and over the fowl of the air, and over every living thing that moveth upon the earth.

— **Genesis 1:28**

Likewise, after God steered the Ark into the same general vicinity of Eden, remarkably, He spoke the same blessing over Noah and his wife, his sons, and their wives (*see* Genesis 9:1) that He spoke over Adam and Eve (*see* Genesis 1:28).

When God said the words, "Be fruitful and multiply and replenish the earth," in that very moment, a supernatural ability was released for Noah, his family, and the animals to quickly multiply and to replenish the earth. This explains why the population of the earth was replenished in a relatively short period of time.

Wouldn't it be just like God to bring Noah and his family back to Eden, the starting place of humanity? As He has done for each of us from time to time in restoring our lives, it seems that God miraculously took Noah and his family back to the starting point where life first began, and through this family of eight, He gave all of creation a fresh start in the original birthplace of humanity. The ingenuity of God is simply amazing!

MOUNT CUDI AND THE VILLAGE OF EIGHT (ARZAP)

Keep in mind, when the Ark first landed, it came to rest atop Mount Cudi at an elevation of approximately 7,000 feet above sea level, and in ancient times, the Silk Road once traversed along the top ridge of this slope. Today, the upper ridge of Mount Cudi is the shared border between Turkiye and Iran.

Because this lower mountain in Ararat is prone to heavy rains that produce mudslides, it is estimated that the Ark has slid down Cudi's slope about 1,200 feet over thousands of years and now rests at about 6,500 feet above sea level. While the slope's features are constantly changing each spring due to fresh mudflows, the ship-shaped formation buried in the earth remains consistent year after year.

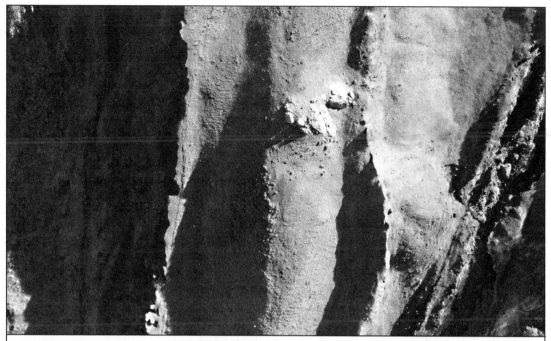

Pictured here is a massive boulder, which at some point in ancient history crashed into the Ark, and it has held the ship-shaped object in place ever since, even though the earth around it continues to move. ERT scans have conclusively shown the boulder is not attached to any underground geology.

At some point in the past, a massive boulder crashed into the Ark, and from that time until now, it has held the ship-shaped object in place, even though the earth around it continues to move.[11] Of course, there have been skeptics who surmised that because there is a massive boulder in the middle of the structure, it proves that the object is simply a geologic formation.

But ground-penetrating radar and ERT scans have conclusively shown otherwise. In fact, the scans show the boulder is not attached to any underground geology. These are the same scans that show images of the ship's hull and numerous right-angle formations, which are not found in nature. Tangible, scientific facts like these provide strong indication that the massive, ship-shaped ruins are a man-made object preserved within the earth — an object that looks exactly like an ancient ship.[12]

Eventually, a time came when Noah and his family left the upper slope of Mount Cudi and moved into the valley below the present location of the Ark's remains.

The "Village of Eight" (Arzap) is so named in commemoration of Noah's family who allegedly lived nearby in years after the Flood. The village is indeed very ancient, and many of the homes constructed there have been built with repurposed stones from preceding ancient generations. In the cemetery are drogue stone fragments that have been collected over thousands of years and used as grave markers.

Now the sons of Noah who went out of the ark were Shem, Ham, and Japheth… These three were the sons of Noah, and from these the whole earth was populated. And Noah began to be a farmer, and he planted a vineyard.

— Genesis 9:18-20 (*NKJV*)

What is exceptionally interesting is that today, in the middle of that valley below the ship-shaped ruins, there is a small village that since ancient times has been called the "Village of Eight" (Arzap), in honor of a distant memory by locals that Noah, his wife, his sons, and their wives once lived there.

The "Village of Eight" (Arzap) — is indeed very ancient, and many of the homes constructed there have been built with repurposed stones from preceding ancient generations. Since Byzantine and Armenian times, this specific area has been commemorated as the location where Noah's family once lived. In the cemetery of that village are fragments of drogue stones that are understood to have hung from the sides of the Ark during its voyage. These fragments have been collected over thousands of

Among ancient stones collected from a Byzantine church that was destroyed by an earthquake is a stone that has one of the earliest-known depictions of Noah's Ark, showing the ship's pointed bow and a rounded stern, exactly like the ship-shaped formation on the lower slope of Mount Cudi.

years and used as grave markers. In Byzantine and Armenian times, ancient peoples engraved crosses on the surface of these stones, and several of these massive stones have been found intact, engraved with eight crosses, which some believe were carved in memory of Noah's family.[13]

In the yard of one of the private homes in that village, the owner has collected ancient stones from either a Byzantine or Armenian church, and he has used them to construct a patio. Among all the ancient stones collected from that church, which was destroyed by an earthquake, are stones that depict church leaders and biblical themes. One stone in particular has one of the earliest-known depictions of Noah's Ark, showing the ship's pointed bow and a rounded stern, exactly like the ship-shaped formation on the lower slope of Mount Cudi.[14]

Also near this "Village of Eight" (Arzap) are the ruins of a Byzantine or Armenian church that was originally built about 1,500 years ago. Church leaders erected this structure in those earlier times because it was believed to be the place where Noah's home was when he became a farmer in the valley below the ship-shaped remains on

Near the "Village of Eight" (Arzap) are the ruins of a Byzantine church that was originally built on this site because Early Church leaders believed it was the location where Noah's home was when he became a farmer in the region after the Flood. Today that church has fallen into ruins, but while most of it is gone, the basic form of the church is still visible.

Several hundred feet from the ruins of that early Byzantine church is an ancient fence constructed of large, archaic stones that seem to intentionally mark off the hill just above and appear to designate a consecrated or holy place.

Beyond the stone fence and further up the hill is a massive square-shaped boulder, which some researchers allege is another altar that Noah and his family used for sacrificial worship when they lived nearby in the flood plain.

the slope of Mount Cudi. Today that church has fallen into ruins, but while most of it is gone, the basic form of the church is still visible. The people who lived in the time period of the Flood documented the places associated with Noah, including the site of his home, which this church seemed to have commemorated.

Several hundred feet from the ruins of that early church is an ancient fence constructed of large archaic stones that seem to intentionally mark off the hill just above it. This rock fence appears to designate a consecrated or holy place that is not to be touched — and just beyond the stone fence up the hill is a massive square-shaped boulder, which some researchers allege is another altar Noah and his family used for sacrificial worship when they lived in the valley nearby.[15]

Although I cannot state categorically that this is the case, the evidence of the ancient church, the ancient fence, the ancient altar, the drogue stones, and the ancient town known for thousands of years as the "Village of Eight" (Arzap), all seem to indicate Noah and his family lived in the area.

THE NATIONS OF THE WORLD WERE BIRTHED THROUGH NOAH'S SONS AND THEIR DESCENDANTS

According to Scripture, Noah was 500 years old when he and his wife began to have children, and it was at that time when God instructed him to build the Ark. When Noah reached the age of 600, the Flood was unleashed upon the earth, and it lasted a little longer than a year. Regarding the remainder of Noah's life, the Bible says:

And Noah lived after the flood three hundred and fifty years. And all the days of Noah were nine hundred and fifty years; and he died.
— Genesis 9:28,29

In the 350 years that Noah lived after the Flood, he worked as a farmer, and his sons Shem, Ham, and Japheth eventually moved out across the region and began to repopulate the earth. Genesis 10, which is referred to by many scholars as the table of nations, gives us these insights concerning the descendants of Noah:

Now these are the generations of the sons of Noah, Shem, Ham, and Japheth: and unto them were sons born after the flood.

The sons of Japheth; Gomer, and Magog, and Madai, and Javan, and Tubal, and Meshech, and Tiras.

And the sons of Gomer; Ashkenaz, and Riphath, and Togarmah. And the sons of Javan; Elishah, and Tarshish, Kittim, and Dodanim. By these were the isles of the Gentiles divided in their lands; every one after his tongue, after their families, in their nations.

And the sons of Ham; Cush, and Mizraim, and Phut, and Canaan.

And the sons of Cush; Seba, and Havilah, and Sabtah, and Raamah, and Sabtechah: and the sons of Raamah; Sheba, and Dedan.

And Cush begat Nimrod: he began to be a mighty one in the earth. He was a mighty hunter before the Lord: wherefore it is said, Even as Nimrod the mighty hunter before the Lord. And the beginning of his kingdom was Babel, and Erech, and Accad, and Calneh, in the land of Shinar.

Out of that land went forth Asshur, and builded Nineveh, and the city Rehoboth, and Calah, and Resen between Nineveh and Calah: the same is a great city.

— Genesis 10:1-12

It's interesting that although a patriarch in any family can follow God in reverential fear, it doesn't guarantee the success of every member in his bloodline. Nimrod, the great-grandson of Noah, grew powerful as a leader who influenced many — but he was defiant against the Lord, who overthrew him, leaving him to be remembered as a failure in God's eyes. A straight path had been paved before Nimrod by Noah, but by Nimrod's actions, we know he erred from that path and failed to lay hold of his godly heritage.

Thank God, we can intercede for our loved ones and claim the promise of salvation for errant ones in our household (*see* Acts 16:31). If that's your situation, be comforted that God gave everyone freedom of choice, so if someone in your family chooses wrongly, it doesn't necessarily mean *you've* done something wrong. Simply yield to the Holy Spirit in prayer and let Him restore your loved one.

But once again, we see this man named Nimrod. He was the son of Cush, the grandson of Ham, and the great-grandson of Noah. Nimrod, whose name means *rebellion*, is the man who instigated the building of the Tower of Babel.

Let's turn again to the writings of the historian Josephus, who wrote the following about this errant descendant of Noah.

> Now it was Nimrod who excited them to such an affront and contempt of God. He was the grandson of Ham, the son of Noah, a bold man, and of great strength of hand. He persuaded them not to ascribe it to God, as if it was through his means they were happy, but to believe that it was their own courage which procured that happiness. He also gradually changed the government into tyranny, seeing no other way of turning men from the fear of God, but to bring them into a constant dependence on his [Nimrod's] **power.**[16]

Scripture says the beginning of Nimrod's kingdom was Babel (*see* Genesis 10:10). Indeed, Babel is the first recorded centralization of power — society's first attempt at a one-world government. God Himself put a stop to Nimrod's defiance and the people's rebellion by confusing everyone's language (*see* Genesis 11:1-9). At Babel, the people scattered into language groups, which became the nations of the world, and in the words of noted historian and prolific author Bill Federer, "Nations were God's invention to postpone a one-world government."[17]

The Bible goes on to tell us about Ham's other grandchildren, saying:

And Mizraim begat Ludim, and Anamim, and Lehabim, and Naph- tuhim, and Pathrusim, and Casluhim, (out of whom came Philistim,) and Caphtorim.

And Canaan begat Sidon his first born, and Heth, and the Jebusite, and the Amorite, and the Girgasite, and the Hivite, and the Arkite, and the Sinite, and the Arvadite, and the Zemarite, and the Hamathite: and afterward were the families of the Canaanites spread abroad. And the border of the Canaanites was from Sidon, as thou comest to Gerar, unto Gaza; as thou goest, unto Sodom, and Gomorrah, and Admah, and Zeboim, even unto Lasha.

These are the sons of Ham, after their families, after their tongues, in their countries, and in their nations. Unto Shem also, the father of all the children of Eber, the brother of Japheth the elder, even to him were children born.

The children of Shem; Elam, and Asshur, and Arphaxad, and Lud, and Aram.

— **Genesis 10:13-22**

At first glance, reading through these verses may seem like an exercise in futility. But the names of Noah's grandsons and their succeeding descendants provided in Genesis 10 comprise the most accurate genealogies of the nations of the world. In fact, when compared with many ancient documents showing the origins of families, a direct connection with several of the biblical names is clearly seen.

One name of great importance is the name *Eber*, who is mentioned three times in Genesis 10:21-25. Eber is a descendant of Shem: Eber is Salah's son, Arphaxad's grandson, Shem's great-grandson, and Noah's great-great-grandson. Eber is significant because he is the father of the Hebrews, from whom Abraham — and ultimately Jesus — descended.

Interestingly, the Bible says, "And unto Eber were born two sons: the name of one was Peleg; for in his days was the earth divided…" (Genesis 10:25). Although some believe this reference to the earth being "divided" in Peleg's time refers to the land breaking apart to form the continents, which may be the case, it's also possible that it points to God dividing up the people by confusing their languages at the Tower of Babel.

Scholars estimate that the total number of languages and people groups that were dispersed from Babel was between 70 and 80. While there are more than 6,900 languages spoken in the world today, language statisticians like *Vistawide World Languages and Cultures* say there are about 94 different language families, that is, groups of languages that share a common origin.[18]

In the next chapter, we will engage in a more detailed study of the life of Noah and his descendants post-Flood, and we will answer the question, "Were there giants on the earth *after* the Flood?"

QUESTIONS TO PONDER

1. God told Noah and his family exactly when to enter and exit the Ark. They didn't go in or leave one day earlier or later. Since God is not a respecter of persons and has no favorites, this means you can trust Him to provide divine direction for your life too. Take a look at these promises He has made and write down what He shows you about receiving His direction. What is *your* part in the process?

   • James 1:5,6

   • Proverbs 3:5-8

   • Psalm 25:4,5,9,12 and 32:8

2. After the Flood, significant changes were made in the new world. Read Genesis 9:2-17 to gain insight regarding God's new guidelines.

   • What laws did God establish to deal with violence among humanity? How about between mankind and the animals? (*See* Genesis 9:5,6.)

   • With whom did God repeatedly say His covenant was established? (*See* Genesis 9:9-17.)

   • What exactly did God promise? (*See* Genesis 9:11,15.)

3. Can you imagine what it would be like not to see dry land for nearly a year? That's what Noah and his family experienced. How do you think you would have responded to not seeing sunlight or dry land for nearly a year?

4. The Bible says the first thing Noah did after exiting the Ark was to offer a sacrifice to the Lord. Worshiping and thanking God for His mercy and kindness were the top priorities to Noah. Be honest — where does God fit on your list of priorities? Do you tend to give Him your first and your best, or do you give Him what's left over when you get around to it?

5. God was extremely merciful to Noah and his family, and Noah knew it. In what ways do you know beyond any doubt that God has shown mercy and kindness to you and your family? Why not take the time right now to *thank Him* and *praise Him* for all He has done to protect you, direct you, and provide for you. He's so worthy of your worship!

We know there were giants — Nephilim — before the Great Deluge. They were the offspring of women who had mated with rebellious angels. But what about Scripture's many instances of the presence of giants *after* the Flood? They did, in fact exist, and we'll explore that in this chapter, as well as God's plan for His people to deal with these ancient menaces who defied God's plans — and purposes — and attacked those He called His own.

CHAPTER THIRTEEN

WERE THERE GIANTS AFTER THE FLOOD?

In the last chapter, we saw that the first thing Noah did when he and his family exited the Ark was to offer a sacrifice to the Lord at an altar (*see* Genesis 8:20). I also noted that near the site of the Ark's original landing place on the upper slope of Mount Cudi, there still exists an ancient stone altar. The local Kurdish people who live there have traced their roots to that area for thousands of years, and they say that it is the very altar used by Noah when he offered the first sacrifices after disembarking from the Ark.

A close-up aerial view of this massive stone altar reveals a "blood channel" that has been chiseled out of the top with ancient tools to allow blood from sacrifices to drain downward. It is simply mind-boggling to think that this stone altar, which is just a few hundred feet from the Ark's original landing place, has been in this same location for thousands of years!

The Bible says that as Noah offered sacrifices to the Lord, "…the Lord smelled a sweet savour…" (Genesis 8:21). The rest of that verse says:

...And the Lord said in his heart, I will not again curse the ground any more for man's sake; for the imagination of man's heart is evil from his youth; neither will I again smite any more every thing living, as I have done.

Moved by Noah's act of worship, God promised that He would never again destroy the earth with a worldwide flood. He made this covenant not only with Noah and his family and all of mankind, but also with every living creature on earth, sealing His covenant oath perpetually with the appearance of a rainbow in the sky whenever it rains (*see* Genesis 9:9-17).

Pre-Flood History Was Known and Honored by Early Civilizations

History documents that the Sumerians were one of the first civilizations after the Flood to occupy the region of southern Mesopotamia. The land where they lived was called *Sumer*, which means *the land of civilized kings*. These people were responsible for segmenting time by dividing day and night into 12-hour periods, hours into 60 minutes, and minutes into 60 seconds.[1]

The Sumerians recognized that there was a pre-Flood civilization preceding their own. This is confirmed by the 1922 discovery of the Weld-Blundell Prism in Babylonia, which can be seen today in the Ashmolean Museum in Oxford, England. This four-sided, clay cuneiform prism was written in about 2100 BC (about 200 years after the Flood) by a scribe named Nur-Ninsubur, and it verifies the extraordinary long life spans of those who existed before the Flood. Amazingly, this tablet contains an extensive history of ten pre-Flood kings and ends with the sobering words, "And the Flood overthrew the land."[2]

A four-sided clay cuneiform prism called the Weld-Blundell Prism, discovered in the ruins of ancient Babylon, can be seen today in the Ashmolean Museum in Oxford, England. It contains an extensive history of ten pre-Flood kings and ends with the sobering words, "And the Flood overthrew the land."

One Babylonian king wrote that he "loved to read the writings of the age before the Flood." Ashurbanipal, who founded the great library of Nineveh, wrote of the great number of "inscriptions of the time before the Flood."

As we saw in Chapter 3, shortly after the Sumerians, the Babylonians and Assyrians also acknowledged the pre-Flood era as a source of superior literature. In fact, one Babylonian king documented that he "loved to read the writings of the age before the Flood." Ashurbanipal, who founded the great library of Nineveh, also alluded to the great "inscriptions of the time before the Flood."

Again, let me be clear that God sent the Flood to cleanse the earth of the widespread wickedness brought about as a result of the fallen angels copulating with women, who then gave birth to hybrid giants that filled the earth with bloodshed and violence. This understanding was held by the Jews, rabbinical writers, the Early Church, Church fathers, and even by certain indigenous groups. And indeed, all flesh on Earth — that is, every living being, *human, beast, fish, and bird* — was destroyed in the Flood, including the nefarious giants (*see* Genesis 7:21-23).

What's puzzling is that the Bible also states there were giants on the earth *after* the Flood, and this fact is verified throughout the Old Testament. What we will see in this chapter is that God made a covenant never to bring about another global flood, and since we know He will not violate an oath, it appears that rather than destroy the earth again, God simply empowered His people — the nation of Israel — to eliminate this subsequent infestation of giants.

THE SECRET THINGS BELONG TO THE LORD

You may be wondering how giants reappeared after the Flood since every living thing had been destroyed. Although the answer is not explicitly stated in Scripture, there are several speculations about how this occurred. For instance, some allege that an extended member of Noah's family, perhaps one of his daughters-in-law, carried a contaminated strain of DNA onto the Ark, and it became a source for the reappearing giants. This, however, is unprovable conjecture, and it goes directly against the

The reasons for some occurrences in the Bible have not yet been revealed, and to venture into those areas would be unwise, because the secret things belong to God (*see* Deuteronomy 29:29).

purpose of God sending the Flood. Think about it: Why would God — who is all-knowing — wipe out all DNA-corrupted lifeforms only to allow seeds of that same corruption to be taken into the post-Flood world via the survivors on the Ark? That makes no sense.

Another major proposal is that a second group of angels abandoned their posts, descended into the earth, and began to cohabit with women, who once again birthed giants. Again, this theory cannot be proven, although it certainly seems this may be the case. But even though the Bible does not explicitly tell us how the reappearance of the giants took place, it does repeatedly confirm that multiple tribes of giants reappeared on the earth after the Flood.

In fact, one would have to be nearly blind, or not believe the authenticity of Scripture, to argue that there were no giants after the Flood. The Old Testament is *filled* with instances of wicked giants contesting the people of God. The purpose of this chapter is not to argue their existence, nor to explain how they proliferated after the Flood. Rather, it is simply to point to Scripture and to early writers concerning the giants' existence and their misdeeds, as well as God's redemptive power to deliver His people and make good on every promise, even in the face of these wicked creatures that opposed them at every turn.

Because we simply do not know how giants reemerged after the Great Flood, I believe it's vital for us to bear in mind the words of Deuteronomy 29:29, which says:

The secret things belong unto the Lord our God: but those things which are revealed belong unto us and to our children for ever....

This verse tells us there are some things that have not yet been revealed, and to venture into those areas would be speculative, at best, and unwise, because the secret things belong to God. Therefore, my focus in this chapter will be on exploring the knowledge God *has* revealed to us. Then in the last two chapters of this book, we will take a look at the dark forces that are meddling once more with the human race.

'IN THOSE DAYS AND ALSO AFTER THAT' THERE WERE GIANTS

Let's look again at a pivotal verse, Genesis 6:4, that talks about the existence of giants before and after the Flood:

> **There were giants in the earth in those days; *and also after that*, when the sons of God came in unto the daughters of men, and they bare children to them, the same became mighty men which were of old, men of renown.**

This verse states there were giants on the earth at two particular time periods — *in those days* and *also after that*. To understand what is being said here, we must remember that God is writing this as history — as "days gone by" — probably through the hands of Moses. Many believe that Moses is the writer and that he likely wrote this sometime in the 40 years between the Exodus from Egypt and his death. Moses was "looking back" and reflecting the mind of God as he described the time just before the Flood. This would likely be telling us that the words "in those days" refers to *the days leading up to the Flood*.

The phrase "and also after that" would then be referring to *the days after the Flood*, which was the time in which Moses was living. Remember, Moses likely wrote all of the first five books of the Bible (also known as the *Pentateuch*) — Genesis, Exodus, Leviticus, Numbers, and Deuteronomy. And in the books of Numbers and Deuteronomy, Moses personally testified of seeing and fighting against giants. Those giants would fall into the category of those on the earth *"also after that."*

The Talmud — which contains rabbinic commentaries, Jewish traditions, and insights on the Torah (laws of Moses) — offers this interesting observation related to the idea of fallen angels producing a race of giants on Earth after the Flood:

The Talmud contains the central text of Rabbinic Judaism and the primary source of Jewish religious law and theology, including observations on a race of giants after the Flood.

> "There were two leaders of the Fallen Angels. One was Shemhazai and the other was Asael. These heaped scorn on the sinfulness of man *after the flood*. They went to earth and also committed sin and were seduced by the beauty of the daughters of men...."[3]

This brings us to the very important word translated in Genesis 6:4 as "when." The verse says, "There were giants in the earth in those days; and also after that, *when* the sons of God came in unto the daughters of men, and they bare children to them...." In this verse and others in the original text, there is a nuance that suggests this word "when" can also mean *whenever*. As such, Genesis 6:4 could be read as follows:

There were giants in the earth in those days; and also after that, WHENEVER the sons of God came in unto the daughters of men, and they bare children to them, the same became mighty men which were of old, men of renown.

The implication here is that at some undetermined point in the days *after* the Flood, another group of angels supposedly descended into the earth's atmosphere and repeated the same rebellious behaviors as the angels who sinned before the Flood. Once again, the result of these fallen angels sexually comingling with mortal women was the birth of *giants*.

These post-Flood giants being talked about in Genesis 6 are not victims of *gigantism*, which is a very rare condition in which a tumor on the pituitary gland causes it to continue to release excess human growth hormone (hGH) and causes a person to grow exceedingly tall and have accelerated growth of muscles, bones, and connective tissue. People with gigantism are most often very weak, have numerous health challenges, and die at a young age. Robert Wadlow, who grew to a height of 8 feet 11.1 inches and died at the age of 22, is a perfect example of gigantism.[4] The post-Flood giants were not physically weak, and they were just as wicked, vicious, tyrannical, and violent as their pre-Flood predecessors.

A Review of Ancient Sources That Verify the Fallen Angels-Giants Narrative

Respected Jewish historians and leaders of the Early Church wrote about the reality of giants both *before* and *after* the Flood. Several of these leaders and their biographical summaries were already provided in Chapter 5. Nevertheless, because their testimonies carry great weight, I'm including what they said about the giants once more, along with their biographical summary, telling who they were and what they did. Again, these were not spurious leaders given to fantasy, but they were serious historians, scholars, and theologians of the Early Church.

As you carefully read through the following insights, note what these trust-worthy individuals understood and shared about the nefarious moment when giants appeared on the earth. Again and again, they inseparably connect the appearance of giants to certain fallen angels who sexually mated with earthly women.

CLEMENT OF ROME
35 – 99 AD

In Chapter 5, we learned that Clement of Rome (also called Pope Clement I) was a member of the Church at Rome in the First Century and was said to have been ordained into the ministry by the apostle Peter. He is listed by Irenaeus and Tertullian as the bishop of Rome, who held office from 88 AD to his death in 99 AD. He is considered one of the apostolic fathers of the Early Church, along with Polycarp of Smyrna and Ignatius of Antioch.

Early tradition says that Clement was imprisoned under Emperor Trajan, but during his imprisonment, he led a ministry among fellow prisoners. *The Liber Pontificalis* states that he later died during Trajan's reign, being executed by having an anchor tied to him and then being thrown into the sea. In Eusebius' famous document *Ecclesiastical History*, he wrote that Clement was the third bishop of Rome and a "co-laborer" of the apostle Paul.

Clement's only credible surviving writing is called *1 Clement*, an epistle that he wrote and sent to the Church at Corinth. That document is one of the oldest that exists outside of the New Testament. Later, a second epistle called *2 Clement* was discovered, but although it was originally attributed to Clement, it is now speculated to have been written by someone else.

Clement was emphatically one of the most formidable, legendary, and illustrious leaders of the Early Church. What he said carried great weight, and his words were taken nearly as seriously as the words of the apostles with whom he personally labored.

Concerning the giants who were allegedly fathered by fallen angels, Clement of Rome wrote:

> …[Angels] **metamorphosed themselves…and partook of human lust, and being brought under its subjection they fell into cohabitation with women; and being involved with them, and sunk in defilement and altogether emptied of their first power, were unable to turn back to the first purity of their proper nature…. But from their unhallowed intercourse spurious men sprang, much greater in stature than ordinary men, whom they afterwards called giants.**[5]

JOSEPHUS
CIRCA 37 – 100 AD

As noted in Chapter 5, Flavius Josephus was a Jewish historian recognized for his multiple historical works, including *The Jewish War* and *The Antiquities of the Jews*. To this day, his writings are considered in Israel to be the most accurate histories, outside of the Bible, of the Jewish people.

Josephus was born in Jerusalem to a father of priestly descent and to a mother who claimed royal ancestry. He served as general of Jewish forces during the first Jewish-Roman War until the army surrendered to Vespasian in 67 AD. Shortly thereafter, Vespasian became impressed by the intellectual prowess of Josephus and took him as a slave. Later, when Vespasian became the Roman emperor in 69 AD, Josephus was granted his freedom. To show his gratitude, Josephus assumed the emperor's family's last name (Flavius), and from that point, he became known as Flavius Josephus.

Eventually Josephus became a Roman citizen and became an advisor to Titus, Vespasian's son and future emperor. He went on to serve as Titus' personal interpreter when Titus laid siege to Jerusalem in 70 AD. Jewish scholars count Josephus' works as the most important, trustworthy source outside of the Bible for the history of Israel. He wrote significant insights concerning the fallen angels who mated with earthly women and then gave birth to monstrous hybrid creatures who roamed the earth.

Concerning these giants, Josephus wrote:

> **For many angels of God accompanied with women, and begat sons that proved unjust, and despisers of all that was good, on account of the confidence they had in their own strength; for the tradition is, that these men did what resembled the acts of those whom the Grecians call giants....[6]**

When recounting a Jewish battle (post-Flood) to exterminate the giants, Josephus said:

> **And when they had taken it, they slew all the inhabitants. There were till then left a race of giants who had bodies so large, and countenances so entirely different from other men, that they were surprising to the sight and terrible to the hearing. The bones of these men are still shewn to this very day; unlike to any credible relations of other men.[7]**

To be clear, Josephus lived during the time of the Early Church — circa 37 to 100 AD. Thus, the bones of the giants were remarkably visible and on display while the books of the New Testament were being written.

TATIAN
CIRCA 120 – 185 AD

As we saw in Chapter 5, Tatian — also known as Tatian of Adiabene, Tatian the Syrian, and Tatian the Assyrian — lived in the Second Century and was an Assyrian Christian. Little is known about the date and place of his birth except what he writes about himself in his treatise called *Oratio ad Graecos*. In that document, Tatian states that he was born in "the land of the Assyrians," which is the Mesopotamian area where the cities of Babylon and Nineveh are located.

His first encounter with the Christian faith took place during a prolonged visit to the city of Rome. According to his own writings, he was disgusted with pagan religions and practices, so he turned to Scripture to seek truth. As he studied the Old Testament, he came to understand the evil of paganism, and over time he converted to Christ and became a disciple of Justin Martyr. Like Justin had done earlier, Tatian eventually opened a Christian school in Rome.

Eventually, Tatian left Rome for various reasons, and it is generally believed that he resided for a time somewhere in Greece or in Alexandria, Egypt, where he instructed Clement of Alexandria. The church leader Epiphanius tells us that Tatian later established a school in Mesopotamia, and its influence reached all the way to Antioch in Assyria and to Cilicia and Pisidia.

In Tatian's work *Oratio ad Graecos*, he vigorously argued that paganism was vile and worthless, and he praised the reasonableness and the antiquity of Christianity. As early as the time of Eusebius, Tatian was referred to honorably for his views of Moses and Jewish law. Among his written works was a "harmony" of the four New Testament gospels, which he called the *Diatessaron*, and which became nearly the only gospel text used in Assyria during the Third and Fourth centuries.

Tatian is believed by the Assyrian Church to have been a strong apostolic force in countries settled around the Euphrates River, and it is understood that he died in Adiabene in about 185 AD.

All this insight affirms that Tatian was viewed as a serious intellectual and a strong spiritual force during his time. As such, he was tremendously respected and considered to be authoritative on issues related to biblical history and to Scripture.

Concerning the giants, Tatian likely quoted Justin Martyr when he wrote:

> ...[Angels] **transgressed their appointment, and were captivated by the love of women, and begat children who are those who are called demons; and besides, they afterwards subdued the human race to themselves, partly by magical writings, and partly by fears and the punishments they occasioned, and partly by teaching them to offer sacrifices, and incense, and libations...and among men they sowed murders, wars, adulteries, intemperate deeds, and all wickedness.**

IRENAEUS
120/140 – 200/203 AD

As noted in Chapter 5, Irenaeus was bishop of Lyons in Gaul, a region which is present-day France. He was originally from Smyrna, which was located in the Roman province of Asia. In Irenaeus' day, Polycarp was the bishop of Smyrna. Thus, Irenaeus heard, knew, and saw Polycarp — the renowned disciple of the apostle John who was famously martyred for his faith in the stadium of Smyrna.

Among the works that Irenaeus authored is *Against Heresies*, which was a series of books in which he combated Gnostic errors. Another well-known book he wrote was a commentary on Paul's epistles. In addition to his monumental work *Against Heresies*, Irenaeus also wrote *The Demonstration of the Apostolic Preaching*. His influence was so great that noted scholars Hippolytus and Tertullian drew from his writings. Additionally, he is noted for devising the three pillars of orthodoxy — *the Scriptures, tradition,* and *the teaching of the apostles' successors*. Indeed, Irenaeus' influence is still felt today, and he is counted among the Early Church fathers.

Like Josephus, Irenaeus was an intellectual noted for his scholarly trustworthiness. Concerning giants, Irenaeus wrote:

> **And for a very long while wickedness extended and spread, and reached and laid hold upon the whole race of mankind, until a very small seed of righteousness remained among them and illicit unions took place upon the earth, since angels were united with the daughters of the race of mankind; and they bore to them sons who for their exceeding greatness were called giants. And the angels brought as presents to their wives teachings of wickedness, in that they brought them the virtues of roots and herbs, dyeing in colors and cosmetics, the discovery of rare substances, love-potions, aversions, amours, concupiscence, constraints of love, spells of bewitchment, and all sorcery and idolatry hateful to God; by the entry of which things into the world evil extended and spread, while righteousness was diminished and enfeebled.[8]**

ATHENAGORAS OF ATHENS
133 – 190 AD

Athenagoras of Athens was a former pagan philosopher who converted to Christianity. It is believed he then went to Alexandria where he eventually taught at the illustrious Catechetical School that was central to the formulation of early Christian doctrine. He, too, is considered to be among the Early Church fathers and was highly respected as an early Christian apologist.

Athenagoras is referred to in several early Christian documents, and his surviving writings demonstrate his intellectual prowess and competency as a philosopher and rhetorician, with a giftedness to fearlessly confront opponents. His enduring written works include the *Embassy for the Christians* (which in Latin is called *Legatio pro Christianis*), and *The Resurrection of the Dead*, which is sometimes referred to as his treatise *On the Resurrection of the Body*.

Like others heretofore mentioned, Athenagoras of Athens was an intellectual giant, recognized and revered for his scholarly trustworthiness. Concerning the giants and the fallen angels, Athenagoras of Athens wrote:

> …These [angels] **fell into impure love of virgins, and were subjugated by the flesh, and he became negligent and wicked in the management of the things entrusted to him. Of these lovers of virgins, therefore, were begotten those who are called giants.**[9]

CLEMENT OF ALEXANDRIA
CIRCA 150 – 215 AD

We saw in Chapter 5 that Clement of Alexandria was considered to be one of the revered Early Church fathers. As a noted Christian theologian, he taught at the Catechetical School in Alexandria, Egypt. He was also an instructor to Origen, an early Christian historian, scholar, and theologian.

Clement also instructed Alexander of Jerusalem, an early bishop who assembled a significant Christian library in Jerusalem, which had access to many ancient records. History documents that Clement of Alexandria eventually died during the persecution of Emperor Decius.

A noted scholar during his time, Clement of Alexandria wrote what was well-known in scholarly circles in his day about fallen angels who mated with mortal women, who then gave birth to giants.

Concerning the giants, Clement of Alexandria wrote:

…[Angels] **partook of human lust, and being brought under its subjection they fell into cohabitation with women…but from their unhallowed intercourse** [fallen angels having sexual relations with mortal women] **spurious men sprang, much greater in stature than ordinary men, whom they afterwards called giants….** [They were] **wild in manners, and greater than men in size, inasmuch as they were sprung of angels; yet less than angels, as they were born of women…not being pleased with purity of food, they longed only after the taste of blood, wherefore they first tasted flesh….**[10]

TERTULLIAN
155/160 – 220/240 AD

Tertullian was from Carthage in the Roman Province of Africa. Although it has never been proven, some suggest that, due to his expert use of legal analogies in his writings, he had been a lawyer. It appears that his conversion to Christianity occurred about 195-196 AD, and even though the details of it are not known, it seems that it was sudden, decisive, and transforming. Being one who had experienced the power of God in his rebirth, he wrote that "Christians are made, not born."

A prolific writer, Tertullian became the first Christian to produce an extensive work of Christian literature in the Latin language. Moreover, he was an apologist, a scholarly historian, and a powerful theologian who used his skills to argue vehemently against heresies — particularly of a Gnostic nature. He is called the Father of Latin Christianity and the Founder of Western Theology.

Thirty-one of Tertullian's works have survived intact. His main body of written materials consist of the *Cluniacense*, *Corbeiense*, *Trecense*, *Agobardinum*, and *Ottobonianus*, and his writings cover a wide theological spectrum, with a special emphasis on combating the errors of Gnostics and pagans. Tertullian is also known for his emphasis on discipline, morals, and the organization of human life on a Christian foundation.

Tertullian is considered impressive in the ranks of the leaders of the Early Church. He was the predecessor of Augustine, who became the chief founder of Latin theology. Jerome wrote that Tertullian lived to an old age, and his eminent writings are deemed by nearly all as being reliable and trustworthy.

Concerning the giants and fallen angels, Tertullian wrote:

> **We are instructed, moreover, by our sacred books how from certain angels, who fell of their own free-will, there sprang a more wicked demon-brood, condemned of God along with the authors of their race...there are the carcasses of the giants of old time; it will be obvious enough that they are not absolutely decayed, for their bony frames are still extent.**[11]

COMMODIAN
Exact lifespan unknown; flourished circa 250 AD

Commodian was a Christian Latin poet who was purportedly from Roman Africa, and he thrived around 250 AD. Ancient writers, such as Gennadius, who was the overseer of the Church of Massilia, referred to him in his *De scriptoribus ecclesiasticis*, and Pope Gelasius mentioned him in his work *Decretum Gelasianum de libris recipiendis et non recipiendis*.

Although the written works of Commodian were at some points deemed controversial, nonetheless, he was noteworthy enough to be referred to by leaders of the Early Church.

Concerning the fallen angels and giants, Commodian wrote:

> **When Almighty God, to beautify the nature of the world, willed that the earth should be visited by angels, when they were sent down they despised His laws. Such was the beauty of women, that it turned them aside; so that, being contaminated, they could not return to heaven. Rebels from God, they uttered words against Him. Then the Highest uttered His judgment against them; and from their seed giants are said to have been born.[12]**

SULPICIUS SEVERUS
360/365 – 420/425 AD

Sulpicius Severus was born to noble parents in Aquitania, which is located in modern-day France, and he was privileged to have educational advantages, which imbued him with cultural learning in Latin letters. He studied law in Burdigala (modern Bordeaux) and was known as an eloquent lawyer, and in his writings, his expert knowledge of Roman law is visible.

In time, Severus became renowned as a Christian writer, and in about 403 AD, he wrote a chronicle of sacred history called *Chronica, Chronicorum Libri duo* or *Historia sacra*. He is also known for his significant historical biography of *Martin of Tours*.

As one who studied law and was famous for his expert legal style in research and writing, Sulpicius Severus is considered to be a legal mind that produced histories that were well-researched, documented, and trustworthy.

Concerning the fallen angels and giants, Sulpicius Severus wrote:

> When by this time the human race had increased to a great multitude, certain angels, whose habitation was in heaven, were captivated by the appearance of some beautiful virgins, and cherished illicit desires after them, so much so, that falling beneath their own proper nature and origin, they left the higher regions of which they were inhabitants and allied themselves in earthly marriages. These angels gradually spreading wicked habits, corrupted the human family, and from their alliance giants are said to have sprung, for the mixture of them of beings of a different nature, as a matter of course, gave birth with monsters.[13]

Again, the purpose in reviewing these historical documents written by prominent ancient voices is to corroborate the events recorded in Genesis 6:4. Furthermore, these happenings were nearly universally believed by both Jews of antiquity and Early Church fathers and Christians alike up until the Third Century AD.

Keep in mind, the word "giants" in Genesis 6:2 and 4 is a translation of the Hebrew word *nephilim*, which some believe means *the fallen ones* or *those who fall* on others. In the Septuagint, which is the Greek version of the Old Testament, the word "giants" is a translation of the Greek word *gigantes*. This word literally means *giants*, and it describes strange creatures that were physically enormous, possessed unnatural strength, and propagated evil and violence throughout the earth.

Genesis 6:4 clearly states that giants were on the earth both *before* and *after* the Flood. Although it is not categorically known how and precisely when the resurgence of giants began to take place post-Flood, the Old Testament is nevertheless filled with passages that refer to numerous races of giants — giants existing post-Flood that we can read about in the Old Testament.

THE OLD TESTAMENT DOCUMENTS
A SECOND WAVE OF GIANTS AFTER THE FLOOD

In the following pages, you will see that before the children of Israel took possession of the Promised Land, it was thickly populated with giants. This section is intended to show numerous biblical proofs where the presence of giants *after* the Flood is clearly referred to in the Old Testament. To begin, let's look at Amos 2:9 and 10, where one group of Amorite giants is referenced. In these verses, the Bible says:

Genesis 6:4 states that there were giants on the earth both before and after the Flood. Although it is not categorically known how — and precisely when — the resurgence of giants took place, the Old Testament is filled with passages that refer to numerous races of giants after the Flood.

Yet destroyed I the Amorite before them, whose height was like the height of the cedars, and he was strong as the oaks; yet I destroyed his fruit from above, and his roots from beneath.

Also I brought you up from the land of Egypt, and led you forty years through the wilderness, to possess the land of the Amorite.

In this passage, God Himself identifies a race of Amorite giants as being present after the Flood and states their height was *as tall as cedars*.[14] Cedars are hardy trees that grow upwards of 100 feet or more, and they can have a trunk diameter of 8 to 10 feet. God compared these Amorite giants to mighty cedars. But in spite of their enormity, they were ultimately wiped out by the children of Israel.

The presence of numerous tribes of giants is also confirmed in the book of Numbers, where we read that Moses sent the 12 spies to search out the land. After 40 days, 10 of the spies returned from the Promised Land and gave a negative, fearful report based on the giants they saw in the land. The Bible says:

And they brought up an evil report of the land which they had searched unto the children of Israel, saying, The land, through which we have gone to search it, is a land that eateth up the inhabitants thereof; and all the people that we saw in it are men of a great stature.

And there we saw the giants, the sons of Anak, which come of the giants: and we were in our own sight as grasshoppers, and so we were in their sight.
— Numbers 13:32,33

Notice that ten of the spies reported that the territory was "a land that eateth up the inhabitants thereof." This suggests that just as giants had insatiable appetites *before* the Flood, giants likewise had insatiable appetites *after* the Flood.[15]

Ancient documents state that when the crops and meat produced by the labors of men were no longer satisfying to the giants, the giants turned on each other, and then they turned against people, cannibalistically eating their flesh and drinking their blood. These barbaric acts of the giants are documented by Eusebius and Clement of Alexandria,[16] who are noted among Jewish and Church historians as being very accurate in what they wrote. Therefore, we may assume that what they wrote about the cannibalistic behavior of the giants is reliable.

Many races of giants are mentioned after the Flood, but throughout the Old Testament, a group called the *Anakim* are referred to the most. They were the descendants of Anak, and these giants made such an impression on the Israelites that they became the yardstick or benchmark that other giants were measured against.

God destroyed the first infestation of giants in the world with the global Flood, but because He promised never to destroy the earth again by water, the second time giants appeared, God tasked His people with exterminating them.

THE ANAKIM WERE A RENOWNED RACE OF GIANTS

Of all the races of giants mentioned after the Flood, a group called the *Anakim*[17] is referred to most throughout the Old Testament. These giants were the descendants of Anak, the son of a man named Arba (*see* Joshua 15:13). Arba was a descendant of Canaan, the son of Ham, which made Arba the great-grandson of Noah. Joshua 14:15 (*NKJV*) says, "…Arba was the greatest man among the Anakim…." In fact, he was so powerful at one time, the city of Kirjath-Arba was named after him (it later became known as the renowned city of Hebron).

Anakim giants made such an impression on the Israelites that they became the yardstick or benchmark that other giants were measured against. The following verses are provided to show how well-known the Anakim were and how frequently they, and their physical sizes, are mentioned in Scripture. You will also notice that scattered among these passages are the names of other groups of giants that we will look at more closely in the pages to come. But notice the frequency with which the dreaded Anakim are mentioned in the book of Deuteronomy:

> **Whither shall we go up? our brethren have discouraged our heart, saying, The people is greater and taller than we; the cities are great and walled up to heaven; and moreover we have seen the sons of the *Anakims* there.**
>
> — **Deuteronomy 1:28**

> **The Emims dwelt therein in times past, a people great, and many, and tall, as the *Anakims*; which also were accounted giants, as the *Anakims*; but the Moabites called them Emims.**
>
> — **Deuteronomy 2:10,11**

> **That** [the land of the Ammonites] **also was accounted a land of giants: giants dwelt therein in old time; and the Ammonites call them Zam-zummims; a people great, and many, and tall, as the *Anakims*; but the Lord destroyed them before them; and they succeeded them, and dwelt in their stead.**
>
> — **Deuteronomy 2:20,21**

> **Hear, O Israel: Thou art to pass over Jordan this day, to go in to possess nations greater and mightier than thyself, cities great and fenced up to heaven, a people great and tall, the children of the *Anakims*, whom thou knowest, and of whom thou hast heard say, Who can stand before the *children of Anak*!**

> **Understand therefore this day, that the Lord thy God is he which goeth over before thee; as a consuming fire he shall destroy them, and he shall bring them down before thy face: so shalt thou drive them out, and destroy them quickly, as the Lord hath said unto thee.**
>
> — **Deuteronomy 9:1-3**

In these four passages, Moses addressed the nation of Israel and recalled three of the groups of giants they'd encountered since the Exodus from Egypt. Along with mentioning the Emim and Zamzummim, Moses cited the Anakim six times and essentially stated that even though they were great in size, strength, and number, God had enabled the children of Israel to decimate them.

We also find that Joshua, Moses' successor, referred to the Anakims. After the Israelites had cut off the Anakim giants from the cities of Hebron, Debir, Anab, and all the mountains of Judah, the Bible says:

There was none of the *Anakims* left in the land of the children of Israel: only in Gaza, in Gath, and in Ashdod, there remained.

— Joshua 11:22

The Old Testament narrative goes on to tell of a moment when Joshua divided the conquered land and assigned it to the various tribes of Israel. In that moment, Caleb suddenly spoke up and said:

Now therefore give me this mountain, whereof the Lord spake in that day; for thou heardest in that day how the *Anakims* were there, and that the cities were great and fenced: if so be the Lord will be with me, then I shall be able to drive them out, as the Lord said.

— Joshua 14:12

Indeed, the Anakim giants (or sons of Anak) were well-known by the children of Israel. As noted, when the 12 spies went in to spy out the Promised Land — one of which was Caleb — it was the descendants of Anak that they saw in numerous cities. As part of their negative, fearful report, 10 of the spies said:

Nevertheless the people be strong that dwell in the land, and the cities are walled, and very great: and moreover we saw the children of Anak there.

The Amalekites dwell in the land of the south: and the Hittites, and the Jebusites, and the Amorites, dwell in the mountains: and the Canaanites dwell by the sea, and by the coast of Jordan.

— Numbers 13:28,29

According to these two verses, the children of Anak — the *Anakim giants* — were made up of subset groups. And these groups were the *Amalekites* in the land of the south; the *Hittites*, *Jebusites*, and *Amorites* that dwelled in the mountains; and the *Canaanites* that dwelled by the coast of Jordan.

The Old Testament reveals that there were numerous tribes of giants living throughout the Promised Land, also known as the land of Canaan.

GIANTS ACTUALLY *PROLIFERATED* AFTER THE FLOOD

A careful study of the Old Testament reveals that there were numerous tribes of giants living throughout the Promised Land (also known as the land of Canaan). These tribes of giants included:

> **Amalekites**
> **Amorites**
> **Avim**
> **Canaanites**
> **Emim**
> **Girgashites**
> **Hittites**
> **Hivites**
> **Horim**
> **Jebusites**
> **Kadmonites**
> **Kenites**
> **Kenizzites**
> **Perizzites**
> **Zamzummim**

In Genesis 14:5 we find the Rephaim, Emim, and Zuzim (a variant of the name Zamzummim) giants were involved in a battle that took place during the time of Abraham between two groups of kings. This verse says:

Along with a mention of the Emims and Zamzummims, the Bible mentions the Anakim six times and states that even though they were great in size, strength, and number, God miraculously enabled the children of Israel to decimate them. God's instructions followed in willing, surrendered obedience will always yield victory, even over the most formidable foes.

And in the fourteenth year came Chedorlaomer, and the kings that were with him, and smote the Rephaims in Ashteroth Karnaim, and the Zuzims in Ham, and the Emims in Shaveh Kiriathaim.

What is fascinating is that while Chedorlaomer and the other kings allied with him defeated the Rephaim, Zuzim, and Emim giants, they could *not* defeat Abraham. The moment Abraham heard that his nephew Lot and his family had been taken hostage, he armed the 318 trained servants born in his household and fought against and defeated Chedorlaomer and the kings fighting with him (*see* Genesis 14:14-16).

Genesis 15 informs us that after this mighty victory, the Lord appeared to Abraham in a vision and promised to give him all the land of Canaan, which included the land from the Nile River in Egypt to the great River Euphrates.

God specifically declared He would give Abraham the land of the notorious giants, which was the land of…

…the Kenites, and the Kenizzites, and the Kadmonites, and the Hittites, and the Perizzites, and the Rephaims, and the Amorites, and the Canaanites, and the Girgashites, and the Jebusites.

— Genesis 15:19-21

Remember, God had destroyed the first infestation of giants in the world with the global Flood. But He promised to never destroy the earth again by water, and the second time giants appeared, God tasked His people with exterminating them.

The descendants of Esau — Jacob's brother — were also successful at annihilating tribes of giants, which is what we read in Deuteronomy 2:9-12.

And the Lord said unto me, Distress not the Moabites, neither contend with them in battle: for I will not give thee of their land for a possession; because I have given Ar unto the children of Lot for a possession.

The Emims dwelt therein in times past, a people great, and many, and tall, as the Anakims; which also were accounted giants, as the Anakims; but the Moabites called them Emims.

The Horims also dwelt in Seir beforetime; but *the children of Esau* succeeded them, when they had destroyed them from before them, and dwelt in their stead; as Israel did unto the land of his possession, which the Lord gave unto them.

This passage informs us of the *Emim* giants who were dwelling among the Moabites[18] and an additional group of giants called *Horims*, living in the region of Seir, which was the large area where the descendants of Esau had settled. As mighty as these hybrid creatures were, Esau's lineage successfully destroyed them and took possession of the land.

Later in this same chapter, the Lord reminded Moses of two additional groups of giants called the *Zamzummim* and the *Avims* and how they too were exterminated by the Ammonites and the Caphtorims.[19]

And when thou comest nigh over against the children of Ammon, distress them not, nor meddle with them: for I will not give thee of the land of the children of Ammon any possession; because I have given it unto the children of Lot for a possession.

(That also was accounted a land of giants: giants dwelt therein in old time; and the Ammonites call them *Zamzummims*; a people great, and many, and tall, as the Anakims; but the Lord destroyed them before them; and they succeeded them, and dwelt in their stead:

As he did to the children of Esau, which dwelt in Seir, when he destroyed the *Horims* from before them; and they succeeded them, and dwelt in their stead even unto this day:

And the *Avims* which dwelt in Hazerim, even unto Azzah, the Caphtorims, which came forth out of Caphtor, destroyed them, and dwelt in their stead.)

— Deuteronomy 2:19-23

OG WAS KING OF THE GIANTS

The giant Og was in a category of his own, a "giant among giants" and notoriously feared throughout the region of 60 cities where he had dominion. Nevertheless, God empowered the children of Israel to defeat him, and the news of his defeat sent shockwaves throughout the land and caused the fear of God and of His people to fall on all the inhabitants. This miraculous victory over the "unconquerable" giant Og emboldened the children of Israel and encouraged them to believe they could inherit any territory the Lord assigned to them.

In the same way Anakim giants were so immense that they became the measuring stick by which all other giants were measured, one specific giant was so immense that he stood in a class all by himself. He is referred to 22 times in 6 books of the Old Testament, and his name was Og, a giant who ruled as the king of Bashan.

We are informed that as Moses led the children of Israel to the entrance of the Promised Land, the Lord instructed him to go through the region of Bashan to fight against Og.

. . . Fear him [Og] not, for I will deliver him, and all his people, and his land, into thy hand....

— Deuteronomy 3:2

The giant Og was so enormous that his bed had to be constructed of iron to support the weight of his body. The Bible says his bed was 9 cubits long and 4 cubits wide, and using an Egyptian cubit (which was likely the measurement Moses used when this text was composed), it would mean Og's bed was nearly 16 feet long by 7 feet wide.

A few verses later, the Bible provides these fascinating details concerning King Og:

For only Og king of Bashan remained of the remnant of giants; behold, his bedstead was a bedstead of iron; is it not in Rabbath of the children of Ammon? nine cubits was the length thereof, and four cubits the breadth of it, after the cubit of a man.

— Deuteronomy 3:11

This verse says Og was so enormous his bed had to be constructed of iron to support the weight of his body. It was 9 cubits long and 4 cubits wide. Using an Egyptian cubit (which was likely the measurement Moses used when this text was composed) would mean Og's bed was nearly 16 feet long by 7 feet wide. Thus, Og was a giant even among giants.

Og is mentioned six times in Joshua's records of the conquests of Canaan, wherein Joshua repeatedly describes the region where this infamous king ruled:

And the coast of Og king of Bashan, which was of the remnant of the giants, that dwelt at Ashtaroth and at Edrei, and reigned in mount Hermon, and in Salcah, and in all Bashan, unto the border of the Geshurites and the Maachathites, and half Gilead, the border of Sihon king of Heshbon.

— Joshua 12:4,5

Joshua 13:12 provides a similar description of Og's domain given to Joshua by the Lord. In that text, God Himself told Joshua:

All the kingdom of Og in Bashan, which reigned in Ashtaroth and in Edrei, who remained of the remnant of the giants: for these did Moses smite, and cast them out.

Indeed, Og was a giant even among giants. His kingdom was immense, and he ruled more than 60 cities (*see* Joshua 13:30; Deuteronomy 3:4). Nevertheless, God empowered the children of Israel to defeat him, and the news of his defeat sent shockwaves throughout the land. We hear this stated in the conversation between Rahab and the two Hebrew spies Joshua sent to spy out the city of Jericho before it was famously defeated (*see* Joshua 2:9-11).[20]

Another race of giants was called the *Rephaim*, and this was a group of giants referred to throughout the Old Testament. The Bible refers to a strip of land where the *Rephaim* lived that was approximately three miles long, known as "the valley of the giants." Both Og of Bashan and Goliath of Gath belonged to this "tribe" of giants.

THE REPHAIM AND THE VALLEY OF THE GIANTS

Another prominent race of giants living in the Promised Land was called the *Rephaim*, which was a group of giants referred to throughout the Old Testament — sometimes directly transliterated as Rephaim and at other times it appears simply as "giants." Both King Og of Bashan and Goliath of Gath are among the Rephaim giants.

As Joshua was setting the boundaries of the land given to the tribe of Benjamin, he specifically referred to a three-mile strip of land along the road to Bethlehem known as "the valley of the giants."

> **And the border came down to the end of the mountain that lieth before the valley of the son of Hinnom, and which is in *the valley of the giants* on the north, and descended to the valley of Hinnom, to the side of Jebusi on the south, and descended to Enrogel.**
>
> **— Joshua 18:16**

In this verse, the word "giants" is the Hebrew word *rephaim*. Like other giants, the Rephaim were physically enormous, and they occupied a section of Canaan that was called "the valley of the giants." This same territory is also referenced as "the valley of Rephaim" in Second Samuel 5:18,22; 23:13, First Chronicles 11:15; 14:9; and in Isaiah 17:5.

Nearly everywhere the children of Israel were settling in the Promised Land, they had to confront giants. Once again, the Bible documents this reality as Joshua was designating the land to be given to Judah:

> **And the border went up by the valley of the son of Hinnom unto the south side of the Jebusite; the same is Jerusalem: and the border went up to the top of the mountain that lieth before the valley of Hinnom westward, which is at the end of *the valley of the giants* northward.**
>
> **— Joshua 15:8**

When the tribes of Ephraim and Manasseh (who were descended from Joseph) began to complain about not having enough land, the Bible says:

> **And Joshua answered them, If thou be a great people, then get thee up to the wood country, and cut down for thyself there in *the land of the Perizzites and of the giants*, if mount Ephraim be too narrow for thee.**
>
> **— Joshua 17:15**

Interestingly, in Joshua 18:16, Joshua 15:8, and Joshua 17:15, the word "giants" is the Hebrew word *rephaim*. Thus, many of Israel's tribes bordered the legendary "valley of the giants."

The most well-known giant was named Goliath, whom David slew with a sling and a stone. The Bible tells us Goliath had a giant brother whose name was Lahmi, and that there were giant sons who were also born to Goliath.

DAVID AND HIS MIGHTY MEN KILLED MORE GIANTS THAN JUST GOLIATH

When thinking of well-known giants, one usually remembers the account of David and his battle against a Philistine giant named Goliath. In addition to Goliath, there were other Philistine giants referred to in Scripture. We find this mentioned in First Chronicles 20:4-8 and then expounded on in Second Samuel 21:15-22, which says:

Moreover the Philistines had yet war again with Israel; and David went down, and his servants with him, and fought against the Philistines: and David waxed faint.

And *Ishbi-benob*, which was *of the sons of the giant*, the weight of whose spear weighed three hundred shekels of brass in weight, he being girded with a new sword, thought to have slain David.

But Abishai the son of Zeruiah succoured him, and smote the Philistine, and killed him. Then the men of David sware unto him, saying, Thou shalt go no more out with us to battle, that thou quench not the light of Israel.

And it came to pass after this, that there was again a battle with the Philistines at Gob: then Sibbechai the Hushathite slew *Saph*, which was *of the sons of the giant*.

337

And there was again a battle in Gob with the Philistines, where Elhanan the son of Jaare-oregim, a Beth-lehemite, slew *the brother of Goliath* the Gittite, the staff of whose spear was like a weaver's beam.

And there was yet a battle in Gath, where was *a man of great stature*, that had on every hand six fingers, and on every foot six toes, four and twenty in number; and *he also was born to the giant.*

And when he defied Israel, Jonathan the son of Shimeah the brother of David slew him.

These four were born to the giant in Gath, and fell by the hand of David, and by the hand of his servants.

In this text, we find there were *at least* four more giants in the time of David. One was Goliath's brother whose name, according to First Chronicles 20:5, was Lahmi. The other three giants were Ishbi-benob, Saph, and a fourth unnamed giant that had 24 "digits" — appendages of fingers and toes — instead of 20.

What's interesting about Ishbi-benob, Saph, and this unnamed giant is that the Bible says each of these were "of the sons of the giant" or "born to the giant."[21] This tells us that at least some of the giants in David's day were fathering offspring just as the fallen angels had done.

Deformities, such as six toes on each foot and six fingers on each hand, are frequently described as characteristics of giants in ancient civilizations. For example, a giant called Cyclops[22] was said to be a cannibalistic giant who had one huge eye in the center of his forehead — or some ancient stories report he had three monstrous eyes. Either way, deformities were often associated with giants. In fact, ancient legends of giants from cultures around the world often report stories of giants with strange physical anomalies.

Again, we see how the roots of ancient mythology can be traced to Genesis 6:1-4 — to a time when the "sons of God" (or fallen angels) saw the daughters of men and comingled with them to produce their own offspring. Although many have alleged these legendary offspring to be nothing more than the product of people's imagination, we have seen that the people groups who wrote about them and bore witness of their existence also gave birth to many of the arts and sciences we still utilize today. In other words, they were not all primitive, uneducated, uncivilized people who were simply given to superstition, gullibility, and over-active imaginations.

The offspring of this angelic-mortal mixture was the original source for all the ancient legends of celestial beings that came down to earth, philandered with women, who then gave birth to "demigods."

ARE MASSIVE ANCIENT STRUCTURES TANGIBLE EVIDENCE OF 'GIANT RACES' THAT ONCE LIVED?

One more thing to consider as we wrap up this chapter on the question of how giants proliferated after the Flood is the presence of ancient monuments that defy explanation, which are scattered in various places all around the world. There are palaces and temples made of cut stones the size of modern boxcars that were transported from quarries hundreds of miles away.

Where did these formations, which are massive in size, and technically advanced in engineering, come from? For centuries, numerous theories have been offered, but the truth is no one really knows how these structures came into existence. Although the list of such constructs is voluminous, take a moment to consider these unexplainable wonders that are still in existence today:

Gilgal Rephaim

Gilgal Rephaim (meaning "Circle of the Giants"). This megalithic monument — also known as Israel's "Stonehenge" — is made of 5 concentric stone circles and is more than 500 feet in diameter. Together, the 40,000-plus stones that make up Gilgal Rephaim weigh nearly 37,500 metric tons (some stones individually weigh 20 tons). It is found in the Golan Heights, about 10 miles east of the Sea of Galilee in Israel and is only distinguishable as an aerial view.[23]

The Megalithic Temples of Malta. The islands of Malta contain several of the world's oldest free-standing structures. These megalithic temples, date to the Fourth and Third Millennium BC, include Mnajdra, Skorba, Tarxien, and Hagar Quim, whose

Megalithic Temples of Malta

name means "worshiping stones." Many of the temples have carvings of animals on the walls and various altars used for animal sacrifices, with bones still intact nearby. The Ggantija Temples of Gozo, which are one of the inhabited three islands of Malta, are a complex believed to have been built by Maltese giants, possibly between 3600-2500 BC. Interestingly, the name Ggantija is Maltese for "belonging to the giant," which supports this native legend. A number of the coralline stones making up the boundary wall around the entire complex are more than 16 feet in height and weigh more than 50 tons.[24]

Göbekli Tepe

Göbekli Tepe. This megalithic excavation site is about the size of 12 football fields. Located on a limestone plateau in southern Turkiye near the border of Syria, it features two huge parallel pillars towering more than 16 feet in the air and weighing nearly 50 tons. More than 100 additional limestone pillars are found in the surrounding wall and throughout the complex, ranging in height from about 5 to 16 feet, many of which exhibit carvings of gazelles, snakes, foxes, and lions.[25] Like the megalithic temples of Malta, Göbekli Tepe — which means "Potbelly Hill" or "Hill with a Naval" — shows evidence of ritualistic animal sacrifices, having several altars and thousands of wild animal bones.

The Great Stones of Baalbek. These humongous stones are located in Lebanon's Beqaa Valley, just north of Beirut. Of the 6 massive megalithic blocks, the 3 smaller ones, weighing between 750 and 800 tons, are part of the podium wall of the temple of Jupiter Baal. The remaining 3 stones include "Stone of the Pregnant Woman" (estimated at 1,000 tons); the "Stone of the South" (estimated at 1,242 tons); and

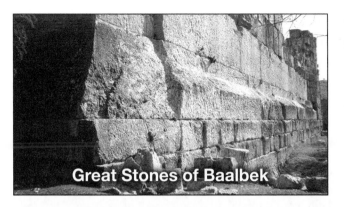
Great Stones of Baalbek

the "Forgotten Stone" (estimated at 1,650 tons). They were never removed from the quarry. The "megalithic gigantism" of these stones are unparalled in antiquity.[26] There is also a massive temple to the storm god Hadad that sits atop the citadel mound in the ancient city of Allepo in Syria. The floor of this temple is equally spectacular, consisting of multiple stones that are each the size of a modern railroad car.[27]

Unexplainable formations and structures like these and many others continue to baffle archaeologists, scientists, and historians. Where did they come from? Who built, carved, and shaped them? How were they transported? And why were they erected? Could the advanced technology be the result of the genius of fallen angels? Were these mysterious structures built by races of giants as many civilizations suggest?

Whatever the case may be, the fact remains that giants lived *before* and *after* the Flood. They are not a myth or fantasy. The Bible repeatedly documents that these hybrid creatures were dominating the land of Canaan during the time of Israel's conquest. The infestation of giants that occurred *before* the Flood was so wicked that God Himself dealt with them by sending the Great Deluge to destroy them. The giants that reappeared *after* the Flood were dealt with primarily by the Israelites whom God empowered to destroy them.

From the beginning of creation, Satan has tempted mankind and instigated rebellion against God's plans, His laws — both natural and spiritual — and His heart. Taking matters further, Satan lured a contingency of watchers (watching angels) that God had assigned to protect mankind, turning those Heaven-sent guardians into predators that God had to deal with severely because of the defilement those rebellious angels brought to His creation.

Similarly, the enemy tries to defile and debase God's people today, turning them aside from His plans and purposes. But God has made a way of escape for us in

Christ — our eternal Ark of Safety, through whom we can be rescued, delivered, and preserved from the storms of judgment that inevitably follow sin like seedtime and harvest. And just as God empowered His people in the Old Testament to decimate the giants and the forces of darkness that tried to withstand them, He empowers us today to stand fast amidst evil and destroy our spiritual opponents as we "prepare ye the way of the Lord" and make ready for His soon return.

In the next chapter, we will study to see that Jesus really prophesied such nefarious events would occur again in some way at the end of the age.

According to Genesis 6:4, there were giants before and after the Flood. How the giants reappeared after the Flood is open to speculation, but the Bible is clear that there was a second infestation, and God commanded His people to follow His instructions and to work with Him to eradicate them from the land.

QUESTIONS TO PONDER

1. What new facts did you learn about Anak and the Anakim? According to Joshua 11:21, who destroyed the majority of the Anakim? Which warrior expelled three of the mightiest sons of Anak from the land? How was he rewarded? (*See* Joshua 14:6-15; 15:13,14.) What does Joshua 11:22 say happened to the Anakim?

2. There is a lot we can learn from David's battle with the Philistine giant Goliath. Take time to reflect on this historic account in First Samuel 17:20-51. In what was David's confidence? Why do you think he picked up five stones from the brook (*consider* 2 Samuel 21:15-22)? What important thing did David do in verses 45-47 of First Samuel 17? How did David actually kill the giant? What else is the Holy Spirit showing you in this passage?

3. After going through this chapter — which is filled with passages confirming the existence of giants *after* the Flood — what is your first reaction? What surprised you most, and what is one of your greatest takeaways?

4. Ever since the time of Adam and Eve's fall in Eden, there has been a "seed war" (*see* Genesis 3:15) taking place. Satan sought to pollute the gene pool of mankind *before* the Flood to stop the birth of the "Seed" that would and did crush his head — Jesus — but why do you think the enemy worked to reinfest the earth with giants during the time of Abraham and the patriarchs?

5. Just as God assigned Israel with the task of exterminating the evil giants from the Promised Land, now God assigned us with the responsibility to push evil out of our lives. What "giants" are you facing right now? Is it sickness? Anxiety? Fear? Financial struggles? Is there a mindset, habit, or behavior that seems to have a tyrannical choke-hold on you? Then it is time for you to pray and release the strength of His mighty Holy Spirit in you and to take the authority Jesus has given you (*see* Luke 10:19) to drive Satan's efforts out of your life! (*See* Matthew 16:19; 18:18.)

6. List the "giants" in your life that need to be exterminated. Is it sickness? An addiction or bad habit? A financial hurdle? A prodigal child or grandchild? Read Ephesians 2:10 (*AMPC*) and take heart that God has a path and a good life that He has prearranged just for you. And He has empowered you to overcome your giants and to enter into all He has ordained for you and your loved ones.

This illustration depicts Jesus speaking to a multitude, but the New Testament demonstrates that Jesus personally addressed His closest disciples about the end times and answered questions regarding what would take place toward the end of the age. Jesus shared with them many end-time signs and activities, once even telling them, "...As the days of Noah were, so shall also the coming of the Son of man be" (Matthew 24:37). Jesus prophesied there would be a "replication" at the end of the age of events that occurred before the Flood.

CHAPTER FOURTEEN

DID JESUS PROPHESY IT WILL HAPPEN AGAIN?

In Matthew 24, Jesus spoke to His disciples about the end times, answering their questions about what would specifically take place toward the end of the age, before the Rapture and before His Second Coming, which will be two separate events. Jesus' discourse of events that will occur can be found in Matthew 24:3-41, and I encourage you to read the entire passage. However, I want to focus in this chapter on one statement Jesus made to His disciples. **But before we go any further, I want to caution you that some of the images in this chapter might be considered offensive to some.**

Please note that Jesus' words in this passage were recorded for *us*, the Church today.

But as the days of Noe [Noah] **were, so shall also the coming of the Son of man be.**

— Matthew 24:37

What did Jesus mean by this statement? Was He prophesying that there will be an exact replication of events that occurred in the time frame preceding the Flood? What activities should we expect to see — and do we see any of these things happening today?

The New Testament clearly teaches that Christ is coming again for His Church at the end of the age. Jesus taught that the earth will experience some type of shocking replication of many of the events that were occurring in the days preceding the Flood. Since God chose us to live in this closing season of this age, we might as well face the fact that we will see some of these evil replications.

Jesus was *exactly* saying in this verse that there would be a "duplicate moment" in time before His return. I'll explain as we look at this verse again.

But as the days of Noe [Noah] **were, so shall also the coming of the Son of man be.**
— **Matthew 24:37**

First, notice Jesus said, "But as."

The Greek word used in the original text means *just exactly as* or *precisely as*, and it describes *a duplicate moment*. When Jesus said, "*But as* the days of Noah were," it essentially meant, "*Exactly as*, *just as*, or *precisely as* it was in the days of Noah." Thus, Jesus prophesied that in some way, those living at the end of the age will experience a replication of what was occurring before the Great Deluge that was released on the earth in the days of Noah.

Second, Jesus said in verse 37, "…So shall also…."

These words literally mean *so it accordingly will be*, or *thus it will be*, or *it will be keeping in line with*. This indicates that the verse could be interpreted, "Exactly and precisely as it was in the days of Noah, *thus it will be* before the coming of the Son of Man."

Third, Jesus said in Matthew 24:37 that these events would occur before His "coming."

The word "coming" is a translation of a Greek word that some argue only describes the Second Coming of Christ when He returns at the end of the Great Tribulation *with* the saints. Although this particular word for "coming" can be used that way, it is not exclusively a word that only applies to Christ's Second Coming. This word is additionally used in the New Testament to describe when Jesus comes to retrieve the Church at the time of the Rapture. Therefore, how this word is used depends on the context.

In any event, the original Greek word for "coming" is a technical expression frequently used in ancient texts to describe *the coming of a king whose arrival and presence alone could deal with a wrong situation and bring order to it.* Thus, the use of this word can refer both to the moment Jesus returns to retrieve His Church and to the time seven years later when He comes back to the earth with the saints at the end of the Tribulation. Both of these events mark a time when Christ activates a final plan to put down evil, deal with the devil, and begin to put everything back in order.

Taking into account all these meanings from the original Greek text, we can gather from Jesus' words in Matthew 24:37 that just before He returns — referring both to the Rapture of the Church and to His Second Coming at the end of the Tribulation — the earth will experience some type of bizarre replication of many of the events that were occurring in the days preceding the Flood. Since God has tagged us to live in this closing season of this age, it is highly likely we will see some of these evil replications.

For the remainder of this chapter, I want to present to you a list of six major events that occurred before the Flood and consider how they compare to what is happening in the world today. Are we already seeing a replication of the days of Noah in our day? I believe the evidence speaks for itself.

6 Major Occurrences in the Days of Noah That Are Outlined in Genesis 6

Scholars believe that the human population exponentially exploded in the days before the Flood. In fact, it is likely that by the time of Noah, there were already millions of people on the earth.

#1: An Exploding Population (Genesis 6:1)

Genesis 6:1 specifically states that in the days that preceded the Flood, "… men began to multiply on the face of the earth…." Hence, the human population was exponentially exploding on the earth. In fact, it is likely that by the time of Noah, there were already several million people on the earth.[1]

Jesus said, "But as the days of Noe [Noah] were, so shall also the coming of the Son of man be" (Matthew 24:37).

Therefore, we must ask:
Is the world today experiencing a population explosion
as it occurred in the days before the Flood?

The following information is provided to help you understand the population growth of the world since the time of Jesus' birth during the First Century to the present.

- **1 AD**: When Jesus was born approximately 2,000 years ago, the global population is estimated to have been roughly 300 million people.[2]

- **1-1500**: During the next 1,500 years, the global population grew very slowly[3] for several reasons, among them being widespread illnesses and plagues that ravaged major population centers and poorer health, in general.

- **1700s**: In the Eighteenth Century and during the Industrial Revolution, the world saw rapid population growth as families began to have more children, and more babies survived their first years.[4]

- **1800s**: Growth of the population finally reached *1* billion people in the early 1800s.[5]

- **1958**: Over the next 100 years from the late Nineteenth Century, the human population doubled so that by 1958, when I was born, there were approximately *3* billion people on the earth.[6] The second half of the Twentieth Century brought along some additional exorbitant growth.

- **1976**: This year, which was the time I enrolled at the university as a student, the global population had skyrocketed from 3 billion (in 1958) to more than 4 billion — *4,142,505,882* to be exact.[7]

- **1976-Present**: From 1976 until now, the world population has doubled again. Today, there are more than 8,000,000,000 — 8 billion people — comprising the global population.[8]

- **Future Projections**: At the current rate of growth, it is projected that the world's population will reach 9.7 billion people by 2050 and 10.4 billion by 2100.[9] Currently, the global population is growing at an average of 1.5 percent annually.

This present, booming period of growth is unprecedented in human history — *except for in the time frame that preceded the Flood.*

This illustration shows the men of Sodom as they approached Lot's house in sexual pursuit of Lot's male guests, who were actually angels sent by God to destroy that wicked city. Today we tend to think of the perversion in Sodom and Gomorrah as the apex of sexual perversion. But in our time, sexual confusion is so rampant that multitudes embrace the lie that there are dozens of genders from which to choose.

#2: GROSS SEXUAL PERVERSION (GENESIS 6:2,11,12)

Genesis 6:2 states, "…The sons of God saw the daughters of men that they were fair; and they took them wives of all which they chose."

In previous chapters, we have determined the "sons of God" were fallen, mutinous angels who began to abandon their God-assigned positions during the time of Jared, Adam's great-great-great-grandson. And as these beings came down to earth and sexually mingled with mortal women, the sexual depravity and perversity raged, reaching an intensity in the days before the Flood that would be impossible to overstate.

The Bible goes on to say that in the days before the Flood, "The earth also was *corrupt* before God, and the earth was filled with violence. And God looked upon the earth, and, behold, it was *corrupt*; for all flesh had *corrupted* his way upon the earth" (Genesis 6:11,12).

Three times the word "corrupt" appears in this text, and as we saw in Chapter 7, it is a translation of an original word that depicts *something that has been blemished, marred, or ruined.* This same word is used throughout the Old Testament and seems to be inseparably linked with sexual sin and perversity. Thus, this *blemishing* and *marring* that was occurring was initiated and accelerated by the fallen angels engaging in forbidden sexual relations with earthly women. Eventually, "all flesh" — even the animals — with the exception of those who eventually boarded the Ark with Noah became contaminated through rampant sexual perversity.

In Chapter 4, we learned that the fallen angels taught sexual "passions" that caused humans to veer from God's original design for sex. These passions included fornication, adultery, homosexuality, bestiality, and every evil act of sexual deviance imaginable.

Again, Jesus said, "But as the days of Noe [Noah] were, so shall also the coming of the Son of man be" (Matthew 24:37).

Therefore, we must ask:
Is the world today experiencing gross sexual perversion
as it occurred in the days before the Flood?

Without question, sexual perversity in society today is unparalleled, as sexual taboos are being thrown to the wind, and what was once considered blasphemous, degenerate, and deviant is now accepted and celebrated. It is unthinkable, but the sex-trafficking and porn industries combined generate nearly $250 billion annually and continue to exponentially grow.[10]

An alarmingly increasing number of individuals allege they are animals, a delusion that has the capacity to ultimately lead to bestiality and to people marrying animals, which we may see happen in the not-so-distant future.

Moral and sexual confusion have reached such an apex that many are confused about whether they are male or female.[11] In fact, there are multitudes that are so mixed up they actually embrace the nonsense that there are *dozens* of genders from which to choose.[12] Confusion is so pandemic that there are even growing numbers of people who believe they are of a different age or race than what is biologically true of them.[13] Moreover, there is an increasing number of individuals who allege that they are animals,[14] a delusion that has the capacity to ultimately lead to bestiality and to people marrying animals, which we may see happen in the not-so-distant future. *All of this is indicative of a deeply delusional societal state or condition.*

It wasn't so long ago that such kinds of thinking and behaving would have been associated with mental illness. But now these behaviors and lifestyles are progressively being legalized and normalized.[15] Rather than treat these deviancies as the insanity they are, courts, educational institutions, fields of medicine, and science are unthinkably endorsing and promoting them[16] — often prosecuting and punishing those who stick to God's prescribed moral values and refuse to bend to the spirit of the age.[17]

This delusional thinking is so prevalent that now, to be admitted to universities, many incoming students are required to sign a document of agreement with new policies of diversity and inclusion as a prerequisite for acceptance.[18] Imagine, to be accepted into many universities, young Christian believers are being required to either compromise what they believe, modify themselves to the new moral agenda, or forego higher education. At this point it must be stated that while we are called to be compassionate and loving toward everyone, we are not called to bend to such delusion in our own beliefs and values.

Only seducing spirits interacting with human beings could convince intelligent people to embrace such absurdity. The moral compass has been skewed so far that now outrageously dressed, cosmetic-riddled transvestites are regularly invited to perform at events for children and to participate in book-reading events for them in public libraries.[19] This is a demonic attempt to desensitize the youngest generation to what is morally right and wrong and to cause children to tolerate and embrace alternate lifestyles that the Bible condemns as abominations.[20] This is the social condition in which we're living.

We are living in a time when minds are being inundated with false information, and there is a widespread celebration of immorality, which is the result of seducing spirits bent on modifying the collective mind of society.

The fact is that we are living in a time when minds are being inundated with false information, and there is an almost across-the-board celebration of immorality. This last-days attack is occurring as seducing spirits, who are bent on modifying the collective mind of society, interact with humans and work to create a way of thinking that is free from moral restraint. This modification process has spread its tentacles into every sector of society so that now even many who grew up in church are becoming affected and are slowly changing what they believe about issues that *should* be set in stone.

This insidious shift in sexual morals has evolved over several decades and has occurred so gradually — and has been so well-disguised as "progressive thinking" — it has become more and more palatable to the masses. This progressive shift has also successfully intimidated many who see that moral values, and society with them, are running amuck — but they are so stigmatized by the new narrative as being hateful and bigoted toward those caught up in the moral haze that they remain quiet about their faith and about the Word and the power of God that could set those captives free.

Indeed, Satan's agenda of deception and intimidation has stepped up in scope and momentum in this end-time season. But to anyone with a sound mind and spiritual eyes to see, it is clear that dark demonic forces are working full-force to numb society and lead our youngest members down a treacherous immoral path.

This level of sexual perversion we are experiencing worldwide is unprecedented in human history — *except for in the time frame that preceded the Flood.*

Before the Flood, the word "inclusion" would have perfectly described the way people were welcoming and embracing a vast array of beliefs and "other gods." In our own time, society is returning to an inclusive and pluralistic mindset, which is deeply indicative of a past system of paganism.

#3: INCREASED DEMONIC ACTIVITY (GENESIS 6:2)

In addition to revealing gross sexual perversion, Genesis 6:2 also shows us that in the time before the Flood, there was an increase in demonic activity, which included humans inclusively worshiping a pantheon of various gods and interfacing with evil on a wide scale.

As fallen angels were entering Earth and interacting with mankind, the pre-Flood population was introduced to many forms of religions and absorbed in dark activities that became widespread in society. Again, Jesus said, "But as the days of Noe [Noah] were, so shall also the coming of the Son of man be" (Matthew 24:37).

Therefore, we must ask:
***Is the world today experiencing increased demonic activity
as it occurred in the days before the Flood?***

In the world before the Flood, the word "inclusion" would have perfectly described the way people were welcoming and embracing a vast array of beliefs. Likewise, in our own time, society is returning to an inclusive and pluralistic mindset, which is deeply indicative of a past system of paganism. By definition, "paganism" is idolatry or heathenism; *the worship of false gods or idols*; and *the rejection of Christianity and of Christ as THE way to ONE God, who is Lord over all.*[21]

There are many examples to demonstrate how today's culture, and even many in the Church, are departing from timeless truth to become more "inclusive" of beliefs and behaviors that are clearly against the teaching of Scripture. Indeed, the moral framework of society is being modified by media, education, government, and other societal institutions. Rather than stay with the scriptural truths that are foundational to a godly society, now the culture is adapting to a new mindset in the name of tolerance and open-mindedness. In an accelerated fashion, modern society is doing away with the Word of God — as God's unalterable will — in order to create a world free of the Bible's authoritative voice.

As the Bible is being displaced societally, moral confusion is raging as never before in our lifetimes. This confusion is no more obvious anywhere than in the debate over gender identity — a manifestation of confusion so severe and bizarre that it stuns most thinking minds.

Unfortunately, many Christians are in this number, gravitating toward more pluralistic, inclusive positions. In fact, the trend toward such thinking is increasing so rapidly among young people in churches that many are wavering on the very basic tenets of the Christian faith. Foundational beliefs — such as the virgin birth, the sinlessness of Christ, the need to repent, the reality of Satan, and a literal Heaven and hell — are all beliefs that are "up for grabs" with the younger generation.

Recent statistical analyses also show that the belief in absolute truth has already declined to such a point that the younger generation generally sees no need to witness to and convert those of a different faith to Christ. Instead of sharing the life-saving message of the Gospel, many young people find ways to rationalize their decision to remain silent, thinking things such as:

- "If what they believe is working for them, why should I bother sharing my beliefs?"

- "Who's to say that Christians are right, and they are wrong?"

- "Isn't it possible that there are alternative ways to God and that Christianity is just our particular way of believing in God?"

This seductive trend toward inclusivism (which is simply paganism with a modern twist) is growing so rapidly that believers are now often hesitant to publicly affirm what they believe for fear of the backlash of being labeled intolerant. But those who remain faithful to the standards of God's Word *must* be prepared to be ostracized as members of a fringe group of non-conforming outcasts. If we adhere to the teaching of the Bible, we will not condone others' immoral life choices, and we must face that our being labeled as "hateful" and "bigoted" as a result is a near certainty.

If today's Church and its leadership don't stand up for *the faith* — regardless of the price required to proclaim it in its purest form — it will be only a matter of time until Christianity is reduced to nothing more than another lifeless religion or philosophy among a cast of many others. Indeed, what pagans believed in the pre-Flood world is creeping back into our homes through education, television, Hollywood entertainment, government, and the courts. Because this trend is having such a dangerous impact on our children and grandchildren — and on our society as a whole — it is vital that we understand what modern paganism is, how to recognize it, and how to guard against it.

Idols of Satan have been permitted to be erected for worship in some public parks and government institutions, and there are public schools now offering "Satan clubs" for kids. Western society is being numbed by the growing prevalence of such diabolic influences because their eyes, minds, and senses are being bombarded with it continually.

In addition to the increasingly pagan mindset of our age, there is also a dramatic increase in dark spiritual activity. To the shock of many, idols of Satan have been permitted to be erected for worship in some public parks and in government institutions.[22] Likewise, there are public schools now offering "Satan clubs" for kids, and some government council meetings are opening with prayer, hailing Satan and asking him to guide the decisions made in their chambers.[23] Add to this the Luciferian-laced themes broadcast to millions during Super-bowl halftime shows and demonic influences proliferating on TV and movies — even in children's cartoons[24] — and we have a recipe for the days of Noah repeating themselves before our eyes.

Western society as a whole has become numbed by the growing prevalence of such diabolic influences because their eyes, minds, and senses are being bombarded with it continually. The regularity of dark images and devilish, occult-related entertainment has modified people to tolerate greater and greater levels of evil until now they no longer see evil as they once did. The toxic effect of it all is searing their minds and hardening their consciences so that what once deeply bothered them now doesn't bother them at all.

The onslaught of pagan-minded inclusiveness and demonic activity in the world today, which is coming from every direction in sophisticated ways, is unprecedented in human history — *except for in the time frame that preceded the Flood.*

Angels rebelled against God and descended into the earth's atmosphere to cohabit with women, and from these unnatural sexual unions, hybrid creatures — something beyond human — were produced.

#4: TRANSHUMANISM
(GENESIS 6:4)

Genesis 6:4 says, "There were giants in the earth in those days; and also after that, when the sons of God came in unto the daughters of men, and they bare children to them, the same became mighty men which were of old, men of renown."

This verse specifically shows us that angels rebelled against God and descended into the earth's atmosphere to cohabit with women, and from these unnatural sexual unions, hybrid creatures — something beyond human — were produced. Some ancient pagan religions referred to these half-angel, half-human entities as demigods. Again, Jesus said, "But as the days of Noe [Noah] were, so shall also the coming of the Son of man be" (Matthew 24:37).

Therefore, we must ask:
Is the world today experiencing a form of transhumanism as it occurred in the days before the Flood?

Today the emergence of a new kind of human and a new type of animal is becoming an unthinkable reality because of genetic engineering and the ramped-up efforts of transhumanists.[25] For the first time in human history, we have the ability to combine the DNA of more than two people, insert it into a human embryo, and create a child. Likewise, we have the capability to combine human DNA with animal DNA and create human-animal hybrids.

The fact is, human-animal hybrids are being grown in laboratories right now all over the world and have been for many years. As we mentioned in Chapter 6, scientists have developed pigs with human blood, mice growing human ears, and sheep growing human hearts.

In fact, *multiple* types of human organs are being grown in pigs and sheep to be harvested and implanted in patients who need them. The mixing of human seed and animal seed is happening right now and is one type of hybridization transhumanists are working to develop.

These actual headlines from around the world make clear some of the endeavors of transhumanists:

- "150 Human Hybrids Grown in…Labs: Embryos Have Been Produced Secretively for the Past Three Years"[26]
- *Transhumanism: Entering an Era of Bodyhacking and Radical Human Modification*[27]
- "Humans Will Be Hybrids By 2030"[28]
- "Super-intelligence and eternal life: transhumanism's faithful follow it blindly into a future for the elite"[29]

In simplest terms, "transhuman" means *beyond human*, which is what transhumanists today are vigorously working to achieve. Producing a new kind of human being that is *over* and *beyond* what any human has ever been is their very forthright goal and intention. And it is proceeding to the comingling of humans with machines — modern computer technology — which we will look at briefly in Chapter 15.

The foundational belief of transhumanism is that human beings are weak and poor, both physically and morally. Therefore, to improve the human experience — which includes overcoming aging, disability, disease, and mental limitations — there must be a convergence between humans and technology to create transhumans that will be stronger and have greater abilities.[30]

The drive of transhumanists to see humans and technology merged has already been achieved in some respects. For example, after interfacing with computers and other forms of technology, some disabled people have regained certain physical features and functions that were once lost,[31] which is a positive development. But that is not the endgame; it is only the beginning.

In addition to the ongoing efforts to merge man and machine, scientists in various nations around the world are also avidly experimenting with splicing human DNA with animal DNA to create superhuman beings. The result of this would be a new species of human-animal hybrid having cells and genetic materials of both humans and animals.[32]

In an article titled, "U.S. SUPER SOLDIERS OF THE FUTURE WILL BE GENETICALLY MODIFIED TRANSHUMANS CAPABLE OF SUPERHUMAN FEATS,"[33] the writer goes on record to say that leading scientists of several first-world countries are working to biologically engineer super soldiers who will…

- Run faster than Olympic gold medalists.
- Not need food or sleep for days.
- Regrow lost limbs.
- Outlift Olympian weightlifters and communicate telepathically.

Even though the development of such human-animal hybrids is the subject of legal, moral, and technological debate, it has not stopped the forward progress of this genetic engineering from taking place. In fact, it is likely that some form

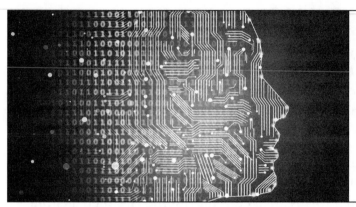

The goal of transhumanists is singularity, which is the occurrence of humanity and technology merging and becoming one. The dream is to so intertwine humans with technology that, eventually, a full convergence of bodies, minds, and emotions takes place. It is yet another manifestation of the arrogance of creation exalting itself against the Creator.

of genetically modified human-animal hybrid has already been produced, but it's being kept out of the public eye until the timing is right to unveil it.[34]

In previous chapters, we learned that there was a time in the ancient past when monstrous hybrid giants and possibly even animal-human hybrids were produced as a result of DNA contamination through illicit sexual activities and the mixing of the seed. Now with the scientific possibilities afforded through AI and things like CRISPR, RNA editing, nanotechnology, bionic implants, and other high-tech advances that exist, it is only a matter of time before a group of "researchers" secretly crosses the threshold and does it again.

Transhumanism is no longer relegated to science fiction. The idea of creating super-soldiers through scientific experimentation is being conducted at this very minute by many leading nations around the world. The question is, what will be the results — and consequences — of such DNA tampering? No one knows for sure, but all of it seems in some way similar to the events that were taking place in the time frame preceding the Flood.

And what about the practice of cloning? It is a well-publicized fact that cloning has already been conducted with animals,[35] and now medical labs are cloning human organs. The fact is that it is entirely possible — and even probable — that some form of human cloning is already secretly underway in remote laboratories where the eyes of the public are not permitted to watch.[36]

Some transhumanists are looking so far into the future (which may not be as far as we think), and they envision a time when mankind as we know it will enter into a *posthuman* period. I know this sounds like the stuff of science fiction, but the fact is there are well-known companies that have already developed computer chips to be implanted into the brain or under the skin to merge humans with AI.[37] This sounds very similar to what John jotted down in the book of Revelation about what will take place during the tribulation (*see* Revelation 13:16; 14:9; 20:4). Hence, we're living in a time where one can not only be transgender, but he or she can also become transhuman.

> **What is the long-term goal of transhumanists? The answer is singularity — the moment when humanity and technology merge and become one and transcend humanity. The dream is to so intertwine humans with technology that eventually a full convergence of bodies, minds, and emotions takes place.[38] Ideally, transhumanists want to escape death and live forever — either through uploading one's mind to computers, cloning, or by other means of technology.**

But be warned: The ultimate ambition and drive behind the transhumanist movement seems much darker than most people realize. In their own words, they want — and believe they have the technological capabilities — *to become like gods.* Sound familiar? Even more disturbing is the statement made by one highly influential, high-profile transhumanist who said, "We don't need to wait for Jesus Christ to come back to earth in order to overcome death. A couple of geeks in the laboratory can do it."[39]

Thinking we can become like God is the same deceptive and depraved lie the serpent sold to Eve in the Garden of Eden — the same temptation she and eventually Adam gave in to that brought death and destruction into the human race and the world (*see* Genesis 3). There is only one God, and we are not Him! As Bible teacher, author, and pastor Jimmy Evans so powerfully put it:

> **"The human seed is sacred and creates humans made in God's image. Man has no right to manipulate or try to improve on what God has done. I'm not talking about good people using medical technology to help people or cure them. I'm talking about arrogant men taking the place of God and trying to improve and immortalize ourselves, so we become our own gods.... What God has done cannot be improved upon, and we should leave the human seed alone except for helping people."[40]**

Altogether, the current level of genetic tampering with God's design for human beings and animals is unprecedented in human history — *except for in the time frame that preceded the Flood.*

In the time frame before the Flood, man degenerated in his imagination into such evil things that "his heart was only evil continually." This evil in the heart of man was especially evident and increased as the pre-Flood population interfaced with the dark spirit world, demonic activity, and engaged in multiple forms of sexual perversion.

#5: CONTINUOUS EVIL IN THE HEART OF MAN (GENESIS 6:5)

Genesis 6:5 says, "And God saw that the wickedness of man was great in the earth, and that every imagination of the thoughts of his heart was only evil continually."

This tells us clearly that in the timeframe before the Flood, man degenerated in his imagination into such evil things that "his heart was only evil continually." This evil in the heart of man was especially evident and increased as the pre-Flood population interfaced with the dark spirit world, and engaged in demonic activity and multiple forms of sexual perversion. Again, Jesus said, "But as the days of Noe [Noah] were, so shall also the coming of the Son of man be" (Matthew 24:37).

Therefore, we must ask:
*Is the world today experiencing a rise of evil in the heart of man
as it occurred in the days before the Flood?*

It is clear we are witnessing an intensification of evil in men's minds and hearts in our own times, and Romans 1:30 states that when lost humanity has their way and continues to go astray, it leads to their becoming "inventors of evil things."

The word "inventors" in this verse is from an original word that means to *contrive* or *invent*, and the word "evil" depicts what is *bad, base, destructive, evil, foul, harmful, injurious, rotten, vile,* or *morally wrong.* When the word "inventions" is used in the Old Testament, it usually has to do with *foul sexual activity.* We find it used this way in Psalm 106:29 and 39 where God was displeased with Israel for going "a whoring" with sexual escapades and sexual inventions in their times.

When Romans 1:30 speaks of "inventors of evil things," it seems to imply a time when the world throws off moral restraint, and inventions of evil things begin to emerge that will include inventions that are base and ugly in the sight of God. Keep in mind, Jesus said that what occurred in the days preceding the Flood would be replicated again at the end of the age. So how does "evil in the heart of man continually" in the pre-Flood society connect with people becoming "inventors of evil things" in our age? Consider the following:

> **The list of evil inventions today is nearly endless, and appearing toward the top of it is pornography and all kinds of highly sophisticated sexual technology that comes with it, including virtual sex.[41] Without getting too explicit, our so-called sophisticated society in which we live has taken the creation of evil fantasy to such a new level that there are new, life-like robots designed to carry out sexual acts however an owner programs them. Recently published articles show that with the push of a button, one can get whatever concoction of sex he or she wants with a robot. People are paying top dollar to engage with robots to meet sexual desires.[42] This bizarre development is a sign of "every imagination of the thoughts of [man's] heart [is] only evil continually" (*see* Genesis 6:5).**

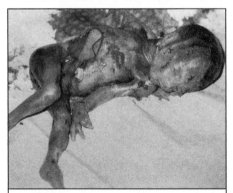

The worldwide slaughter of *more than two billion babies and counting* shows that we are not more civilized — rather, barbarism is escalating on an unthinkable scale.

An Evil Invention That Has Killed Billions

Bloodshed was also widespread before the Flood, which begs the question: How is it being replicated in our time at the end of the age? The answer could lead us to many horrific societal trends, but one practice it painfully brings to mind is the mass killing of the unborn in our generation. Today, easy accessibility to abortion has taken this form of bloodshed to an entirely different level than ever existed in previous generations.

In my book *Last-Days Survival Guide,* the documented, unembellished statistics of abortion around the world (at the time of my writing) are outlined. To help you grasp the intensity that this spirit of death has on our culture, consider the following:

> **Because accurate numbers of abortions were not kept in the Soviet Union before 1957, if we count from 1957 to the collapse of the Soviet Union in 1991 — in those 34 years, approximately 306,457,000 abortions were performed in the Soviet Union. This number is *larger* than the entire population of the USSR when the USSR dissolved in 1991.**
>
> **When we turn our attention to China to see how many abortions have been performed there, we find that the best records for the numbers of abortions performed in China before 1970 are unavailable, so research must begin with 1971, when the best information became available. Those records reveal that from 1971 to 2020 — a span of nearly 50 years — nearly 490,000,000 abortions were carried out in China.**
>
> **To help you comprehend that number, the current population of the United States is approximately 328 million. This means from 1971 to 2020, China aborted the equivalent of the entire population of the United States, *plus nearly 162 million more*. That second number is almost equivalent to the entire populations of Canada and Mexico combined. So if you add the 328 million and 162 million abortions carried out in China, the total number of infants killed in the womb during that time period is actually approaching the equivalent of the entire human population from the Arctic to the southern border of Mexico! That is the magnitude of the number of babies who were aborted in China in an almost 50-year span of time.**
>
> **Turning our attention to the United States, we see that since 1973 when abortion was legalized by the Supreme Court in the famous case of Roe v. Wade, nearly 62 million abortions have been performed.**
>
> **Altogether, the most solid information shows that the worldwide number of abortions between 1980 and 2020 (the last approximately 40 years) is estimated to have exceeded 2 billion. Think of that horrifying landmark number modern society has reached — *2 billion abortions* carried out globally in a span of 40 years!**

> **To help you grasp that number, try to imagine this: If *all* the people were killed who are currently living in North America, Central America, and South America — *plus* all of Europe, Russia, and Australia! — the total number of deaths still would not amount to the number of babies who have been aborted worldwide in this 40-year-window of time!**
>
> **Although these statistics are already mind-boggling, by the time you read this, they will be outdated because approximately 125,000 abortions are carried out *every day* worldwide.**

So while some contend that the world today is more technologically advanced and more sophisticated, this slaughter of more than *two billion babies and counting* shows that we are *not* more civilized; rather, barbarism is escalating on an unthinkable scale. Infants are routinely brutally burned to death by chemicals injected into a mother's womb, torn to pieces in the womb by medical devices, or aborted — their lives snuffed out — by means of an easily ingested pill.[43]

Almost every minute of every day in sterilized hospitals and clinics around the world, this barbaric act occurs.[44] This is worldwide savagery of the worst kind that — due to the sheer number of these acts against the innocent and defenseless — makes other holocausts and genocides smaller in comparison, though still grievous. It is murder on a scale so massive that no fiction writer could have ever imagined it. Yet this is *reality* in our present day and age.

So although we may think the mass killings that occurred at the hands of past infamous dictators or cruel leaders were barbaric and cruel — a fact no one would argue — those barbaric actions do not come close to the magnitude of the horrific number of lives for which abortion providers as a whole are responsible. Murdering more than *two billion babies* through the act of abortion is the mass annihilation of those who cannot scream, who cannot be heard, and who cannot defend themselves. The tiny bodies of these image-bearers of God are mutilated and thrown into garbage cans, sold for parts to the highest bidder, or recycled to be used in shampoos or cosmetics.[45]

When godly advocates raise their voices against this genocide, those who are pro-choice (which could also be called pro-death or pro-murder) often portray objectors to this atrocity as narrow-minded, right-wing fanatics. These advocates for life are attacked with a vengeance by the pro-choice faction that wants to intimidate, silence, and render powerless any and all opposition in order to retain the legal right to terminate the life of a child.[46]

Make no mistake — this present generation is tainted with the blood of innocent children. And one could argue that as a whole, it is largely guilty of the most heinous and barbaric behavior, perhaps in the entire history of mankind, because of the murder of more than two billion unborn children.

ALL GENDER RESTROOM

An evil is occurring as medical procedures are being regularly performed in an attempt to change people's gender. The preposterous notion that a person's gender can be creatively "reassigned" is a recurring message being shoved down the throats of modern society until the shock factor of gender reassignment is diminished and people begin to accept the idea that changing a person's gender isn't so bad or physically and emotionally damaging.

ALONG WITH ABORTION, THE EVIL INVENTION OF GENDER REASSIGNMENT IS DESTROYING LIVES

In addition to abortion, think of the evil occurring as medical procedures are being regularly carried out in an attempt to change people's gender.[47] The preposterous notion that a person's gender can be creatively "reassigned" is a recurring message being shoved down the throats of everyone in modern society.

Satan, the god of this world, is deceptively working overtime through educational institutions, the courts, many forms of the media, and the entertainment industry to wear people down until the shock factor of gender reassignment diminishes and society begins to adjust to and accept the idea that changing a person's gender isn't so bad or physically and emotionally damaging, but that it is, in fact, a good thing.

This is a blaring signal that delusion is oozing into the mainstream of society at an ever-increasing rate. In my book *How To Keep Your Head on Straight in a World Gone Crazy*, I discuss this topic of gender dysphoria compassionately.

This seduction and deception has woven its way into the fabric of society from nearly every angle, and even the Church has been affected. Besides what's being blasted over the airwaves on televisions, one of the primary ways the minds of the young are being swayed is through public education.

Curriculum is being written for the classroom that promotes and pushes a narrative that includes all-things ungodly — sex without limitations, abortion, same-sex attraction, gender fluidity, and pretty much anything else that undermines respect for God, Jesus, and the authority of the Bible.

This so-called "progressive" curriculum blurs the lines of truth, incites confusion, obliterates common sense, and punishes individual thinking. Any thinking that is outside the box of the "kinder, gentler" world of progressive humanism is not only frowned on, but is often met with violent, punitive resistance.

As incredibly challenging as this is, we as Christians need to know that it's *okay* and *right* to recognize and acknowledge that such assertions belong in a world gone mad — not in the life of the Body of Christ. If you are still standing *for* biblical truth and *against* the lunacy that has been loosed in this last-days society to destroy it — congratulations on maintaining your spiritual fire and not caving and becoming numbed and desensitized to the changes in the moral tide that we've experienced over the last 50 years.

To a rational thinker who still believes that science — which includes our anatomy and DNA — dictates our gender at birth,[48] gender fluidity and gender reassignment sounds like insane nonsense. But this delusional line of thinking, which not long ago was considered preposterous, is rapidly spreading across the stratum of society in an end-time bid to become "the norm."

> Let me be clear and say gender confusion is a real and complicated spiritual and psychological problem[49] that *cannot* be remedied by cutting off a man's penis to create an artificial vagina or cutting off a woman's breasts and/or surgically altering her private anatomy to try to turn it into a penis. This is not a reasonable answer to such a deep spiritual and psychological issue. In fact, it is *delusionary*. Those who struggle with the serious issue of gender confusion need mental and emotional healing — not surgery to try to make their physical makeup match their mental confusion. We need to help them with the *right* tools, not a surgeon's scalpel.

All that said, we must admit that the lid has been removed from reason, and commonsense thinking has been thrown to the wind, replaced with the whims of ever-fluctuating times. We can therefore soundly forecast that without a merciful and miraculous intervention by God Himself, in the not-so-distant future, society will begin implementing even more bizarre ideas and actions that would have been inconceivable abominations to previous generations.

To most of us, it seems that the level of evil that is now manifesting is unprecedented in human history. And it is — *except for in the time frame that preceded the Flood.*

The apostle Paul forecasted that society would turn violent at the end of the age. As barbaric and violent as society has been in past times and in the days before the Flood, the level of violence that will mark the end of the age will be greater than what we have ever known in our generation.

#6: WIDESPREAD VIOLENCE (GENESIS 6:11,13)

The sixth phenomenon that was taking place before the Flood was widespread violence across the earth. In fact, violence was so prevalent that God ultimately concluded that the only way to cleanse the earth of it was to send a Flood. In Genesis 6:11 and 13, we read:

The earth also was corrupt before God, and the earth was filled with violence.... And God said unto Noah, The end of all flesh is come before me; for the earth is filled with violence through them; and, behold, I will destroy them with the earth.

Once more, we look to Matthew 24:37, where Jesus said: "But as the days of Noe [Noah] were, so shall also the coming of the Son of man be."

Therefore, we must ask:
Is the world today experiencing widespread violence as it occurred in the days before the Flood?

Today, violence and corruption run rampant in our schools, our streets, and even our homes — it is everywhere. Nearly 2,000 years ago, the apostle Paul forecasted that society would turn violent at the end of the age (*see* 2 Timothy 3:1-9), and his Holy Spirit-inspired predictions support Jesus' prophetic warning that the things that occurred before the Flood would be repeated in the days before Christ's return. As barbaric and violent as society has been in past times, the level of violence that will mark the end of the age will be greater than this world has ever known.

In today's world of entertainment, violence is one of the hottest-selling tickets. It can be found all over the Internet, embedded in music, and vividly portrayed in video games.[50] To demonstrate just how sinisterly barbaric our world has become, consider these insights from my book *Last-Days Survival Guide*:

> **In our own time — at a time in modern history when we seem to be so sophisticated — we have taken the barbaric behavior of the ancient world to a new, unprecedented level. We may seem to be more sophisticated. But in reality, we no longer have to visit stadiums and other venues to experience violence and bloodshed, because now we bring huge doses of violence directly into our homes through television, digital devices, and the Internet. Although the means by which we receive our entertainment may be more technologically sophisticated, this generation is as barbaric, or even more so, than previous generations. It is simply barbarism manifesting in a different form.**
>
> **We can look back at ancient Roman society and wonder how they tolerated such savagery and cruelty. Yet in Second Timothy 3:1-4, the Holy Spirit pointed His prophetic finger toward the future and prophesied that in the last of the last days, violence would become *even more* widespread and commonplace in society. And we are seeing this come to pass.**
>
> **This present generation has seen so much brutality *as entertainment* on screens in front of them that they have become numb to its hideousness. Today people purchase tickets to movie theaters to watch scenes of human carnage play out before their eyes as thrilling entertainment.**
>
> **So I ask you — if we regularly feast our eyes, minds, and emotions on enacted scenes of human bloodshed, does that really make us more civilized, even though more sophisticated, than the ancient world that once reveled in some of the same live scenes played out before them?**

...Current statistics prove that if a person watches enough violence on television, his sensitivity to violence will become dulled and he will become numbed to acts that would otherwise prick his conscience and vex his soul. The same statistics reveal that if a person watches pornography, in time, that person will lose his sensitivity to the wrongness of this behavior; once again, he will become *numb* to it.

Consider these facts:

- The escalation of violence in entertainment is now so widespread that by age 18, a child will have seen more than 200,000 acts of violence on television and witnessed more than 40,000 simulated murders.

- The average seventh-grader watches more than 4 hours of television per day — with more than 60 percent of the programs containing violence.

- The same average seventh-grader plays electronic games 4 hours per week — with more than 50 percent of games categorized as "violent."

- In most of the industrialized world, 90 percent of homes with children have more than one television, not to mention video-game equipment, a personal computer, and high-tech cell phones with the capability of showing movies. This means parents can watch television in one room while their children sit unsupervised in another room with access to "entertainment" that projects violence into their young minds.

- Violent video games have created a thirst for violence. In fact, statistics now reveal the majority of children select "fantasy violence" as their favorite type of video games.

- Further studies reveal that the more frequently children practice fantasy acts of violence on video games, the more likely it becomes that they will carry out real acts of violence.

- These games are so similar to the programs used in real military training that one expert has stated, "We're not just teaching kids to kill; we're teaching them to like it." Advertising boldly tells children,

"Let the slaughter begin!" and awards them points for each person slaughtered during the game.

- The desensitizing effect of these words and images on young minds is proven to numb them to the seriousness of brutal acts committed against others.

- Today's music is filled with violence. All we have to do is listen to popular music or stroll down the aisle of almost any music or computer-game store to have this truth confirmed.

- The average teenager now listens to more than 10,500 hours of music during the years between the seventh and twelfth grades — much of which is violence-related.

- This means violent words and acts are being routinely poured into the minds of teenagers under the guise of music. This destructive influence is very difficult for parents to control, and many of them have no idea what their children are listening to on their devices — on the radio, satellite, and the Internet.

- As a result of the widespread use of the Internet, youth are regularly exposed to violent words, violent music, violent images, and pornography. There are literally *thousands* of websites specifically dedicated to foster racial hate, bigotry, violence, and pornography to the younger generations.

- Research shows — beyond any shadow of doubt — that violence in the media has a direct link to youth violence. One expert stated it well: "To argue against it is like arguing against gravity."

In this present-day culture, this escalation of violence has spread beyond the Internet and the screens of movie theaters, television, digital devices, and computers. It is now infiltrating society as shooters take aim at innocent people in public venues across the nation. One would think in this time when terrorism and bloodshed is so widespread that people would shun such entertainment. In reality, the opposite is true. Entertainment based on violence has only increased in popularity, and great masses of

> people are finding pleasure in "thrillers" filled with carnage. Just as the ancient Romans had a taste for blood, modern society pays money to sit and be entertained by murder, barbarism, and bloodshed.

The slower, kinder, safer world many of us grew up in is nearly gone, and with every new day it seems like society is being inundated with more violence. Our culture is so obsessed with images of violence that statisticians show it is seeping into the mainstream. Anyone with spiritual eyes opened is aware of this increase. In fact, we live in a world today where many enjoy and are so wholly given to violence, we have become a society known for our violent, reckless, and emotional overindulgence.

We are now reaping the long-term impact of violence on society as acts of violence steadily increase in every part of modern culture, which should make us question:

- When future historians look back on *our* time, what will they write about *us*?

- Will we be remembered as we remember the Romans and their taste for violence?

Unfortunately, our "sophisticated" and "technologically advanced" generation has become the generation that is most wholly given to violence in human history. Who would have ever thought it might be dangerous to go shopping at the mall or go watch a movie at the theater.[51] Nevertheless, because there have been so many shootings and killings in the past decades, many people who frequent these types of public places are now taking the time to scope out the closest emergency exits in case a shooter shows up and goes on a rampage.

Indeed, the levels of violence we are witnessing today may be unprecedented in human history — *except for in the time frame that preceded the Flood.*

We Are Witnessing the Onset of a Duplicate Moment as in the Days Before the Flood

Once more, consider the words of Jesus in Matthew 24:37:

But as the days of Noe [Noah] were, so shall also the coming of the Son of man be.

For 100 years, Noah preached to a perverse generation that judgment would eventually come — but the world around him went on nonchalantly as if they heard nothing. Jesus prophesied that at the end of the age people will also live nonchalantly in the face of judgment. Just as God used Noah to preach to an erring generation, God's Spirit beckons us to speak as His voice to a last-days generation.

Again, the meaning of the original text here is the equivalent of Jesus saying, "Exactly and precisely as it was in the days of Noah, thus it will be in the days preceding My coming, when I will set all things right upon My arrival."

Friend, as I've mentioned many times, what once *was* in history will once again *be*. Times are changing, along with the culture of each new generation. But the plans of the enemy to make society lawless and to turn people away from Christ as their "Ark of Safety" is still fully in play — and it will increase in severity in the days ahead.

But God has not left us without hope and without a way of escaping the temptation to just passively go along with the enemy's insanity that has penetrated sin-affected minds and society. In the name of "walking in love," which we should indeed do as believers, many have turned aside from loving God and His Word in favor of craving the world's applause and refusing to confront erring humanity with the truth spoken in love that could save them. This spiral of compromise has jeopardized the eternal well-being of those around them who are lost without Christ — while in their own lives, spiritual slumber enfolds them like a weighted blanket that impairs their movement and their effectiveness for God's Kingdom.

As much as we would like to think otherwise, the world will not grow brighter, but will dim to darker degrees as we approach the very end of the age. The Holy Spirit said through the apostle Paul that these times would be perilous (2 Timothy 3:1). And as we saw in Matthew 24, Jesus Himself said that deception would abound, and then He gave a list of calamitous events we should expect as we look up, expecting our final redemption.

But in the midst of darkness and chaos, our task is not to hide His light as we await His coming, but to shine as His glorious Church and do the works of Jesus while there's still time. While the world calls evil "good" and good "evil," the Church has been tasked with staying the course of righteousness and standing our ground on the absolute truth of God's Word. Nothing less will be worthy of Christ's name and His shed blood that was poured out to redeem us. As we continually *draw* near and *live* near to Him, He will surely give us the power to stand.

In the next chapter, we will see what Jesus said about the world going on nonchalantly at the end of the age. And we will examine two very important, yet mysterious, signs He told us would appear at the outer edge of the last days.

Additionally, we will look at what Peter urged us to pay attention to regarding Noah and the Flood and how that momentous event serves as a prophetic, telltale sign of the last days. There is so much we can learn from this story! And if we are open and listening, the Holy Spirit will use it to prepare us for living victoriously in these last of the last days.

QUESTIONS TO PONDER

1. Jesus said the things that were occurring before the Flood would be repeated in some way in the days before His return. In what specific ways are you seeing the "days of Noah" duplicated in society today? Specifically, what events do you see that are at least similar in some way to the bloodshed, evil, darkness, perverseness, and violence that was prevalent in the days prior to the Flood?

2. What is Jesus' return compared to repeatedly in First Thessalonians 5:1-4; Second Peter 3:10; Matthew 24:42-44; and Revelation 3:3; 16:15? Think carefully about this illustration. How does it help you better understand how the Lord will come to rapture His Church?

3. In light of your answer to the last question, what does God tell us we are to do to be ready at all times for Christ's return? (*See* Matthew 24:42-51; Luke 12:35-44; 1 Thessalonians 5:4-11; 2 Peter 3:10-14.) Pray and ask the Holy Spirit for His grace daily to be awake, watchful, and ready.

4. In this chapter, we saw that Jesus said the last days of the age would be *exactly like* the days of Noah. What images does that conjure in your mind concerning society in the end of days?

5. What is the remedy to a last-days scenario that rivals the days of Noah? Review some of the following verses and list ways believers can be "preachers of righteousness" like Noah before judgment came in his day: Matthew 24:24; 28:19,20; Mark16:15-18; John 3:3; 14:6; Acts 4:12; Romans 10:13-18; Second Corinthians 5:20; Philippians 2:15,16; Second Timothy 2:24-26.

6. Have you ever wondered what your place is in the last-days Church — the place God has called you to "for such a time as this"? Why not simply ask Him, "Lord, what would You have me do?" and then earnestly seek Him in prayer and the Word as you expect an answer. Praying the prayers in Ephesians 1:16-23 and Ephesians 3:16-21 would be a great place to start.

People before the Flood heard the warnings given by Noah, but they continued to live nonchalant lives, carrying on in their daily routines in a "business as usual" sort of way, even though a cataclysmic event lay directly before them. According to Jesus, this attitude of apathy and indifference will be replicated in the very last days leading up to the return of Christ.

CHAPTER FIFTEEN

NONCHALANT LIVING IN THE FACE OF JUDGMENT; SIGNS FROM THE HEAVENS; MONSTERS AND SCOFFERS; AND THE LONGSUFFERING OF GOD

As we have seen, Jesus explicitly said, "As it was in the days of Noah, so it will be at the coming of the Son of Man" (Matthew 24:37 *NIV*). Jesus forewarned that events in the time just before His coming would be similar to events that occurred in the time frame before the Flood in the days of Noah. He also warned that in spite of all the nefarious activities that will occur in a world going increasingly mad at the end of the age, people will largely continue their lives indifferently, oblivious to Jesus' end-time warnings.

But after referring to the days of Noah to describe the end of the age, Jesus gave us these additional details about what was going on in the time before the Flood.

For as in the days that were before the flood they were eating and drinking, marrying and giving in marriage, until the day that Noe [Noah] **entered into the ark.**

— **Matthew 24:38**

In this verse, the words "for as" mean *for in the same identical manner*. Jesus used these words to let us know that *in the same identical manner* the people before the Flood were living their lives is the same way people will be living their lives before Christ returns.

The use of Jesus' words "for as" indicates that just as the people before the Flood heard Noah's righteous preaching and continued living sinful lives — nonchalant in their attitude toward Noah's preaching and the things of God — people at the end of the age will also shrug off warnings of a judgment to come. Specifically, Jesus said that before the Flood, they were "eating and drinking, marrying and giving in marriage."

People lived as though they had never heard the preaching of Noah, carrying on in their "eating and drinking, marrying, and giving in marriage." But they had been told that a judgment would soon be released upon the earth.

Let's look at these words in the Greek for "eating," "drinking," and "marrying and giving in marriage."

Eating: The tense of this word "eating" is continuous in the original text, which means people were *eating and eating and eating*, and it depicts overeating or gluttony. This informs us that people in the time frame before the Flood were all about enjoying themselves in the "here and now" and were not concerned about a future judgment.

Drinking: Jesus also said people were "drinking," and just like the word "eating," the tense here is a continuous form, which means the people were *drinking and drinking and drinking*, and it indicates people were partying, drinking alcohol without moderation. They were given to enjoying themselves fully, without a care in the world about the days ahead of them, outside their present moment.

Marrying and Giving in Marriage: Once more we see the continuous tense in the original word for "marrying." Hence, it would better be translated *marrying and marrying and marrying*, which implies that the pre-Flood population was living and planning their personal futures with no thought or anticipation of a coming judgment. Jesus then added that the people were "giving in marriage," which is also in a continuous form, and it alerts us that the pre-Flood world was *giving and giving in marriage*. This expression might convey the idea of *a casual view of marriage*, of *broken marriages,* and of *remarriage*. It pictures people living with no thought of consequences or eternal ramifications.

Altogether, these ongoing actions of eating, drinking, marrying, and giving in marriage all point to a time when people lived very nonchalantly, carrying on in their daily routines in a "business as usual" sort of way, even though a cataclysmic flood lay directly before them.

According to Jesus, this attitude of apathy and indifference will be replicated at the very end of the age in the days just before the return of Christ. People will have heard the truth — that the end is coming and the need to repent and get right with God is at hand. But many will respond in the very same manner as people responded, or *failed* to respond, before the Flood. Even though they hear the message that a tumultuous time is rapidly approaching for all who are living on Earth, they will shrug it off and go on about their lives nonchalantly.

When Noah, his family, and the animals, entered into the Ark, and God shut the door, they trusted that God would direct the currents of the Flood to carry them to safety, which is exactly what He did.

'UNTIL THE DAY NOAH ENTERED THE ARK'

If you're wondering how long the pre-Flood population acted indifferently and nonchalantly toward Noah's righteous preaching and warnings, Jesus said it was "...until the day that Noe [Noah] entered into the ark" (Matthew 24:38). The word "until" in the original text means *right up until* and pictures people living unresponsive and uninterested right up to the final moment when Noah and his family entered the Ark.

The book of Genesis, which is largely attributed to Moses as the author, contains the biblical account of Noah and the Ark. It is noteworthy that the word "ark" used in Matthew 24:38 is the same word Moses used in Exodus 2:3 when he wrote of the *ark* of bulrushes his mother constructed and placed him in on the Nile River as an infant so he could escape Pharoah's death decree to the male Hebrew babies.

As we know from the book of Exodus, Moses' mother placed him into the little ark made of bulrushes that was covered with pitch so it would float and not sink. When she released it into the waters of the Nile, she was trusting God to direct the currents of the river to carry her little baby to a safe place. When writing the story of the Flood, Moses used the same word for "ark" to let us know that when Noah, his family, and the animals, entered into the Ark and God shut the door, they, too, trusted God to direct the currents of the Flood to carry them to safety, which is exactly what He did.

Although people lived in the shadow of the Ark, they did not take it seriously that God would send judgment. Jesus stated that at the very end of the age, although people will have heard righteous preaching for many years declaring a coming judgment, the world will nonchalantly turn a deaf ear to the message, just as the people did in the days preceding the Flood.

ALTHOUGH THE PEOPLE HAD BEEN WARNED, THEY WERE INDIFFERENT

In Matthew 24, as Jesus continued to describe the similarities between the days of Noah and the last days before His return, He stated that even though people had heard Noah's warnings — and the Ark stood before them as a vivid confirmation of his inspired words — they were indifferent. They continued *so* indifferent, in fact, that they became clueless as to what was about to happen. Jesus said that they were living on the precipice of judgment.

For as in the days that were before the flood they were eating and drinking, marrying and giving in marriage, until the day that Noe [Noah] **entered the Ark.**

— Matthew 24:38

Those are powerful words that are appropriate to our own day and age. Jesus used the word "until," which in the original text means *up to* or *right up until.* Although people heard the faithful preaching of Noah for 100 years and lived in the shadow of the Ark being built, they didn't take him seriously and were blind to what was coming — *right up until* the moment it came. In the same way, Jesus stated that at the very end of the age, although people have heard for many years righteous preaching that declared the coming of the Great Tribulation and judgment, they will nonchalantly turn a deaf ear to the message — just as the people did in the days preceding the Flood.

Jesus also stated that because the people did not heed Noah's message, the Flood came and "took them all away" (v. 39). This phrase is interpreted from two original words, the first meaning *to remove, to move from its place,* or *to prune* — and the second word means *absolutely all of them, each and every one of them,* or *all of them together.*

This lets us know that God intended for the Flood to be a pruning operation to prune the earth of all wickedness and corruption that had resulted from the mutinous angels intermingling with mortal women — as well as the alleged monstrous beasts that were supposedly birthed through the sexual defilement of the animals by the giants.

Basically, Jesus warned us that just as the Flood was a pruning operation in the old world, "...so shall also the coming of the Son of man be" (*see* Matthew 24:39). The phrase "so shall also" in Greek means *in keeping in line also.* This informs us that when Jesus comes to get His Church in the Rapture and seven years later in His

Second Coming, a new era will be initiated when He will clean house and straighten out all that is wrong in the world.

Jesus said in Matthew 24:40 that two will be working in the field when one will be taken, and the other will be left.

'ONE TAKEN, THE OTHER LEFT'

Jesus went on to describe a moment in the future when "…one shall be taken, and the other left" (Matthew 24:40).

Then shall two be in the field; the one shall be taken, and the other left.

This verse is interpreted in different ways by many, but some propose this can be viewed as a picture of the Rapture of the Church. The word "taken" is interestingly translated from a very endearing Greek word that means *to embrace, to receive to one's side*, or *to personally snatch*. Could this describe a future moment when Jesus will come and *embrace us, take us to His side, and snatch us away*?

This brings us to the second part of what Jesus said: "…and the other left." The word "left" is from an original Greek word that carries the sense of *being sorrowfully left behind*. Its use here indicates that those who did not pay heed to the warning of the coming judgment, but who instead carried on nonchalantly, will be left behind and experience a sense of regret and deep sorrow when they wake up and realize what has occurred.

Jesus' next statement in Matthew 24:41 seems to mirror His words in verse 40:

In Matthew 24:41, Jesus said two women will be grinding at the mill, and one will be taken, and the other will be left.

Two women shall be grinding at the mill; the one shall be taken, and the other left.

Again, we see the word "taken" and the word "left." The meanings of these words in the original text are the same as we saw in verse 40. Here, Jesus gives us a picture of two women who will be working side-by-side and going about their daily routines, when suddenly one will be *snatched away*, but the other will be painfully left behind and experience regret and sorrow as a result. Without question, those who ignore the warnings of God's coming wrath will be filled with indescribable regret and sorrow once the Rapture takes place and they realize they have been left behind.

WATCH — BE ON GUARD! NO ONE KNOWS THE HOUR

After describing these events, Jesus spoke with great urgency and said:

Watch therefore: for ye know not what hour your Lord doth come.
— Matthew 24:42

The word "watch" is translated from an original Greek word that means *to be attentive, to be on your guard*, or *to be watchful*. It conveys the attitude of one who is on the lookout and who is on high alert.

Jesus warned of our need to be ready at any moment for the time when He comes to take the Church. The reason Jesus said we must be continually on the lookout and on high alert is because we "…know not what hour your Lord doth come" (Matthew 24:42).

It pictures a person who has been informed that something is coming and who is watchful so he's not taken off guard by it.

The next word in this verse is "therefore," which means *accordingly*. Jesus used this word to emphasize our need to hear what He was saying about the Rapture and His Second Coming as well as our need to be on the lookout and watch for it. The reason Jesus said we must continually be on the lookout and on high alert is because we "…know not what hour your Lord doth come."

The word "hour" in the original text would be better translated *day*. This means we do not know the exact *day* when the Lord — which means our *Supreme Master* who is personally directing our lives — will come. But this does not mean we cannot have a *sense* of when He's coming.

If we study the Scriptures that particularly have to do with end-time events and observe what is happening in society and in the world around us, we are able to recognize that we are living in the season of the Lord's return. Although we cannot know the exact day, we can be spiritually attuned to the reality that we are living in the end-time season just before Jesus returns.

GET READY AND *LIVE* READY

Jesus wrapped up this urgent warning with this command:

Therefore, be ye also ready: for in such an hour as ye think not the Son of man cometh.

— Matthew 24:44

The opening word of this verse — "therefore" — could be interpreted *on account of this* or *in response to this*. Thus, after stating that His coming for the Church will be a stealth operation (*see* Matthew 24:43), Jesus then essentially said, "On account of all I've said, this needs to be your response…"

> **He then commanded, "Be ye ready," which are words translated from a phrase that means *to be constantly prepared, to be constantly ready for action*, and it depicts *a continual state of readiness*. Jesus thus declared that we are to live in a constant state of readiness because "…in such an hour as ye think not the Son of man cometh" (Matthew 24:44). In Greek, the phrase "in such an hour as ye think not" means *in the very hour you are not giving seriousness and due weight to this issue*, that may be the very moment when the Lord will come.**

The fact is, there is nothing stopping Jesus from coming right now, which is why we are to live on the lookout for Him and be in a constant state of readiness. Jesus said that when we see the kinds of things happening as they were happening in the days of Noah just before the Flood, "…Look up and lift up your heads, because your redemption draws near" (Luke 21:28 *NKJV*).

In Matthew 24, Jesus' disciples asked Him very candidly, "...What shall be the sign of thy coming, and of the end of the world?" (Matthew 24:3). They wanted the inside scoop from Jesus as to what visible "signs" would appear along the prophetic road to let them know that the time of His return and the end of the age was about to occur.

JESUS NAMED MULTIPLE SIGNS
THAT WILL APPEAR AT THE END OF THE AGE

It is interesting to note that at the beginning of Matthew 24, before Jesus compared the end of the age and the time of His return to the days of Noah, He had a riveting conversation with His disciples, who had asked Him very candidly, "...What shall be the sign of thy coming, and of the end of the world?" (Matthew 24:3).

People in general have always been fascinated with knowing the future, and there's something especially intriguing about knowing when "the end of the world" is going to take place. Since the beginning of time, individuals have sought soothsayers, fortune-tellers, astrologers, and horoscopes in an effort to satiate their inner need to know what the future holds.

Jesus' disciples were no different. They wanted the inside scoop from Jesus as to what visible "signs" would appear along the prophetic road to let them know when

the time for His return and the end of the age would be near.

What's interesting is that the word "sign" in Matthew 24:3 is translated from the Greek word used to describe *signposts* that helped travelers know exactly where they were when they were on their journey. Today we have these same kinds of authenticating road markers on our modern roads. For example, I see signs every day as I drive into the city of Moscow, and you see signs as you travel to your various destinations each day.

The disciples wanted to know what would be the "sign" that would alert them that the time of Christ's return was drawing near. They also wanted to know the road marker confirming that they had reached "the end of the world" (*see* Matthew 24:3).

It is important to note that the phrase "end of the world" is a translation of words that mean *the closure or wrap-up of the age*. Every age has a concrete beginning and a concrete end. When this present age — which many refer to as the Church age or the age of grace — ends, it will give way to the next age, which the Bible calls the Great Tribulation, a time when God's wrath will be poured out on all the ungodly who willfully rejected Jesus and His offer of salvation.

Not wanting any of us to be caught off guard, Jesus warned us of events that will occur at the end of the age, communicating them in such a way that those times would be easily recognizable and not obscure or difficult to understand. In fact, He gave us specific markers to let us know for sure where we are on the prophetic timeline and approximately how close we are to His return and the end of the age.

A BIBLICAL LIST OF LAST-DAYS SIGNS

Of all the subjects the Bible covers, about one-third of all Scripture deals with prophecy, and much of this centers on the return of Christ and the end of the age. This topic is so important, it is recorded in three of the four gospels — Matthew 24:4-14; Mark 13:5-13; and Luke 21:8-19. By reading these passages and comparing what Christ said in each, we can assemble a list of happenings Jesus said we would see as we approach the territory of the *very last* of the last days.

The following is a summary of the *signposts* Christ enumerated to let us know where we are on our journey toward eternity. Although these things have been occurring throughout the ages, Jesus forecasted these particular signs would *escalate in intensity and be widespread in the world* as we approached the very end of the age:

- **Widespread deception**
- **Deception in the Church**
- **Wars**
- **Rumors of wars**
- **Commotions**
- **Widespread terrorism**
- **Warring political systems**
- **Clashing of cultures**
- **Ethnic conflicts**
- **Famines**
- **Economic instability**
- **Pestilences**
- **Emergence of unknown diseases**
- **Great seismic activity**
- **Widespread persecution**
- **Legal prosecution of Christians**
- **Imprisonment of believers**
- **Emergence of false prophets and false religious movements**
- **The love of many waxing cold**
- **Fearful sights**
- **Signs from the heavens**
- **Worldwide preaching of the Gospel**

It is my personal conviction that we are living in the last "moments" of this present age. We have the keen ability to see and understand end-time scriptures more clearly than ever before, and I believe it is because *we are living in the season of their fulfillment*. Evidence continues to mount all around us of what Jesus forecasted so long ago. Because of where we are on the prophetic timeline, we are seeing and experiencing up-close what other generations could only see from a distance.

Clearly, these signs Jesus prophetically enumerated have the potential to either trouble our hearts or ignite our faith. Personally, my faith is *ignited* to think that God has chosen us to live in these very last days that have been long foretold in Scripture. With the equipping power of God's Word and the Holy Spirit, we are going to see Him move mightily as the last days of this age come to a close.

Jesus also warned in Matthew 24:36, "But of that day and hour knoweth no man, no, not the angels of heaven, but my Father only." Those who have tried to fix dates on Christ's coming have embarrassingly learned that no one is able to pinpoint the exact day or hour of His return. Nevertheless, the fact that we are seeing the simultaneous manifestation of numerous signs that Jesus predicted should put us on notice that we are living in the season of the Lord's soon return.

Likewise, because many similar events are occurring now that took place in the time frame before the Flood, it is a glaring announcement we may be living in *the very last of* the last days of this present age.

JESUS PREDICTED 'FEARFUL SIGNS' WILL APPEAR AT THE END OF THE AGE

There's something Jesus said that's recorded in Luke's gospel regarding a specific sign that will appear in the last days that isn't found in any of the other gospels. After Jesus warned us of the rise of false prophets, wars and commotions, nation rising against nation and kingdom against kingdom, earthquakes in diverse places, famines, and pestilences, He prophesied that there will be "…fearful sights and great signs shall there be from heaven" (Luke 21:11).

In this verse, the words "fearful sights" are derived from an original Greek word that depicts *fright, horror,* or *something that is scary.* Interestingly, Greek writers of antiquity actually employed this word to describe *monsters.* Certainly, the births of giants and monstrous hybrid creatures was taking place in the time before the Flood.

So what exactly was Jesus referring to in Luke 21:11?

Although it is not clear and Bible scholars cannot pinpoint or agree on what the words "fearful sights" entail, it seems that Jesus was saying that the last-days society would see things that are "monstrous" in the eyes of God and to the minds of men.

COULD THESE 'FEARFUL SIGHTS' BE...?

Natural disasters? One possibility that has been offered is that the words "fearful sights" refers to some form of catastrophic, monstrous natural disaster. However, we must note that when Jesus prophesied about the very *end of the* last days, He specifically listed several types of natural disasters by name (*see* Matthew 24:7; Luke 21:11). This seems to indicate that His warning of "fearful sights" as a category is separate from the natural disasters He specifically enumerated.

Devastation through technology? Another possibility that was previously unimaginable, but that has arisen in our modern age is that "fearful signs" could be a *horrific scientific or technological development*. The idea that technology could unleash profound devastation comes as no surprise in our modern era.

The Twentieth Century saw the first atomic bombs dropped at the close of World War II and the subsequent proliferation of nuclear weapons across the globe. Today many countries possess the means to wreak unthinkable devastation upon their enemies, and any such attack would have a profound impact on the fragile stability of the geopolitical system, not to mention the earth itself.

To date, no such attack has occurred since the U.S. atomic bomb attack on Hiroshima and Nagasaki in 1945. However, rising geopolitical tensions have begun to erode this sense of safety, and many analysts speculate the world is closer to the brink of a nuclear catastrophe than at any time since the Cold War.

Certainly, the total destruction unleashed by a nuclear blast and the ensuing aftermath caused by radioactive fallout would classify as *horrific*, *monstrous*, and *scary*. But again, I must point out that Jesus gave specific categories for these military conflicts (*see* Matthew 24:6,7; Luke 21:10). So it would seem the "fearful sights" are likely something altogether different.

Tragedy through transhumanism? We saw in the previous chapter that we are living in a day when DNA tampering and the genetic engineering of humans and animals are on the rise, and transhumanists are attempting to create a synchronous singularity between humans and technology. Could it be that a global monstrosity arises from the transhumanism movement?

The consequences of such experimentation, along with AI, that becomes out of control could certainly lead to monstrous human developments. Perhaps this is what Jesus was referring to when He foretold of "frightful sights."

Other possibilities exist as well, such as highly contagious superbugs and weaponized chemical agents that have been engineered at the behest of nations. Although such biological weaponry is presently kept under lock and key, the results of releasing these biological or chemical concoctions would be catastrophic if a population was ever exposed to them.

The original Greek word translated as "fearful sights" that Jesus used in Luke 21:11 is actually a word that was used by ancient Greeks to describe *monsters*. Therefore, we must ask: What would have been considered a "monster" at the time Jesus used this word and prophesied that "fearful sights" (monsters) would appear at the end of this age?

People's Appearance Can Sometimes Seem 'Monstrous'

In the ancient world, there were many cultural beliefs and stories and tales about monsters. These were bizarre creatures that were *frightening*, *strange*, and *unnatural*. Such monsters at that time were *deviant animals*, *creatures*, or even *people* that in some way became *distorted*, *hideous*, *outrageous*, *revolting*, and *twisted*.

> **The Latin word for a "monster" is derived from *monstrum*, and it likewise denotes something that is *contrary to the usual course of nature*. Most often ancient writers used various words for monsters to depict a being, creature, or person who *departed from the normal course of nature*, and this departure caused others to look upon it as *abnormal* and *shocking*.**

The reality is that there are many different scenarios one could imagine that would fall under the umbrella of Jesus' warning of "fearful sights." Any ideas will remain firmly in the realm of conjecture because Jesus purposefully kept this warning vague. However, one thing is certain: As a child of God, you do not need to fear these impending developments, and neither should you be surprised by them.

Regardless of exactly what these "fearful sights" are that Jesus prophesied about in Luke 21:11, these monsters or monstrous events He is alluding to will in some way be similar to the events that occurred in the days before the Flood when monstrous hybrid creatures roamed the earth and brought widespread violence and bloodshed to humanity. That is what Jesus said in Matthew 24:37 — that what occurred in the days of Noah would be replicated at the end of the age. Therefore, we must be prepared for the appearance of something monstrous as we speed toward the return of Christ and the wrap-up of this age.

Jesus Also Predicted 'Great Signs' From the Heavens Before His Return

Along with fearful sights, Jesus also prophesied that at the very end of the last days:

...Great signs shall there be from heaven.

— Luke 21:11

Here we find yet another mysterious sign for which there is no clear explanation. The word "great" in the original text depicts something that has a *monumental*, *far-reaching*, and *deep impact* on the earth and its citizenry. Whatever these "great signs" are, Jesus said they will appear "from heaven." Here, the word translated as "from" in the original text means *directly from*, which tells us the *monumental, far-reaching* signs will come directly from the *heavens* or from the *sky*, and whatever they are, much of the human race will be deeply impacted by it.

The fact that this word "from" is included in this verse adds great intrigue to what Jesus is saying. In the original text, the words "from heaven" implies something *from above* or something that will be *descending* from the heavens. This certainly agrees with Jesus' prophecy in Matthew 24:37, where He said the events at the end of the age and before His return will be a replication of the events that were occurring in the time frame before the Flood.

COULD THESE 'GREAT SIGNS' FROM HEAVEN BE...?

Nuclear bombs? Some claim that the "great signs from heaven" refers to nuclear bombs that descend from above and fall to the earth, bringing untold death and destruction. As I said earlier, many countries now possess nuclear weapons with the capability of unleashing unthinkable devastation upon their enemies. Any such attack would have a profound impact on the fragile stability of both the planet and the people of the world.

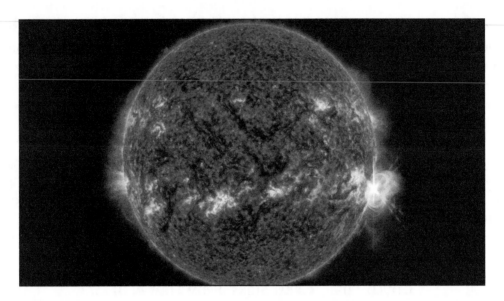

Solar flares? Others suggest the "great signs from heaven" Jesus spoke of may be solar flares that some scientists have already predicted will have the capacity of short-circuiting electrical connections and communications — including completely shutting down the Internet — a cataclysmic event that would disrupt life in many far-reaching ways.

Like tornadoes and other natural disasters, solar flares are natural occurrences. Generally speaking, solar flares are a type of "solar activity" in which certain explosions from the sun's surface emit bursts of electromagnetic radiation.

Solar flares are classed in a similar way earthquakes are measured on the Richter scale — and in the way tornadoes are classified on the "Fujita Scale" or the "Enhanced Fujita Scale" (from EF0 to EF5). For example, the smallest solar flares are A-class, followed in intensity by B-class, C-class, M-class, and X-class. Using x-ray data from satellites, space and weather organizations are able to predict the occurrence of solar flares to some degree. A- and B-classed flares don't significantly affect the earth — but M- and X-classed flares can trigger geomagnetic storms, resulting in electrical and radio blackouts, which could disrupt the technological world depending on their degree of severity.

Although solar flares don't hold enough energy to destroy a planet the size of Earth, they *can* create a great sight, or sign, from the skies — *the heavens*. As I said, no one really knows what Jesus' words meant as recorded in Luke 21:11, but I present *solar flares* as one possibility.

Meteors or asteroids? Still others contend that the "great signs from heaven" Jesus spoke of were His way of prophetically describing a meteor or an asteroid that will collide with the earth and create vast destruction. What's interesting is that there are indeed potentially dangerous asteroids that NASA has identified. One of them has been given the name "Apophis," which is the Greek name for the Egyptian god *Apep*, the god of *chaos*. Is such an asteroid, which is forecasted to come uncomfortably close to Earth in April of 2029, a fulfillment of the "great signs from heaven"?[1]

Could the phrase "great signs from the heavens" be Jesus' way of prophetically speaking about a meteor or an asteroid that collides with the earth and creates vast destruction? Or could these signs be something beyond the scope of our present imagination?

One thing is certain — the words Jesus chose in Luke 21:11 emphatically mean these "great signs" will descend from the heavens. In other words, before this age concludes, there will be some type of event, or series of events, descending from the heavens that will have a great impact on the population of the earth.

Luke 21:11 holds a mystery that Bible scholars and commentators haven't been able to unravel or explain. But what we do know with complete certainty is that "earthquakes, fearful sights, and great signs" will occur as we near the end of the age. Whatever these "fearful sights in the earth" and "great signs from heaven" are, the Bible tells us that they will be horrific and monstrous to those who witness them.

The return of fallen angels? In this book, we have shown that fallen angels were *descending* onto the earth at the time before the Flood and that as these spiritual beings sexually comingled with mortal women, giants were born from their illicit union — giants that brought widespread wickedness, violence, and bloodshed to the world.

This begs the question by some: Are these "great signs from heaven" possibly a return of fallen angels that somehow begin to tamper with the DNA of mankind to produce another hybrid race?

Or perhaps these "signs" will descend from the skies in the form of other rebellious angels that will beguile people to participate with them in some other nefarious fashion. Since angels can take on various appearances, could they suddenly begin to make appearances from the skies, purporting to be an interplanetary race of alien beings?

These types of scenarios that have been suggested both by theologians and by adventure-seekers are only conjecture and speculation. No one can conclusively say with any degree of certainty or credibility what these "fearful sights" and "great signs" will be. What we do know is that every word of God will prove true, and that it is a certain fact that these things will indeed appear as we approach the very end of the age.

UFOs and aliens? Some say the "great signs from heaven" Jesus prophesied may refer to UFOs (unidentified flying objects) or UAPs (unidentified aerial phenomena), which is the newest label for such unexplainable occurrences. In most recent years, the subject of UFOs and UAPs has become so prevalent that the Internet is now filled with reports of eyewitness accounts.

Was Jesus predicting *supernatural phenomena*, as opposed to natural occurrences in our solar system, that could become visibly apparent as a "great sign"? If He was, we know that these supernatural signs from above — such as UFOs or UAPs or so-called "space aliens" — will be of an evil, ungodly nature sent to deceive and distract mankind away from a desire for God and His Gospel — for "His only begotten Son," whom He sent as the only means of eternal reconciliation to the Father.

If an evil contingency of angelic beings transforms into "unidentified" signs from above in the very last days, they could potentially be as welcomed as the *watcher* angels were welcomed in Noah's day. As those mutinous angels descended to intermingle with humankind, they were welcomed with great fascination as god-like and divine. Could something similar happen in the end of days on the earth?

Again, no one has ever concluded with certainty what Jesus was referring to in Luke 21:11 concerning "signs in the heavens." But whatever these "signs" are, when we begin to see them, may we remember Jesus' words and at the same time remember to look up for Him, for our redemption will most certainly be near (*see* Luke 21:28).

Equally alarming is the fact these phenomena have also been the subject of military, congressional, and senate hearings. In a recent UFO hearing before the U.S. Congress, whistleblower and former intelligence official David Grusch said under oath that "non-human biologics" were found at a number of crash sites and recovered by the government. Grusch noted that these entities are "interdimensional," and his findings are based on "extensive interviews with high-level intelligence officials."[2]

Additional testimony was given by two former Navy personnel:

- **David Fravor, a former Navy commander, testified that he saw a strange object in the sky while on a training mission in 2004.**

- **Ryan Graves, a retired Navy pilot gave witness that he saw UAPs off the Atlantic coast "every day for at least a couple years" and that such sightings were "not rare or isolated." Military air crews and commercial pilots "whose lives depend on accurate identification," report witnessing these UAPs regularly.**

To the surprise of many, the military has finally and unequivocally stated on record that a great number of craft that have been seen are not ours and that man does not have the technology to make vehicles that move at such supersonic speeds,

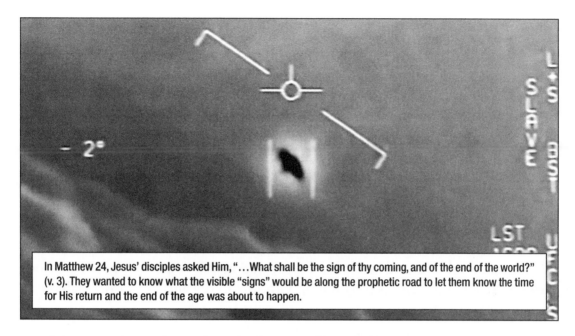

In Matthew 24, Jesus' disciples asked Him, "…What shall be the sign of thy coming, and of the end of the world?" (v. 3). They wanted to know what the visible "signs" would be along the prophetic road to let them know the time for His return and the end of the age was about to happen.

much less at right angles at those high rates of speed. Operators on the USS Princeton, part of the Nimitz carrier group, tracked one UAP accelerating from a standing position to traveling 60 miles in a minute — an astounding 3,600 miles an hour. No human pilot could survive traveling at such a speed.[3] Not only have these sightings been witnessed, but they have been recorded by highly sophisticated naval equipment, shown to the Congress, and widely distributed to the general public.

Some so-called "alien theorists" on far-fetched TV programs speculate that aliens are visiting the earth just as they claim aliens did in ancient times. However, we have already seen in this book that such claims are a twisted version of what is actually recorded in Genesis 6:1,2, and 4. Those who descended in times past were not aliens, but were mutinous angels. Again, I ask, is it possible that rebellious beings will attempt to come down to earth once more and replicate in some way the activities of the fallen angels before the Flood?

Or could these "great signs from the heavens" be something beyond the scope of our present imagination? The speculation and theories about these words are nearly endless.

One thing is certain: The words Jesus chose in Luke 21:11 emphatically mean that before this age concludes, there will be some type of event, or a series of events, that *descends directly from the heavens* and deeply impacts the population of the earth.

Moreover, these happenings will be *horrific* and *monstrous* to those who experience them.

Regardless of what these signs are, we need to realize that because we're living at the end of the age, it means we are likely on the threshold of seeing something we've never encountered before. Since strange events occurred before the Flood, then it is more than just probable that strange events will occur again before the coming of the Lord Jesus, just as He prophesied in Matthew 24:37.

This underscores how imperative it is that we fill our hearts and minds with the Word of God to maintain peace in our lives. Only then can we be instruments of comfort, healing, and deliverance to a generation that will witness these cataclysmic events. This is not a time for us as believers to cower in fear — it's a time for us to be filled with the Spirit of God and to reach a generation that desperately needs the Good News of Jesus Christ. This is truly our opportunity to rise and shine (*see* Isaiah 60:1).

IS THE REAPPEARANCE OF NOAH'S ARK A WONDER AND A WARNING THAT WE'RE IN THE LAST DAYS?

In Chapter 1, I began by making the statement that the story of the Flood and Noah's Ark is not a fantasy, but a reality. This was an event that really happened, and the ruins of Noah's Ark that are visible today on the slopes of the lower mountains of Ararat are proof. There are many significant eyewitnesses from antiquity who wrote about the Ark and documented the details of what they saw. The discovery of the Ark's ruins is significant because if there was an Ark and a Flood, there was a man named Noah who found favor with God and was saved from the Flood along with his family.

This means there actually was a time frame before the Flood — the period which Jesus referred to as "the days of Noah." Jesus prophesied in Matthew 24:37, "But as the days of Noe [Noah] were, so shall also the coming of the Son of man be." Again, according to this verse, events at the end of the age will be very similar to what was occurring on the earth in the days prior to the Flood.

The fact that we are living at the end of the age and the remains of Noah's Ark have reappeared is a glaring last-days reminder of Jesus' words in this pivotal verse. Is it possible that God saved the Ark's revealing to the world as a prophetic sign of the times we are living in right now?

The ruins of Noah's Ark are visible today on the slopes of the lower mountains of Ararat. Jesus prophesied in Matthew 24:37 (*NKJV*), "But as the days of Noah were, so also will the coming of the Son of Man be." Is it possible that God saved the Ark's revealing to the world as a prophetic sign of the times we are living in right now?

The Bible states that in the last days scoffers will come mocking those who believe we are living in the last days. Thus, one way to know that we've come to the end of this age is the presence of scoffers who arise to disdain and mock those who believe in Christ's soon return.

The apostle Peter wrote about the last days and said:

Knowing this first, that there shall come in the last days scoffers, walking after their own lusts, and saying, Where is the promise of his coming? for since the fathers fell asleep, all things continue as they were from the beginning of the creation.

— 2 Peter 3:3,4

The words "knowing this first" in the original text is the equivalent of Peter saying, *"First, foremost, and above all else, you need to know this…."* What does Peter emphatically want us to know above all else? *That in the last days, scoffers will come.* Thus, one sure-fire way we can know that we've come to the end of this age is the presence of scoffers on the scene who mock those who believe biblical prophesies such as the ones you've read in this book.

SCOFFERS DENY THE TRUTH OF WHAT THE BIBLE SAYS

The word "scoffers" in Second Peter 3:3 in the original text depicts *those who make fun of something through mockery.* In the days before the Flood in the time of

Noah, he and his family were surrounded by scoffers who mocked them and their warnings about a coming judgment.

Likewise, in our own time, there are scoffers — just as Peter predicted — who ridicule those who believe these really are the last days and that Jesus' return is near. This group says, "If Christ was going to come, He would have come by now. The world hasn't really changed that much over the years. We simply have better news coverage, so we're more aware of the darkness and tragedy in the world."

Furthermore, these "dissenters" argue that the heralding of Christ's soon return is based on fictitious prophetic utterances that have no basis in reality and that people have been talking about "the last days" for 2,000 years. Consequently, they allege that those who believe the return of Christ and the end of the age are near are living in a fantasy.

Technically, these mockers are correct when they state we've been calling it the last days for the past 2,000 years. Biblically, the last days officially started 2,000 years ago when the Holy Spirit was poured out on the Day of Pentecost. Acts 2:17 informs us that on that day, Peter quoted Joel 2:28 in which the prophet Joel prophesied about the supernatural happenings in the last days. Peter said:

> **And it shall come to pass in the last days, saith God, I will pour out of my Spirit upon all flesh....**
>
> **— Acts 2:17**

The outpouring of the Holy Spirit on the Day of Pentecost triggered the prophetic time frame called "the last days" that we've been living in for nearly 2,000 years. If you measure time according to Scripture, the time between Creation and the birth of Christ is about 4,000 years, and from the time of Christ until now, another 2,000 years have passed. Could it be that each 1,000 years signifies a "day" on God's prophetic calendar? Consider what Peter wrote in Second Peter 3:8:

> **But beloved, be not ignorant of this one thing, that *one day is with the Lord as a thousand years*, and *a thousand years as one day*.**

If indeed *one day* symbolizes 1,000 years, then from the time of Creation until now, humanity has experienced six "days" — four "days" *before* Christ's birth and two "days" *after* His birth. Thus, the two "days" (2,000 years) since His resurrection are the "last days" of the six total days, which means we are now in *the last of the last days*.

We Have Come to the Very End of the Last Days

The apostle Paul wrote about the *last* of the last days in his final letter to his spiritual son Timothy. With great urgency, he said:

This know also, that in the last days perilous times shall come.
— **2 Timothy 3:1**

The original word for "last" in this verse depicts something that is *final* and points to the *very last* or the *ultimate end* of a thing. This word was specially used by ancient Greeks to describe the point that was *furthest away*.

In the ancient world, this word "last" was used as a seafaring term to describe *the last port of call for a ship*. Although a ship in transit stops at many ports en route to its final destination, there was one *ultimate, final port* at the very end of the journey, and that is what the word translated "last" was used to depict. This last stopping-off point signified that it was the end of the road and the journey was finished. Thus, this word translated "last" indicated, *"This is the end, and you can go no further."*

> When discussing the end of this age and the return of Jesus, the word "last" points to the *very last* of a long, last-days season, or *the last of the last days*. Although we have been living in what is theologically called the period of *the last days* for some 2,000 years, we are now living in the ultimate end of the last days — the time when Jesus prophesied bizarre events that occurred before the Flood would happen again before His return.

The scoffing and mocking we are seeing today are a mere replication of what took place in the days preceding the Flood. When Noah preached and warned that judgment was coming, people in that age scoffed and mocked him and lived indifferently even though total devastation was soon to be released in the form of a flood.

Peter prophesied about these last-of-the-last-days scoffers, telling us some of the specific things about which they will attack and ridicule God's people:

They purposely ignore the fact that long ago God gave a command, and the heavens and earth were created. The earth was formed out of water

and by water, and it was also by water, the water of the flood, that the old world was destroyed.

— 2 Peter 3:5,6 *GNT*

In this passage, Peter said that last-days scoffers will willingly deny two things: that God is the Creator and that there was a global flood that once destroyed the world. This is exactly what we are dealing with today. Through the introduction of Darwin's theory of evolution in 1859 and ensuing ideas that the earth and everything in it has slowly evolved over millions of years, society at large has reasoned away the existence of God and the fact that He judged the earth by way of the Flood.

In the days of Noah, he and his family were surrounded by scoffers who mocked them and their warnings about a coming judgment. Although the people ridiculed them and rejected the warnings they gave, God protected and preserved Noah and his family through the Flood, but all the scoffers perished in the old world that overflowed with water.

THE PURPOSE FOR GOD POSTPONING JUDGMENT: HE IS PATIENTLY WAITING FOR PEOPLE TO REPENT

Someone may ask, "Why is God taking so long to wrap up this period and move on to the next prophetic phase? What is He waiting for?" Peter answers this question in his second epistle.

The Lord is not slack concerning His promise, as some count slackness; but is longsuffering to us-ward, not willing that any should perish, but that all should come to repentance.

— 2 Peter 3:9

The word "slack" in the original text means to be *tardy*, *slow*, *delayed*, or *late* in time. By using this word, the Holy Spirit informs us that God is not slow regarding the promises He has made — including the promises of Christ's return. He made them, and He will fulfill them. The reason for the wait is that God is "longsuffering." For the sake of those who still need to come to repentance, He is patiently waiting just as He did in the days before the Flood.

The word "longsuffering" in Second Peter 3:9 is from an original word that means to be *longsuffering* and *patient*. It is the Holy Spirit who *could* take revenge on a sin-ridden

Christ will come to retrieve His people in what is commonly referred to as "the Rapture." Thereafter judgment will be released upon the earth.

society, but He *utterly refuses* to do so. The *delay* of God's judgment is due to His *long-suffering* and *patience* with those who are unsaved. He is not tardy, delayed, or slow in fulfilling His promise to return and get us and bring an end to this age. He is simply holding out and purposely waiting for the last soul to be saved.

God is never in a rush to judge and is "…not willing that any should perish…" (2 Peter 3:9). Furthermore, He Himself has said, "…I take no pleasure in the death of wicked people. I only want them to turn from their wicked ways so they can live…" (Ezekiel 33:11 *NLT*). Nevertheless, the end of this age will come the *instant* the last person who is going to be saved is brought into the Kingdom.

Although it's true that not all will be saved, God is nevertheless patiently waiting for the Gospel to reach the ends of the earth and for that last person who will respond to His call. This shows just how *long* the longsuffering of God is toward humanity.

Just as God waited patiently in the days of Noah, He is waiting patiently again. But a time will finally come when the clock stops ticking and this age will end. When that occurs, Christ will come and retrieve His people, and thereafter judgment will be released upon the earth. Those who are safe inside the Ark of Jesus Christ will be unaffected, but those who have rejected Christ and mocked His warnings will be left behind and experience the Great Tribulation.

Until then, God calls each of us to faithfully proclaim the truth of Christ's coming and of the end of the age whether people listen to us or not. *Will God find us faithful, as Noah was, to proclaim the truth to the generation around us?* May God give us His grace to actively share the Good News of Jesus and endure to the end!

QUESTIONS TO PONDER

1. Nearly 2,000 years ago, the Holy Spirit prophesied through Paul in detail what society would be like at the end of the age. Take a moment to read these prophetic passages and jot down a quick summary of what each describes. Are you seeing any of these conditions in the world today?

   • 1 Timothy 4:1-3

   • 2 Timothy 3:1-9

   • 2 Timothy 4:3,4

2. What does God's Word instruct you and your family to do to guard yourselves from falling away from the faith (the last-days apostasy) and from being sucked into the godless behavior of the world? (*Consider* Second Timothy 3:14-17; Psalm 119:9,11,105; James 1:21-25; Hebrews 12:1,2; Ephesians 6:10-18; and Jude 20,21.)

3. Peter prophesied something very specific about the last days in Second Peter 3:3-6. What did he forewarn us that the people would be like? What will be the motivating force in their life (*see* verse 3)? What will they specifically scoff and mock at? What things will they purposely forget? Are you seeing any of these God-inspired words being fulfilled? What does this tell you?

4. Did you know that Jesus said we would see "fearful sights and great signs shall there be from heaven" (Luke 21:11)? What comes to mind when you hear that the end of the age will be a time of *"monsters,"* and that *monstrous* things will descend directly from the heavens to the earth? What connection do you think there might be between Jesus' words in Luke 21:11 and Luke 21:25 and 26?

5. Do you think Noah's Ark has reappeared at this specific time to remind the world of what Jesus said would occur at the end of the age? What does the news of Noah's Ark personally say to you?

6. As you finish this book, get quiet in the Lord's presence to see what He is speaking to you through these chapters. What actions do you sense Him prompting you to take? What adjustments do you sense Him asking you to make in the way you think, speak, and live your life? Take time to write down what the Holy Spirit is telling you and ask Him for the grace to obey His instructions.

Here, I am pictured standing on the top of the ruins of Noah's Ark on the slope of Mount Cudi at the Durupinar site, in the eastern mountains of Turkiye, with the cloud-covered Greater and Lesser Ararat in the distance behind me.

CHAPTER 16

A FINAL WORD

Without question, the world around us has entered a very dark and deviant time. Yet while the freefall into confusion and chaos continues and catastrophes abound, those who are in the Ark of Christ are protected in God's own hands (*see* John 10:28,29). Indeed, the signs all around us indicate the end date for this age is fast approaching and may be closer than we think.

JESUS IS COMING SOON FOR YOU AND ME!

The countdown to the catching away — Christ's rapture of His Church — is ticking. Jesus Himself has promised to come and get you and me before the wrath of God is poured out on the earth. Shortly before going to the Cross, Jesus encouraged His disciples by saying:

> **...I go to prepare a place for you. And if I go and prepare a place for you, I will come again, and receive you unto myself; that where I am, there ye may be also.**
> **— John 14:2,3**

This promise of Christ's coming is echoed throughout the New Testament, but is conveyed very clearly by the apostle Paul in his first letter to the believers in Thessalonica, where he writes:

According to the Lord's own word, we tell you that we who are still alive, who are left until the coming of the Lord, will certainly not precede those who have fallen asleep.

For the Lord himself will come down from heaven, with a loud command, with the voice of the archangel and with the trumpet call of God, and the dead in Christ will rise first. After that, we who are still alive and are left will be caught up together with them in the clouds to meet the Lord in the air. And so we will be with the Lord forever.

Therefore encourage one another with these words.
— 1 Thessalonians 4:15-18 *NIV*

For those who've made Jesus their Lord and Savior and eagerly await His return, *the best is yet to come!* Our job, according to Jesus, is to *watch* and *pray always* "… that [we] may be accounted worthy to escape all these things that shall come to pass, and to stand before the Son of man" (Luke 21:36). Make no mistake — if you are in Christ, a "great escape" awaits!

'The Great Evacuation' and the Devil's *Counterfeit Delusion*

The enemy is aware of Christ's promise to snatch His people away, into the air, receiving us to Himself. He knows God's Word and the promise to all believers that we will be "caught up" with Jesus. Perhaps this is why he has been methodically preparing society for years to buy a lie that explains away the Rapture of the Church. For decades, Hollywood has pumped out movies and television programming with storylines of aliens invading from outer space, inserting all sorts of ideas into people's heads. Are these simply artistic expressions, or is there a deeper plan of deception at work?

Some say the ball got rolling with the October 1938 legendary radio broadcast of "War of the Worlds," in which a dramatized radio program had many people believing we had actually been invaded by Martians.[1] From there, a steady flow of other offerings hit the big screen like *Invasion of the Body Snatchers, Close Encounters of the Third Kind, Alien, E.T., Independence Day, Signs, Predator*, and the list goes on and on.[2] Today, superior advances in CGI effects and AI generated images make

408

the latest releases more lifelike than ever before. Many wonder if these sensational box-office successes, seen by the masses are "coincidental" or a part of a master plan devised by the enemy.

The fact is, the subject of UFOs and aliens is an integral part of the occult and New Age belief system. One of the basic lines of thinking this system presents is that at some point in the future, the earth will undergo a season of great calamity. But before these catastrophic changes take place, we are going to see a "mass disappearance" of people. Some call it "The Great Evacuation" that will cleanse the earth of individuals whose existence is hindering the onset of the utopian world for which humanity waits.

In her book *Bringers of the Dawn*, renowned New Age author and channeler Barbara Marciniak claims to share insights she gained after 400 hours of channeling and receiving "wisdom" from so-called enlightened beings she calls the Pleiadians. She says:

> "There will be great shiftings within humanity on this planet… It will seem that great chaos and turmoil are forming, that nations are rising against each other in war, and that earthquakes are happening more frequently… Earth is shaking itself free, and a certain realignment or adjustment period is to be expected…. The people who leave the planet during the time of Earth changes do not fit here any longer, and they are stopping the harmony of earth…. When the time comes that perhaps twenty million people leave the planet at one time, there will be a tremendous shift in consciousness for those who are remaining…."[3]

Occult and New Age leaders like Marciniak encourage their adherents who will be "left behind" not to be concerned or alarmed because they are the "chosen ones" who were specially selected to help usher in a New World Order. Many of these leaders also claim that aliens will be the ones to help save humanity from itself and enable us to put an end to our Earth-destroying ways.

I am not saying this is the case, but some wonder if it is possible that a future media-spun story to explain away the Rapture of the Church will include the idea that aliens snatched away people's loved ones. Will it be said that these extraterrestrials — who will also likely be known as our more highly-evolved "space brothers" — came and removed from earth the millions of people who were unable to transition into the new utopian world?

One who carefully investigates the endgame of those involved in the occult will discover that their focused agenda is to establish a one-world government, a one-world religion, under a one-world ruler. Interestingly, this one-world everything is also the shared goal of many high-profile elites and billionaires around the world who are feverishly seeking to usher in a global Luciferian society. If this scenario sounds familiar, it's because the Bible — especially Revelation and Second Thessalonians 2 — are replete with similar details, all describing the kingdom of the Antichrist and the rise of the "beast system" (*see* Revelation 13:17).

ARE ALIENS REAL?

In the last chapter, I mentioned that the subject of UFOs (also known as UAPs) has become extremely prevalent. In fact, in some of the more recent data, 2022 was registered as a peak year, documenting 9,973 UFO sightings in the U.S. The county of Lincoln in Nevada, near the notorious Area 51 military base, is still the hotspot, recording more than 820 UFO sightings per 100,000 people.[4]

This begs the question: Are UFOs simply unidentified objects in the air, or are they other-worldly? It's been stated by many that the majority of UFO sightings have nothing to do with other-worldly entities. Whether that statement is true is up for debate across the board — by scientists, intellectuals, and thrill-seekers alike.

American physicist and science communicator Michio Kaku confirms this stating, *"95 percent of all UFO sightings can be immediately identified."* But then Kaku added, *"It's the 5 percent that give you the willies."*[5]

- Could it be that UFOs are the "great signs from heaven" Jesus prophesied we would see in the days before His return? (*see* Luke 21:11).

- And what about aliens? Are they real? Are they connected with fallen-angel activity?

Knowing from Scripture that there is nothing new under the sun (*see* Ecclesiastes 1:9,10) and that the enemy often comes as an angel of light (*see* 2 Corinthians 11:14), it is possible the "aliens" of today are nothing more than demons in a new disguise. This is not my pronouncement — I am simply presenting it to you for consideration. And it's not an original theory; rather, it is the united assessment of many secular experts who have worked extensively with those who claim to have had some kind of alien encounter.

Consider what these leading researchers have stated:

> • **Dr. Pierre Guerin**, distinguished scientist with the French National Council for Scientific Research said, "UFO behavior is more akin to magic than to physics as we know it. The modern UFOnauts and the demons of past days are probably identical."[6]
>
> • **John Keel**, renowned and highly informed journalist on the topic of UFOs said, "The manifestations and occurrences described in this imposing literature on *demonology* are similar if not entirely identical to the UFO phenomenon itself.... The UFO manifestations seem to be, by and large, merely minor variations of the age-old demonological phenomenon."[7]
>
> • **Dr. Jacques Vallee**, legendary scientist in the fields of astrophysics, computers, and aerial phenomena stated, "I do not believe anymore that UFOs are simply the spacecraft of some race of extraterrestrial visitors.... This notion is too simplistic to explain their appearance, the frequency of their manifestations through recorded history.... An impressive parallel can be made between UFO occupants and the popular conception of demons."[8]

If modern-day aliens are "real," they are nothing more than demons in disguise — and the devil has somehow cleverly reclothed his minions in such a way that they are accepted by society, thusly achieving his goals of deception.

Now here's the great news: In the powerful, matchless name of Jesus Christ, God has given believers all authority over all demonic forces! In Luke 10:19, Jesus said, "Behold, I give unto you power to tread on serpents and scorpions, and *over all the power of the enemy*: and nothing shall by any means hurt you." Just as the Lord rebuked evil spirits and they obeyed His commands, Jesus has given us that same power to defeat the devil and his minions in our lives.

For All Unbelievers...

The countdown to the end of this current age is well underway, and the rise of the Antichrist's kingdom and the beast's system is almost here. For all who reject

God's merciful and generous gift of salvation through Christ, the worst is yet to come. Rather than escape the coming wrath, the unsaved will be ensnared by it. Paul makes this clear in First Thessalonians 5:3.

> **For when they shall say, Peace and safety; then sudden destruction cometh upon them, as travail upon a woman with child; and they shall not escape.**

To All Believers…

God has called us to *occupy* until Christ comes (*see* Luke 19:13). Jesus said, "We must quickly carry out the tasks assigned us by the one who sent us. The night is coming, and then no one can work" (John 9:4 *NLT*). Some of these "works" the Lord has called us to do include:

- "Keep yourselves in the love of God, looking for the mercy of our Lord Jesus Christ unto eternal life." (Jude 1:21)

- "…Be ready always to give an answer to every man that asketh you a reason of the hope that is in you with meekness and fear." (1 Peter 3:15)

- "…Of some have compassion, making a difference: And others save with fear, pulling them out of the fire; hating even the garment spotted by the flesh." (Jude 1:22,23)

As you abide in the Ark of Christ, you will avoid the snares of deception and be ready for His soon return. The day *is* coming when true Christians will vanish from the face of the earth as Jesus catches them away in the Rapture. The Bible says, "In a moment, in the twinkling of an eye, at the last trump: for the trumpet shall sound, and the dead shall be raised incorruptible, and we shall be changed" (1 Corinthians 15:52).

The cause of the disappearance won't be alien abduction. It will be Jesus Himself descending into the sky to snatch His Bride out of harm's way, just in the nick of time! The rapture of the Church is the next event on God's prophetic calendar — and it will be a *great escape* for those who believe in the Lord Jesus Christ and are looking and longing for His return.

> "Even so, come, Lord Jesus. The Spirit and the bride say, Come!"
> (*See* Revelation 22:20; 22:17.)

ENDNOTES

Chapter 1

[1] Michael Castellano, "ARK SIGHTINGS: Both Literary and Eye Witnesses," Ark on Ararat, https://www.arkonararat.com/ark-sightings/. Accessed January 13, 2024.

[2] Dan Eden for ViewZone, "Noah's Ark Has Been Found. Why Are They Keeping Us In The Dark?," Sunny Skyz, December 13, 2013. https://www.sunnyskyz.com/good-news/470/Noah-s-Ark-Has-Been-Found-Why-Are-They-Keeping-Us-In-The-Dark-. Accessed January 13, 2024.

[3] Ibid.

[4] *LIFE Magazine: Hemingway: 'The Dangerous Summer,' Part 1*, (New York City, NY: Henry Luce, September 5, 1960), Page 112, https://www.originallifemagazines.com/product/life-magazine-september-5-1960/. Accessed January 13, 2024; "NOAH'S ARK? Boatlike form is seen near Ararat," *LIFE Magazine*, September 5, 1960, https://adventurefolio.com/wp-content/uploads/2022/04/Noahs-Ark-Life-Magazine.jpg. Accessed January 27, 2024.

[5] "NOAH'S ARK – THE EARLY YEARS," Wyatt Archaeological Research, https://wyattmuseum.com/noahs-ark-the-early-years/2011-697. Accessed January 13, 2024.

[6] "WHY ARE WE BEING KEPT IN THE DARK ABOUT THE DISCOVERY OF NOAH'S ARK?," Impact Lab, https://www.impactlab.com/2013/12/23/why-are-we-being-kept-in-the-dark-about-the-discovery-of-noahs-ark/. Accessed January 13, 2024.

[7] Ibid.

[8] Bill Crouse, "The landing place," https://dl0.creation.com/articles/p044/c04471/j15_3_10-18.pdf. Accessed January 14, 2024.

[9] "WHY ARE WE BEING KEPT IN THE DARK ABOUT THE DISCOVERY OF NOAH'S ARK?," Impact Lab, https://www.impactlab.com/2013/12/23why-are-we-being-kept-in-the-dark-about-the-discovery-of-noahs-ark/. Accessed January 13, 2024.

[10] Ibid.

[11] Ibid.

[12] Eric Bermingham, "The Search for Noah's Ark," The Kolbe Center for the Study of Creation, October 12, 2009, https://kolbecenter.org/the-search-for-noahs-ark/. Accessed January 19, 2024.

[13] Prof. Dr. Faruk Kaya, Prof. Dr. Oktay Belli, Prof. Dr. Randall W. Younker, *7th INTERNATIONAL SYMPOSIUM on MOUNT ARARAT and NOAH'S ARK: ABSTRACT BOOK* (Turkey: Agri Ibrahim Cecen Universitesi, 2023), page 44.

[14] Dan Eden for ViewZone, "Noah's Ark Has Been Found. Why Are They Keeping Us In The Dark?," Sunny Skyz, December 13, 2013. https://www.sunnyskyz.com/good-news/470/Noah-s-Ark-Has-Been-Found-Why-Are-They-Keeping-Us-In-The-Dark-. Accessed January 13, 2024.

15 John Larsen, "THE RESULTS OF THE SUBSURFACE IMAGING PROJECT OF NOAH'S ARK," NoahsArkScans.nz, https://noahsarkscans.nz/. Accessed January 15, 2024.

16 Discovered Media, "Science Channel investigates the Noah's Ark site!," YouTube, https://www.youtube.com/watch?v=FNKRqFwcLow. Accessed January 15, 2024.

17 "History Channel filming in Noah's Ark area," Hurriyet Daily News, November 18, 2021, https://www.hurriyetdailynews.com/history-channel-filming-in-noahs-ark-area-169430. Accessed January 15, 2024.

18 Bill Crouse, "The landing place," https://dl0.creation.com/articles/p044/c04471/j15_3_10-18.pdf. Accessed January 14, 2024.

19 Kurt Readman, "Mount Ararat: Where is Noah's Ark, Then?," Historic Mysteries, October 3, 2023, https://www.historicmysteries.com/myths-legends/mount-ararat/36824/. Accessed February 1, 2024.

20 Ethan Russell, "9 things to know about Google's maps data: Beyond the Map," Google Maps Platform, September 30, 2019, https://mapsplatform.google.com/resources/blog/9-things-know-about-googles-maps-data-beyond-map/. Accessed March 9, 2024; "Mount Ararat," Google Maps, https://www.google.com/maps/place/Mount+Ararat/@39.7024699,44.2784764,4046m/data=!3m2!1e3!4b1!4m6!3m5!1s0x4014d232638342ad:0xaaa6fa54b6b1247c!8m2!3d39.7024393!4d44.2990761!16zL20vMDF0a3c5?entry=ttu. Accessed February 2, 2024.

21 Mount Ararat Weather: Current Forecasts and Conditions, Two Ararat, https://www.twoararat.com/information/climb-preparation/mount-ararat-weather-forecasts/. Accessed March 9, 2024.

22 "Ararat," Smithsonian Institution, National Museum of Natural History, Global Volcanism Program, https://volcano.si.edu/volcano.cfm?vn=213040. Accessed January 18, 2024.

23 NOAA: National Centers for Environmental Information, Significant Earthquake Information, https://www.ngdc.noaa.gov/hazel/view/hazards/earthquake/event-more-info/1823. Accessed January 18, 2024; "1840 Ahora earthquake," Wikipedia, https://en.wikipedia.org/wiki/1840_Ahora_earthquake. Accessed March 21, 2024.

24 "NOAH'S ARK: FACT or FICTION?," Discovery World, https://www.discovery.global/noahs-ark-fact-or-fiction. Accessed January 29, 2024.

25 Del Tackett, "The Violence of the Pre-Flood World," Soli Deo Gloria, February 13, 2016, https://www.deltackett.com/resources/2656/the-violence-of-the-pre-flood-world. Accessed January 19, 2024.

Chapter 2

1 "How was the world populated before the flood?," Never Thirsty, https://www.neverthirsty.org/bible-qa/qa-archives/question/how-was-the-world-populated/. Accessed January 20, 2024.

2 Brett Hooper, "The Gospel in Genesis 5," Biblical Fidelity Publishing, January 17, 2019, https://biblicalfidelity.com/2019/01/17/the-gospel-in-genesis-5/. Accessed January 20, 2024.

3 Fr. Stephen De Young, "The Book of the Watchers," The Whole Counsel Blog, Ancient Faith Ministries, July 31, 2020, https://blogs.ancientfaith.com/wholecounsel/2020/07/31/the-book-of-the-watchers/. Accessed January 23, 2024.

[4] "Explore Sources: A database of excerpts from ancient documents that retell the story of the Nephilim & the 'sons of God'.," Chasing the Giants, https://chasingthegiants.com/sources/. Accessed January 20, 2024.

[5] Brett Hooper, "The Gospel in Genesis 5," Biblical Fidelity Publishing, January 17, 2019, https://biblicalfidelity.com/2019/01/17/the-gospel-in-genesis-5/. Accessed January 20, 2024.

[6] "Explore Sources: A database of excerpts from ancient documents that retell the story of the Nephilim & the 'sons of God'.," Chasing the Giants, https://chasingthegiants.com/sources/. Accessed January 20, 2024.

[7] Brett Hooper, "The Gospel in Genesis 5," Biblical Fidelity Publishing, January 17, 2019, https://biblicalfidelity.com/2019/01/17/the-gospel-in-genesis-5/. Accessed January 20, 2024.

[8] Rebecca Denova, "Enoch," World History Encyclopedia, September 16, 2021, https://www.worldhistory.org/Enoch/. Accessed January 20, 2024.

[9] "The Book of Enoch," Translated by R.H. Charles, Sacred-Texts, 1917, https://sacred-texts.com/bib/boe/. Accessed January 21, 2024.

[10] Brett Hooper, "The Gospel in Genesis 5," Biblical Fidelity Publishing, January 17, 2019, https://biblicalfidelity.com/2019/01/17/the-gospel-in-genesis-5/. Accessed January 20, 2024.

[11] Ibid.

[12] "LIFESPANS BEFORE THE FLOOD: HOW DID PEOPLE LIVE TO BE 900 YEARS OLD BEFORE THE FLOOD?," Genesis Apologetics, https://genesisapologetics.com/faqs/lifespans/. Accessed January 21, 2024.

[13] "The Pre-flood Atmosphere," Genesis Park, https://www.genesispark.com/exhibits/early-earth/atmosphere/. Accessed January 21, 2024.

[14] Ibid.

[15] Peter Goeman, "What Was the Population of Earth Before the Flood?," The Bible Sojourner, February 12, 2022, https://petergoeman.com/population-earth-flood/. Accessed January 21, 2024.

Chapter 3

[1] Peter Goeman, "What Was the Population of Earth Before the Flood?," The Bible Sojourner, February 12, 2022, https://petergoeman.com/population-earth-flood/. Accessed January 21, 2024.

[2] "Explore Sources: A database of excerpts from ancient documents that retell the story of the Nephilim & the 'sons of God'.," Chasing the Giants, https://chasingthegiants.com/sources/. Accessed January 20, 2024.

[3] Chuck Missler, "Mischievous Angels or Sethites?," Koinonia House, August 1, 1997, https://www.khouse.org/personal_update/articles/1997/mischievous-angels-or-sethites. Accessed May 15, 2024.

[4] "About Septuagint.Bible," The Septuagint: LXX, THE GREEK TRANSLATION OF THE HEBREW SCRIPTURES, Greek Orthodox Archdiocese of America, https://www.septuagint.bible/. Accessed January 22, 2024.

[5] Dr. Elmer Towns, "WERE THE 'SONS OF GOD' FALLEN ANGELS?," Bible Sprout, https://www.biblesprout.com/articles/heaven/angels/sons-of-god/. Accessed January 22, 2024.

6 Peter Colón, "The Septuagint: The First of the Bible Translations," Israel My Glory, November/December 2012, https://israelmyglory.org/article/the-septuagint-the-first-of-the-bible-translations/. Accessed January 22, 2024.

7 Joshua J. Mark, "Alexander the Great," World History Encyclopedia, November 14, 2013, https://www.worldhistory.org/Alexander_the_Great/. Accessed January 22, 2024.

8 "The Origins and Significance of the Septuagint," Christian Discipleship Lessons, https://www.cocdiscipleship.org/early-church/the-origins-and-significance-of-the-septuagint/. Accessed January 23, 2024.

9 "Explore Sources: A database of excerpts from ancient documents that retell the story of the Nephilim & the 'sons of God'.," Chasing the Giants, https://chasingthegiants.com/sources/. Accessed January 20, 2024.

10 John Drummond, "The Nephilim and the Sons of God," Biblical Archaeology Society, July 25, 2023, https://www.biblicalarchaeology.org/daily/biblical-topics/hebrew-bible/the-nephilim-and-the-sons-of-god/. Accessed January 22, 2024.

11 Fr. Stephen De Young, "The Book of the Watchers," The Whole Counsel Blog, Ancient Faith Ministries, July 31, 2020, https://blogs.ancientfaith.com/wholecounsel/2020/07/31/the-book-of-the-watchers/. Accessed January 23, 2024.

12 "Explore Sources: A database of excerpts from ancient documents that retell the story of the Nephilim & the 'sons of God'.," Chasing the Giants, https://chasingthegiants.com/sources/. Accessed January 20, 2024.

13 Phillip J. Long, "When was 1 Enoch Written?," Reading Acts, May 20, 2016, https://readingacts.com/2016/05/20/when-was-1-enoch-written/#. Accessed January 22, 2024.

14 "The Book of Enoch," Britannica, https://www.britannica.com/topic/biblical-literature/The-Book-of-Enoch. Accessed January 22, 2024.

15 Christen Coulter, "Enoch: Its History and Role in New Testament Understanding," Kesher: A Journal of Messianic Judaism, April 30, 2023, https://www.kesherjournal.com/article/enoch-its-history-and-role-in-new-testament-understanding/. Accessed January 23, 2024.

16 Richard Gottheil, Enno Littmann, "ENOCH, BOOKS OF (Ethiopic and Slavonic)," Jewish Encyclopedia.com, https://www.jewishencyclopedia.com/articles/5773-enoch-books-of-ethiopic-and-slavonic. Accessed January 22, 2024.

17 HD Clump, "ANCIENT ALIENS – S19 E16 | THE GODS OF GREECE," HD Clump, August 13, 2023, https://hdclump.com/ancient-aliens-s19-e16-the-gods-of-greece/. Accessed January 24, 2024.

18 "Tower of Babel," Jewish Virtual Library: A Project of AICE, https://www.jewishvirtuallibrary.org/tower-of-babel. Accessed January 24, 2024.

19 James Hardy, "The 10 Most Important Sumerian Gods: Nammu, Enki, Enlil, and More!," History Cooperative, April 22, 2022, https://historycooperative.org/sumerian-gods/. Accessed January 29, 2024.

20 History.com Editors, "Mesopotamia," History.com, April 24, 2023, https://www.history.com/topics/ancient-middle-east/mesopotamia. Accessed February 10, 2024; Joshua J. Mark, "The Mesopotamian Pantheon," World History Encyclopedia, February 25, 2011, https://www.worldhistory.org/article/221/the-mesopotamian-pantheon/. Accessed February 10, 2024.

21 Joshua J. Mark, "Egyptian Gods – The Complete List" [Note: Different names, similar attributes], World History Encyclopedia, April 14, 2016, https://www.worldhistory.org/article/885/egyptian-gods---the-complete-list/. Accessed February 13, 2024.

22 History.com Editors, "Mesopotamia," History.com, April 24, 2023, https://www.history.com/topics/ancient-middle-east/mesopotamia. Accessed February 10, 2024; Joshua J. Mark, "The Mesopotamian Pantheon," World History Encyclopedia, February 25, 2011, https://www.worldhistory.org/article/221/the-mesopotamian-pantheon/. Accessed February 10, 2024.

23 "About Babylonian Mythology," Cliffs Notes, https://www.cliffsnotes.com/literature/m/mythology/about-babylonian-mythology. Accessed January 29, 2024; Joshua J. Mark, "The Mesopotamian Pantheon," World History Encyclopedia, February 25, 2011, https://www.worldhistory.org/article/221/the-mesopotamian-pantheon/. Accessed February 10, 2024.

24 Mark Cartwright, "Greek Mythology," World History Encyclopedia, July 29, 2012, https://www.worldhistory.org/Greek_Mythology/. Accessed January 24, 2024.

25 Donald L. Wasson, "Roman Mythology," World History Encyclopedia, May 8, 2018, https://www.worldhistory.org/Roman_Mythology/. Accessed January 24, 2024.

26 Cierra Tolentino, "Incan Gods and Goddesses: 14 Ancient Deities of the Inca Pantheon," History Cooperative, March 11, 2024, https://historycooperative.org/incan-gods/. Accessed April 26, 2024.

27 Jesus Santillan, "Similarities Between Mayan and Aztec Gods and Goddesses," The Collector, January 5, 2020, https://www.thecollector.com/similarities-between-mayan-and-aztec-gods-and-goddesses/. Accessed January 30, 2024; Joshua J. Mark, "The Mayan Pantheon: The Many Gods of the Maya," World History Encyclopedia, July 7, 2012, https://www.worldhistory.org/article/415/the-mayan-pantheon-the-many-gods-of-the-maya/. Accessed April 26, 2024.

28 Arushi Gupta, "The Parallels of Two Countries: The Indian and Mexican Connection," June 30, 2021, https://himjournals.com/article/articleID=224. Accessed January 24, 2024; Swarupa, *Cultural Similarities between the Ancient Hindu & Indigenous Civilizations of the Americas,* thegr8wall.wordpress.com, March 23, 2013, https://thegr8wall.wordpress.com/2013/03/23/cultural-similarities-between-the-ancient-hindu-indigenous-civilizations-of-the-americas/. Accessed March 9, 2024.

29 Cierra Tolentino, "Chinese Mythology: History, Culture, Myths, and Heroes," History Cooperative, January 15, 2024, https://historycooperative.org/chinese-mythology/. Accessed January 24, 2024.

30 Daniel Kershaw, "Key Characteristics of Japanese Mythology," History Cooperative, August 16, 2023, https://historycooperative.org/japanese-mythology/. Accessed January 24, 2024.

31 Claudine Cassar, "Uncovering the Mythology of Native American Culture," Anthropology Review, March 12, 2023, https://anthropologyreview.org/anthropology-archaeology-news/native-american-mythology/. Accessed January 24, 2024.

32 Louise Pryke, "Ishtar," World History Encyclopedia, May 10, 2019, https://www.worldhistory.org/ishtar/. Accessed January 24, 2024.

33 Derek Gilbert, "The Spiritual Origins of Islam," Blog – Latest News, All Pro Pastors International, November 11, 2019, https://allpropastors.org/the-spiritual-origins-of-islam/. Accessed January 30, 2024.

34 Joshua J. Mark, "Astarte," World History Encyclopedia, November 9, 2021, https://www.worldhistory .org/astarte/. Accessed January 24, 2024.

35 Joshua J. Mark, "Sauska," World History Encyclopedia, January 5, 2015, https://www.worldhistory .org/Sauska/. Accessed January 24, 2024.

36 Joshua J. Mark, "Astarte," World History Encyclopedia, November 9, 2021, https://www.worldhistory .org/astarte/. Accessed January 24, 2024.

37 Morris Jastrow, Jr., George A. Barton, "ASHTORETH," Jewish Encyclopedia.com, https://www .jewishencyclopedia.com/articles/2005-ashtoreth. Accessed January 25, 2024.

38 Mark Cartwright, "Ancient Greek Inventions," World History Encyclopedia, December 20, 2017, https://www.worldhistory.org/article/1165/ancient-greek-inventions/. Accessed January 25, 2024.

39 Ray Pritchard, Keep Believing Ministries, "What is the Protoevangelium (Protoevangelion)?," Christianity.com, March 10, 2011, https://www.christianity.com/jesus/is-jesus-god/old-testament -prophecies/what-is-the-protoevangelium-protoevangelion.html. Accessed January 25, 2024.

Chapter 4

1 Dr. Elmer Towns, "WERE THE 'SONS OF GOD' FALLEN ANGELS?," Bible Sprout, https://www .biblesprout.com/articles/heaven/angels/sons-of-god/. Accessed January 22, 2024.

2 Fr. Stephen De Young, "The Book of the Watchers," The Whole Counsel Blog, Ancient Faith Ministries, July 31, 2020, https://blogs.ancientfaith.com/wholecounsel/2020/07/31/the-book-of-the-watchers/. Accessed January 23, 2024.

3 Christen Coulter, "Enoch: Its History and Role in New Testament Understanding," Kesher: A Journal of Messianic Judaism, April 30, 2023, https://www.kesherjournal.com/article/enoch-its-history-and-role-in -new-testament-understanding/. Accessed January 23, 2024.

4 Charles R. Swindoll, "Jude," Insight for Living Ministries, 2010, https://www.insight.org/resources /bible/the-general-epistles/jude. Accessed January 25, 2024.

5 TDL, "THE 'CHURCH FATHERS' AND THE BOOK OF ENOCH," Torah Driven Life, August 27, 2012, https://torahdrivenlife.org/the-church-fathers-and-the-book-of-enoch/. Accessed January 25, 2024.

Chapter 5

1 "Explore Sources: A database of excerpts from ancient documents that retell the story of the Nephilim & the 'sons of God'.," Chasing the Giants, https://chasingthegiants.com/sources/. Accessed January 20, 2024.

2 Melissa Petruzzello, "Nephilim," Britannica, https://www.britannica.com/topic/Nephilim. Accessed January 25, 2024.

3 John Drummond, "The Nephilim and the Sons of God," Biblical Archaeology Society, July 25, 2023, https://www.biblicalarchaeology.org/daily/biblical-topics/hebrew-bible/the-nephilim-and-the-sons-of -god/. Accessed January 22, 2024.

[4] Adam Stokes, "The Fall of the Giants and Their Fate According to Ancient Texts," Ancient Origins: Reconstructing the Story of Humanity's Past, April 26, 2020, https://www.ancient-origins.net/myths-legends-americas/giants-0013621. Accessed January 25, 2024.

[5] "Tertullian on Apostolic Tradition – Original Latin Text with English translation," Early Church Texts, https://www.earlychurchtexts.com/public/tertullian_on_apostolic_tradition.htm. Accessed February 3, 2024.

[6] "Pope Clement 1," The Famous People, https://www.thefamouspeople.com/profiles/pope-clement-i-37430.php. Accessed February 3, 2024.

[7] "Clement of Rome," Theopedia, https://www.theopedia.com/clement-of-rome. Accessed February 3, 2024.

[8] Ryan Nelson, "Who Was Clement of Rome?," OverviewBible.com, August 31, 2018, https://overviewbible.com/clement-of-rome/. Accessed February 3, 2024; "Church History (Book III)," Translated by Arthur Cushman McGiffert, NewAdvent.org, https://www.newadvent.org/fathers/250103.htm. Accessed May 23, 2024.

[9] Ibid.

[10] "Homily 8," Translated by Peter Peterson, NewAdvent.org, https://www.newadvent.org/fathers/080808.htm. Accessed February 3, 2024.

[11] Rebecca Denova, "Josephus on Christianity," World History Encyclopedia, October 8, 2021, https://www.worldhistory.org/article/1848/josephus-on-christianity/. Accessed February 1, 2024.

[12] Ibid.

[13] "Quotes from Josephus concerning Giants," Generation Word, https://www.generationword.com/notes/bible-topics/josephus_giants.htm. Accessed January 26, 2024.

[14] Jules Lebreton, "Gospel of Luke" [Note: Article title does not reflect content which actually refers to Justin Martyr], Early Christian Writings, http://www.earlychristianwritings.com/info/justin-cathen.html. Accessed February 1, 2024.

[15] Philip W. Comfort, "EARLY CHRISTIANITY: Justin Martyr (c. 100-110 – c.165 AD) – Early Christian Apologist and Philosopher," Christian Publishing House, February 22, 2022, https://uasvbible.org/2022/02/22/early-christianity-justin-martyr-c-100-110-c-165-ad-early-christian-apologist-and-philosopher/. Accessed February 1, 2024.

[16] "Saint Justin, Martyr," Living Space, Sacred Space, https://livingspace.sacredspace.ie/F0601s/. Accessed February 1, 2024.

[17] Jeff Riddle, "Eusebius, EH.4.16-18: Justin Martyr," Stylos, October 10, 2019, http://www.jeffriddle.net/2019/10/eusebius-eh416-18-justin-martyr.html. Accessed February 1, 2024.

[18] "Justin Martyr," Knowing Jesus Ministries, July 31, 2022, https://www.knowingjesusministries.co/sermons/justin-martyr/. Accessed February 1, 2024.

[19] "JUSTIN MARTYR & THE ANGELS THAT TRANSGRESSED," Chasing the Giants, https://chasingthegiants.com/justin-martyr-the-angels-that-transgressed/. Accessed February 1, 2024.

[20] "Tatian the Assyrian," Good Reads, https://www.goodreads.com/author/show/2170.Tatian_the_Assyrian. Accessed February 4, 2024.

[21] Ibid.

[22] Ibid.

[23] "Tatian," Alchetron, September 3, 2022, https://alchetron.com/Tatian. Accessed February 4, 2024.

[24] "Tatian the Assyrian," Good Reads, https://www.goodreads.com/author/show/2170. Tatian_the_Assyrian. Accessed February 4, 2024.

[25] James R. Payton, Jr., "Who is Irenaeus of Lyons?," The Gospel Coalition Canada, August 29, 2023, https://ca.thegospelcoalition.org/article/who-is-irenaeus-of-lyon/. Accessed January 30, 2024.

[26] "IRENAEUS OF LYONS AND 'ILLICIT UNIONS' OF ANGELS," Chasing the Giants, https://chasingthegiants.com/irenaeus-of-lyons-and-illicit-unions-of-angels/. Accessed January 30, 2024.

[27] "Saint Athenagoras of Athens," Orthodox Church in America, https://www.oca.org/saints/lives/2023/07/24/206388-saint-athenagoras-of-athens. Accessed January 30, 2024; "Athenagoras," Encyclopedia.com, https://www.encyclopedia.com/religion/encyclopedias-almanacs-transcripts-and-maps/athenagoras.Accessed January 30, 2024.

[28] "Athenagoras of Athens," Translated by Rev. B.P. Pratten, Early Christian Writings, http://www.earlychristianwritings.com/text/athenagoras-plea.html. Accessed January 30, 2024.

[29] "Clement of Alexandria," History of the Early Church, https://earlychurch.com/clement-of-alexandria/. Accessed January 26, 2024; Linwood Fredericksen, "St. Clement of Alexandria," Britannica, January 25, 2024, https://www.britannica.com/biography/Clement-of-Alexandria. Accessed January 26, 2024.

[30] "Homily 8," Translated by Peter Peterson, NewAdvent.org, https://www.newadvent.org/fathers/080808.htm. Accessed January 26, 2024.

[31] Johnson Thomaskutty, "Tertullian, the Father of Latin Western Theology and an Advocate of 'Freedom of Religion'," EarlyChurch.org.uk, https://earlychurch.org.uk/article_tertullian_thomaskutty.html. Accessed February 3, 2024.

[32] "Tertullian," The Voice of Healing, https://voh.church/resources/tertullian-biography_235449/. Accessed February 3, 2024.

[33] "The Text Tradition," Tertullian.org, February 26, 2000, https://tertullian.org/manuscripts/index.htm. Accessed February 3, 2024.

[34] Paul Pavao, "The Trinity: Doctrine, Development, and Definition," Christian History for Everyman, https://www.christian-history.org/the-trinity.html. Accessed February 3, 2024.

[35] James O'Donnell, "St. Augustine," Britannica, January 5, 2024, https://www.britannica.com/biography/Saint-Augustine. Accessed February 3, 2024.

[36] "Tertullian (145-220): Apology, Chapter 22," Translated by S. Thelwall, LogosLibrary.org, https://www.logoslibrary.org/tertullian/apology/22.html. Accessed February 3, 2024; "Death Changes, Without Destroying, Our Mortal Bodies Remains of the Giants.," On the Resurrection of the Flesh – Tertullian, Bible Hub, https://biblehub.com/library/tertullian/on_the_resurrection_of_the_flesh/chapter_xlii_death_changes_without_destroying.htm. Accessed February 3, 2024.

[37] "COMMODIAN," Pantheon, https://pantheon.world/profile/person/Commodian/. Accessed February 3, 2024.

[38] "COMMODIANUS ON THE INTERACTIONS OF ANGELS AND HUMANITY IN GENESIS," Chasing the Giants, https://chasingthegiants.com/comodianus-on-the-interactions-of-angels-and -humanity-in-genesis/. Accessed February 3, 2024.

[39] Rebecca Denova, "Eusebius on Christianity," World History Encyclopedia, October 15, 2021, https:// www.worldhistory.org/article/1854/eusebius-on-christianity/. Accessed January 30, 2024.

[40] OT, "Socrates Scholasaticus of Constantinople," Fourth-Century Christianity, February 8, 2017, https://www.fourthcentury.com/socrates-scholasaticus-of-constantinople/. Accessed January 30, 2024; "Socrates of Constantinople," Wikipedia, December 3, 2023, https://en.wikipedia.org/wiki/Socrates _of_Constantinople. Accessed January 30, 2024.

[41] "Sozomen: Christian Lawyer," Britannica, https://www.britannica.com/biography/Sozomen. Accessed February 11, 2024.

[42] "The Works of Theodoret," The Ecclesiastical History of Theodoret – Theodoret, Bible Hub, https:// biblehub.com/library/theodoret/the_ecclesiastical_history_of_theodoret/viii_the_works_of_theodoret .htm. Accessed February 11, 2024; Philip Wood, "Review: *Making Christian History: Eusebius of Cae-sarea and His Readers*, by Michael J. Hollerich," University of California Press, February 1, 2023, https://online.ucpress.edu/SLA/article/7/1/166/195780/Review-Making-Christian-History-Eusebius-of. Accessed February 11, 2024.

[43] Walter John Burghardt, "St. Jerome," Britannica, January 30, 2024, https://www.britannica.com/biography /Saint-Jerome. Accessed January 30, 2024.

[44] "Church History (Book 1)," Translated by Arthur Cushman McGiffert, NewAdvent.org, https://www .newadvent.org/fathers/250101.htm. Accessed January 31, 2024.

[45] "St. Jerome," Patheos, https://www.patheos.com/faith-figures-database/s/st-jerome. Accessed Febru-ary 5, 2024.

[46] "Jerome," Jewish Virtual Library: A Project of AICE, https://www.jewishvirtuallibrary.org/jerome -x00b0. Accessed February 5, 2024.

[47] "St. Jerome," Christian Classics Ethereal Library, https://www.ccel.org/ccel/jerome. Accessed Febru-ary 5, 2024.

[48] "The Church of the Nativity," Enjoy Bethlehem, https://enjoybethlehem.com/see/the-church-of-the -nativity. Accessed February 5, 2024.

[49] Louis Saltet, "St Jerome," NewAdvent.org, https://www.newadvent.org/cathen/08341a.htm. Accessed February 5, 2024.

[50] "St. Jerome," Patheos, https://www.patheos.com/faith-figures-database/s/st-jerome. Accessed Febru-ary 5, 2024.

[51] "Letter x. To Paul, an Old Man of Concordia," The Principal Works of St. Jerome – St. Jerome, Bible Hub, https://biblehub.com/library/jerome/the_principal_works_of_st_jerome/letter_x_to_paul_an.htm. Accessed February 6, 2024.

[52] J.S. Reid, "Sulpicius Severus: Early Christian writer," 1902 Encyclopedia, https://www.1902encyclopedia .com/S/SEV/sulpicius-severus.html. Accessed February 4, 2024; Nicholas Weber, "Sulpicius Severus," NewAdvent.org, https://www.newadvent.org/cathen/14332a.htm. Accessed February 4, 2024; SMT,

"Sulpicius Severus," Fourth-Century Christianity, April 25, 2012, https://www.fourthcentury.com/sulpicius-severus/. Accessed February 4, 2024.

[53] "SULPICIUS SEVERUS: THE NEPHILIM AND THE ANGELS THAT FORSOOK GOD," Chasing the Giants, https://chasingthegiants.com/sulpicius-severus-the-nephilim-and-the-angels-that-forsook-god/. Accessed February 4, 2024.

[54] "The Authentic Annals Of The Early Hebrews – Is It The "Real" Book of Jasher?," Christian Classics Ethereal Library, https://ccel.org/ccel/anonymous/jasher/jasher.ii.html. Accessed February 6, 2024.

[55] "The Book of Jasher," Good Reads, https://www.goodreads.com/book/show/40541164-the-book-of-jasher. Accessed February 6, 2024.

[56] "The Book of Jasher," Sacred-Texts, 1613, https://sacred-texts.com/chr/apo/jasher/index.htm. Accessed February 6, 2024.

[57] History Academy, "The Book of Jubilees: From Creation to Exodus of the Children of Israel," Google Books, 2021, https://books.google.com/books/about/The_Book_of_Jubilees.html?id=XxxjzgEACAAJ. Accessed February 7, 2024.

[58] "VERSIONS AND ORIGINAL LANGUAGE," Sacred-Texts, https://sacred-texts.com/bib/jub/jub04.htm. Accessed February 7, 2024.

[59] Fr. Stephen De Young, "The Book of Jubilees," The Whole Counsel Blog, Ancient Faith Ministries, October 30, 2019, https://blogs.ancientfaith.com/wholecounsel/2019/10/30/the-book-of-jubilees/. Accessed February 7, 2024.

[60] "THE BOOK OF JUBILEES AND THE WATCHERS," Chasing the Giants, https://chasingthegiants.com/the-book-of-jubilees-and-the-watchers/. Accessed February 7, 2024.

Chapter 6

[1] History.com Editors, "Mesopotamia," History, April 24, 2023, https://www.history.com/topics/ancient-middle-east/mesopotamia. Accessed February 10, 2024; Joshua J. Mark, "The Mesopotamian Pantheon," World History Encyclopedia, February 25, 2011, https://www.worldhistory.org/article/221/the-mesopotamian-pantheon/. Accessed February 10, 2024.

[2] Ibid.

[3] Joshua J. Mark, "Egyptian Gods – The Complete List," World History Encyclopedia, April 14, 2016, https://www.worldhistory.org/article/885/egyptian-gods---the-complete-list/. Accessed February 13, 2024.

[4] Joshua J. Mark, "Elam," World History Encyclopedia, August 27, 2020, https://www.worldhistory.org/elam/. Accessed February 10, 2024; Joshua J. Mark, "The Mesopotamian Pantheon," World History Encyclopedia, February 25, 2011, https://www.worldhistory.org/article/221/the-mesopotamian-pantheon/. Accessed February 10, 2024.

[5] History.com Editors, "Greek Mythology," History, August 15, 2023, https://www.history.com/topics/ancient-greece/greek-mythology. Accessed February 14, 2024; Maryn Liles, "30 Most Mythical Creatures From Folklore, Legends and Fairytales," Parade, September 29, 2022, https://parade.com/1056247/marynliles/mythical-creatures/. Accessed February 14, 2024.

[6] "Hittite Religion," Encyclopedia.com, https://www.encyclopedia.com/environment/encyclopedias-almanacs-transcripts-and-maps/hittite-religion. Accessed February 10, 2024; Joshua J. Mark, "The Mesopotamian Pantheon," World History Encyclopedia, February 25, 2011, https://www.worldhistory.org/article/221/the-mesopotamian-pantheon/. Accessed February 10, 2024.

[7] John F. Walvoord, "6. The Medes And The Persians," Bible.org, January 1, 2008, https://bible.org/seriespage/chapter-vi-medes-and-persians. Accessed February 14, 2024; Joshua J. Mark, "Twelve Ancient Persian Mythological Creatures," World History Encyclopedia, December 10, 2019, https://www.worldhistory.org/article/1484/twelve-ancient-persian-mythological-creatures/. Accessed February 14, 2024.

[8] "History of the Hurrians and the State of Mitanni," History and Culture of Ancient Civilizations, https://ancient-civilization.com/mesopotamia/history-of-the-hurrians-and-the-state-of-mitanni.html. Accessed February 15, 2024; "Hittite Religion," Encyclopedia.com, https://www.encyclopedia.com/environment/encyclopedias-almanacs-transcripts-and-maps/hittite-religion. Accessed February 10, 2024; Joshua J. Mark, "The Mesopotamian Pantheon," World History Encyclopedia, February 25, 2011, https://www.worldhistory.org/article/221/the-mesopotamian-pantheon/. Accessed February 10, 2024.

[9] Patrick Scott Smith, M.A., "Parthian Religion," World History Encyclopedia, June 30, 2020, https://www.worldhistory.org/Parthian_Religion/. Accessed February 14, 2024; Alonso Constenla Cervantes, "Sasanian Empire," World History Encyclopedia, May 17, 2013, https://www.worldhistory.org/Sasanian_Empire/. Accessed February 14, 2024; Joshua J. Mark, "Twelve Ancient Persian Mythological Creatures," World History Encyclopedia, December 10, 2019, https://www.worldhistory.org/article/1484/twelve-ancient-persian-mythological-creatures/. Accessed February 14, 2024.

[10] Joshua J. Mark, "Twelve Ancient Persian Mythological Creatures," World History Encyclopedia, December 10, 2019, https://www.worldhistory.org/article/1484/twelve-ancient-persian-mythological-creatures/. Accessed February 14, 2024.

[11] Cierra Tolentino, "Roman Mythology: The Legends, Deities, Heroes, Culture, and Religion of Ancient Rome," History Cooperative, November 8, 2023, https://historycooperative.org/roman-mythology/. Accessed February 14, 2024; Faiq Azam, "The Most Famous Roman Mythology Creatures (From Antiquity)," Vidzhome.com, March 30, 2022, https://vidzhome.com/roman-mythology-creatures/#. Accessed February 14, 2024.

[12] Alonso Constenla Cervantes, "Sasanian Empire," World History Encyclopedia, May 17, 2013, https://www.worldhistory.org/Sasanian_Empire/. Accessed February 14, 2024; Joshua J. Mark, "Twelve Ancient Persian Mythological Creatures," World History Encyclopedia, December 10, 2019, https://www.worldhistory.org/article/1484/twelve-ancient-persian-mythological-creatures/. Accessed February 14, 2024.

[13] History.com Editors, "Mesopotamia," History, April 24, 2023, https://www.history.com/topics/ancient-middle-east/mesopotamia. Accessed February 10, 2024; Joshua J. Mark, "The Mesopotamian Pantheon," World History Encyclopedia, February 25, 2011, https://www.worldhistory.org/article/221/the-mesopotamian-pantheon/. Accessed February 10, 2024.

[14] Mark Cartwright, "Urartu Religion," World History Encyclopedia, February 9, 2018, https://www.worldhistory.org/Urartu_Religion/. Accessed February 14, 2024.

[15] Cierra Tolentino, "Hindu Mythology: The Legends, Culture, Deities, and Heroes," History Cooperative, January 23, 2024, https://historycooperative.org/hindu-mythology/. Accessed February 15, 2024.

[16] Cierra Tolentino, "Norse Mythology: Legends, Characters, Deities, and Culture," History Cooperative, September 8, 2023, https://historycooperative.org/norse-mythology/. Accessed February 15, 2024; James Brigden, "7 TERRIFYING MONSTERS FROM NORSE MYTHOLOGY," Sky History, https://www.history.co.uk/articles/terrifying-monsters-from-norse-mythology. Accessed February 15, 2024.

[17] C. Todd Lopez, "DARPA Director Talks Promise of Life Sciences Research," U.S. Department of Defense, September 24, 2019; https://www.defense.gov/News/News-Stories/article/article/1969741/darpa-director-talks-promise-of-life-sciences-research/. Accessed May 24, 2024.

Chapter 7

[1] Dan Eden for ViewZone, "Noah's Ark Has Been Found. Why Are They Keeping Us In The Dark?," Sunny Skyz, December 13, 2013. https://www.sunnyskyz.com/good-news/470/Noah-s-Ark-Has-Been-Found-Why-Are-They-Keeping-Us-In-The-Dark-. Accessed January 13, 2024.

[2] "Noah's Ark: Fact or Fiction?," Discovery World, https://www.discovery.global/noahs-ark-fact-or-fiction. Accessed February 15, 2024; Bill Crouse, "The landing place," https://dl0.creation.com/articles/p044/c04471/j15_3_10-18.pdf. Accessed February 15, 2024.

[3] "Homily 8," Translated by Peter Peterson, NewAdvent.org, https://www.newadvent.org/fathers/080808.htm. Accessed February 15, 2024.

[4] "THE BOOK OF ENOCH: WATCHER ANGELS & THEIR GIANT SONS," Chasing the Giants, https://chasingthegiants.com/the-book-of-enochs-story-of-the-watchers-sins-the-giants/. Accessed February 15, 2024.

[5] *The Works of Josephus*, Translated by William Whiston (Hendrickson Publishers, 1987, 1994) p.32.

[6] "Book of Jubilees," Bible Gateway, https://www.biblegateway.com/resources/encyclopedia-of-the-bible/Book-Jubilees. Accessed February 15, 2024.

[7] Gabriel Oussani, "Book of Jubilees," NewAdvent.org, https://www.newadvent.org/cathen/08535a.htm. Accessed February 15, 2024.

[8] "The Book of Jubilees: The Little Genesis," Good Reads, https://www.goodreads.com/book/show/29334071-the-book-of-jubilees. Accessed February 15, 2024.

[9] "Dead Sea Scrolls," Encyclopedia.com, May 23, 2018, https://www.encyclopedia.com/philosophy-and-religion/bible/bible-general/dead-sea-scrolls. Accessed February 15, 2024.

[10] The Editors, "The World's Oldest Writing," Archaeology: A Publication of the Archaeological Institute of America, May/June 2016, https://www.archaeology.org/issues/213-features/4326-cuneiform-the-world-s-oldest-writing. Accessed February 16, 2024.

[11] "Cuneiform Tablets: From the Reign of Gudea of Lagash to Shalmanassar III," LIBRARY: Library of Congress, https://www.loc.gov/collections/cuneiform-tablets/about-this-collection/. Accessed February 16, 2024.

Chapter 8

[1] Emil G. Hirsch, W. Muss-Arnolt, Hartwig Hirschfeld, "FLOOD, THE," JewishEncyclopedia.com, https://www.jewishencyclopedia.com/articles/6192-flood-the. Accessed February 16, 2024.

[2] Bill Gifford, "How Old Can Humans Get?," ScientificAmerican.com, July 31, 2023, https://www.scientificamerican.com/article/how-old-can-humans-get/. Accessed February 16, 2024.

[3] "Oldest person ever," Guinness World Records, https://www.guinnessworldrecords.com/world-records/oldest-person/. Accessed February 17, 2024.

Chapter 9

[1] "Berossus (Babylonian Bel-Re'Ushu) in Wikipedia," Bible-History.com, https://bible-history.com/links/berossus-babylonian-bel-reushu-2282. Accessed February 18, 2024.

[2] "THE HUNT FOR NOAH'S ARK," JasonColavito.com, https://www.jasoncolavito.com/the-hunt-for-noahs-ark.html. Accessed February 18, 2024.

[3] "Abydenus," Wikipedia, https://en.wikipedia.org/wiki/Abydenus. Accessed February 19, 2024.

[4] "THE HUNT FOR NOAH'S ARK," JasonColavito.com, https://www.jasoncolavito.com/the-hunt-for-noahs-ark.html. Accessed February 18, 2024.

[5] "Nicolaus of Damascus: Life of Augustus: - sections 91-139, and the fragments of the Autobiography of Nicolaus," Translated by C.M. Hall, attalus.org, http://www.attalus.org/translate/nicolaus2.html#NicAug. Accessed February 18, 2024.

[6] "Nicholas of Damascus," Jewish Virtual Library: A Project of AICE, https://www.jewishvirtuallibrary.org/nicholas-of-damascus-x00b0. Accessed February 18, 2024.

[7] "Josephus: The Complete Works: CHAPTER 3. CONCERNING THE FLOOD; AND AFTER WHAT MANNER NOAH WAS SAVED IN AN ARK, WITH HIS KINDRED, AND AFTERWARDS DWELT IN THE PLAIN OF SHINAR,," Christian Classics Ethereal Library, https://ccel.org/ccel/josephus/complete.ii.ii.iii.html. Accessed February 18, 2024.

[8] Rebecca Denova, "Josephus on Christianity," World History Encyclopedia, October 8, 2021, https://www.worldhistory.org/article/1848/josephus-on-christianity/. Accessed February 1, 2024.

[9] Ibid.

[10] "Josephus: The Complete Works: CHAPTER 3. CONCERNING THE FLOOD; AND AFTER WHAT MANNER NOAH WAS SAVED IN AN ARK, WITH HIS KINDRED, AND AFTERWARDS DWELT IN THE PLAIN OF SHINAR,," Christian Classics Ethereal Library, https://ccel.org/ccel/josephus/complete.ii.ii.iii.html. Accessed February 18, 2024.

[11] Patricia Claus, "The Suda, The Greek Encyclopedia Written in the Year 1100," Greek Reporter, November 23, 2023, https://greekreporter.com/2023/11/23/suda-byzantine-encyclopedia-written-1100/. Accessed February 18, 2024.

[12] "Julius Africanus," Christian Classics Ethereal Library, https://ccel.org/ccel/juliusafricanus. Accessed February 18, 2024.

[13] "Sextus Julius Africanus – Encyclopedia," Encyclopedia Britannica 1911, https://theodora.com/encyclopedia /a/sextus_julius_africanus.html. Accessed February 18, 2024.

[14] "Fragment iv. On the Deluge. …," The Writings of Julius Africanus – Julius Africanus, Bible Hub, https://biblehub.com/library/africanus/the_writings_of_julius_africanus/fragment_iv_on_the_deluge_.htm. Accessed February 18, 2024.

[15] Johann Peter Kirsch, "St. Hippolytus of Rome," NewAdvent.org, https://www.newadvent.org/cathen /07360c.htm. Accessed February 19, 2024.

[16] "Hippolytus Romanus," Dictionary of Christian Biograph, Christian Classics Ethereal Library, https:// www.ccel.org/ccel/wace/biodict.h.html?term=hippolytus+romanus. Accessed February 19, 2024.

[17] "1911 Encyclopædia Britannica/Hippolytus (writer)," Wikisource, https://en.wikisource.org/wiki /1911_Encyclop%C3%A6dia_Britannica/Hippolytus_(writer). Accessed February 19, 2024.

[18] Ibid.

[19] "Hippolytus of Rome," The Refutation of All Heresies – Book X, Early Christian Writings, https:// earlychristianwritings.com/text/hippolytus10.html. Accessed February 19, 2024.

[20] Patricia Claus, "The Fascinating History of Romaniote Jews in Greece's Ioannina," Greek Reporter, October 8, 2023, https://greekreporter.com/2023/10/08/greece-ioannina-romaniote-jews-history/. Accessed February 20, 2024.

[21] "ST. EPIPHANIUS OF SALAMIS," Vela de Jerusalén: www.santosepulcro.co.il, https://santosepulcro.co .il/en/saints/st-epiphanius-of-salamis/. Accessed February 20, 2024.

[22] Ibid.

[23] "THE HUNT FOR NOAH'S ARK," JasonColavito.com, https://www.jasoncolavito.com/the-hunt-for -noahs-ark.html. Accessed February 18, 2024.

[24] Mavro, "JOHN CHRYSOSTOM: THE 'GOLDEN-MOUTHED', MAN OF GOD AND TEO-LOGICIAN," ASH – Abrahamic Study Hall, September 14, 2018, https://www.abrahamicstudyhall .org/2018/09/14/john-chrysostom-golden-mouthed-man-of-god-saint-teologician/. Accessed February 20, 2024; Mary Fairchild, "John Chrysostom, the Golden-Tongued Preacher," Learn Religions, September 3, 2019, https://www.learnreligions.com/john-chrysostom-4764128. Accessed February 20, 2024.

[25] Ibid.

[26] "Homily 8 on First Thessalonians," Translated by John A. Broadus, NewAdvent.org, https://www .newadvent.org/fathers/230408.htm. Accessed February 20, 2024.

[27] James R. Russell, "FAUSTUS" [Note: FAUSTUS also known as P'AWSTOS BUZAND or FAUSTUS OF BYZANTIUM], Encyclopædia Iranica, January 24, 2012, https://iranicaonline.org/articles/faustus-. Accessed February 20, 2024; "Faustus of Byzantium," Wikipedia, https://en.wikipedia.org/wiki/Faustus _of_Byzantium. Accessed February 20, 2024.

[28] Bill Crouse and Gordon Franz, "MOUNT CUDI – TRUE MOUNTAIN OF NOAH'S ARK," www.biblia .work, https://www.biblia.work/sermons/mountcudi-true-mountain-of-noahs-ark/. Accessed February 20, 2024.

[29] "ST. ISIDORE OF SEVILLE," Vela de Jerusalén: www.santosepulcro.co.il, https://santosepulcro.co.il/en/saints/st-isidore-of-seville/. Accessed February 21, 2024; John Bonaventure O'Connor, "St. Isidore of Seville," NewAdvent.org, https://www.newadvent.org/cathen/08186a.htm. Accessed February 21, 2024.

[30] Ibid.

[31] Lucas Van Rompay, "Theophilos of Edessa (d.785) [Maron.]," Gorgias Encyclopedic Dictionary of the Syriac Heritage: Electronic Edition, https://gedsh.bethmardutho.org/Theophilos-of-Edessa. Accessed February 22, 2024.

[32] "THE HUNT FOR NOAH'S ARK," JasonColavito.com, https://www.jasoncolavito.com/the-hunt-for-noahs-ark.html. Accessed February 18, 2024.

[33] "Hayton – Encyclopedia," Encyclopedia Britannica 1911, https://theodora.com/encyclopedia/h/hayton.html. Accessed February 22, 2024.

[34] "Jean Chardin," Alchetron, November 9, 2023, https://alchetron.com/Jean-Chardin. Accessed February 22, 2024.

[35] Ibid.

[36] "Sir John Chardin," Westminster Abbey, https://www.westminster-abbey.org/abbey-commemorations/commemorations/sir-john-chardin#i13236. Accessed February 22, 2024.

[37] "THE HUNT FOR NOAH'S ARK," JasonColavito.com, https://www.jasoncolavito.com/the-hunt-for-noahs-ark.html. Accessed February 22, 2024.

[38] "1911 Encyclopædia Britannica/Oelschläger, Adam," Wikisource, https://en.wikisource.org/wiki/1911_Encyclopædia_Britannica/Oelschläger,_Adam. Accessed February 22, 2024.

[39] Ibid.

[40] "Near Eastern Languages & Civilizations: Assyriology," Yale University, https://nelc.yale.edu/graduate/specializations/assyriology. Accessed February 23, 2024; "Assyriology," Wikipedia, https://en.wikipedia.org/wiki/Assyriology. Accessed February 23, 2024.

[41] John M. Cunningham, "Claudius James Rich," Britannica, https://www.britannica.com/biography/Claudius-James-Rich. Accessed February 23, 2024.

[42] Patricia E. Daniels, "Biography of Czar Nicholas II, Last Czar of Russia," ThoughtCo., January 22, 2020, https://www.thoughtco.com/nicholas-ii-1779830. Accessed February 23, 2024.

[43] Helen Azar, "TSAR NICHOLAS II: DIARY OF THE ABDICATION" [Note: dates correspond with Old Style/Julian calendar used in that time], The Romanov Family, June 21, 2018, https://www.theromanovfamily.com/tsar-nicholas-ii-diary-of-the-abdication/. Accessed February 23, 2024.

[44] "Exploring The Historic Silk Road In Turkey," Explore More Turkey, November 29, 2023, https://exploremoreturkey.com/whats-new/exploring-the-historic-silk-road-in-turkey/. Accessed February 23, 2024; C. Griffith Mann, "*Armenia!* In the Shadows of Mount Ararat," The Met, October 15, 2018, https://www.metmuseum.org/blogs/now-at-the-met/2018/armenia-mt-ararat. Accessed February 23, 2024; HIRC, "Marco Polo: Ancient Historical Figures Write About and Reveal Location of Noah's Ark | Matthew 7:7," Hebrew Israelite Research Center, August 3, 2022, https://www.hebrewisraeliteresearchcenter

.org/marco-polo-ancient-historical-figures-write-about-and-reveal-location-of-noahs-ark-matthew-77/. Accessed February 23, 2024.

Chapter 10

[1] A.J. Monty White, "Stories from around the world verify Noah's Flood," Educate for Life: Kevin Conover, October 7, 2013, https://educateforlife.org/stories-around-world-verify-noahs-flood/. Accessed February 24, 2024.

[2] Eric Lyons and Kyle Butt, "Legends of the Flood," Apologetics Press, November 1, 2003, https://apologeticspress.org/legends-of-the-flood-64/. Accessed February 24, 2024; Mark Isaak, "Flood Stories from Around the World," The TalkOrigins Archive, September 2, 2002, http://www.talkorigins.org/faqs/flood-myths.html. Accessed February 24, 2024; "Flood Legends From Around the World," NW Creation Network, https://www.nwcreation.net/noahlegends.html. Accessed February 26, 2024; Roger Marshall, "Ancient Flood Legends Compared to the Biblical Account of Noah's Flood," Project Probe, May 8, 2017, https://www.projectprobe.org/blog/ancient-flood-legends-compared-to-the-biblical-account-of-noahs-flood/. Accessed January 29, 2024.

[3] Prof. Dr. Faruk Kaya, Prof. Dr. Oktay Belli, Prof. Dr. Randall W. Younker, *7th INTERNATIONAL SYMPOSIUM on MOUNT ARARAT and NOAH'S ARK: ABSTRACT BOOK* (Turkey: Agri Ibrahim Cecen Universitesi, 2023), page 2.

[4] Prof. Dr. Faruk Kaya, Prof. Dr. Oktay Belli, Prof. Dr. Randall W. Younker, *7th INTERNATIONAL SYMPOSIUM on MOUNT ARARAT and NOAH'S ARK: ABSTRACT BOOK* (Turkey: Agri Ibrahim Cecen Universitesi, 2023), page 7.

[5] Prof. Dr. Faruk Kaya, Prof. Dr. Oktay Belli, Prof. Dr. Randall W. Younker, *7th INTERNATIONAL SYMPOSIUM on MOUNT ARARAT and NOAH'S ARK: ABSTRACT BOOK* (Turkey: Agri Ibrahim Cecen Universitesi, 2023), page 39.

[6] "THE EPIC OF GILGAMESH," Academy for Ancient Texts, http://www.ancienttexts.org/library/mesopotamian/gilgamesh/. Accessed February 25, 2024.

[7] Adam Augustyn, "Gilgamesh," Britannica, https://www.britannica.com/topic/Gilgamesh. Accessed February 25, 2024; Carolina López-Ruiz, "Anonymous, *The Epic of Gilgamesh*," edblogs: a blog for every Columbia course, Columbia University: In the City of New York, https://edblogs.columbia.edu/worldepics/project/gilgamesh/. Accessed February 25, 2024.

[8] "Gilgamesh – The Epic Tale of King Gilgamesh of Uruk," World History, July 11, 2017, https://worldhistory.us/ancient-history/ancient-near-east/gilgamesh-the-epic-tale-of-king-gilgamesh-of-uruk.php. Accessed February 25, 2024; "The Sumerian King List," California State University, Northridge, https://www.csun.edu/~hcfll004/sumking.html. Accessed February 25, 2024; A. Sutherland, "Sumerian King List – Ancient Record Of Kingship That Has Long Been Of Great Interest," AncientPages.com, January 22, 2016, https://www.ancientpages.com/2016/01/22/sumerian-king-list-ancient-record-of-kingship-that-has-long-been-of-great-interest/. Accessed February 25, 2024.

[9] "Gilgamesh tomb believed found," BBC News, April 29, 2003, http://news.bbc.co.uk/2/hi/science/nature/2982891.stm. Accessed February 25, 2024.

10 "The Epic of Gilgamesh," American Historical Association, https://www.historians.org/teaching-and-learning/teaching-resources-for-historians/teaching-and-learning-in-the-digital-age/creation-stories-and-epics/the-epic-of-gilgamesh. Accessed February 25, 2024.

11 Osama Shukir Muhammed Amin, "Flood Tablet of the Epic of Gilgamesh," World History Encyclopedia, April 7, 2016, https://www.worldhistory.org/image/4821/flood-tablet-of-the-epic-of-gilgamesh/. Accessed February 25, 2024.

12 "CHAPTER XVI. THE STORY OF THE FLOOD AND CONCLUSION.," Sacred-Texts, https://sacred-texts.com/ane/caog/caog19.htm. Accessed February 25, 2024; Rob Bradshaw, "Chaldean Account of Genesis by George Smith," Biblical Archaeology Blog, BiblicalArchaeology.org.uk, April 23, 2021, https://biblicalarchaeology.org.uk/blog/chaldean-account-of-genesis-by-george-smith/. Accessed February 25, 2024.

13 Frank Lorey, "The Flood of Noah and the Flood of Gilgamesh," The Institute for Creation Research, March 1, 1997, https://www.icr.org/article/noah-flood-gilgamesh/. Accessed February 25, 2024.

14 John D. Morris, "Why Does Nearly Every Culture Have a Tradition of a Global Flood?," The Institute for Creation Research, September 1, 2001, https://www.icr.org/article/why-does-nearly-every-culture-have-tradition-globa/. Accessed February 26, 2024; "Flood Legends From Around the World," NW Creation Network, https://www.nwcreation.net/noahlegends.html. Accessed February 26, 2024; Eric Lyons and Kyle Butt, "Legends of the Flood," Apologetics Press, November 1, 2003, https://apologeticspress.org/legends-of-the-flood-64/. Accessed February 26, 2024.

15 "Pitching Noah's Ark – and its implications," Reasons to Believe, February 5, 2008, https://reasons.org/explore/publications/rtb-101/pitching-noahs-ark-and-its-implications. Accessed February 26, 2024.

16 Ryan Nelson, "Moses: The Old Testament's Greatest Prophet," OverviewBible.com, July 27, 2020, https://overviewbible.com/moses/. Accessed February 26, 2024.

17 Mark H. Stone, "The Cubit: A History and Measurement Commentary," Hindawi: Journal of Anthropology, January 30, 2014, https://doi.org/10.1155/2014/489757. Accessed May 24, 2024.

18 "Why Are We Being Kept in the Dark About the Discovery of Noah's Ark?," Impact Lab, https://www.impactlab.com/2013/12/23/why-are-we-being-kept-in-the-dark-about-the-discovery-of-noahs-ark/. Accessed January 13, 2024.

19 7th INTERNATIONAL SYMPOSIUM ON MOUNT ARARAT AND NOAH'S ARK, www.ismana.agri.edu.tr, https://ismana.agri.edu.tr/default.aspx?dil=en-US. Accessed February 26, 2024.

20 Nicholas McEntyre, "Samples from 'Noah's Ark' site in Turkey reveal human activity dating back to biblical era, scientists claim," New York Post, October 28, 2023, https://nypost.com/2023/10/28/news/noahs-ark-site-rock-samples-reveal-human-activity-dating-back-thousands-of-years/. Accessed February 26, 2024. "It was believed to belong to Noah's Ark! The remains have been examined, here are the first results...," Translated by Google, Hürriyet.com.tr, October 26, 2023, https://www.hurriyet.com.tr/gundem/nuhun-gemisine-ait-olduguna-inaniliyordu-kalintilar-incelendi-iste-ilk-sonuclar-42351635. Accessed February 26, 2024; Walla!, "New research might point out to location, remains of Noah's Ark," The Jerusalem Post, November 1, 2023, https://www.jpost.com/archaeology/article-770948. Accessed February 26, 2024; "Samples From Noah's Ark Site In Turkey Indicate Human Presence In Biblical Times," The Times of India, October 29, 2023, https://timesofindia.indiatimes.com/home/science/samples-from-noahs-ark-site-in-turkey

-indicate-human-presence-in-biblical-times/amp_articleshow/104787871.cms. Accessed February 26, 2024; Joseph Shavit, "Ancient Discovery: International team of scientists may have found Noah's Ark," The Brighter Side of News, December 30, 2023, https://www.thebrighterside.news/post/ancient-discovery -international-team-of-scientists-may-have-found-noah-s-ark. Accessed February 26, 2024.

[21] "Noah's Ark Location," Holy Land Site, https://www.holylandsite.com/noah-ark-location. Accessed February 27, 2024; "The Village of Eight and the Sea Anchor Stones," Ark Discovery International, https://www.arkdiscovery.com/noahsarkstones.htm. Accessed February 27, 2024.

[22] Ibid.

[23] "Noah's Ark Location," Holy Land Site, https://www.holylandsite.com/noah-ark-location. Accessed February 27, 2024; "The Village of Eight and the Sea Anchor Stones," Ark Discovery International, https://www.arkdiscovery.com/noahsarkstones.htm. Accessed February 27, 2024; "Noah's Ark: Fact or Fiction?," Discovery World, https://www.discovery.global/noahs-ark-fact-or-fiction. Accessed February 27, 2024.

[24] "Exploring The Historic Silk Road In Turkey," Explore More Turkey, November 29, 2023, https://exploremoreturkey.com/whats-new/exploring-the-historic-silk-road-in-turkey/. Accessed February 27, 2024; C. Griffith Mann, "*Armenia!* In the Shadows of Mount Ararat," The Met, October 15, 2018, https://www.metmuseum.org/blogs/now-at-the-met/2018/armenia-mt-ararat. Accessed February 27, 2024.

[25] "Noah's Ark Location," Holy Land Site, https://www.holylandsite.com/noah-ark-location. Accessed February 27, 2024; Rizwan Choudhury, "Noah's Ark mystery: Researchers find human signs near boat-like site," Interesting Engineering, November 3, 2023, https://interestingengineering.com/culture/noahs-ark -mystery-researchers-find-human-signs-near-boat-like-site. Accessed February 27, 2024.

Chapter 11

[1] Kurt Readman, "Mount Ararat: Where is Noah's Ark, Then?," Historic Mysteries, October 3, 2023, https://www.historicmysteries.com/myths-legends/mount-ararat/36824/. Accessed February 29, 2024; "Movies about Noahs Ark," Movie Flavor, https://www.movieflavor.com/type/movies-about-noahs+ark. Accessed February 29, 2024; Rick Lanser, "THE LANDING-PLACE OF NOAH'S ARK: TESTIMO-NIAL, GEOLOGICAL AND HISTORICAL CONSIDERATIONS: PART TWO," Associates for Biblical Research, October 24, 2011, https://biblearchaeology.org/research/contemporary-issues/2553-the-landingplace -of-noahs-ark-testimonial-geological-and-historical-considerations-part-two. Accessed February 29, 2024.

[2] "Has the Ark Been Found? Site Five: Ararat-NAMI Expedition," Ark Encounter, January 9, 2015, https://arkencounter.com/blog/2015/01/09/has-the-ark-been-found-site-five-ararat-nami-expedition/. Accessed January 29, 2024; Amy L. Beam, Ed.D., "The Turkish Guides and the Noah's Ark Discovery Fraud," Mountain Ararat Trek, February 24, 2012; http://mountainararattrek.com/ark/kurdishguides _noahsark.pdf. Accessed January 29, 2024.

[3] Henry Morris, Ph.D., *The Remarkable Record of Job* (Green Forest, AR: Master Books, Inc., 2000, 2007) pp. 28-29.

[4] Craig von Buseck, "Where Did All That Water Come From?," CBN, https://cmsedit.cbn.com/biblestudy /where-did-all-that-water-come-from%3F. Accessed March 27, 2024.

[5] Ibid.

6 Steven J. Robinson, "The Flood in Genesis: What Does the Text Tell Geologists," The Proceedings of the International Conference on Creationism: Vol. 4 , Article 40 (Cedarville, OH; Centennial Library: Cedarville University, 1998) pp. 467, 468

7 Steven J. Robinson, "The Flood in Genesis: What Does the Text Tell Geologists," The Proceedings of the International Conference on Creationism: Vol. 4 , Article 40 (Cedarville, OH; Centennial Library: Cedarville University, 1998) p. 466

8 "Exodus 16 Bible Commentary," John Gill's Exposition of the Bible, Christianity.com, https://www.christianity.com/bible/commentary/john-gill/exodus/16. Accessed February 29, 2024.

9 "Greatest rainfall in 24 hours," Guiness World Records, https://www.guinnessworldrecords.com/world-records/greatest-rainfall-24-hours. Accessed March 11, 2024.

10 "Mount St. Helens: The New and Little Grand Canyon!," Discovery World, https://www.discovery.global/mount-st-helens-the-new-and-little-grand-canyon. Accessed March 26, 2024.

11 "The Channeled Scablands," The Seven Wonders of Washington State, http://www.sevenwondersofwashingtonstate.com/the-channeled-scablands.html. Accessed March 26, 2024; "The Channeled Scablands," Historical Geology, https://opengeology.org/historicalgeology/case-studies/channeled-scablands/. Accessed March 26, 2024.

12 "Ararat," Smithsonian Institution, National Museum of Natural History, Global Volcanism Program, https://volcano.si.edu/volcano.cfm?vn=213040. Accessed January 18, 2024; NOAA: National Centers for Environmental Information, Significant Earthquake Information, https://www.ngdc.noaa.gov/hazel/view/hazards/earthquake/event-more-info/1823 . Accessed January 18, 2024.

13 Mark Cartwright, "Urartu Civilization," World History Encyclopedia, February 8, 2018, https://www.worldhistory.org/Urartu_Civilization/. Accessed March 1, 2024; David Allen Deal, "NAXUAN, THE LOST CITY OF NOAH FOUND!," Noah's Ark Search, https://www.noahsarksearch.com/davedeal.htm. Accessed March 1, 2024; Robert Michelson, angel-strike.com, http://angel-strike.com/sepdac/6Durupinar.html. Accessed March 1, 2024; "Armenia: The Forgotten Paradise," PeopleofAr.com, December 2, 2013, https://www.peopleofar.com/2013/12/02/armenia-the-forgotten-paradise/. Accessed March 1, 2024.

14 "Mount Judi," Atlas Obscura, May 19, 2016, https://www.atlasobscura.com/places/mount-judi. Accessed March 2, 2024.

15 Robert Bowie Johnson, "Evidence that Noah's Ark Landed on a Mountain 17 Miles South of Ararat," Ancient Origins, September 9, 2021, https://www.ancient-origins.net/human-origins-religions/noahs-ark-south-ararat-009725. Accessed March 2, 2024.

16 Ibid.

17 "An Earthquake Story," Anchor Stone International, November 15, 2005, https://anchorstone.com/an-earthquake-story/. Accessed March 2, 2024; David Allen Deal, "NAXUAN, THE LOST CITY OF NOAH FOUND!," ThroneofGod.com, https://www.throneofgod.com/NoahsArk/naxuan.html. Accessed March 2, 2024.

Chapter 12

1 *The Works of Josephus*, Translated by William Whiston (Hendrickson Publications, Inc.,1987, 1994) p. 34.

ENDNOTES

ENDNOTES

[2] Henry Morris, Ph.D., *The Remarkable Record of Job* (Green Forest, AR: Master Books, 2000, 2007) p.103.

[3] John D. Morris, Ph.D., "The Real Nature of the Fossil Record," Institute for Creation Research, February 1, 2010, https://www.icr.org/article/real-nature-fossil-record/. Accessed March 5, 2024.

[4] "Fossils," Grand Canyon: National Park Arizona, National Park Service, https://www.nps.gov/grca/learn/nature/fossils.htm. Accessed March 5, 2024.

[5] Michelle Roberts, "Scientists Unearth 4 Million Year Old Whale Remains in Santa Cruz Mountains," NBC BAY AREA, September 19, 2015, https://www.nbcbayarea.com/news/local/scientists-unearth-4-million-year-old-whale-remains-in-santa-cruz-mountains/66404/. Accessed March 8, 2024.

[6] History.com Editors, "Tsunami devastates Indian Ocean coast," History.com, https://www.history.com/this-day-in-history/tsunami-devastates-indian-ocean-coast. Accessed March 5, 2024; Dave Roos, "The 2004 Tsunami Wiped Away Towns with 'Mind-Boggling' Destruction," History, June 1, 2023, https://www.history.com/news/deadliest-tsunami-2004-indian-ocean. Accessed March 5, 2024; "Indian Ocean tsunami of 2004," Britannica, https://www.britannica.com/event/Indian-Ocean-tsunami-of-2004. Accessed March 5, 2024.

[7] "The Village of Eight and the Sea Anchor Stones," Ark Discovery International, https://www.arkdiscovery.com/noahsarkstones.htm. Accessed March 8, 2024.

[8] Joshua J. Mark, "Fertile Crescent," World History Encyclopedia, March 28, 2018, https://www.worldhistory.org/Fertile_Crescent/. Accessed March 4, 2024; "Garden of Eden," BibleHub.com, https://biblehub.com/topical/g/garden_of_eden.htm. Accessed March 4, 2024.

[9] *The Works of Josephus*, Translated by William Whiston (Hendrickson Publications, Inc.,1987, 1994) pp. 29,30.

[10] "Armenia: The Forgotten Paradise," PeopleofAr.com, December 2, 2013, https://www.peopleofar.com/2013/12/02/armenia-the-forgotten-paradise/. Accessed March 4, 2024; Eric H. Cline, "The Garden of Eden," The Bible and Interpretation, bibleinterp.arizona.edu, October 2009, https://bibleinterp.arizona.edu/articles/2009/10/eden357918. Accessed March 4, 2024; Clint Wagner, "Where does the river Euphrates begin and end?," NCESC.COM/geographic-faq, February 25, 2024, https://www.ncesc.com/geographic-faq/where-does-the-river-euphrates-begin-and-end/. Accessed March 4, 2024.

[11] "UNDERSTANDING THE REMAINS OF NOAH'S ARK," Wyatt Archaeological Research, https://wyattmuseum.com/understanding-the-remains-of-noahs-ark/2011-693. Accessed March 4, 2024.

[12] John Larsen, "THE RESULTS OF THE SUBSURFACE IMAGING PROJECT OF NOAH'S ARK," NoahsArkScans.nz, https://noahsarkscans.nz/. Accessed March 4, 2024.

[13] "The Village of Eight and the Sea Anchor Stones," Ark Discovery International, https://www.arkdiscovery.com/noahsarkstones.htm. Accessed March 4, 2024.

[14] "Noah's Ark Location," Holy Land Site, https://www.holylandsite.com/noah-ark-location. Accessed March 4, 2024.

[15] "The Village of Eight and the Sea Anchor Stones," Ark Discovery International, https://www.arkdiscovery.com/noahsarkstones.htm. Accessed March 4, 2024.

[16] *The Works of Josephus*, Translated by William Whiston (Hendrickson Publications, Inc.,1987, 1994) p. 35.

[17] "Special Insight on how we got here what Comes Next! w/ Bill Federer Mark Cowart – Full Disclosure!," Z Ministries, February 4, 2024, https://video.josephz.com/channel/ZMinistries/video/1248 /special-insight-on-how-we-got-here-what-comes-next-w-bill-federer-mark-cowart-full-disclosure-on -04-feb-24-02-00-23. Accessed February 23, 2024.

[18] "World language families," Vistawide World Languages & Cultures, https://www.vistawide.com /languages/language_families_statistics1.htm. Accessed March 5, 2024.

Chapter 13

[1] Joshua J. Mark, "Sumerians," World History Encyclopedia, October 9, 2019, https://www.worldhistory .org/Sumerians/. Accessed March 8, 2024.

[2] "Ancient Assyria – Weld Prism," AncientReplicas.com, https://www.ancientreplicas.com/weld-prism .html. Accessed March 8, 2024; Dennis R. Petersen, *Unlocking the Mysteries of Creation* (El Dorado, CA: Creation Resource Publications, 2002) p. 203.

[3] "Jewish Concepts: Angels & Angelology," Jewish Virtual Library: A Project of AICE, https://www .jewishvirtuallibrary.org/angels-and-angelology-2. Accessed May 24, 2024.

[4] Sanj Atwal, "The tragic death of Robert Wadlow, the tallest man ever," Guiness World Records, June 30, 2022, https://www.guinnessworldrecords.com/news/2022/6/the-tragic-death-of-robert-wadlow-the -tallest-man-ever-708849. Accessed March 5, 2024.

[5] "Homily 8," Translated by Peter Peterson, NewAdvent.org, https://www.newadvent.org/fathers/080808 .htm. Accessed February 3, 2024.

[6] "Quotes from Josephus concerning Giants," Generation Word, https://www.generationword.com/notes /bible-topics/josephus_giants.htm. Accessed January 26, 2024.

[7] Ibid.

[8] "IRENAEUS OF LYONS AND 'ILLICIT UNIONS' OF ANGELS," Chasing the Giants, https:// chasingthegiants.com/irenaeus-of-lyons-and-illicit-unions-of-angels/. Accessed January 30, 2024.

[9] "Athenagoras of Athens," Translated by Rev. B.P. Pratten, Early Christian Writings, http://www .earlychristianwritings.com/text/athenagoras-plea.html. Accessed January 30, 2024.

[10] "Homily 8," Translated by Peter Peterson, NewAdvent.org, https://www.newadvent.org/fathers/080808 .htm. Accessed January 26, 2024.

[11] "Tertullian (145-220): Apology, Chapter 22," Translated by S. Thelwall, LogosLibrary.org, https:// www.logoslibrary.org/tertullian/apology/22.html. Accessed February 3, 2024; "Death Changes, Without Destroying, Our Mortal Bodies Remains of the Giants.," On the Resurrection of the Flesh – Tertullian, Bible Hub, https://biblehub.com/library/tertullian/on_the_resurrection_of_the_flesh/chapter_xlii _death_changes_without_destroying.htm. Accessed February 3, 2024.

[12] "COMMODIANUS ON THE INTERACTIONS OF ANGELS AND HUMANITY IN GENESIS," Chasing the Giants, https://chasingthegiants.com/commodianus-on-the-interactions-of-angels-and-humanity-in-genesis/. Accessed February 3, 2024.

[13] "SULPICIUS SEVERUS: THE NEPHILIM AND THE ANGELS THAT FORSOOK GOD," Chasing the Giants, https://chasingthegiants.com/sulpicius-severus-the-nephilim-and-the-angels-that-forsook-god/. Accessed February 4, 2024.

[14] "Origins of the Amorites," Ancient Origins, March 31, 2021, https://www.ancient-origins.net/videos/origins-amorites-0015138. Accessed March 7, 2024.

[15] "THE BOOK OF ENOCH: WATCHER ANGELS & THEIR GIANT SONS," Chasing the Giants, https://chasingthegiants.com/the-book-of-enochs-story-of-the-watchers-sins-the-giants/. Accessed March 7, 2024; "The Rephaim – Who were they?," CompellingTruth.org, https://www.compellingtruth.org/Rephaim.html. Accessed March 7, 2024.

[16] "Explore Sources: A database of excerpts from ancient documents that retell the story of the Nephilim & the 'sons of God'.," Chasing the Giants, https://chasingthegiants.com/sources/. Accessed March 7, 2024; "Church History (Book 1)," Translated by Arthur Cushman McGiffert, NewAdvent.org, https://www.newadvent.org/fathers/250101.htm. Accessed March 7, 2024; "Homily 8," Translated by Peter Peterson, NewAdvent.org, https://www.newadvent.org/fathers/080808.htm. Accessed March 7, 2024.

[17] "What do we know about the Anakim?," CompellingTruth.org, https://www.compellingtruth.org/Anakim.html. Accessed March 7, 2024.

[18] Stephen Baker, "Who Were the Moabite People in the Bible – The Good, Bad, and Ugly," BibleStudyTools.com, August 19, 2021, https://www.biblestudytools.com/bible-study/topical-studies/who-were-the-moabite-people-in-the-bible.html. Accessed March 7, 2024.

[19] Emil G. Hirsch, M. Seligsohn, "GIANTS," JewishEncyclopedia.com, https://www.jewishencyclopedia.com/articles/6658-giants. Accessed March 8, 2024.

[20] Michael A. Milton, "The Scarlet Cord: Rahab's Bible Story & Our Story," Crosswalk.com, January 21, 2020, https://www.crosswalk.com/faith/bible-study/the-scarlet-cord-rahabs-bible-story-and-our-story.html. Accessed March 8, 2024.

[21] Zachary Garris, "GIANTS IN THE LAND: A BIBLICAL THEOLOGY OF THE NEPHILIM, ANAKIM, REPHAIM (AND GOLIATH)," Knowing Scripture, July 2, 2019, https://knowingscripture.com/articles/giants-in-the-land-a-biblical-theology-of-the-nephilim-anakim-rephaim-and-goliath. Accessed March 8, 2024.

[22] Mike Greenberg, "The Cyclops: Greek Mythology's One-Eyed Monster," Mythology Source, February 22, 2021, https://mythologysource.com/cyclops-one-eyed-monster/. Accessed March 8, 2024.

[23] Dr. Dennis G. Lindsay, *Giants, Fallen Angels and the Return of the Nephilim* (Shippensburg, PA: Destiny Image Publishers, Inc., 2015, 2018) pp. 91,92.

[24] "Historical and Architectural Detail," The Virtual Malta Project, http://virtualmalta.weebly.com/ggantija-history-and-architecture.html. Accessed April 3, 2024.

[25] Ronnie Jones III, "Göbekli Tepe," World History Encyclopedia, May 7, 2015, https://www.worldhistory.org/G%C3%B6bekli_Tepe/. Accessed April 3, 2024.

26 "Baalbek Stones," Wikipedia, https://en.wikipedia.org/wiki/Baalbek_Stones. Accessed May 25, 2024.

27 Stephen Quayle, *Genesis 6 Giants* (Bozeman, MT: End Time Thunder Publishers, 2002, 2015) p. 174.

Chapter 14

1 Peter Goeman, "What Was the Population of Earth Before the Flood?," The Bible Sojourner, February 12, 2022, https://petergoeman.com/population-earth-flood/. Accessed March 11, 2024.

2 C Haub, "How many people have ever lived on earth?," National Library of Medicine, February 1995, https://pubmed.ncbi.nlm.nih.gov/12288594/. Accessed March 11, 2024; Lambert Dolphin, "World Population Since Creation," https://www.ldolphin.org/popul.html. Accessed March 11, 2024.

3 Lambert Dolphin, "World Population Since Creation," https://www.ldolphin.org/popul.html. Accessed March 11, 2024; Max Roser and Hannah Ritchie, "Two centuries of rapid global population growth will come to an end," Our World in Data, March 18, 2023, https://ourworldindata.org/world-population -growth-past-future. Accessed March 12, 2024.

4 Amber Pariona, "Worldwide Population Throughout Human History," World Atlas, April 25, 2017, https://www.worldatlas.com/articles/worldwide-population-throughout-human-history.html. Accessed March 12, 2024; "Population change," Britannica, https://www.britannica.com/topic/modernization /Population-change. Accessed March 12, 2024.

5 Ibid.

6 "World Population by Year," WorldOMeter, https://www.worldometers.info/world-population /world-population-by-year/. Accessed March 12, 2024.

7 Ibid.

8 Ibid.

9 "Growing at a slower pace, world population is expected to reach 9.7 billion in 2050 and could peak at nearly 11 billion around 2100," United Nations, Department of Economic and Social Affairs, June 17, 2019, https://www.un.org/development/desa/en/news/population/world-population-prospects-2019.html. Accessed March 12, 2024.

10 Hope for Justice, "How much money is made by human trafficking and modern slavery?," Hope for Justice, August 10, 2023, https://hopeforjustice.org/news/how-much-money-is-made-by-human-trafficking -and-modern-slavery/. Accessed March 12, 2024; Torie Pfau, "THE LINK BETWEEN PORNOGRA-PHY & HUMAN TRAFFICKING," Dressember, https://www.dressember.org/blog/thepornographylink. Accessed March 12, 2024.

11 Sarah Marsh and Guardian readers, "The gender-fluid generation: young people on being male, female or non-binary," The Guardian, March 23, 2016, https://www.theguardian.com/commentisfree/2016 /mar/23/gender-fluid-generation-young-people-male-female-trans. Accessed March 12, 2024.

12 "Gender," Psychology Today, https://www.psychologytoday.com/us/basics/gender. Accessed March 12, 2024.

13 Emi Tuyetnhi Tran, "Inside the online world of people who think they can change their race," NBC News, July 30, 2023, https://www.nbcnews.com/news/asian-america/race-change-to-another-trend-online -rcna93759. Accessed March 12, 2024.

[14] "Clinical lycanthropy: people who believe they become animals," en.yestherapyhelps.com, March 3, 2024, https://en.yestherapyhelps.com/clinical-lycanthropy-people-who-believe-they-become-animals-14305. Accessed March 13, 2024; Angela Chen, "Community of people who believe they are animals," FOX26 Houston, May 24, 2016, https://www.fox26houston.com/news/community-of-people-who-believe-they-are-animals. Accessed March 13, 2024.

[15] Nate Raymond, "Parents cannot challenge school gender identity policy, US court rules," Reuters, August 14, 2023, https://www.reuters.com/legal/government/parents-cannot-challenge-school-gender-identity-policy-us-court-rules-2023-08-14/. Accessed March 13, 2024; Sandra Hearth, "Is Therian A Mental Illness? Discover What the Experts Say," Wellbeing Port, September 20, 2023, https://wellbeingport.com/is-therian-a-mental-illness-discover-what-the-experts-say/. Accessed March 13, 2024.

[16] "Marriage Equality Around the World," Human Rights Campaign, https://www.hrc.org/resources/marriage-equality-around-the-world. Accessed March 13, 2024; Fan Liang, M.D., "Gender Affirmation Surgeries," Johns Hopkins Medicine, https://www.hopkinsmedicine.org/health/wellness-and-prevention/gender-affirmation-surgeries. Accessed March 13, 2024; Laura Meckler, "Gender identity lessons, banned in some schools, are rising in others," The Washington Post, June 3, 2022, https://www.washingtonpost.com/education/2022/06/03/schools-gender-identity-transgender-lessons/. Accessed March 13, 2024.

[17] Carlos Granda, "SoCal teacher says she was fired for not hiding students' gender preferences from parents," Eyewitness News: ABC7, March 14, 2023, https://abc7.com/jurupa-valley-high-school-teacher-fired-students-gender-identity/12950847/. Accessed March 13, 2024; Mark Walsh, "Court Backs Firing of Teacher Who Refused to Use Transgender Students' Names," Education Week, April 10, 2023, https://www.edweek.org/policy-politics/court-backs-firing-of-teacher-who-refused-to-use-transgender-students-names/2023/04. Accessed March 13, 2024; Joe Hernandez, "A Virginia Teacher Was Put on Leave After Opposing New Rights For Trans Students," NPR, June 2, 2021, https://www.npr.org/2021/06/02/1002479412/a-virginia-teacher-was-put-on-leave-after-opposing-a-new-policy-for-trans-studen. Accessed March 13, 2024; Jesse O'Neill, "Father arrested for discussing child's gender transition in defiance of court order," New York Post, March 18, 2021, https://nypost.com/2021/03/18/man-arrested-for-discussing-childs-gender-in-court-order-violation/. Accessed March 13, 2024; Virginia Allen, "New Canadian Law Could Send Parents to Jail for Not Affirming Gender Identity," The Daily Signal, February 11, 2022, https://www.dailysignal.com/2022/02/11/new-canadian-law-could-send-parents-to-jail-for-not-affirming-gender-identity/. Accessed March 14, 2024.

[18] Walter Olson, "Required Diversity Statements on Campus: Are They Constitutional?," CATO Institute, September 23, 2022, https://www.cato.org/blog/required-dei-diversity-equity-inclusion-statements-campus-analogy. Accessed March 14, 2024; Elizabeth Wolfe, "Trans and nonbinary students have long had a place at women's colleges. Here's what they want you to know," CNN, May 7, 2023, https://edition.cnn.com/2023/04/30/us/transgender-womens-colleges-admissions-experiences/index.html. Accessed March 14, 2024; "2023 Equity & Inclusion Colleges of Distinction," Colleges of Distinction, https://collegesofdistinction.com/equity-inclusion-colleges-of-distinction/. Accessed March 14, 2024.

[19] Mary Kay Linge and Jon Levine, "Over $200K being spent on drag queen shows at NYC schools, records show," New York Post, June 11, 2022, https://nypost.com/2022/06/11/over-200k-being-spent-on-drag-queen-shows-at-nyc-schools/. Accessed March 13, 2024; "Libraries Respond: Drag Queen Story Hour," American Library Association, https://www.ala.org/advocacy/libraries-respond-drag-queen-story-hour. Accessed March 14, 2024; Erin Blakemore; "Drag Queens Are Public Libraries'

Newest Storytellers," Smithsonian Magazine, May 18, 2017, https://www.smithsonianmag.com/smart-news/drag-queens-are-public-libraries-newest-storytellers-180963341/. Accessed March 14, 2024.

[20] The Bible Study Tools Staff, "Abomination in the Bible," Bible Study Tools, February 19, 2024, https://www.biblestudytools.com/topical-verses/abomination-in-the-bible/. Accessed March 14, 2024.

[21] Adapted from *Noah Webster's 1828 American Dictionary of the English Language* (San Francisco, CA: The Foundation for American Christian Education, 1967, 1995).

[22] Anna Swartz, "Satanists are putting up the first public Satanic monument in the US," MIC, May 5, 2017, https://www.mic.com/articles/176377/satanists-are-putting-up-the-first-public-satanic-monument-in-the-us. Accessed March 14, 2024; Victoria Reyna-Rodriguez and Noelle Alviz-Gransee, "'Disgusting' Satanic Temple display at state capitol in Iowa sparks free speech battle," USA Today, December 12, 2023, https://www.usatoday.com/story/news/nation/2023/12/12/satanic-display-iowa-capitol-free-speech-battle/71897091007/. Accessed March 14, 2024.

[23] Michele Gile, "Satan Club at Orange County elementary school stirs controversy," CBS News, January 23, 2024, https://www.cbsnews.com/losangeles/news/satan-club-at-orange-county-elementary-school-stirs-controversy/. Accessed March 14, 2024; Talia Wise, "Satanist Opens County Meeting With Invocation Hailing Satan: 'A Struggle Between Good and Evil'," CBN, January 19, 2024, https://www2.cbn.com/news/us/satanist-opens-county-meeting-invocation-hailing-satan-struggle-between-good-and-evil. Accessed March 14, 2024; Trevor Hughes, "After School Satan Clubs and pagan statues have popped up across US. What's going on?," USA Today, December 19, 2023, https://www.usatoday.com/story/news/nation/2023/12/16/satanic-temple-christian-controversy/71919541007/. Accessed March 14, 2024.

[24] Bailee Abell, "'Ex-Witch' Warns Parents of Disney's New Show: 'Be Careful!'," ITM: InsidetheMagic.com, January 21, 2020, https://insidethemagic.net/2020/01/the-owl-house-demonic-ba1/. Accessed March 14, 2024; Mandy Parker, "Amazon Debuts Cartoon Series Celebrating Demons & Lucifer," Bleeding Fool, January 21, 2024, https://bleedingfool.com/movies-tv-film/amazon-debuts-cartoon-series-celebrating-demons-lucifer/. Accessed March 14, 2024.

[25] "Human Enhancement: The Scientific and Ethical Dimensions of Striving for Perfection," Pew Research Center, July 26, 2016, https://www.pewresearch.org/science/2016/07/26/human-enhancement-the-scientific-and-ethical-dimensions-of-striving-for-perfection/. Accessed March 15, 2024.

[26] Daniel Martin for The Daily Mail and Simon Caldwell for MailOnline, "150 human animal hybrids grown in UK labs: Embryos have been produced secretively for the past three years," DailyMail.com, July 22, 2011, https://www.dailymail.co.uk/sciencetech/article-2017818/Embryos-involving-genes-animals-mixed-humans-produced-secretively-past-years.html. Accessed May 27, 2024.

[27] Emma Tumilty and Michele Battle-Fisher, Editors, *Transhumanism: Entering an Era of Bodyhacking and Radical Human Modification* (Springer Cham Publisher, 2022)

[28] Jillian Eugenios, "Ray Kurzweil: Humans will be hybrids by 2030," CNN Business, June 4, 2015, https://money.cnn.com/2015/06/03/technology/ray-kurzweil-predictions/. Accessed May 27, 2024.

[29] "Super-intelligence and eternal life: transhumanism's faithful follow it blindly into a future for the elite," The Conversation, July 31, 2017, https://theconversation.com/super-intelligence-and-eternal-life-transhumanisms-faithful-follow-it-blindly-into-a-future-for-the-elite-78538. Accessed May 27, 2024.

30 "Human Enhancement: The Scientific and Ethical Dimensions of Striving for Perfection," Pew Research Center, July 26, 2016, https://www.pewresearch.org/science/2016/07/26/human-enhancement-the-scientific-and-ethical-dimensions-of-striving-for-perfection/. Accessed March 15, 2024.

31 Ibid.

32 Tim Newcomb, "Scientists Put Tardigrade DNA Into Human Stem Cells. They May Create Super Soldiers.," Popular Mechanics, April 4, 2023, https://www.popularmechanics.com/science/animals/a43509580/tardigrade-dna-human-stem-cells-super-soldiers/. Accessed March 15, 2024.

33 "Pastor Jimmy Evans - Tipping Point - Technology at a Tipping Point (Lesson 3)" [Note: article in question begins at video timestamp 15:55], YouTube, https://www.youtube.com/watch?v=lxcYa9SdfIs. Accessed March 1, 2024.

34 Josh Hrala, "The First Human-Pig Hybrid Embryo Has Been Created in The Lab," Science Alert, January 27, 2017, https://www.sciencealert.com/it-s-alive-the-first-human-pig-hybrid-has-been-created-in-the-lab. Accessed March 17, 2024; Dan Robitzski, "SCIENTISTS ALARMED BY LAB-GROWN HUMAN-ANIMAL HYBRIDS," Neoscope, April 26, 2021, https://futurism.com/neoscope/scientists-alarmed-lab-grown-human-animal-hybrids. Accessed March 17, 2024; Mark Oliver, "10 Experiments That Have Created Real Human-Animal Hybrids," Listverse.com, June 25, 2018, https://listverse.com/2018/06/25/10-experiments-that-have-created-real-human-animal-hybrids/. Accessed March 17, 2024.

35 Lily Rothman, "This Is How Dolly the Sheep Was Cloned," TIME, July 5, 2016, https://time.com/4384947/dolly-sheep-cloning-history/. Accessed March 15, 2024.

36 Rob Stein, "How genetically modified pigs could end the shortage of organs for transplants," NPR, February 29, 2024, https://www.npr.org/sections/health-shots/2024/02/29/1231699834/genetically-modified-pigs-organs-human-transplant. Accessed March 15, 2024.

37 "Human Enhancement: The Scientific and Ethical Dimensions of Striving for Perfection," Pew Research Center, July 26, 2016, https://www.pewresearch.org/science/2016/07/26/human-enhancement-the-scientific-and-ethical-dimensions-of-striving-for-perfection/. Accessed March 15, 2024.

38 Ibid.

39 "Yuval Noah Hararai – 'We Don't Need to Wait for Jesus Christ in Order to Overcome Death'," YouTube, https://www.youtube.com/watch?v=tw-ZeDMtHIE. Accessed March 15, 2024.

40 "Pastor Jimmy Evans - Tipping Point - Technology at a Tipping Point (Lesson 3)," YouTube, https://www.youtube.com/watch?v=lxcYa9SdfIs. Accessed March 1, 2024.

41 Bernard Marr, "Future of Intimacy: Sex Bots, Virtual Reality, And Smart Sex Toys," Forbes, November 30, 2020, https://www.forbes.com/sites/bernardmarr/2020/11/30/future-of-intimacy-sex-bots-virtual-reality-and-smart-sex-toys/?sh=78c7b00238fa. Accessed March 15, 2024.

42 Ibid.

43 "Induction Abortion," ProFemina, April 12, 2023, https://www.profemina.org/en-us/abortion/induction-abortion#overview. Accessed March 15, 2024; "Vacuum Aspiration," ProFemina, December 11, 2023, https://www.profemina.org/en-us/abortion/vacuum-aspiration. Accessed March 15, 2024; "Abortion Pill FAQ," ProFemina, March 14, 2024, https://www.profemina.org/en-us/abortion/abortion-pill. Accessed March 15, 2024; Ginny Montalbano, "She Survived a Saline Abortion. Here's Her Story," The Daily

Signal, February 12, 2019, https://www.dailysignal.com/2019/02/12/she-survived-a-saline-abortion -heres-her-story/. Accessed March 15, 2024; Sarah Terzo, "Quotes from Abortion Clinic Workers and Doctors: Abortion Providers React," EPM: Eternal Perspective Ministries with Randy Alcorn, March 2, 2010, https://www.epm.org/resources/2010/Mar/2/quotes-abortion-clinic-workers-and-doctors-abortio/. Accessed March 15, 2024.

44 "Abortions worldwide this year," WorldOMeter, https://www.worldometers.info/abortions/. Accessed March 15, 2024.

45 Damien Cave, "Behind the Scenes: Picturing Fetal Remains," The New York Times, October 9, 2009, https://archive.nytimes.com/lens.blogs.nytimes.com/2009/10/09/behind-19/. Accessed March 15, 2024; "Planned Parenthood Testimony On Selling Baby Parts Unsealed, New Videos Released," CMP: The Center for Medical Progress, May 26, 2020, https://www.centerformedicalprogress.org/2020/05/planned -parenthood-testimony-on-selling-baby-parts-unsealed-new-videos-released/. Accessed March 15, 2024; Stephanie Hauer, "Fetal Cells in the Cosmetics, Food, and Medical Industries," Rehumanize International, November 14, 2020, https://www.rehumanizeintl.org/post/fetal-cells-in-the-cosmetics-food-and-medical -industries. Accessed March 15, 2024.

46 Emma Colton, "Data show there have been 22 times more attacks on pro-lifers than pro-choice groups since Supreme Court leak," FOX News, November 1, 2022, https://www.foxnews.com/us/data -show-there-have-been-22-times-more-attacks-on-pro-lifers-pro-choice-groups-since-supreme-court-leak. Accessed March 16, 2024; Micaiah Bilger, "Radical Extremists Attacked 230 Churches, Pro-Life Groups in Wave of Pro-Abortion Violence in 2022," LifeNews.com, December 30, 2022, https://www.lifenews .com/2022/12/30/radical-extremists-attacked-230-churches-pro-life-groups-in-wave-of-pro-abortion -violence-in-2022/. Accessed March 16, 2024.

47 Jennifer Whitlock, "Gender Confirmation Surgery (GCS)," Very Well Health, October 7, 2021, https:// www.verywellhealth.com/gender-confirmation-surgery-gcs-3157235. Accessed March 16, 2024.

48 "Geneticists make new discovery about how a baby's sex is determined," University of Melbourne, Science Daily, December 15, 2018, https://www.sciencedaily.com/releases/2018/12/181215141333.htm. Accessed March 16, 2024.

49 Jack Turban, M.D., M.H.S., "What is Gender Dysphoria?," American Psychiatric Association, August 2022, https://www.psychiatry.org/patients-families/gender-dysphoria/what-is-gender-dysphoria. Accessed March 16, 2024.

50 Alex MacGillis, "How Social Media Apps Could Be Fueling Homicides Among Young Americans," ProPublica, August 9, 2023, https://www.propublica.org/article/social-media-violence-young-americans. Accessed March 16, 2024; Craig Anderson, Ph.D., "Violent Music Lyrics Increase Aggressive Thoughts and Feelings, According to New Study," American Psychological Association, 2003, https://www.apa .org/news/press/releases/2003/05/violent-songs. Accessed March 16, 2024; Jeffrey L. Wilson, "The Most Violent Video Games of All Time," PC Mag, July 12, 2013, https://www.pcmag.com/news/the-most -violent-video-games-of-all-time. Accessed March 17, 2024; Brian Charles Clark, "The evidence that video game violence leads to real-world aggression," Washington State Magazine, Fall 2019, https:// magazine.wsu.edu/web-extra/the-evidence-that-video-game-violence-leads-to-real-world-aggression/. Accessed March 17, 2024.

51 Jake Bleiberg and Gene Johnson, "What to know about the mass shooting at a Texas mall," AP: The Associated Press, May 10, 2023, https://apnews.com/article/shooting-outlet-mall-allen-texas -200f1ffadf7daefa42cfbe45510b083f. Accessed March 17, 2024; History.com Editors, "Aurora shooting leaves 12 dead, 70 wounded," History.com, https://www.history.com/this-day-in-history/12-people-killed -70-wounded-in-colorado-movie-theater-shooting. Accessed March 17, 2024.

Chapter 15

1 Aristos Georgiou, "What Apophis Means as God of Chaos Asteroid Has Close Encounter with Earth," Newsweek, March 5, 2021, https://www.newsweek.com/what-apophis-means-god-chaos-asteroid-earth -1574044. Accessed March 5, 2024.

2 Léonie Chao-Fong, "UFO hearings: whistleblower David Grusch says 'non-human biologics' found at alleged crash sites – as it happened," The Guardian, July 26, 2023, https://www.theguardian.com/world /live/2023/jul/26/ufo-hearing-congress-david-grusch-whistleblower-live-updates. Accessed March 6, 2024.

3 Greg Daugherty and Missy Sullivan, "These 5 UFO Traits, Captured on Video by Navy Fighters, Defy Explanation," History.com, June 5, 2019, https://www.history.com/news/ufo-sightings-speed-appearance -movement. Accessed March 6, 2024.

Chapter 16

1 "Orson Welles's 'War of the Worlds' radio play is broadcast," History.com, https://www.history.com /this-day-in-history/welles-scares-nation. Accessed March 7, 2024.

2 JustJonAllen, "The 20 Best Alien Movies of All Time," IMDb, December 4, 2016, https://www.imdb .com/list/ls066689833/. Accessed March 7, 2024.

3 Billy Crone, "Aliens & UFOs: The Great Deception," Get A Life Media, https://www.getalifemedia .com/video/apologetics/video/ufo10.htm. Accessed March 7, 2024.

4 John O'Sullivan, "UFO map shows extraterrestrial reporting hotspots in the United States," MSN .com, https://www.msn.com/en-us/news/technology/ufo-map-shows-extraterrestrial-reporting-hotspots-in-the -united-states/ar-BB1ikrWh?cvid=41a1b4fd5fd04bf3b4a8c44489eb576c&ocid=winp2fptaskbarhover&ei =16. Accessed March 7, 2024.

5 Billy Crone, "Aliens & UFOs: The Great Deception," Get A Life Media, https://www.getalifemedia. com/video/apologetics/video/ufo10.htm. Accessed March 7, 2024.

6 Ibid.

7 Ibid.

8 Ibid.

ILLUSTRATION AND PHOTO CREDIT ACKNOWLEDGMENTS

RENNER Ministries would like to thank the following picture libraries as well as individual copyright owners for permission to reproduce their images. Copyright inquiries should be directed to RENNER Ministries, social@renner.org.

Many photographs were shot on-site by photographer Alexander Dovgan, Mark Dovgan, William Renner and other team photographers during various research trips to Turkey. Such photos are credited as Private Collection — RENNER.

Photo credits are listed by chapter and page.

COVER/DUST COVER:

Cover Art: *Painting of David and Goliath*, Generated with AI © Bargais/Adobe Stock; *Heaven and hell with many lost souls, angels fight*, background image, Generated with AI © giorgi/Adobe Stock; *Beyond the Deluge: Unraveling the Threads of Noah's Ark and the Ancient Mesopotamian Sagas of Atranasis, Ziusudra, and Utiapishtim*, Generative AI, Generated with AI © furyon/Adobe Stock; *Noah's Ark (stormy ocean)*, isolated transparent background, Generated with AI © Mr.PNG/Adobe Stock.

FRONT MATTER:

Special Permission

xxx *Perry Stone*, Courtesy of Voice of Evangelism Ministries.

xxxi *Joseph Z*, Courtesy of Joseph Z Ministries.

xxxiii *Andrew Jones*, Courtesy of Andrew Jones, NoahsArkScans.com.

INTRODUCTION:

Royalty-Free

1 *Noah's Ark (stormy ocean)*, isolated transparent background, generated with AI © Mr.PNG/Adobe Stock.

CHAPTER 1:

Alamy

19 *Friends hiking towards Mount Ararat on sunny day*, Photo by: Westend61 © Westend61/GmbH/Alamy Stock Photo.

Andrew Jones, Noah's Ark Scans

7 *Captain Durupinar* © Andrew Jones/ NoahsArkScans.com.

10 *Ribs of the Ark* © Andrew Jones/ NoahsArkScans.com.

11 *Petrified Wood* © Andrew Jones/ NoahsArkScans.com.

12 *Survey Aerial View 1* © Andrew Jones/ NoahsArkScans.com.

13 *Radar 3* © Andrew Jones/ NoahsArkScans.com.

13 *Angular Scan* © Andrew Jones/
NoahsArkScans.com.

17 *Ark Comparisons Chart* © Andrew Jones/
NoahsArkScans.com.

18 *Mount Ararat snow peak* © Andrew Jones/
NoahsArkScans.com.

19 *Mt Ararat Low Snow* © Andrew Jones/
NoahsArkScans.com.

23 *Aerial View 28* © Andrew Jones/
NoahsArkScans.com.

GoodSalt

24 *Noah and the Ark* © Pacific Press/GoodSalt,
Inc.

Public Domain

21 *Kurdish-inhabited area by CIA*, August
1992, from Perry-Castaneda Library Map
Collection at the University of Texas at Austin,
Central Intelligence Agency, Source: Wikimedia Commons (Kurdish-inhabited area by CIA
(1992) box insert removed)/Public Domain.

Ron Wyatt, Wyatt Archaeological Research

9 *Ron Wyatt Image 1*, Wyatt Archaeological
Research (used by permission);
https://www.ronwyatt.com/.

9 *Wyatt Rivet* © Wyatt Archaeological
Research (used by permission);
https://www.ronwyatt.com/.

9 *Vertical Petrified Timbers* © Wyatt Archaeological Research (used by permission);
https://www.ronwyatt.com.

10 *Metal Detection Surveys* © Wyatt Archaeological Research (used by permission);
https://www.ronwyatt.com/.

Royalty-Free

5 *Noah's Ark (stormy ocean)*, isolated transparent background, generated with AI ©
Mr.PNG/Adobe Stock.

Private Collection — RENNER

22 *RENNER travel team 2023.*

Science Photo Library

19 *Mount Ararat, Turkey* (satellite image)
© Airbus Defense and Space/Science Photo
Library.

20 *Stratovolcano eruption* (illustration)
© Tumeggy/Science Photo Library.

Special Permissions

4 *Satellite Image RWL*, Noah's Ark Visitor's
Center (used by permission).

6 *Satellite Image WTL*, Noah's Ark Visitor's
Center (used by permission).

7 *Image 1*, Noah's Ark Visitor's Center
(used by permission).

8 *Image 2*, Noah's Ark Visitor's Center
(used by permission).

8 *Satellite Image DCL*, Noah's Ark Visitor's
Center (used by permission).

13 *Ship Hull Scan* © John Larsen.

14 *Underside Scan* © John Larsen.

14 *Ship Full Scan* © John Larsen.

CHAPTER 2:

Alamy

26 *The Rising of the Waters from John Milton's
Paradise Lost.* 1667, black & white engraving,
Doré, Gustave. 1832-1883 © Timewatch
Images/Alamy Stock Photo/Public Domain.

29 *Detail from the Angel Visiting Adam and Eve in Paradise from John Milton's Paradise Lost.* 1866, engraving, Doré, Gustave. 1832-1883 © Timewatch Images/Alamy Stock Photo/ Public Domain.

51 *The Creation of Light,* Gen. 1:1-5, The engraving depicts a literal representation of Genesis 1:1 'Let there be light', Creation of Light © The Picture Art Collection/Alamy Stock Photo.

Getty Images

30 *Seth, third son of Adam and Eve,* human biblical figure, engraving, Epitome, Gai, Bartolomeo. 1751, Rome. Photo by Icas94/DEA © De Agostini Picture Library/Getty Images.

32 *Enos or Enosh, son of Seth,* human biblical figure, engraving, Epitome, Gai, Bartolomeo. 1751, Rome. Photo by Icas94/DEA © De Agostini Picture Library/Getty Images.

33 *Portrait of Kenan, son of Enos or Enosh,* human biblical figure, engraving from, Epitome, Gai, Bartolomeo. 1751, Rome. Photo by Icas94/DEA © De Agostini Picture Library/Getty Images.

34 *Portrait of Jared, son of Mahalalel,* human biblical figure, engraving, Epitome, Gai, Bartolomeo. 1751, Rome. Photo by Icas94/DEA © De Agostini Picture Library/Getty Images.

36 *Portrait of Enoch, son of Jared,* human biblical figure, engraving, Epitome, Gai, Bartolomeo. 1751, Rome. Photo by Icas94/DEA © De Agostini Picture Library/Getty Images.

37,42 *Portrait of Methuselah, son of Enoch,* human biblical figure, engraving, Epitome, Gai, Bartolomeo. 1751, Rome. Photo by Icas94/DEA © De Agostini Picture Library/ Getty Images.

43 *Portrait of Lamech, son of Methuselah,* human biblical figure, engraving, Epitome,

Gai, Bartolomeo. 1751, Rome. Photo by Icas94/DEA © De Agostini Picture Library/ Getty Images.

45 *Portrait of Noah, son of Lamech,* human biblical figure, engraving, Epitome, Gai, Bartolomeo. 1751, Rome. Photo by Icas94/DEA © De Agostini Picture Library/Getty Images.

Private Collection — RENNER

48 *Genealogy Chart* created by Vincent and Allison Newfield, www.newfieldcreativeservices.com.

Public Domain

39 *God Took Enoch.* 1728, illustration, Bizzell Bible Collection from *Figures de la Bible,* Hoet, Gerard. 1648-1733, P. de Hondt in The Hague, Source: Wikimedia Commons (Enoch)/Public Domain.

Royalty-Free

27 *Noah's Ark (stormy ocean),* isolated transparent background, generated with AI © Mr.PNG/Adobe Stock.

CHAPTER 3:

Alamy

54 *Illustration of Genesis 28:12 from the Bible, The Children's Bible in Color,* 1968, The Hamlyn Publishing Group LTD © Del Anson/ Alamy Stock Photo.

57 *Illustration for Paradiso* by Dante Alighieri. Canto XXXI, lines 1 to 3, Doré, Gustave. 1832-1883 © Classic Image/Alamy Stock Photo.

58 *Jean de Gerson Jo gerson cancellarius parisiensis,* letterpress/woodcut, Wolgemut, Michel. 1434-1519, Pleydenwurff, Wilhelm. 1460-1494, Liber Chronicarum (Nuremberg

Chronicle). 1493 © Art World/Alamy Stock Photo/Public Domain.

58 *Saint Augustine of Hippo*, born 354 died 430, Bishop of Hippo Regius aka St Augustine or St Austin Berber philosopher and theologian, Crabbes Historical Dictionary, 1825 © Classic Image/Alamy Stock Photo.

64 *Library At Alexandria*, as imagined in a 19th-century engraving © Pictorial Press/Alamy Stock Photo.

67 *Holy Bible in Amharic language*, 2 May 2021, Photo by Zoonar/ArtushFoto © Zoonar GmbH/Alamy Stock Photo.

68 *Dead Sea Scrolls Before Unraveled* © History and Art Collection/Alamy Stock Photo/Public Domain.

69 *Tablet with Cuneiform Inscription* LACMA M.79.106.2 © MCLA Collection/Alamy Stock Photo/Public Domain.

74 *The Goddess Ishtar holding her weapon*, 2nd millennium 1500 BC, Eshnunna, Mesopotamia, Iraq. © Peter Horree/Alamy Stock Photo.

78 *The Confusion of Tongues or The Tower of Babel.* 1866 (engraving), Doré, Gustave © Alex Ramsay/Alamy Stock Photo.

Archaeology Illustrated (Balage Balogh)

77 *Roman Forum*, 3rd-4th century AD © Balogh, Balage (archaeologyillustrated.com).

Creative Commons

75 CC SA-BY 4.0: *La dispute de Minerve et de Neptune au sujet d'Athenes (Minerva and Neptune's dispute over Athens).* 1821, oil on canvas, Blondel, Merry-Joseph. 1781-1853, Musée du Louvre (The Louvre Museum), Source: Wikimedia Commons (La dispute de Neptune et Athéna) © Merry-Joseph Blondel.

Getty Images

59 *Portrait of Seth, third son of Adam and Eve*, human biblical figure, engraving, Epitome, Gai, Bartolomeo. 1751, Rome. Photo by Icas94/DEA © De Agostini Picture Library/Getty Images.

Private Collection — RENNER

76 *Chart Greek Roman* created by LMoore.

Public Domain

62 *God speaks from the whirlwind* (Job 38:1). 1909, Russell, Walter, *The Bible and Its Story, Taught by One Thousand Picture Lessons*, Charles Horne and Julius August Brewer. 1909/Public Domain.

64 *Engraving of a bust of Lucius Cornelius Sulla Felix*, Source: 123rf.com © morphart/Public Domain.

64 *Detail Alexander Mosaic*, House of the Faun, Pompeii. circa 100 BC, Image courtesy of *The Guardian* (DEA/G Nimatallah/De Agostini/Getty Images), Source: Wikimedia Commons (Alexander Mosaic)/Public Domain.

71 *Angels fighting against fallen angels during the War in Heaven from John Milton's Paradise Lost.* 1866, engraving, Doré, Gustave. 1832-1883, Source: Wikimedia Commons (Paradise Lost 24)/Public Domain.

Royalty-Free

55 *Noah's Ark (stormy ocean)*, isolated transparent background, generated with AI © Mr.PNG/Adobe Stock.

66 *King Nebuchadnezzar*, engraving, 19th Century, *The Prize Bible* (Wells Gardner, Darton & Company). Circa 1890, Source: Look and Learn History Picture Archive/Courtesy

ILLUSTRATION AND PHOTO CREDIT ACKNOWLEDGMENTS

of Look and Learn, Elgar Collection. All rights reserved. © 2005-2024 Look and Learn.

72 *Old worn paper sheet and scroll isolated on white* © Andrey Kuzmin/Adobe Stock.

79 *Picture of black and white close up of stone snake statue trodden in Brussels cathedral Being Tread by Holy Mary's Foot*, Brussels, Belgium, 18 October 2014 © Wirestock/depositphotos.

Chapter 4:

akg-Images

90 *Paradise.* 1530, oil on poplar, Cranach, Lucas (The Elder). 1472-1553, Gemäldegalerie Alte Meister, Dresden, Germany © akg-images.

Alamy

84A *The Temple Scroll, one of the longest Dead Sea Scrolls*, Qumran, Photo by: Zev Radovan/BibleLandPictures © Zev Radovan/Alamy Stock Photo.

84B *5470. Codex Sinaiticus*, 4th Century (manuscript), Greek Bible. Written between 330-350. Discovered in 1844 by Constantine Tischendorf in St. Catherine's Monastery, Sinai, Photo by: Zev Radovan/BibleLandPictures © Zev Radovan/Alamy Stock Photo.

88 *The Sermon on the Mount* (Matthew 5:1). 1866, Germany © bilwissedition Ltd. & Co. KG/Alamy Stock Photo.

Getty Images

102 *High on a Throne of Royal State* from John Milton's *Paradise Lost.* 1866, engraving, Doré, Gustave. 1832-1883, Photo by duncan1890/DigitalVision Vectors via Getty Images.

Public Domain

82 *Michael casts out rebel angels* from John Milton's *Paradise Lost.* 1866, engraving, Doré,

Gustave. 1832-1883, Book VI, lines 874-875, Source: Wikimedia Commons (Paradise Lost 1)/Public Domain.

87 *John Milton's Paradise Lost.* 1866, engraving, Doré, Gustave. 1832-1883, Source: Wikimedia Commons (Paradise Lost 28)/Public Domain.

93 *Abraham Receiving the Three Angels (Abraham and the Three Angels)*, 1667, painting (oil on canvas), by Murillo, Bartolomè Esteban (1677-1682), National Gallery of Canada (#4900), Source: Wikimedia Commons (Murillo Abraham)/Public Domain.

94 *Lot Invites Two Angels to Enter His Home.* 1723, etching, Robert-de-Seri, Paul Ponce Antione. 1686-1917, Source: metmuseum.org © Harris Brisbane Dick Fund. 1917/Public Domain.

Royalty-Free

83 *Noah's Ark (stormy ocean)*, isolated transparent background, generated with AI © Mr.PNG/Adobe Stock.

86 *Old worn paper sheet and scroll isolated on white* © Andrey Kuzmin/Adobe Stock.

96 *Angry Mob at Lot's door* (Genesis 19:4-7), woodcut after drawing by Julius Schnorr von Carolsfeld (German painter, 1794-1872), published in 1877 © ZU_09/iStockphoto L.P.

103 *Angels in Chains*, AI generated by DLee, iStockphoto L.P.

Chapter 5:

Alamy

111 *Clemens I*, 1030, Byzantine Mosaics, © Artgen/Alamy Stock Photo/Public Domain.

117 *SAINT IRENAEUS*, Greek prelate and Bishop of Lugdunum (Lyons). Known for

Wikimedia Commons (Eusebius of Caesarea)/
Public Domain.

CHAPTER 6:

Alamy

139 *Undated photo released by U.S. Salk Institute shows a 4-week-old pig embryo containing human cells.* 26 Jan 2017, Washington, USA. Credit: U.S Salk Institute/Xinhua/Alamy Live News © Xinhua/Alamy Stock Photo.

141 *LIGRON, CROSS BETWEEN TIGER AND LION* © gerald lacz/Alamy Stock Photo.

141 *Panther or Black Jaguar Panthera Onca.* 16 July 2014 © Amazon-Images/Alamy Stock Photo.

141 *The Lion Who Just Can't Change His Spots*, circa 1960, Kobe, Japan. Photo by: Mirrorpix © Trinity Mirror/Mirrorpix/Alamy Stock Photo.

144 *The Temple Scroll, one of the longest Dead Sea Scrolls*, Qumran, Photo: Zed Radavan/ BibleLandPictures © Zed Radavan/Alamy Stock Photo.

146 *Destruction of humanity by the Flood* © BTEU/RKMLGE/Alamy Stock Photo/Public Domain.

Creative Commons

141 CC BY-SA 4.0: *The Zorse mare (Zebroid) Eclyse Horse*, born 2006, Safariland, Stukenbrock, Source: Wikimedia Commons (Zorse Elclyse, Safariland, Stukenbrock) © Fährtenlesser.

141 CC BY-SA 3.0: *Donkey/zebra hybrid*, Colchester Zoo, England, 2 June 2004, Source: Wikimedia Commons (Zeedonk 800) © sannse.

Royalty-Free

131 *Noah's Ark (stormy ocean)*, isolated transparent background, generated with AI © Mr.PNG/Adobe Stock.

133 *Old worn paper sheet and scroll isolated on white* © Andrey Kuzmin/Adobe Stock.

144 *An ancient Torah scroll on white background*, top view © Eran Yardeni/ Dreamstime.com.

145 *Open Pandora's Box with green smoke on a wooden background*, digital illustration (Generative AI) © Ilugram/Adobe Stock.

Hotspot Media/Doug Perrine

141 *Killer Smile, The Whale Grins*, false killer whale, Pseudorca crassidens (c,de), Source: Mirror UK/Image: Hotspot Media © Doug Perrine.

Public Domain

130 *Destruction of Leviathan.* 1865 (engraving), by Doré, Gustave (1832-1883), Source: Wikimedia Commons (Destruction of Leviathan)/Public Domain.

143 *The Dream of Countess Marguerite of Flanders.* 1795, Viganò, Salvatore, illustration after the ballet pantomime *Riccardo Cuor de Leone*, Source: Wikimedia Commons (Incubus)/ Public Domain.

CHAPTER 7:

Alamy

156 *Eusebius of Caesarea* © Niday Picture Library/Alamy Stock Photo.

157 *Saint Clements of Alexandria (Titus Flavius Clemens).* Circa 150-215 © Timewatch Images/Alamy Stock Photo/Public Domain.

158 *The Temple Scroll, one of the longest Dead Sea Scrolls*, Qumran, Photo: Zed Radovan/ BibleLandPictures © Zed Radovan/Alamy Stock Photo.

159 *Josephus, aka Flavius Josephus.* circa 37-100 AD © Lebrecht Author/Lebrecht Music & Arts/Alamy Stock Photo.

160 *5503. PART OF THE ISAIAH SCROLL, THE LONGEST & OLDEST*, circa 100 B.C., of the Dead Sea Scrolls found in Qumran, Photo by: Zev Radovan/bibleland © Zev Radovan/Alamy Stock Photo.

Creative Commons

163 CC BY-SA 3.0: *Large Cuneiform inscription from the Persian king Xerxes.* Van, Turkey, Source: Wikimedia Commons (Xerxes Cuneiform Van) © Bjørn Christian Tørrissen.

GoodSalt

153 *Noah's Ark in the Flood* © Pacific Press/ GoodSalt, Inc.

Museum of the Bible

161 *The Torah Scroll, Image 5*, circa 1500, ink on parchment, Courtesy of Museum of the Bible, Green Collection. All rights reserved. © Museum of the Bible, 2020.

Royalty-Free

151 *Noah's Ark (stormy ocean)*, isolated transparent background, generated with AI © Mr.PNG/Adobe Stock.

155 *Angel flying from earth to heaven giving light in darkness* (Generative AI) © Fantastic Studio/Freepik Company S.L.

Public Domain

150 *Nephilim Namebase*, 27 January 2023, Source: cartographersassets.com/assets/27540/ nephilim-namebase//NewMar/Public Domain.

161 *Dead Sea Scrolls and caves and Qumran Excavations of Essene Monastery*, scroll from "the war of the sons of light against the sons of darkness," circa 1947-1967, negative, Photo: G. Eric and Edith Matson Photograph Collection, Library of Congress (ID matpc. 13011), Source: Wikimedia Commons (Dead Sea Scrolls and Caves and Qumran Excavations of Essene Monastery. Scroll from "the war of the sons of light against the sons of darkness LOC matpc.13011)/Public Domain.

163 *Norandino and Lucina Discovered by the Ogre.* 1624, oil on canvas, Lanfranco, Giovanni. 1582-1647, from the Galleria Borghese Collection, Art Renewal Center, Source: Wikimedia Commons (Giovanni Lanfranco Norandino and Lucina Discovered by the Ogre)/Public Domain.

CHAPTER 8:

Alamy

174 *Death of Eli* (book of Samuel, Old Testament), 19th Century, engraving, Illustration from *History of the Bible*, 1833 © Old Books Images/Alamy Stock Photo.

174 *Nathan Before King David*, 19th Century, engraving, illustration for *Tales Told for Sunday*, Cassell, 1897 © Reading Room 2020/Alamy Stock Photo.

176 *'Then fell she down straightway at his feet, and yielded up the ghost'*, Acts 5:10, 19th Century (biblical scene) © The Print Collector/ Alamy Stock Photo.

177 *Thumb for happiness on the Statue of Gregory of Nin.*1929, Split, Croatia © Branko Ostojic/Alamy Stock Photo.

194 *Aaron and Hur holding up Moses' hands* © Historic Collection/Alamy Stock Photo.

Julius, 1794-1872), German painter © ZU_09/iStockphoto LP.

195 *Bald eagle flying above the clouds* © Steve-Collender/iStockphoto LP.

Public Domain

173 *Holzschnitt aus "Die Bibel in Bildern," Kain erschlägt Abel*, Woodcut from "Die Bibel in Bildern," Cain slays Abel. 1860, Schnorr von Carolsfeld, Julius (1794-1872), Source: Wikimedia Commons (Schnorr von Carolsfeld Bibel in Bildern 1860 013)/Public Domain.

CHAPTER 9:

Alamy

204 *Sea Storm Lightning*, 7 June 2019 © mif. photos/Alamy Stock Photo.

206 *Building of the Ark, Noah's Ark.* 1928, Photo: All Star Picture Library © WARNER BROS./All Star Picture Library Limited/Alamy Stock Photo.

215 *John Chrysostom (John of Antioch)*, circa 349, Antioch on the Orontes © bilwissedition Ltd. and Co. KG/Alamy Stock Photo.

216 *Isidore of Seville*, 560-636 © bilwissedition Ltd. and Co. KG/Alamy Stock Photo.

217 *Israel, Jerusalem, Church of the Holy Sepulchre.* 14 March 2016 © Jane Sweeney/Alamy Stock Photo.

218 *Jean Chardin*, 1643-1713, born Jean-Baptiste Chardin (aka Sir John Chardin), published in *Crabb's Historical Dictionary.* 1825 © Classic Image/Alamy Stock Photo.

220 *Adam Olearius [Oelschlager]*, line engraving © Well/BOT/Alamy Stock Photo/Public Domain.

222 *Tsar Nicholas II*, The Romanov Dynasty © CBW/Alamy Stock Photo.

Andrew Jones

224 *Aerial Mount Cuidi*, © Andrew Jones/NoahsArkScans.com.

Creative Commons

208 CC BY-SA 4.0: *Presunto ritratto di Berosso (Portrait of Berossus).* 2015, Rizzotto, Mark, Source: Wikimedia Commons (Beroso) © Mark Rizzotto.

216 CC BY-SA 2.0: *Movses Khorenatsi*, Source: Wikimedia Commons (St. Movses Khorenatsi) © Ashnag.

Getty Images

212 *Europe, Greece, Plain of Thessaly, Valley of Penee*, World Heritage of UNESCO, since 1988, Orthodox Christian Monasteries of Meteora, Monastery of Saint-Nicolas, Photononstop Collection © Emilie CHAIX via Getty Images.

Royalty-Free

201 *Noah's Ark (stormy ocean)*, isolated transparent background, generated with AI © Mr.PNG/Adobe Stock.

209 *Abydenus*, generated with AI, DLee.

209 *Nicolaus of Damascus*, generated with AI by DLee.

211 *Orthodox icon of the Byzantine style of St. Paisius*, Odessa Region, Ukraine © hramikona/Shutterstock, Inc.

218 *Hayton*, generated with AI, DLee.

Private Collection — RENNER

200 *On Location.*

Public Domain

210 *Flavius Josephus, 36-100 CE.* 1817, engraving, *The Works of Flavius Josephus,* Whiston, William (19th Century), Source: Wikimedia Commons (Josephus)/Public Domain.

214 *Epiphanius of Salamis, church father,* circa 310-403, fresco, Gracanica Monastery, Liplijan, Kosovo, Cultural Heritage Site of Serbia (CK 1367), Source: Wikimedia Commons (Epiphanius-Kosovo)/Public Domain.

221 *Claudius James Rich*, 1787-1820, Phillips, Thomas, 1770-1845, Source: Wikimedia Commons (Claudius James Rich)/Public Domain.

223 *Karawane auf der Seidenstraße.* Seite 10, Atlas Catalan, Caravan on the Silk Road. Sheet 10, Atlas catalan, 1375, Abraham, Cresques, 1325-1387, published in Katalanischer *Weltatlas* (*Catalan World Atlas*), Source: Wikimedia Commons (Katalanischer Atlas 01)/Public Domain.

CHAPTER 10:

Alamy

231 *Winged lion bas-relief at the entrance to an Assyrian temple,* Photogravure 19th Century © North Wind Picture Library/Alamy Stock Photo.

Andrew Jones

247 *Ancient Silk Road* © Andrew Jones/NoahsArkScans.com.

Bridgeman Images

236 *Noah directs the animals to the Ark,* colour lithograph, Coller, Henry (1886-1958), from *The Wonder Book of Bible Stories,* published by Ward Lock, 1953, Private Collection © Bridgeman Images.

Creative Commons

233 CC BY-SA 4.0: *Tablet V of the Epic Gilgamesh*, Old Babylonian period, 2003-1595 BCE, The Sulaymaniyah Museum, Iraq, Source: Wikimedia Commons (The Newly Discovered Tablet of the Epic Gilgamesh) © Osama Shatir Muhummed Amin FRCP (Glasg).

Lev Kaplan, Artist and Illustrator

226 *Ark at Rest on Ararat* © Lev Kaplan, illustration, Special Commission, Renner 2024 (https://www.kaplan-art.de/).

240 *A Look Inside the Ark* © Lev Kaplan, illustration, Special Commission, 2024 (https://www.kaplan-art.de/).

246 *Drogue Stones On the Ark* © Lev Kaplan, illustration, Special Commission, Renner 2024, (https://www.kaplan-art.de/).

246 *Drogue Stones On the Mountain* © Lev Kaplan, illustration/ Special Commission, 2024, (https://www.kaplan-art.de/).

Royalty-Free

227 *Noah's Ark (stormy ocean)*, isolated transparent background, generated with AI © Mr.PNG/Adobe Stock.

Special Permissions

244 *The Seventh International Symposium on Mount Ararat and Noah's Ark* 2023, (used by permission), https://ismana.agri.edu.tr/.

Private Collection — RENNER

235 *Chart A* created by Chart adapted by Vincent and Allison Newfield (www.newfield-creativeservices.com) from A. J. Monty White, Ph.D., "Flood Legends," *Answers* magazine, p. 20. Answers in Genesis, Hebron, Kentucky.

States, 27 July 2017 © John Andrus/Alamy Stock Photo.

293 *Noah's Sacrifice,* 1853, Maclise, Daniel, 1806-1870, Irish history, literary and portrait painter and illustrator © World History Archive/Alamy Stock Photo.

Andrew Jones

299 *Aerial View 15* © Andrew Jones/ NoahsArkScans.com.

Creative Commons

288 CC BY-SA 3.0: *Priscacara liops fossil fish,* class actinopterygii, order perciformes: family priscacaridae, eocene, Green River Formation, Kemmerer, Wyoming (18 inch layer), 5 inches long, 10 February 2007, Source: Wikimedia Commons (Priscacara liops) © User:SNP.

Institute for Creation Research

287 *Henry M. Morris,* Christian apologist, scientist, and engineer, Ashcraft, Source: Wikipedia (Henry M. Morris photo) Content © Institute for Creation Research.

Lev Kaplan, Artist and Illustrator

280 *Ark in the Storm* © Lev Kaplan, illustration, Special Commission, 2024 (https://www.kaplan-art.de/).

284 *Dove with Olive Leaf* © Lev Kaplan, illustration, Special Commission, 2024 (https://www.kaplan-art.de/).

Private Collection — RENNER

282 *Drogue Stone in the Valley,* 2023.

291 *Rick Renner.*

292 *Sacrificial Stone.*

300 *Drogue Stones 8.*

301 *Ark Depiction in Stone Carving.*

302 *Ruins of Byzantine Church 1.*

302 *Ruins of Byzantine Church 2.*

302 *Rock 16.*

Public Domain

281, 305 *Flavius Josephus,* 36-100 CE. 1817, engraving, *The Works of Flavius Josephus,* Whiston, William (19th Century), Source: Wikimedia Commons (Josephus)/Public Domain.

Royalty-Free

281 *Noah's Ark (stormy ocean),* isolated transparent background, generated with AI © Mr.PNG/Adobe Stock.

285 *Entry into the ark,* 19th Century, illustration © clu/iStockphoto.

288 *dangerous AI tsunami,* earthquake sea waves illustration, GENERATED WITH AI © Sternfahrer/Adobe Stock.

295 *Beautiful evening sunset with rainbow,* Source: iStockphoto L.P. © Victor Asheien.

296 *Pe'epe'e falls on the Wailuku River with dramatic light,* Hilo, Big Island, Hawaii © Eachat/ iStockphoto L.P.

CHAPTER 13:

Alamy

315 *Clemens I,* 1030, Byzantine Mosaics © ARTGEN/Alamy Stock Photo.

319 *SAINT IRENAEUS,* prelate and bishop of Lugdunum (Lyons), circa 130-200 © Chronicle/Alamy Stock Photo.

Bridgeman

310 *Baked Clay Prism ('Weld Blundell Prism') with the Sumerian King List giving rulers from 'before the Flood' to King Sin-magir of Isin (circa 1827-17 BC),* inscribed in cuneiform script (20 cm), Larsa, Iraq (stone). Ashmolean Museum, University of Oxford, UK © Ashmolean Museum/Bridgeman Images.

333 *Capture of Og, King of Bashan*, colour lithograph, Twidle, Arthur (1865-1936)/ English, from *Bible Heroes*, published by The Religious Tract Society, 1929, Private Collection © Bridgeman Images.

Creative Commons

311 CC BY-SA 4.0: *Assyrian King Ashurbanipal on his horse thrusting a spear onto a lion's head*, Alabaster bas-relief, North Palace, Nineveh, Mesopotamia, Modern-day Iraq, Neo-Assyrian Period 645-635 BCE, British Museum Collection, Source: Wikimedia Commons (Assyrian king Ashurbanipal on his horse thrusting a spear into a lion's head. Alabaster bas-relief from Nineveh. Dating back to 645-635 BCE and is currently housed in the British Museum, London) © Osama Shukir Muhammed Amin FRCP (Glasg).

339 CC BY-SA 4.0: *Rujm el-Hiri*, Bronze Age, Golan Heights, Syria/Israel, Graicer, Abraham, 2010, Source: Wikimedia Commons (RUJM EL-HIRI AERIAL) © Abraham Graicer.

340 CC BY-SA 4.0: *Hagar Qim, outer wall*, Malta. Gunter, Michael, 1998, Source: Wikimedia Commons (Hagar Qim, Maltahq5) © Michael Gunter.

341 CC BY-SA 3.0: *Trilithon of Baalbek*, 2009, Source: Wikimedia Commons (Trilithonof-Baalbek3) © Brattarb.

Public Domain

313 *The Great Mesorah,* manuscript Hebrew Bible with full vocalization, accentuation, and Masorah annotation, circa 1300, Spain, illustrated in color, silver, and gold, National Library of Israel, Ktiv, Source: Wikimedia

Commons, Bible from 1300 (20)/Public Domain.

316 *Flavius Josephus*, 36-100 CE, 1817, engraving, *The Works of Flavius Josephus* by William Whiston, 19th Century, Source: Wikimedia Commons (Josephus)/Public Domain.

317 *Clemens Von Alexandrien*, Source: Wikimedia Commons (ClemensVonAlexandrien)/ Public Domain.

320 *Libanius the Orator (Libanius the Sophist)*, circa 18th Century, woodcut, unknown artist, Source: Wikimedia (Libanius_the_Sophist)/ Public Domain.

321 *Saint Clement of Alexandra (Titus Flavius Celems)*, circa 150-215, Christian theologian and philosopher. Head of the Catechetical School of Alexandria © Timewatch Images/ Alamy Stock Photo/Public Domain.

321 *Portrait of Tertullian*, prolific early Christian author from Carthage, 1784, Thevet, Andre, Source: Wikimedia (Tertullian2)/Public Domain.

342 *El Coloso (The Colossus)*, oil on canvas, circa 1808, Fransico de Goya,1746-1828, Meseo de Prado Collection, Spain, Source: Wikimedia Commons (El coloso)/Public Domain.

Royalty-Free

308 *Painting of David and Goliath* © Bargais/ Adobe Stock.

309 *Noah's Ark (stormy ocean)*, isolated transparent background, generated with AI © Mr.PNG/Adobe Stock.

312 *Mysterious pandora box opening with rays of light,* high contrast image 3D rendering illustration. Pro photo © scofano/2024 Eezy LLC.

322 *Commodian 250*, generated with AI by DLee.

325 *Genesis 6 Giant*, generated with AI by DLee.

326 *Anakim*, generated with AI by DLee.

327 *Renowned Giants*, generated with AI by DLee.

330 *Attacking Giant*, generated with AI by DLee.

331 *Giant 22*, generated with AI by DLee.

334 *The Giant Og*, generated with AI by DLee.

335 *Spies Valley*, generated with AI by DLee.

337 *David and Goliath battling on a land in high definition with a beautiful sky*, generated with AI © Marco/Adobe Stock.

340 *Archaeological findings in Göbekitepe excavation site in Turkey*, pro-pottery neolithic period, 9500-8000 BCE © EnesTaha/Adobe Stock.

Science Photo Library

323 *Suetonius writing the Twelve Caesars*, 1691, Johannes G. Graevius,1622-1703, Source: sciencephoto.com © Middle Temple Library/ Science Photo Library.

CHAPTER 14:

Alamy

347 *Standard of Ur - War* © Art Collection 2/ Alamy Stock Photo.

352 *Homer, The Odyssey*. Ulysses (Odysseus), Nestor, king of Pylos and former warrior in the Trojan war, sacrifice bulls to Neptune (Poseidon) - God of the sea, circa 800-600 BCE, Trojan War, epic; illustration after Flaxman © Lebrecht Music & Arts/Alamy Stock Photo.

354 *A vertical shot of the Statue of Baphomet, New England, Massachusetts*, Wirestock © Wirestock, Inc./Alamy Stock Photo.

355 *Polyphemus Cave*, conceptual reproduction based on the old painting by Jacob Jordaens entitled *Cave of Polifemo*, oil on canvas (1635). Pushkin Museum of Fine Arts © Kadumago/ Alamy Stock Photo.

361 *London, England, UK. Anti-abortion campaigners with graphic poster of aborted fetus*, 8 April 2014 © PjrNews/Alamy Stock Photo.

Getty

350 *RIPLEY'S BELIEVE IT OR NOT! Times Square Odditorium Opening Night, Ripley's Time Square, New York, NY*, 21 June 2007. Photo by: Rob Rich/Everett Collection © Everett Collection Inc/Getty Images.

Royalty-Free

344 *Sermon on the Mount*, generated with AI, Source: Dreamstime.

345 *Noah's Ark (stormy ocean)*, isolated transparent background, generated with AI © Mr.PNG/Adobe Stock.

346 *Jesus From Heaven*, generated with AI by DLee.

349 *Sodomites in the Street*, generated with AI by DLee.

351 *Same Sex LGBT Lesbian Gay Women Exchanging Rings During Wedding Ceremony - two brides* © Jaimie/Adobe Stock.

353 *Book stock photo, old book in fire* © D-Keine/iStockphoto L.P.

358 *Technology and engineering concept stock photo* © Peshkova/iStockphoto L.P.

360 *Sodomites*, generated with AI by DLee.

364 *Gender Neutral or All Gender Restroom Sign Illustration with man woman and human figures*, illustrated © John Mantell Photo/ Adobe Stock.

366 *Sodomites 3*, generated with AI by DLee.

371 *Poignant portrait biblical figure Noah stands hopeful anticipation, eyes fixed on horizon.* GENERATED WITH AI © Ruslan Batiuk/ Adobe Stock.

CHAPTER 15:

Alamy

374 *A Roman Banquet, Ancient Rome, Roman Empire.* Italy, Europe, old 19th Century engraved illustration, El Mundo Ilustrado 1881 © Old Books Images/Alamy Stock Photo.

376 *Romans drink at banquet* © Chronicle/ Alamy Stock Photo.

377 *Entering Noah's Ark, flood narrative, Bible, Old Testament, First Book of Moses, Genesis, historical illustration*, 1850. Illustrated magnificent Bible or the Complete Holy Scriptures of the Old and New Testaments, after the German translation by D. Martin Luther. Numerous illustrations and explanatory notes by Otto Delitsch. Englische Kunst-Anstalt of A.H. Payne in Leipzig and Dresden, 1850 © Wolfgang Deiderich/Alamy Stock Photo.

380 *Two Women Shall Be Grinding at the MILL, Elmore Alfred* © Artmedia/Alamy Stock Photo.

391 *A test nuclear explosion codenamed "Baker" at Bikini Atoll in the Marshall Islands*, July 25, 1946. © mccool/Alamy Stock Photo.

392 *The beauty of the universe: The sun and its flares* - Element of this image provided by NASA's Goddard Space Flight Center/SDO, 10 January 2019 © Equatore/Alamy Stock Photo.

Archaeology Illustrated (Balage Balogh)

383 *Jesus and His Disciples in the Kidron Valley* © Balage Balogh/archaeologyillustrated.com. All rights reserved.

Andrew Jones

399 *Aerial View of the Ark*, ©Andrew Jones/ NoahsArkScans.com.

Creative Commons

387 CC BY-SA 2.5: *Montage of examples of severe weather, from left to right, starting at the stop: F5 tornado, wildfire, thunderstorm, lightning, flooding, hurricane, ice storm, and giant hail*, 3 June 2010, Source: Wikimedia Commons (Severe weather montage) © Fallshirmjäger.

Getty Images

395 *Alien spaceship landing on rural road*, Tetra Images Collection © Chris Clor/Getty Images.

Private Collection — RENNER

384 *Sign*; LMoore.

Public Domain

378 *Bible Primer, Old Testament*, for use in the primary department of Sunday schools, 1919. by Hult, Adolf (1869-1943) from Augusta Synod (old catalog), published by Rock Island, Ill. Augustana book concern, Library of Congress, Source: Wikimedia Commons (Bible Primer, Old Testament, for use in the primary department of Sunday schools (1919) (1459348790)/Public Domain.

380 *The Gleaners*, 1857, oil on canvas, Jean-François Millet, 1814-1875, Musée d'Orsay, Paris, Source: Wikimedia Commons (Jean-François Millet -Gleaners - Google Art Project 2)/Public Domain.

397 *Gimbal, The First Official UAP Footage from the USG for Public Release*, military video of unidentified aerial phenomena (UAP), 21 January 2015, United States Navy/Public Domain.

Royalty-Free

375 *Noah's Ark (stormy ocean)*, isolated transparent background, generated with AI © Mr.PNG/Adobe Stock.

381 *Crowd of people during the rapture being accepted in heaven,* created with generative AI © Andrew Hudson/Adobe Stock.

388 *Red word Error on digital computer background,* internet hacking concept © Vladimir Boronzenets/Shutterstock, Inc.

389 *Man with blue biotech integration on neck and face.* Biohack concept. Generated with AI © Sunshine Design/Adobe Stock.

393 *Prophecy of the blood moon* © Yuri_Arcurs/iStockphoto L.P.

394 *fallen angels,* AI generated art, generative AI © Feel Surreal/Adobe Stock.

400 *Soccer fans angry screaming at camera during match,* Generated with AI © Cavan/Adobe Stock.

404 *The Rapture* © Benjamin Haas/Adobe Stock.

Special Permissions

396 *Ryan Graves, executive director of Americans for Safe Aerospace, David Grusch, former National Reconnaissance Office representative on the Defense Department's Unidentified Aerial Phenomena Task Force, and retired Navy commander David Fravor attend House Oversight and Accountability Committee's National Security, the Border, and Foreign Affairs Subcommittee's hearing on "Unidentified Anamalgous Phenomena: Implications on National Security, Public Safety, and Government Transparency"* at the U.S. Capitol Hill in Washington, U.S. on 26 July 2023 © REUTERS/Elizabeth Frantz.

CHAPTER 16:

Private Collection — RENNER

406 *Rick Renner and the Ark* 2024.

Royalty-Free

407 *Noah's Ark (stormy ocean)*, isolated transparent background, generated with AI © Mr.PNG/Adobe Stock.

BACK MATTER:

Images provided courtesy of Andrew Jones ©Andrew Jones/NoahsArkScans.com.

PRAYER OF SALVATION

When Jesus Christ comes into your life, you are immediately emancipated — totally set free from the bondage of sin! If you have never received Jesus as your personal Savior, it is time to experience this new life for yourself. The first step to freedom is simple. Just pray this prayer from your heart:

Lord, I can never adequately thank You for all You did for me on the Cross. I am so undeserving, Jesus, but You came and gave Your life for me anyway. I repent for rejecting You, and I turn away from my life of rebellion and sin right now. I turn to You and receive You as my Savior, and I ask You to wash away my sin and make me completely new in You by Your precious blood. I thank You from the depths of my heart for doing what no one else could do for me.

Thank You, Jesus, that I am now redeemed by Your blood. On the Cross, You bore my sin, my sickness, my pain, my lack of peace, and my suffering. Your blood has removed my sin, washed me whiter than snow, and given me rightstanding with the Father. I have no need to be ashamed of my past sins because I am now a new creature in You. Old things have passed away, and all things have become new because I am in Jesus Christ (2 Corinthians 5:17).

Because of You, Jesus, today I am forgiven; I am filled with peace; and I am a joint-heir with You! Satan no longer has a right to lay any claim on me. From a grateful heart, I will faithfully serve You the rest of my days!

If you prayed this prayer from your heart, something amazing has happened to you. As a result of your decision to turn your life over to Jesus Christ, your eternal home has been decided forever. Heaven will now be your permanent address for all eternity. God's Spirit has moved into your own human spirit, and you have become the "temple of God" (1 Corinthians 6:19). What a miracle! To think that God, by His Spirit, now lives inside you! And He has become your Heavenly Father. You are a child of God!

Now you have a new Lord and Master, and His name is Jesus. From this moment on, the Spirit of God will work in you and supernaturally energize you to fulfill God's will for your life. Everything will change for you as you yield to His leadership in your life — and it's all going to change for the best!

ABOUT THE AUTHOR

Rick Renner is a highly respected Bible teacher and leader in the international Christian community. He is the author of a long list of books, including the bestsellers *Dressed To Kill* and *Sparkling Gems From the Greek 1* and *2*, which have sold millions of copies in multiple languages worldwide. Rick's understanding of the Greek language and biblical history opens up the Scriptures in a unique way that enables his audience to gain wisdom and insight while learning something brand new from the Word of God. Rick and his wife Denise have cumulatively authored more than 40 books that have been distributed worldwide.

Rick is the overseer of the Good News Association of Churches, founder of the Moscow Good News Church, pastor of the Internet Good News Church, and founder of Media Mir and of TBV — a national Russian Christian TV channel that reaches into homes across all of Russia's 11 time zones. He is the president of GNC (Good News Channel) — the largest Russian-speaking Christian satellite network in the world, which broadcasts the Gospel 24/7 to countless viewers worldwide via multiple satellites and the Internet. Rick is the founder of RENNER Ministries in Broken Arrow, Oklahoma, and host to his TV program, also seen around the world in multiple languages. Rick leads this amazing work with Denise — his wife and lifelong ministry partner — along with their sons and committed leadership team.

CONTACT RENNER MINISTRIES

For further information
about RENNER Ministries,
please contact the office nearest you,
or visit the ministry website at:
www.renner.org

**ALL USA
CORRESPONDENCE:**
RENNER Ministries
1814 W. Tacoma St.
Broken Arrow, OK 74012
(918) 496-3213
Or 1-800-RICK-593
Email: renner@renner.org
Website: www.renner.org

MOSCOW OFFICE:
RENNER Ministries
P. O. Box 789
101000, Moscow, Russia
+7 (495) 727-1467
Email: blagayavestonline@ignc.org
Website: www.ignc.org

RIGA OFFICE:
RENNER Ministries
Unijas 99
Riga LV-1084, Latvia
+371 67802150
Email: church@goodnews.lv
Website: www.goodnews.lv

OXFORD OFFICE:
RENNER Ministries
Box 7, 266 Banbury Road
Oxford OX2 7DL, United Kingdom
+44 1865 521024
Email: europe@renner.org

WITH US!

 facebook.com/rickrenner • facebook.com/rennerdenise
 youtube.com/rennerministries • youtube.com/deniserenner
 instagram.com/rickrrenner • instagram.com/rennerministries_
instagram.com/rennerdenise

Books by Rick Renner

Apostles & Prophets
Build Your Foundation*
Chosen by God*
Christmas — The Rest of the Story
Dream Thieves*
Dressed To Kill*
Fallen Angels, Giants, Monsters, and the World Before the Flood
The Holy Spirit and You*
How To Keep Your Head on Straight in a World Gone Crazy*
How To Receive Answers From Heaven!*
Igniting a Powerful Prayer Life
Insights on Successful Leadership*
Last-Days Survival Guide*
A Life Ablaze*
Life in the Combat Zone*
A Light in Darkness, Volume One,
　　Seven Messages to the Seven Churches series
The Love Test*
My Peace-Filled Day
My Spirit-Empowered Day
No Room for Compromise, Volume Two,
　　Seven Messages to the Seven Churches series
Paid in Full*
The Point of No Return*
Repentance*
Renner A to Z — Comments and Quotes by Rick Renner on 400 Bible Topics A to Z!
Signs You'll See Just Before Jesus Comes*
Sparkling Gems From the Greek Daily Devotional 1*
Sparkling Gems From the Greek Daily Devotional 2*
Spiritual Weapons To Defeat the Enemy*
Ten Guidelines To Help You Achieve Your Long-Awaited Promotion!*
Testing the Supernatural
365 Days of Increase
365 Days of Power
Turn Your God-Given Dreams Into Reality*
Unlikely — Our Faith-Filled Journey to the Ends of the Earth*
Why We Need the Gifts of the Holy Spirit*
The Will of God — The Key to Your Success*
You Can Get Over It*

*Digital version available for Kindle, Nook, and iBook.
Note: Books by Rick Renner are available for purchase at:
www.renner.org

IF YOU'RE INTERESTED IN SEEING THE NOAH'S ARK SITE FIRSTHAND…

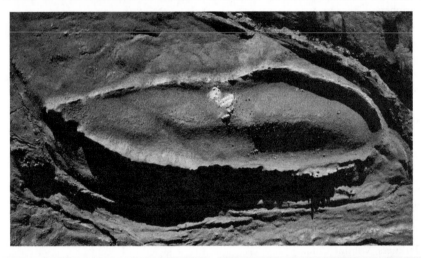

Since the time I filmed at the Durupinar site for my first series of programs on the subject of Noah's Ark, I have received many inquiries about touring this location firsthand.

I am pleased to refer those interested in a tour to my friend Andrew Jones, who assisted my team and me in our own visit to eastern Turkiye to investigate and to film. Andrew, an expert on this site for many years, wrote the Special Message on page xxxiii of this book and regularly conducts tours of this special site in the Ararat mountain range.

For more information on securing a reservation for an individual or group tour, please contact Andrew directly at **www.NoahsArkScans.com/tours** for information on the itinerary, dates, and pricing.

— *Rick Renner*

RENNER A TO Z

COMMENTS AND QUOTES BY RICK RENNER
ON 400 BIBLE TOPICS A TO Z!

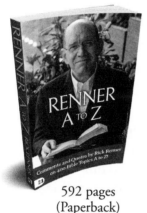

592 pages
(Paperback)

Has your mind ever buzzed with questions about the Bible that you couldn't find answers for? Have you wished you had a resource to turn to for quick answers to life's perplexing problems?

With more than 45 years of ministry experience, prolific author Rick Renner shares hundreds of his own comments and quotes on hundreds of topics to bring you helpful advice on how to answer life's questions with God's wisdom and to live a committed life in Christ.

In this book, *Renner A to Z — Comments and Quotes by Rick Renner on 400 Bible Topics A to Z!*, you will find 1,780 alphabetically arranged comments and quotes packed full of practical, Spirit-filled counsel you can meditate on and apply to your life.

This comprehensive resource is sure to answer long-held questions and bring insight to a wide variety of topics. Whether you're looking to deepen your personal study of the Bible or you're interested in what Scripture has to say on a particular subject, this book is fun and easy to use and is sure to be an invaluable addition to your Christian library.

To order, visit us online at: **www.renner.org**
Book resellers: Contact Harrison House at 800-722-6774
or visit **www.HarrisonHouse.com** for quantity discounts.

IGNITING A POWERFUL PRAYER LIFE

A Sparkling Gems From the Greek
Guided Devotional Journal

256 pages
(Paperback)

Igniting a Powerful Prayer Life: A Sparkling Gems From the Greek Guided Devotional Journal can take you from feeling overwhelmed by the signs of the times to enjoying a serene sense of wholeness and well-being as you walk and live in God's presence.

You are not impotent against the struggles of broken families and relationships, decaying morality, rumors of wars, and unstable economies! The Father longs for you to release His power in your sphere through prayer. You only need to know how.

In *Igniting a Powerful Prayer Life*, Rick Renner uses scriptural principles and spiritual wisdom that can set ablaze in your heart a passion for potent prayer. Each lesson in this 31-day journal also includes a prayer and a confession to put the Word in your mouth and stimulate a fervent, effectual prayer life.

Don't stand by and let the enemy oppress or destroy you *or* your family. Use this guided journal to ignite your prayer life and set your world *on fire* with the power of God!

To order, visit us online at: **www.renner.org**
Book Resellers: Contact Harrison House at 800-722-6774
or visit **www.HarrisonHouse.com** for quantity discounts.

MY PEACE-FILLED DAY

A SPARKLING GEMS FROM THE GREEK
GUIDED DEVOTIONAL JOURNAL

256 pages
(Paperback)

Do you feel like you're on a merry-go-round of stress and anxiety that just won't stop? Do you feel like the circumstances around you are shouting *loudly* as you search for peace and calm?

Help is here! You *can* live in peace — fearless and free!

In *My Peace-Filled Day: A Sparkling Gems From the Greek Guided Devotional Journal*, Rick Renner shares 31 teachings, expounding from his thorough knowledge of the Greek language, to help you take hold of the God-given peace that belongs to you. As you devote yourself to the scriptural truths in each devotional — and journal your answers to thought-provoking questions — the power of God will melt away the fears, anxieties, and cares of this world until His peace takes centerstage in your life.

Don't let the turmoil of this world swirl you into an emotional frenzy. As you encounter God on every page of this devotional journal, you will find yourself living the peace-filled life your loving Heavenly Father wants for you!

To order, visit us online at: **www.renner.org**
Book Resellers: Contact Harrison House at 800-722-6774
or visit **www.HarrisonHouse.com** for quantity discounts.

APOSTLES AND PROPHETS
THEIR ROLES IN THE PAST, THE PRESENT, AND THE LAST DAYS

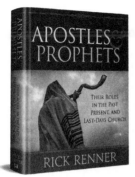

804 pages
(Paperback)

Did the offices of the apostle and prophet pass away with the last of Jesus' disciples? *They did not!*

In his book *Apostles and Prophets — Their Roles in the Past, the Present, and the Last Days,* Rick Renner biblically defines and historically traces these ministry gifts from the time of the Early Church to TODAY!

Containing 20 pages of vivid illustrations that narrate Old and New Testament history as you have perhaps never seen it, this book answers such questions as:

- Why is the Church referred to in Scripture as a *vineyard*, a *body*, and a *temple* or *building*?

- What is Christ's real intention and masterful plan for His last-days Church?

- Does every member of the Church have a priestly ministry to fulfill?

- Shouldn't *every* believer be prophetic?

- What is an apostle — and what is a *false* apostle?

- What signs must accompany the ministry of a true apostle?

- What is a prophet — and what is a *false* prophet?

- What signs must accompany the ministry of a true prophet?

To order, visit us online at: **www.renner.org**
Book Resellers: Contact Harrison House at 800-722-6774
or visit **www.HarrisonHouse.com** for quantity discounts.

CHRISTMAS
THE REST OF THE STORY

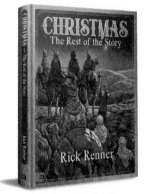

304 pages
(Hardback)

In this storybook of biblical history, Rick takes you on the "magical" journey of Christ's coming to earth in a way you've probably never heard it before. Featuring full-color, original illustrations, *Christmas — The Rest of the Story* gives the spellbinding account of God's masterful plan to redeem mankind, and vividly portrays the wonder of the Savior's birth and His "ordinary" life marked by God's *extraordinary* plan.

If you want to be taken back in your imagination to this earth-shaking course of events that changed the history of the whole world, this book is a *must-have* not just for the Christmas season, but for all time. *Topics include:*

- Why God chose Mary and Joseph.
- The significance of the *manger* and *swaddling clothes*.
- Why angels viewed *God in the flesh* with such wonderment.
- Why King Herod was so troubled by this historical birth.
- How we can prepare for Christ's *next* coming.

Christmas — The Rest of the Story is sure to be a favorite in your family for generations to come! Jesus' birth is truly *the greatest story on earth* — perhaps never more uniquely told than in the pages of this book.

LAST-DAYS SURVIVAL GUIDE

A Scriptural Handbook
To Prepare You for These Perilous Times

496 pages
(Paperback)

In his book *Last-Days Survival Guide*, Rick Renner masterfully expands on Second Timothy 3 to clearly reveal the last-days signs to expect in society as one age draws to a close before another age begins.

Rick also thoroughly explains how not to just *survive* the times, but to *thrive* in the midst of them. God wants you as a believer to be equipped — *outfitted* — to withstand end-time storms, to navigate wind-tossed seas, and to sail with His grace and power to fulfill your divine destiny on earth!

If you're concerned about what you're witnessing in society today — and even in certain sectors of the Church — the answers you need in order to keep your gaze focused on Christ and maintain your victory are in this book!

To order, visit us online at: **www.renner.org**
Book Resellers: Contact Harrison House at 800-722-6774
or visit **www.HarrisonHouse.com** for quantity discounts.

SPARKLING GEMS FROM THE GREEK 1

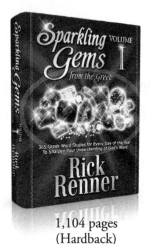

1,104 pages
(Hardback)

Rick Renner's *Sparkling Gems From the Greek 1* has gained widespread recognition for its unique illumination of the New Testament through more than 1,000 Greek word studies in a 365-day devotional format. *Sparkling Gems 1* remains a beloved resource that has spiritually strengthened believers worldwide. As many have testified, the wealth of truths within its pages never grows old. Year after year, *Sparkling Gems 1* continues to deepen readers' understanding of the Bible.

SPARKLING GEMS FROM THE GREEK 2

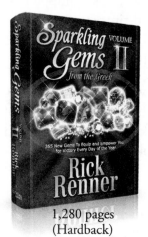

1,280 pages
(Hardback)

Rick infuses into *Sparkling Gems From the Greek 2* the added strength and richness of many more years of his own personal study and growth in God — expanding this devotional series to impact the reader's heart on a deeper level than ever before. This remarkable study tool helps unlock new hidden treasures from God's Word that will draw readers into an ever more passionate pursuit of Him.

DRESSED TO KILL
A Biblical Approach
to Spiritual Warfare and Armor

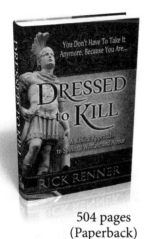

504 pages
(Paperback)

Rick Renner's book *Dressed To Kill* is considered by many to be a true classic on the subject of spiritual warfare. The original version, which sold more than 400,000 copies, is a curriculum staple in Bible schools worldwide. In this beautiful volume, you will find:

- 504 pages of reedited text in paperback
- 16 pages of full-color illustrations
- Questions at the end of each chapter to guide you into deeper study

In *Dressed To Kill*, Rick explains with exacting detail the purpose and function of each piece of Roman armor. In the process, he describes the significance of our *spiritual* armor not only to withstand the onslaughts of the enemy, but also to overturn the tendencies of the carnal mind. Furthermore, Rick delivers a clear, scriptural presentation on the biblical definition of spiritual warfare — what it is and what it is not.

When you walk with God in deliberate, continual fellowship, He will enrobe you with Himself. Armed with the knowledge of who you are in Him, you will be dressed and dangerous to the works of darkness, unflinching in the face of conflict, and fully equipped to take the offensive and gain mastery over any opposition from your spiritual foe. You don't have to accept defeat anymore once you are *dressed to kill*!

HOW TO KEEP YOUR HEAD ON STRAIGHT IN A WORLD GONE CRAZY

DEVELOPING DISCERNMENT FOR THESE LAST DAYS

400 pages
(Paperback)

The world is changing. In fact, it's more than changing — it has *gone crazy*.

We are living in a world where faith is questioned and sin is welcomed — where people seem to have lost their minds about what is right and wrong. It seems truth has been turned *upside down*.

In Rick Renner's book *How To Keep Your Head on Straight in a World Gone Crazy*, he reveals the disastrous consequences of a society in spiritual and moral collapse.

In this book, you'll discover what Christians need to do to stay out of the chaos and remain anchored to truth. You'll learn how to stay sensitive to the Holy Spirit, how to discern right and wrong teaching, how to be grounded in prayer, and how to be spiritually prepared for living in victory in these last days.

Leading ministers from around the world are calling this book essential for every believer.

To order, visit us online at: **www.renner.org**
Book Resellers: Contact Harrison House at 800-722-6774
or visit **www.HarrisonHouse.com** for quantity discounts.

Equipping Believers to Walk in the Abundant Life

John 10:10b

Connect with us for fresh content and news about forthcoming books from your favorite authors...

Facebook @ HarrisonHousePublishers

Instagram @ HarrisonHousePublishing

www.harrisonhouse.com